D0820376

Historical Thought and Literary Representation
in West Indian Literature

Historical Thought and Literary Representation in West Indian Literature

Nana Wilson-Tagoe

University Press of Florida

Gainesville · Tallahassee · Tampa · Boca Raton
Pensacola · Orlando · Miami · Jacksonville

The Press University of the West Indies

Barbados / Jamaica / Trinidad and Tobago

James Currey

Oxford

Published by the University Press of Florida (ISBN 0-8130-1582-0, cloth)
Published simultaneously in the Caribbean by The Press
University of the West Indies (ISBN 976-640-062-8, paper)
Published simultaneously in the United Kingdom and British Commonwealth
by James Currey Ltd., 73 Botley Road, Oxford OX2 0BS (ISBN 0-85255-553-9, paper)

03 02 01 00 99 98 6 5 4 3 2 1
Library of Congress Cataloging-in-Publication Data (UPF)
Wilson-Tagoe, Nana.
Historical thought and literary representation in West Indian
literature / Nana Wilson-Tagoe.
p. cm.
Includes bibliographical references (p.) and index.
ISBN 0-8130-1582-0 (alk. paper)
1. West Indian literature (English)—History and criticism. 2. Literature and history—
West Indies—History. 3. West Indies—Historiography. 4. Historiography—
West Indies. 5. West Indies—In literature. I. Title.
PR9210.W55 1998 98-5412
810.9'9729—dc21

03 02 01 00 99 98 6 5 4 3 2 1
Cataloguing-in-Publication Data (UWI)
Wilson-Tagoe, Nana.
Historical thought and literary representation in West Indian
literature / Nana Wilson-Tagoe.
p. cm.
Includes bibliographical references.
ISBN 976-640-062-8
1. West Indian literature (English)—History and criticism.
2. West Indian Literature (French)—History and criticism.
3. Literature and history—West Indies—History.
4. Historiography—West Indies.
5. West Indies—Historiography. 6. West Indies—In literature.
PR9210.W55 1998 810.9'9729

03 02 01 00 99 98 6 5 4 3 2 1
British Library Cataloguing in Publication Data (James Currey)
Wilson-Tagoe, Nana
Historical thought & literary representation in West Indian literature
1. West Indian literature (English)—History and criticism 2. History in
literature 3. West Indies—Historiography I. Title
810.9'9729
ISBN 0-85255-553-9

For my parents,
James and Charlotte Tete-Marmon of Cape Coast, Ghana,
and for Ma Violet Matthew of Gonzalez, Trinidad

Contents

Preface and Acknowledgments

In the West Indian literary context a book on the relationship between historical thought and literary perception hardly needs to justify itself. No subject has occupied and engrossed the West Indian writer as consistently and painfully as the subject of history. No eyebrows need be raised on this account, because in relation to what is conventionally understood as "history," no society occupies the uniquely ironic position that the West Indies occupies. On one hand it is a society created entirely by history. Its super-structures and values reveal such evidence of history that even the writers who confine themselves to the present can find their writing forcibly confronted by history. Yet on the other hand, in the sense in which we normally approach and possess a historic past, the West Indies may appear totally lacking in history. It has no artifacts or monuments, and no ancient epics connect it imaginatively to the landscape to reveal a continuous, tiered concept of a past.

The literal-minded historian, confounded by these absences, shrieks his judgment, condemning the region to a historical limbo: "There are no people there, in the true sense of the word, with a character and purpose of their own,"[1] the British historian James Froude has said, beginning a controversy on history which continues both in the historiography and the imaginative literature of the region. Even in the twentieth century, these absences can still confound: "History is built on creation and achievement and nothing was created in the West Indies."[2] V. S. Naipaul's literal judgment of the region has become almost a whining, hackneyed statement in the wake of the vigorous thinking on the subject in West Indian literature and historiography. Yet his assessment can still prick a nerve of self-doubt and anguish, and both it and Froude's nineteenth-century statement contributed in a large way to the soul-searching and the exciting original literature that the confrontation with history has inspired.

My decision to explore the relationship between West Indian writing and West Indian conceptions of history has been inspired by the theoretical and ideological possibilities inherent in such a study. For an imaginative interpretation of the past offers leeway for creating meanings over and above the existing historiography. Such a construction of history is also in part an act of definition, and in a region which had for a long time been seen through other eyes, where systems of subjugation have engendered self-distrust and dependency, self-definition and creativity are both valid and urgent.

My decision has also been encouraged by the discovery that whereas almost every West Indian writer has dealt with history, and West Indian historiography itself has been vigorous and exciting especially in the latter half of this century, there has as yet not been a sufficiently comprehensive body of criticism that has explored the subject of history in relation to West Indian writing. Until Barbara Webb's *History and Myth in Caribbean Fiction,* which concentrates only on Wilson Harris, Alejo Carpentier, and Edouard Glissant, there had only been scattered critical insights on imaginative interpretations of history in the literature of the region.

There is, in the first place, Wilson Harris's major article "History, Fable, and Myth in the Caribbean and Guianas," which identified the stasis in the method of conventional historiography with regard to the Caribbean and suggested possibilities for exploring figurative meanings beyond the "prison" of linear history. In the related area of concepts, of history as dialectic, there have been several essays which have sometimes provided conceptual frameworks for exploring "history" in the region's imaginative literature. There are Walcott's three crucial essays, "What the Twilight Says," "The Muse of History," and "The Caribbean, Culture or Mimicry?"; there is Brathwaite's "Timehri" and his numerous other insights on history in the region; there is Lamming's *The Pleasures of Exile;* Glissant's *Caribbean Discourse;* Naipaul's *The Loss of El Dorado;* C. L. R. James's *The Black Jacobins;* and Denis Williams's *Image and Idea in the Arts of Guyana.*

In the area of critical approach, particularly in relation to the historical novel in the West Indies, the debate between Kenneth Ramchand and Sylvia Wynter in the 1970s raises crucial questions still relevant to analysis and interpretation.[3] During the 1960s and 1970s, the reexaminations inspired by Naipaul's novels, black consciousness, and the published research of West Indian historians and sociologists have generated much critical interest in the relationship between West Indian writing and West Indian conceptions of history. I refer particularly to Edward Baugh's article, "The West Indian Writer and His Quarrel with History," which identified a relationship between conceptions of history and the forms of West Indian writing; to the same author's book on Derek Walcott's poetry, *Derek Walcott: Memory as Vision: Another Life;* to Jessie Noel's "Historicity and Homelessness in Naipaul"; and to Gordon Rohlehr's "The Historian as Poet."

Recently, with the vigorous interrogations and reassessments of contemporary postcolonial critical theory, several essays and discussions have pointed to the need for a critical perspective that is relevant to ex-colonial societies. Peter Hulme's *Colonial Encounters,* Michael Dash's essay "Redefining the Subject in Caribbean Literature," Homi Bhabha's "Representation and the Colonial Text," Davies and Fido's *Out of the Kumbla,* Evelyn O'Callaghan's *Woman Version,* Simon Gikandi's *Writing in Limbo: Modernism and Caribbean Literature,* and indeed, the entire critical focus of the publication *After Europe* present arguments which benefit from dialectical engagements with history.

In the West Indian critical context what seems to be needed at the moment is a study that explores the convergence of the historical and the literary in West Indian writing. A critical study exploring West Indian writers in relation to their perception and use of history will reveal both the depth of rethinking and the innovative literary strategies inspired by the confrontation with history. Each writer's vision of the region's history would be reflected in imaginative perception and artistic form, and the entire body of writing would reveal itself as a complex, growing, and definable activity. It will uncover the often blurred similarities between the writers and reveal a shared preoccupation and vision. West Indian writing can then be seen to cohere, to reveal itself as a literature shaped in many respects by the search for historical meanings as a spur to redefinition.

My idea of history and the assumptions behind its use in the book need explaining. For though I have been broadly aware of history in a literal sense as the events that have shaped life and values in the West Indies, I have used it mostly in a dialectical sense as a concept, implying a writer's sense of the meaning of history and the historical process. My elaboration and extension of this meaning have been guided by an awareness of new ideas and thinking on history as a method and discipline. The epistemological certainties and the objectivity long claimed by the discipline have been considerably undermined by new insights which have revealed the historical method as a literary construction similar to the artist's creation of story and narrative. The writing of history may be seen as subject to the particular emplotments and ideologies of narrative, and the creative writer in this context stands in a better position to write new meanings into the Caribbean past.

My definition of the West Indies and the ease with which I sometimes interchange "West Indian" and "Caribbean" needs explaining, since my conception of the region extends beyond the merely geographical and linguistic. The West Indies is in the context of this book a historical entity extending beyond the islands to cover Guiana and other parts of South and North America (the extended Caribbean), an entity with a common history involving the settlement of migrants, the decimation of aboriginal populations, the importation of slaves, and the creation of plantation societies and latifundia. This is the overall geographic and historical configuration that shapes the study in spite of its concentration on the Anglophone Caribbean. It would be noticeable then that both Wilson Harris and Edouard Glissant, whose theories feature in the framework of the book's analyses, represent different geographic and linguistic areas of the Caribbean and that in spite of the emphasis on Anglophone West Indian writing, the work of the Francophone writer Simone Schwarz-Bart is central to the discussion of the female historical imagination in chapter 9. This vision of a historical unity, I notice, is also shared by West Indian writers themselves, and since this is a book solidly based in history, the historical extensions of the term "West Indies" should be considered valid.

As is usual with studies completed over a stretch of time, I have in the course of researching and putting the book together received immeasurable support and encouragement from several people, and I must record gratitude and appreciation to a few of these. First, to Professor Alistair Hennessy, director of the Centre for Caribbean Studies, University of Warwick and general editor of the Macmillan-Warwick series, for support, encouragement, and insightful comments; to Dr. Stewart Brown of the University of Birmingham for a thorough and critical reading of the manuscript and very insightful suggestions; to Dr. Michael Gilkes and Dr. Al Creighton for critical and enthusiastic readings of the manuscript and suggestions that helped me to rethink ideas; to Dr. David Dabydeen of the University of Warwick for unwavering support and encouragement; to my family, immediate, extended, and adopted; and especially to the Eshuns of Reynard Way, Northampton, and the Bennehs of St. George's Way, Peckham; to Mrs. Grace Trenchard for the peace of her beautiful house in Bournville, Birmingham, as I did the final work on the manuscript; and to Mrs. Barbara Owens, John Mulwa, and Mercy for the arduous task of processing the manuscript in the U.K. and Kenya.

There are in addition intellectual debts which must be recorded: to historians and critics, especially Edward Brathwaite, Wilson Harris, Kenneth Ramchand, Gordon Rohlehr, Edward Baugh, Michael Gilkes, Simon Gikandi, Marjorie Thorpe, Patricia Ismond, Carole Boyce-Davies, Elaine Fido, Evelyn O'Callaghan, and Carolyn Cooper, whose work in the area has both inspired and deepened mine. There is special gratitude to Professor Kenneth Ramchand, my supervisor at the University of the West Indies, and to Dr. Richard Burton of the Department of French, University of Sussex, for introducing me to Caribbean literature and for supporting my inspiration to go to the West Indies; also, importantly, to Professors Kofi Senanu and A. N. Mensah of the University of Ghana, whose papers on the subject first fired my imagination about the literature of the Caribbean, and to Craig Tapping and Fergus Foley for all the ideas we have shared on Caribbean literature. There are, finally, financial debts: debts to the University of Cape Coast, Ghana, for study leave at the Universities of Sussex and the West Indies; to the American Association of University Women for a Marion Riley International Fellowship that supported me in Trinidad for a year; and to the Universities of London, Warwick, and Birmingham for visiting fellowships.

Introduction

The Critical Context
Defining Subject and Form

A critical study dealing with the perception, interpretation, and use of history in West Indian literature must necessarily confront the literary implications of relationships between ideologies and texts. Within this context ideology encompasses not merely those systems of belief that make up coherent doctrines but the very conditions of our experience of life, those combinations of social, economic, and political conditions which constitute what Althusser has termed our social formation.[1] The ways in which a text constructs these contexts and analyzes relations within them represents an ideological discourse, and in most imaginative literature such a discourse shapes the nature and representation of experience as well as its transformations within the text.

In evaluating such interactions, the critic must not only extract perceptions and meanings but also demonstrate the working of ideological discourse as it informs the entire conception and form of the work. For contrary to the "formalist" belief that a text selects only the contexts that will reinforce its form, this study's premise accepts that formal structures in texts are themselves selected by particular ideologies; that while there may not be strict, unifying correlations between form and ideology, there may still be demonstrable impact that reveals and explains even the contradictions in their interactions. After all, the purpose of writing is, as Foucault has argued, not necessarily to exalt the act of writing or to pin a subject within language, but to create spaces into which the writing subject constantly disappears.[2] The critic's business, then, is to bring out the work's relation to this space, to reconstruct experience and thought from the intersection between ideology and form in a text.

In the context of this study the broad ideological thrust is the nature, meaning, and impact of history in the West Indies. The discourse on history, while confronting fundamental assumptions behind European perceptions and interpretations of the region's history, is really inspired by the imperatives of redefinition and subjectification which are basically colonial impulses. Traumatized by history, the West Indian writer is yet continually haunted by its specter and perpetually engaged with redefining it. As Michael Dash has observed, "The task of consciousness becomes necessary in a world that is the product of others' dreams, where systems of knowledge and signification are enforced in order to produce docility, constraint and helplessness.[3] Active self-formation or "subjectification," a major concern of modern critical theory, is thus a necessary and frequent discourse in Caribbean writing.

For the West Indian writer reconceptualizations of the past and the creation of consciousness are part of what Michael Dash calls "a new authority or authorship," and the methodologies of these processes interestingly reflect poststructuralist and postmodernist destabilization of centered authority. The "colonial" writer's attempts at redefinition and self-formation exhibit the same skepticism towards self-contained traditions that poststructuralist methodologies demonstrate towards homogenizing categories of critical discourse. The literary idea of the text as a self-contained unity (whether this unity resides entirely in the consciousness of the author or in the text) parallels the static gestalt and total models articulated by most colonizing cultures. The West Indian writer faced with such models and aware of their bias finds it necessary, in Harris's words, "to descend beneath the 'surface mind' of a culture into other *structures* that alter emphases upon vague and elusive formations suppressed by static gestalt institution."[4]

Poststructuralist criticism, decentering the text as the single most dominant source of meaning, focuses on the plurality of the text, on the text as the source of several possible meanings. "The text is not an empty space, filled with meaning from outside itself, any more than it is the transcription of an authorial intention, filled with meaning from outside language . . . The intertextual relations of the text are never purely literary. Fiction draws not only on other fiction but on knowledges of its period, discourses in circulation which are themselves sites of power and the contest for power."[5]

The focus on plurality is really the critic's way of creating other focuses, other possible meanings that would undermine the dogmatic, self-certain subject. Correspondingly, the art of criticism has moved beyond the domain of expression and formal transformation to center on the cultural and exterior ramifications of the subject, in most cases deflating the author's individualist hold on fictive structures. Foucault has elaborated this new critical perspective in several essays and argued that as the exterior historical and cultural context of art gains credence, the individualist and realist idea of the author as the voice, the orbit of the fictive world diminishes, giving centrality to the "subject" as a presence and a shaping force.[6]

The focus on the subject (i.e., background, cosmos, collective) has been crucial in highlighting other variables beyond the orbit of author and the known, and particularly in the literature of the West Indies, this perspective on art and artistic representation has become pertinent as an additional dimension to "text," "author," and the interplay of style in a work of art. For a people whose circumstances and consciousness have been shaped by systems of domination and dependency and who must therefore create their own subjectification, plurality of text means a great deal more than the representation of multiple experiences behind the text. It means a historically and culturally grounded text which would include not only the known and literary forms of apprehending and registering experience but also the unknown and nonliterary.

This multiple perspective on context and artistic representation is a reflection of differing relations to history and experience and their impact on West Indian self-definition. Michael Dash has explored the implications of these differing relations to history and identified two contrasting perceptions:

There are those who focus on the known and the real as an exclusive area of concern and who can explain all structures as part of rational knowable order. The self-certain subject, free to confer meaning on his or her world, to wrest the land from Prospero's signifying grasp, is the exemplary figure in this fiction. For other writers the world exists prior to and independent of subject. They concentrate on that area of experience which exceeds explanation, on the deconstruction of the sovereign subject. The constructive subject's grasp of the world is always inadequate . . . In the first instance, the structuring ego longs for a world of alternative stable meanings, of fixed values. The second provides a radical critique of the privileged subject. In this view, the individual subject is simply the site, the threshold where collective subject finds articulation, where private and public, individual and group interact. The apotheosis of the subject and the decentered subject, the poetics of rupture and "relation," are the determining factors in a Caribbean literary tradition.[7]

The two perspectives on Caribbean definition are manifested in the interaction between historical perception and imaginative writing. For the perception and interpretation of a Caribbean relation to history is perhaps the single most consistent and crucial preoccupation in a West Indian literary endeavor. Michael Dash's differentiation between the two major perspectives may therefore approximate the underlying critical focus of this book. For the imaginative writer history can be both a nightmare and a challenge; a nightmare if his or her relation to it remains imprisoned in the fixed relations and attitudes of the region's linear past; a challenge if he or she exploits the artist's freedom to endow history and experience with figurative meanings and explores other areas of experience beyond the rational linear order.

The West Indian writer's relation to history moves between these perceptual perspectives, generating a dialectic which dictates and shapes both theme and form in the region's literature. The dialectic of the known and the linear accepts the ordinarily linear quality of our experience of time and history, making a straightforward correlation between cause and effect and therefore between past, present, and future. In conformity with its assumptions, writers assume particular relationships to space and time. Time is conceived of as a linear movement, and history becomes a chronicle of progress and development in a particular space and time.

In West Indian writing such conceptions of time and history have come against several disadvantages. For the history of slavery and colonialism conceived in such linear terms inevitably presents an image of the West Indian as a victim rather than a creator of history, and invariably writers have either had to struggle to transcend "history" and reconstruct new identities or accept the despairing conclusion that displacement and violation have been historically determined and are therefore unconquerable.

The choice between stasis and transformation, between determinism and re-visioning is always a matter of individual perspective. For the novelist V. S. Naipaul, the past brings on a crucial self-knowledge which is nevertheless futilely circumscribed in a vision of West Indian man as chained to past violations. Although Naipaul himself urges West Indian writers to engage with self-definition by confronting their history,[8] this definition seems only to confirm the realities of violation and their permanent repercussions on the West Indies. The image of the West Indian as displaced and shipwrecked is never really countered in Naipaul's works. Rather, it is balanced by a historical understanding that enables characters to impose some personal order on their history. In spite of a sense of his displaced condition, the protagonist in *The Mimic Men* believes he has achieved an imaginative order and understanding that could free him from further illusions and simplifications. "By this recreation the event became historical and manageable; it was given its place; it will no longer disturb me. And this became my aim: from the central fact of this meeting . . . to impose order on my own history, to abolish that disturbance, which is what a narrative in sequence might have led me to."[9]

This kind of wry understanding is eventually all that is possible for Naipaul's protagonist. The recognition of the processes that determine one's place in history, it appears, leads to a better self-awareness and identity than the sense of unexamined continuity which characterizes certain relations to history.[10] Writing becomes then a way of gaining understanding and controlling the chaos of the known as the writer pitches an ideal of stable values against disorder.[11]

West Indian writers, engaged with history and definition, have explored alternative perceptions, moving away from a cloying material time, investing history with figurative connotations, and creating a whole new corpus of sensibility by relating to other spaces and other inarticulate presences in the region. It was Wilson Harris who first recognized the limitations of the linear vision and its novelistic expression in the realistic novel of persuasion. The idea that a novelist must consolidate his or her characters by persuading us to believe in their lifelike portrayal, the entire apparatus of verisimilitude which was the focal point of nineteenth-century European realism, proves inadequate as a medium for registering the difference of the colonial subject. The idea of representation as a natural and gradual unfolding of reality and consciousness would be limiting in a colonial context in which the exigencies of representation may require not a mimetic representation of the transcendental subject or a given preconstituted reality but the production of meaning within it.[12] In Caribbean writing figurations of new meanings in history have engaged with presences often excised from recorded history. Harris has argued that inarticulate layers of the region as well as the subtle and far-reaching renaissance that took place among displaced people in the region have generated variables of myth and legend which are crucial for a sense of community and which need their historical and artistic correlation in both the historiography and imaginative writing of the region. A literature of renaissance and reconstruction, Harris argues, needs to move beyond the behavioristic and deterministic limitations of the realistic novel and invest in "an art of memory which dislocates, in some measure, an idolatrous plane of realism by immersing us in a peculiar kind of ruined fabric."[13] Such an art "may help to free us from a consensus of bestiality; monolithic helplessness, monolithic violence."[14] It may help us to "visualise the globe within a new corpus of sensibility wherein the function of character within the interior of the novel will begin to displace a helpless and hopeless consolidation of powers."[15]

The subject of history and the West Indian artist's relation to it becomes then a source not just for defining subject and perspective in the region's literature but also a spur to a new radical art, an inner art, a drama of consciousness which rises above "story line" to visualize other depths of experience, in several cases, primordial realms of broken recollections (as in Lamming, Brathwaite, Harris) which are often a spur to the acquisition of image and vision and to the envisioning of community. In the literature of the West Indies the groping towards such an art has been gradual, varied, and supremely complex, registering variations from genre to genre and from writer to writer, revealing a literature that shapes and defines its own context and artistic form.

The complex artistic processes involved in these explorations make up the subject of this book, which is basically a study of the interplay between historical thought and literary perception in the Caribbean region. Each chapter examines a particular writer's relationship to the phenomenon of history as well as his or her mode of representing this relationship in fiction, poetry, or drama. Although the book explores the separate genres of fiction, poetry, and drama under the common umbrella of the historical imagination, its delineations show a critical awareness of their separate histories and ramifications in the development of literature, recognizing the different natures, demands, and orientation of each genre as well as the impulses of vision that lead a writer to choose a particular artistic medium. It is aware, for instance, of fiction's approximation of life, especially its attempts to give an illusion of reality by evoking a full span of life in which characters appear in constant interaction with their environment and with each other. It takes note of the artistic effects of this orientation in the organization of facts and events in the novel, particularly of the ways in which these are linked by time, place, circumstance, and the cause and effect of action.

In comparison, the book distinguishes the different nature, orientation, and form of drama and poetry, demonstrating, for instance, drama's concentration on dramatic collision, that particular reflection of life around which all action, all manifestations of life must gravitate. By identifying the essentially allusive and selective nature of drama, which reduces the artistic experience to the particular human, moral problem that the collision heightens, the book's explorations differentiate dramatic form from fictive form, especially in its relation to historical perception. Thus it demonstrates that whereas the novel's broad enactment of a span of life encapsulates the method of history, drama's concentration on collision focuses on the complex ramifications of a particular problem, making its medium less amenable to history's linear portrayal of events and their causal links. It recognizes drama's performance aspect and sees its ability to mobilize and disperse emotions within performance as a different way of relating to history.

In the same way the sections on poetry reveal the poetic medium as different in form and orientation from the novel and drama. By highlighting poetry's unique way of perceiving and articulating experience, its patterned projection of the idea or intuition, its dependence on verbal organization and the connotations of words to communicate experience, the book distinguishes poetic form from the realistic enactment of fiction, showing its suitability for capturing flashes of insight and intuition outside the linear realism of fiction and history.

Finally, the book establishes a correlation between the artist's vision and his or her medium of expression, showing how a particular artistic medium affects a writer's relation to history. In this respect it is quite cautious, refusing to pin a definitive historical vision on any writer and instead laying bare the sheer range, complexity, and difference in attitude as the writers themselves shift from medium to medium. Thus, for instance, rather than limit itself to Brathwaite's historical vision as is revealed in his poetry, the book delineates as well a contrasting perspective in the poet's academic history, showing the variations in vision as Brathwaite moves from the medium of history to the poetic mode. The two chapters on Walcott's poetry and drama attempt a similar juxtaposition, showing how in both cases the medium of exploration impacts on Walcott's relation to the historical process in the Caribbean region. It is my awareness of these important correlations between vision and medium that impels me to put the three genres together in this wide-ranging book. I have worked with the conviction that in spite of the critical risks involved, the methodology has the obvious advantage of deepening the imaginative grappling with the phenomenon of history in the region of the Caribbean.

By encapsulating my critical explorations within the intersection of history and the imagination, I am, of course, assuming a double-edged interpretation of imagination, regarding it on one hand as a subjective creation of images and symbols and on the other as an understanding that orders and objectifies images in the cognitive process. In other words, I am accepting that there is an impulse of imagination that conjures various impressions of sense and subjectively creates a work of art while at the same time there exists an aspect of imagination that logically orders facts and images as part of the processes of knowing and consciousness. There is a sense, then, in which the historical imagination operates on two very similar levels in the argument of this book. There is on one hand the imaginative construction of historical material involved in historical knowledge and encompassing history as a discipline. Here the imagination works to arrange and order events and relics of the past, reconstructing a sequential picture of an age. Since the past is never an account to begin with, it is the historian who must order and synthesize the events, relics, and debris of the past, performing an imaginative and philosophical act almost parallel to the narrative organization of the novelist. Thus, as Hayden White argues, the process of writing history involves an artistic component which exercises the imagination in characterizing events according to certain motifs, sometimes literally inventing story, drama, mood, and situation in the interest of historical explanation.[16]

Yet even in this artistic representation, the historian, unlike the fiction writer, must work towards conclusions based on questions raised about a particular history (i.e., what happened and why). Thus, over and above the artistic presentation of narrative and story, the historian must present another level of argument that would seek to explain what happened by invoking principles and laws of historical explanation. At all these levels of historical perception and understanding, the historian is bound by a particular space and time and by a constant need to be truthful to fact and evidence. There is a sense, then, in which the imaginative leeway available to the historian may be limited by his or her motif or by the demands of the historical discipline itself; and in this book the historian's imaginative interpretation exists side by side with what I term the imaginative writer's conception and treatment of history. The juxtaposition is both pertinent and revealing, especially in the way it demonstrates the writer's capacity to transcend the boundaries of space and time to explore a timeless pattern that explains at the same time the present, the past, and the future.

From a contrasting perspective the juxtapositions also enable me to explore the West Indian writer's consciously historical conception of the present, an engagement which interprets contemporary social structures in terms of the region's history, opening out possibilities for redefinitions of West Indian experience. It is from the standpoint of these juxtapositions that the reader can appreciate the importance and relevance of the chapter on West Indian historiography. For as a framework of Eurocentric and Caribbean-centered historiography, it enacts the progress of historical thought and writing in the region and becomes both a premise of the argument and a refutation of it, showing on one hand the scope and limits of historical writing and at the same time presenting the imaginative explorations of writers as reactions to the bias and inevitability that govern western assumptions about history in the region.

The arrangement of chapters in the book attempts another kind of progression in its correlation of historical vision and artistic representation. The "literary" chapters begin with the West Indian writer's most obvious and straightforward relationship to history: the historical novel, the novel as history, a mode of representation in which the writer constructs a plot around historical events and presents characters as living in the same world with historical persons, revealing a conception of the past in the way in which characters' lives are shaped at specific moments of history and how this shaping reveals the texture and character of a particular age.

Because of the book's basically critical focus, explorations of the historical novel also raise the crucial issue of the tension between historical truth and the writer's imaginative freedom. For to be able to convey by imaginative sympathy the nature and character of a particular age a writer must also describe and interpret accurately, and such a need may clash with the imaginative impulse to follow the inner workings of plot and character as well as with the impulse to put new meanings and interpretations on the past.

The chapters exploring the West Indian writer's consciously historical conception of the present reveal the most complex and varied relationships to history in the entire literature of the region. The leeway provided by an imaginative interpretation of history opens up possibilities for producing meanings, for investing the past with figurative meanings, for extending the connotations of history in the region, and for evolving new modes of representing them in fiction, poetry, and drama. Thus, we move from the linear deterministic visions of the past and their artistic correlations in the realistic novels of V. S. Naipaul through the novels of George Lamming, where the novel of space and time, the novel of persuasion, is also punctuated with other modes of apprehending history as well as criteria for representing these in fiction. Lamming believes that the imaginative writer has the freedom to put new meanings on history, and the contrasting states of consciousness represented in his novels as well as the metaphors of possession and descent into submerged history and consciousness represent other apprehensions and interpretations which enlarge his idea of history in the region. Although Lamming remains solidly within the mode of the novel of persuasion his metaphor of the "backward glance" registers apprehensions of the past and of community which represent areas of experience and self often suppressed, often outside the known and recorded history of colonial relations yet energizing a vision of self beyond restricted colonial definitions. These are the new meanings, the contrasting states of consciousness, the "vision and stress of transplantation in the person out of one world into another,"[17] which push Lamming's relation to the past beyond that uniform pattern of imperialism which tends to constrict the vision of a novelist like Naipaul.

It is indeed in relation to the vision of the two novelists that Wilson Harris's perception and interpretation of West Indian history emerges as novel and unique, and the book arranges itself to present this comparison. For Harris's explorations, especially in the *Guiana Quartet*, reveal a dissatisfaction with the imperial and material confines of the region's history and with the sense of inevitability that governs and limits the dialectic on history in the region. His apprehension of a world of the spirit which unites men in a common pursuit and in which economic and political bonds pale into insignificance, reveals an engagement with dimensions of history beyond the hollow ground of conquest. His immaterial vision opens a gateway to several paradoxes in Caribbean history and experience: paradoxes of space, personality, and vision which make up a multidimensional and fluid perception of the region's history. The chapter on Harris examines these paradoxes in relation to his transformation of the novel form, especially his success in breaking through the boundaries of the realist novel, the form which throughout the nineteenth and early twentieth centuries had appeared to be the definitive form of the novel genre.

The book's transition from the novel genre to poetry elicits further comment. For in relation to argument and progression of subject the evolution of vision and poetic style in Walcott and Brathwaite reveals the subtle interplay between interpretation of history and poetic form. The two chapters make repeated references to each other, pointing to the complementary visions of both poets and laying bare the tenuous differences in perception of history, conception of the imagination, and relation to poetic form. For in their somewhat differing interpretations of history their poetic art nevertheless reveals what Harris has characterized as the nature and purpose of creative endeavor in the West Indies: the energizing of the diminished man. "What sort of art is the outcome of this environment? The art of the skeleton or cell, the lonely, diminished structure of man . . . [Yet] we have to move that diminished creature through our work in a manner that is disturbing, so disturbing that vitality and power are realized as a very strong possibility."[18]

Both Walcott and Brathwaite, in complementary ways (though from different angles), give energy to the faceless, diminished man of the West Indies. Walcott talks of striding

from the magnetic sphere of legends,
from the gigantic myth,
To change the marble sweat which pebbled
the wave-blow of stone brows
for this sweat-drop on the cedar plank,
for a future without heroes,
to make out of these foresters and fishermen
heraldic men![19]

Brathwaite commits himself equally to the paradoxical energy and strength of his song, the song of the skeleton.

But if to live here
is to die
clutching ashes

the fist tight
the skull dry
I will sing songs of the skeleton.

I will return to the pebble
to the dumb seed
The unlighted faces of the fetish in the vegetable kingdom.[20]

The two poetry chapters demonstrate the close relationship between historical perception, conception of the imagination, and poetic style, revealing Walcott and Brathwaite not so much as poets in opposition to each other but as artists relating with differing emphases on aspects of history in the region. Thus Walcott's philosophy of elation, even his propensity for and ambivalence towards metaphor, paradox, and ambiguity are in the long run as much an attempt to energize the diminished man as Brathwaite's aesthetic of renaissance.

The chapter on configurations of history in the writing of West Indian women presents contrasting perspectives on an important and significant voice that has frequently been deflated both in the theorization of the region's literature and in the construction of its central canon. It is indeed an irony of history that women's historical visions came to be deflated and supplanted in early postcolonial refigurations of history. For as griots, spiritual foremothers, and culture heroes, their perspectives and the values derived from them were instrumental in the African's initial negotiation of Caribbean space. In that transitional period between displacement and appropriation of new space when enslaved Africans were compelled to "verify a self's being in the world,"[21] women's voices, folk wisdom, and refigurations of knowledge from the past were instrumental in nurturing a sense of self. Those rich resources of memory and oral traditions transformed and transmitted through the generations are crucial aspects of Caribbean relations to history even though they have been continually devalued within the creolized and colonial worlds of the Caribbean. Thus, in contrast to the written postcolonial literatures inspired by nationalist ideologies and dominated by male writers, the orally transmitted knowledge has remained within a submerged oral culture and is only now being retrieved and refigured in the contemporary writing of Caribbean women.

It is this historical background that explains the relative absence of women's voices in the early debates on history and subjectification in the region's literature. Disadvantaged educationally and often unable to express their experiences in the new language and forms of representation, women remained marginal to the literary debates on history. However, their belated perceptions and explorations have introduced different and important dimensions that reveal the incompleteness of the perspective of male writers.

Placed almost at the end of the discussions, women's writing opens several avenues for investigating the larger question of gender and history and for exploring the ways in which women's distinctive figurations of history break new ground in the representation of the colonial subject. The chapter locates the power of this writing in the way it valorizes and at the same time disrupts the conventional images that define the women's sphere.

The final chapter presents a fresh look at a much aired but often inadequately examined aspect of the West Indian writer's relation to history. Africa has existed in the historical imagination of the West Indian writer on two broad levels: as symbol and vision of the ancestor and as an aspect of continuity and submerged history—song, dance, word, ritual—which writers feel can be activated in a new definition of the "African" man in the Caribbean. Thus, beginning with Denis Williams' vigorously argued article on Caribbean man's relation to the ancestor,[22] the chapter examines the imaginative confrontation with Africa in his *Other Leopards,* in Walcott's *Dream on Monkey Mountain,* Harris's *The Secret Ladder,* Dennis Scott's *An Echo in the Bone,* and Paule Marshall's *Praisesong for the Widow,* revealing how the engagement leads to greater self-knowledge whether or not it points to identification with or separation from Africa.

Although the book works logically towards an end, it never pretends to be definitive about vision and perception, since the very open-endedness of the subject precludes such conclusions. The concluding chapter is therefore a summary of deductions, highlighting focuses, trends, and developments that eventually reveal the West Indian engagement with history as a dynamic aspect of a literature continually growing and shifting perspectives and forms as it grapples with the ramifications of history in the region of the Caribbean.

Chapter One

The Scope and Limits of West Indian Historiography

> History in pursuing a continuous wall as its domain, in consolidating na-
> tional or local political and economic self-interest, becomes the servant of a
> material vision of time. As such it has not realized criteria to assess the subtle
> discontinuities which point to the originalities of man as a civilization-mak-
> ing animal who can alter the architectural complex of an age. Such an alter-
> ation or dialectic of alteration would seem to me the cornerstone for a phi-
> losophy of history in the Third World of the Caribbean. It would bring into
> play the inspiration for new criteria within the dead-end of economic and
> political institutions.
>
> Wilson Harris, "History, Fable and Myth in the Caribbean and Guianas"

When we talk of the historical imagination we talk in terms of particular
modes of apprehending and conveying the past. We imply that history is an
inquiry into human action, change, and development in the past and that a
certain process of enactment and unfolding can make this past intelligible.
The processes that bring the past to life and make it understandable constitute a concept of the historical imagination; the most common of these in
Western thought are historiography, philosophy, and literature. All three
modes have influenced the tenor and character of the historical imagination in the West Indies precisely because, since the seventeenth century,
historical writing in the region has been dominated by European and Euro-
pean-centered visions of what constitutes history. As a result, our understanding and appreciation of present trends in West Indian historiography
and of current reconceptualizations of history in the imaginative literature
of the region would be impossible without a knowledge of the European
historical consciousness as it emerged and has developed.

The idea of the past as a distinct territory from the present was central to this consciousness and was indeed a secularization of Jewish and Christian traditions in religion. The belief that man's life on earth had a design and direction imposed by God, that events had a particular progression and purpose, gave a distinctive meaning to the past. It could be envisaged now as an autonomous phenomenon with a beginning, a movement, and a goal. The movement was towards transcendence, a religious goal which, though challenged by Renaissance and rationalist philosophers, remains fundamental to European historical thought. For what the secular philosophical traditions really did was replace the religious motive with a rationalist explanation. This perspective, which envisioned the laws of history as dictated by dialectics, implied that the meaning of history lay in this world and that a certain metaphysical determinism held the key to this meaning.

Though this was a far-reaching perspective that enabled a critical and analytical engagement with the past, it also ordered and regulated temporal distances between events and imposed a chronology of historical facts on the act of memory itself. Its concern with the theory and the logic of narration and its analysis of the necessity of events were to be challenged in the nineteenth century by a historicist perspective, which argued for the multiplicity of individual and cultural manifestations. The rise of historicism introduced new dimensions into historical thinking, though the fundamental idea of transcendence still remained. For the historicists the essence of history was man's reality and humanness, and historical writing was thus to deal with nations and peoples, with their expressions, customs, institutions, thoughts, and myths and their transformations through time.[1]

Yet this humanistic and multidimensional perspective ironically coexisted with the ideological biases behind the very idea of categorizing and describing other peoples and cultures. The dawn of historicism was also the crystallization of a European self-consciousness about race and about its own superior position within a hierarchical chain of being. In addition, empiricist methodologies that framed reconstructions of the past demanded rigorous standards of evaluation and verification, introducing a mode of scientific analysis that overshadowed other nonscientific perceptions of the past. This combination of ideology and methodology was important in European conceptualizations about peoples and cultures of the New World. The epistemological categories developed for their expression influenced historical writing by both metropolitan and settler historians.

To talk of a West Indian historiography is therefore to talk of the convergence of these factors in European historical writing and of their continued impact on the historiography of the region. It is also to talk of the successive stages and cumulative development of historical writing and of how each age has perceived, conveyed, and used the past. In the West Indies the fundamental framework for such writing has been the colonial context. West Indian historiography followed patterns dictated by the circumstances and exigencies of conquest and by the political, economic, and social implications of slavery and colonialism. The early West Indian historians were also in the main European colonists and planters, often writing from the point of view of conquerors celebrating imperial glories and defending the validity of their social institutions.

The early forms of this writing, mostly descriptive accounts by Spanish colonists, were "unhistorical" in the sense in which history itself had come to be regarded in Europe by the nineteenth century. Writers such as Colon, Ovieto, La Casas, and Herrera were really chroniclers, recorders of contemporary events which they knew at first hand.[2] They were men, making and writing history, and their narratives of Spanish voyages and conquests, of aboriginal Indians and of the European creation of a new society in the Caribbean, established the point of view which has consistently underlain historical writing in the area. It was a point of view that ascribed creativity to European colonists and projected them as the creators of history in the region. Most narratives, especially those of European voyages, projected an image of the heroic European battling against hostile forces to establish supremacy in the area; and in spite of the dissenting voice of La Casas, vociferous in his indictment of Spanish brutality, this perspective remained part of the historical tradition of "settler" historians, becoming an integral part of historical interpretation and the yardstick by which the racial differences of aborigines and slaves were frequently explained.

By the seventeenth century the past had become sufficiently remote to be identified and explained, and historians like Du Tertre and Rochefort could re-create the world and atmosphere of the early colonists and attempt to explain the new society.[3] This was a period in which English, French, and Dutch colonists struggled for footholds in the Caribbean, and the contemporary historical writing attempted to describe and analyze the strange mixture of people and cultures and the new relations between them. The very nature of the society, its newness and strangeness to Europeans, necessitated a methodology beyond ordinary narrative. It called for analysis and explanation, and the rather unusual coexistence of colonists, free Indians, slaves, Catholics, heretics, and others provided both a background and a challenge.

The historical methodology was still the descriptive narrative, but the understanding of the scope and possibilities of history were considerable, because the historical narrative did more than record the characteristics of a new society. It created a historical world where landscape, manners, and customs stood in comparative relationships to each other, promising an analysis of the forces at work in a new colonial society. Because their authors attempted to mirror, explain, and elucidate the development of a whole society, these historical writings tended to be all-embracing and comprehensive, touching on all aspects of man in society as well as on the problems of human relationships. The history they portray is the history of man in his world, a humanist perspective which was also a reflection of the European ethos of the time and of then-current ideals of equality. These early chroniclers were not professional historians or empiricists in the sense in which we assess historians in the present day; although they established a certain need for a narrative which should be true to facts, their judgments of these facts were often widely varied and colored by current European ideas and ideologies.

"In the writing of West Indian history the most potent atmosphere underlying interpretation have often been drawn from outside the subject."[4] Elsa Goveia's remark clarifies a major and persistent characteristic of West Indian historiography as it emerged and progressed, an aspect which also underlies its greatest irony: that a comprehensive, almost encyclopedic array of distinctly local material should have been analyzed and judged not in terms of the region's particularity and future but by ideas and beliefs developed in the context of other societies and other futures.

This mode of historical writing bequeathed to West Indian historiography has undergone various phases and crises, not as chronological changes determined by a movement from one period to another but as responses to social situations and change in the region. In the eighteenth century, for instance, various social conditions gave a context and a character to West Indian historical writing. The consolidation of the institution of slavery, the creolization of slave society, the crisis of West Indian relationships with metropolitan England, and the upheaval created by the American Revolution and humanitarian movements opposed to slavery generated the social and ideological context from which most historical interpretations were made.

The age gave birth to the planter historian, the West Indian "Creole," frequently conscious of the distinctiveness of his society but, ironically, also aware of the metropolis as the bigger, more real world. It was an irony that also informed the tenor of historical writing and gave eighteenth-century West Indian historiography its paradoxical perspective. For there was, on one hand, the local historian with distinctly West Indian sympathies and loyalties, living in a society based on slavery, conscious of the variety of social groupings and of peculiarly West Indian institutions; and there was on the other, the larger metropolitan world to which most planter historians were also linked, a world of larger institutions and larger ideas, the world which originally created those institutions now being creolized.

The historian of the period had inherited a historical methodology based on description and analysis as a supplement to the narration of events, and his history attempted to understand the nature of his society through an examination of its various institutions and their historical development. The historical writing of Edward Long and Bryan Edwards, the dominant planter historians of the period, embody both this consciousness and its methodology.[5] Long's history was, for instance, inspired by a belief in the possibility of an internally autonomous Jamaica. It analyzed the island's political, constitutional, and economic development, showing it as the peculiar progress of a society with a different past and future from metropolitan England. Yet, ironically, the assumptions that governed Long's analysis were metropolitan assumptions and principles such as Locke's theory on the limits of the sovereign power and its dependence on the will of the people, an idea of political relations and political liberty developed in a society of free men.

As an idea, the vision of constitutional rights and political freedom implied in Long's analysis was a radical and revolutionary view of what Jamaica could become; but it is obvious that in practice it did not lead Long to an understanding and interpretation of a slave-based society, developing in a certain pattern, creating certain social groupings, and fostering particular group and individual relations. Did liberal principles, for instance, also apply to slaves? Long only resolved these problems by taking refuge in defensive arguments, attempting to convince himself that the liberal principles he championed applied only to free men. It was as if he was analyzing only an idea of Jamaica, as if the social order of plantation slavery had not changed society and people. It was altogether as if Locke's political theory was being held in some vacuum.

Long's analysis was indeed a failure of historical interpretation which blocked his understanding of the dynamics of slave society and led him to see slavery almost as a divinely ordered and changeless institution with no relation to the quality of Jamaican life. Its defects are a reflection of a historical imagination that derived its inspiration and framework from outside its subject instead of deriving them from within it. This outer, Eurocentered perspective and framework is, to my mind, the most characteristic aspect of West Indian historiography in the eighteenth century. It explains the different perspectives and biases with which the same material was interpreted by historians of varied persuasions. Long's liberal framework could be matched or balanced, for instance, with the humanist perspective of Edmund and William Burke, who argued the common humanity of all men yet were unable to offer a "humanist" analysis of slavery or the measure of amelioration or tolerance possible within its systems.[6] It could as well be matched with the philosophical approach of Robertson's *History of America*, carefully documented and humanist in approach yet unable to analyze the true significance of slavery or account for its existence and persistence in South America.

On the other hand, Long's framework could be put beside the humanitarianism of Abbé Raynal, whose historical imagination was nursed by the rationalist concepts of liberty and reason and by the new awareness of the relativity of social institutions fostered in Europe, ironically, by the discovery of the New World and its diversity of religions and cultures.[7] Raynal's history, written in the context of the new rationalism, may have offered a radical reinterpretation of his material. But it too was compromised by the very fact that it operated within a slave society and a mercantilist system and often utilized material already used in historical arguments that supported and justified slavery. Thus, though the concepts of liberty and reason from which he examined the geography, peoples, manners, and institutions of the West Indies enabled him to reject slavery outright, the entire framework of rationalist thought which he imposed on his material led paradoxically to purely theoretical considerations: views of slavery instead of the real and material conditions of the slave as they shaped men through history; the idea of slavery instead of the slave himself.

The diversity of assumptions and biases imposed on historical interpretations may be glimpsed even in like-minded planter historians like Long and Edwards. For if Long's perspective was of the constitutional rights of Jamaica argued within the framework of the liberal principles of seventeenth-century England, Edwards's was a "Creole" defense against the English humanitarians and abolitionists. It was a Creole and colonial perspective committed to the mercantilist system and the institution of slavery which supported it. As such, its dichotomies sprang, as in most of the other histories, from his naive attempts to reconcile the claims of order and justice in a slave-based institution. Generally, however, Edwards perceived man's action in the West Indies from the point of view of a civilizing act and saw history in the region as the progress and development of a higher civilization. In this context the decimation of aborigines could be seen merely as a cultural battle, a Christian country's defeat of a savage people; slavery itself could, by the same token, be justified in these terms. Thus Edwards rejected Long's racial arguments only to substitute a bias of cultural interpretations in which progress, development, and civilization could proceed only in the rule of the wise over the unwise, the Christian over the savage.

The basic argument, then, is that West Indian historiography was shaped both by a European historical consciousness and by economic systems and ideologies in Europe. This background presented a paradoxical situation in historical writing. For the very mode of a European historical sense and methodology fostered an active consciousness of man in history, an awareness not just of day-to-day events that happened to men in their environment but of the relationships between them, of those circumstances and forces which either conditioned men's actions or constrained their will. This consciousness was reflected in the vigor with which historical writing attempted to describe, explain, and analyze the past as a way of understanding a new society. But the colonial context was also a restraint in the sense that it imposed an apparatus of perceptions, a system of thoughts, ideas, and ideologies from which the internal workings of the society were often perceived and explained, and the result was that history failed as an engagement with the whole of society and assumed the perspectives and biases of the group with power.

What happened then to the nature of historical perception and writing when the mercantilist system itself was undermined and its great structure crumbled in the early nineteenth century? Earlier historians had, of course, been influenced by a respect for the social order and by an anxiety to preserve its social structure; nineteenth-century historians, without this compulsion and need, appeared to have broken free (for a short period at least) from the tradition of historiography established in the eighteenth century. The conditions of the islands had changed appreciably enough for men to perceive history in a different light. The collapse of slavery had weakened the foundations of political and economic life in the colonies, and antislavery agitation and strategies had identified humanitarianism with imperial control of the colonies, not trusting the West Indian planter oligarchy to initiate change. Threats of imperial control of the colonies through Crown Colony government brought the islands into a new colonial relationship with the metropolis, and the vigorous Whig tradition of politics, with its consciousness of separateness and internal autonomy, came to be rejected even among West Indians as a planter-class imposition. Internally, West Indian societies were themselves in a state of flux. The disappearance of such a major social order had to have some effect on the texture of society. A large West Indian peasantry made up of ex-slaves had emerged, more willing to establish small subsistence holdings than to work on plantations for small wages. Beside them a mulatto peasantry had also emerged, economically significant and poised to make some substantial difference to the social composition of the society.

These social conditions naturally affected the historiography of the period. Historians seemed to have been liberated from the eighteenth-century bondage to the social structure of slavery and were able now to examine the institution impartially. West Indian historiography tended now to have a social thrust and was directed more stringently towards social analysis. Historians were at last defining an attitude to an emerging society, explaining the course of events in terms of the influence and ingredients of a given environment and grasping (for instance) the importance of emancipation, which led to a massive ex-slave exodus from the plantations. But for all its social direction, the analysis of the period tended to be divided by two perspectives: a perspective that still analyzed the society as an economic commodity and conceived of the ex-slave as a productive agent of plantation economy, and a perspective that envisaged him as a free and component member of a developing society, free like other men to exercise personal desires and preferences.

It was this later perspective that distinguished the work of a historian like Montgomery Martin, whose analysis began from a common base of humanity and explained the expectations of the newly emancipated slave.[8] Because of Martin's humanitarian bias, he was able to appreciate the creation of a postemancipation West Indian peasantry and to understand the thinking and consciousness of the new peasant. His assumption that the ex-slave has as much right as others to profitable cultivation of the land was reflected in a sympathetic understanding of the Jamaican peasant's new attitude to labor and capital. What was interesting, though, was the way in which it was now possible to hold a humanist position and carry it through analysis. Historians who argued from a single standard of common humanity seemed more able than eighteenth-century historians to hold a humanist position and maintain it through actual social analysis. The composition had changed and so had the climate of thinking, and with the institution of slavery no longer dominant, it was becoming possible to envisage other social relations and possibilities.

Perspectives like Martin's were not new and were indeed only part of other historical positions encroaching on West Indian historiography, especially in the wake of Crown Colony government and the new threat of imperial control.[9] The tendency sprang from a general British attitude towards history which helped to define relationships with other nations and peoples. It was an essentially optimistic view which projected history as following a gradual path of development and progress. "The true field of historical study," declared the historian William Stubbs, "is the history of those nations and institutions in which real growth of humanity is to be traced, in which we can follow the development, the retardations and perturbation, the ebb and flow of human progress."[10] The idea that modern history was a gradual progress in the direction of organized freedom and that British history itself had followed this path of development became a major theme in the writing of British historians of the time. Macaulay, Acton, and Freeman all lent their support to a view which was later to be used in justification of an imperialism based on the thesis of inequality propounded by Arthur Gobineau.[11] "Subjection to a people of a higher capacity for government," declared Lord Acton, "is itself no misfortune, and it is to most countries the condition for their political advancement."[12]

Here was a view which could logically and easily support imperial control, Crown Colony government, and the reestablishment of old plantation relationships, and it could not but affect West Indian historiography. Thus, in spite of the postemancipation analysis and interpretations of historians like W. G. Sewell[13] urging that the shift in emphasis of West Indian economic life (though it threatened the sugar industry) involved a healthy social transformation, the thrust of historical thinking in the late nineteenth century was towards the ethnological and racialist interpretations that had marred historical thinking in the eighteenth century. Carlyle, Trollope, and Froude, neither settlers nor planters, wrote with an imperial concern for British domination in the islands, explaining the economic situation of the plantations and the Negro's refusal to work on the plantations only in terms of what they called his native indolence and incapacity.[14] Their point of view favored the old plantation relationships and the subjection of the entire society to a strong and wise imperial government.

Froude's history presented itself as an analysis of the course of social and economic development in the West Indies before and after emancipation, but as its title suggests, it was through its inconsistencies and contradictions an apologia for the protection of British planter interests and for the continuation of an authoritarian Crown Colony government. As a nineteenth-century historian he had conceived of history as progress and development and had seen this development as the quickening and growth of human physical and intellectual energy in an atmosphere of the rule of the strong over the weak. These faculties, he argued, had grown not in the freedom in which the modern society takes delight, but under the sharp rule of the strong over the weak. Thus ex-slaves, naturally indolent and inferior, were incapable of progress, unfit for the franchise, and deserving to be subjugated. It was a proslavery argument more characteristic of Long and the eighteenth century than of a period which, though not very different from the previous age, was less congenial to that way of thinking.

It was not surprising then that a contemporary historian, W. G. Sewell, in *The Ordeal of Free Labour,* presented a different picture and analysis to Froude's position and that a significant rebuttal of Froude's book was made by the black scholar J. J. Thomas.[15] Sewell's history took account of the emerging peasantry which Froude and Trollope had ignored. It analyzed the implications of the twenty thousand freeholders on the land and looked to a society of freeholders to arrest the ruin brought on by the planters. It showed a superior social perception to Froude through its awareness of social change and its sensibility to alternate relationships to the master-slave relationship and indeed stands as a revelation of all the possibilities from which Froude and Trollope were excluded by their peculiar biases.

Thomas's challenge was a more elaborate argument that rejected Froude's historical positions, putting forward a philosophy of history to validate the Negro's place and potential in the West Indies. It was on one hand a vigorous indictment of Froude's historical premise and on the other, a systematic re-evaluation of the Negro ex-slave's place in history. Thomas's response to Froude had in so many ways shaped his own historical position. For in response to Froude's argument about the nature and conditions of man's development, he had insisted that a historical law must account for the uniformity characteristic of successive generations of mankind; that without this law history became what the historian chose to make it, a story of privilege that ignored whatever progress the weak had made.

Froude conceived of West Indian realities as absolute and saw no merit in change. For him any society such as the West Indies that functioned and had a structure did not require change. Thomas, on the other hand, argued the relativity of West Indian realities. He pointed to a consistent advancement and progress among ex-slaves and systematically illustrated the ways in which they had made progress in the pre- and postemancipation settings.

But progress for Thomas simply meant advancement in the context of the existing social structure which had supported slavery and which now seemed little changed in its assumptions and relationships. Thomas analyzed change not in relation to the obvious defects of the system but in terms of the personal attributes and individual failures of successive governors of the colony. He could not envisage fundamental changes in the structure of society because his vision of its possibilities did not rise very much above a vision of nineteenth-century economic realities. As far as he could see, pre-emancipation West Indies was an economic society in which white, colored, and black, if they were free, engaged in economic activities in which all were equal: "the skin-discriminating policy induced as regard the colored/subjects of the Queen since the abolition of slavery did not, and could not, operate when colored and white stood on the same level as slave owners and ruling potentates in the Colonies."[16]

Discrimination on account of color, it would appear from Thomas's argument, only entered West Indian personal relationships with the abolition of slavery and the decline of the economic activity in which the free and well-off had been engaged. Thus Thomas apparently saw no deep disturbance, no psychological paralysis from the after-effects of slavery. He could see negative tendencies and possible neurosis only in situations in which racial obstacles stood in the way of the gifted, the strong, the brave.

Yet for all his belief in upward mobility within a social context which still retained characteristics of a slave-based society, Thomas did have a perspective on the inherent movements and possibilities of West Indian development, as his analysis of the revolution in San Domingue reveals. The understanding and appreciation of the fundamental features of Negro people which his analysis demonstrated made possible the self-awareness and reevaluations of his time. There is a sense then in which this consciousness of possibility may clash with Thomas's assessment of Negro progress mostly within the values of a plantation system, and though C. L. R. James is right in arguing that Thomas had revealed a social conception and a historical method superior to Froude's,[17] there still remain some areas in which both Thomas and Froude were united in a similar historical perspective, such as in their attitude to property relations and their view that economic and social relationships, based on property, were essential for the social structure and stability of civilization in the West Indies. Unlike Froude, Thomas did envisage change in the situation of the Negro, but he saw this change as advancement within a system that remained fundamentally unchanged. Both he and Froude were thus unable, in Harris's words, "to deepen the ornament of (their) age in such a way that unpredictable intuitive resources would affect the prison of the object and therefore the person of the object."[18] As men of the nineteenth century, they both shared a nineteenth-century perception of history as continuity and progress.

Within this context Froude maintained that accident and natural development quickened human faculties only under the sharp rule of the strong over the weak. Thomas, on the other hand, placed the Western Negro in the context of this progress, rejecting the strong-weak dichotomy as it applied to color and tracing a beneficent revolution in social conditions from his displacement to the present day, an experience in which the Western Negro, no longer a despicable member of the human race, gradually bettered his social conditions in a modern system and survived.

Thomas's position is indeed amply clarified by James in his introduction to the New Beacon edition of *Froudacity:*

We of the Caribbean are a people more than any other people, constructed by history, and therefore any attempt not only to analyze but
to carry out political or social activity in connection with ourselves
and in relation to other peoples, any such attempt has got to begin
and constantly to bear in mind how we came into being, where we
have reached, who we are and what we are. We were brought from
Africa and thrown into a highly developed modern industry and a
highly developed modern language . . . We are not dealing with ab-
stractions that concern people who are intellectuals and historians,
we are dealing with concrete matters that penetrate into the very immediate necessity of a social existence.[19]

But both James and Thomas talk of progress and development as though continuity is the most conspicuous feature of history in the West Indies; as though the displacement of people and the discontinuities of culture are all part of a continuum in human affairs. Their perspective creates an illusion of a steady continuous flow in history, which is certainly at variance with the displacement and dislocations characteristic of migrations into the New World. Man's history in the region is, after all, not wholly a story of conti-nuity and development. Indeed, considered from aboriginal, African, In-dian, even British perspectives, there is a sense in which dislocations also involved original reconstructions and re-creations, phenomena that cannot be explained, understood, or utilized if history is judged as one long, unbro-ken progressive movement. Thomas's historical imagination, it seems to me, excludes, even censures, these subtle responses. Yet they are responses which create deeper realities beyond the thin scraps of recorded history and which one believes can be explored and activated to inspire new sensibili-ties. Their manifestations do not belong in records, documents, or relics but rather in the subconscious imagination and its reflection in the arts of the imagination. Their time is not the linear time of historical analysis; it is an inner time not necessarily measured in terms of chronology and space.

Admittedly, Thomas did not possess the criteria or the methodology for exploring this aspect of history. He was a nineteenth-century scholar, and his historical argument, for all its earnest validation of the Western Negro's place in history, revealed an imagination shaped by his age. As a nine-teenth-century European scholar, he believed that he could understand the nature of anything by examining its development. To place West Indian man in history he had therefore placed him in an African context and placed Africa itself in world history, explaining its past and future in terms of a general theory of historical development, of the ceaseless progression of temporal existence towards an existence that is eternal. This had been the pattern of Europe's history, he had argued; it could be the pattern of Africa's development as well.

From this perspective Thomas had attempted to explore African lives in the New World but had not gone much beyond that sense of solidarity in bondage which had created strong attachments among slaves in the West Indies. His history of the African in the West Indies had been unable to deal with the trauma of displacement, with those discontinuities which had inspired responses in the West Indian imagination. To explore these, Thomas would have had to be able to perceive beyond his time, to be aware of what Wilson Harris calls "significant vestiges" of the subconscious imagination, of perspectives of renaissance able to translate and accommodate Africa and other legacies within a new architecture of cultures. For only such an apprehension can bring into play a wider figurative meaning beyond recorded history. Without this wider reality the African's history in the West Indies is constricted within the relatively small arena of enslavement and progress in a world created by conquerors and slave owners.

Harris identifies this construction as an aspect of the historical stasis which afflicts the West Indian sensibility and sees it as reflected even in the West Indian historiography of the twentieth century. This is ironical, because the twentieth century more than previous centuries has been the most traumatized by change and upheaval and the most pressed to reexamine perspectives and conceptions of history. The upheavals of migration, displacement, and revolution have made it obvious that history is not always a story of continuity governed by an evolutionary law. Everywhere people are having to learn that their inherited assumptions no longer fit the reality they experience, and in the West Indies the situation has been even more remarkable. Those realities of social structure and relationships which Froude had seen as absolute crumbled within a space of fifty or so years, and the economic eclipse of planter and merchant lessened the influence of the planter class and brought West Indian societies into new colonial relationships with Great Britain.

It is therefore within the context of colonial relations and anticolonial perspectives that the twentieth-century historiography of the region can be located. It is history written by descendants of slaves and colonials under different circumstances and meant as a reinterpretation of historical realities that had shaped their lives. Thus, in both perspective and methodology, it has attempted to reexamine institutions, structures, and relationships not just from the point of view of economic motivation and political and social development but also from the point of view of the conscious lives of mass numbers of slaves as they sought to make adjustments in the society. There were greater attempts now to analyze the nature and dynamics of plantation society. Historians pieced the lives of slaves together and attempted to create images of life and relationships within slave society. Plantations were conceived as models of socialization, and slaves, virtually invisible in the histories of eighteenth- and nineteenth-century historians, now became the focus of analysis. For the first time it was possible to see history from the point of view of the underdog: the slave, the aborigine, groups hitherto depicted as objects of history in the historiography of the region.

C. L. R. James's monumental history of the San Domingue rebellion and the fortunes of Toussaint L'Ouverture introduced several new perspectives on West Indian historiography. James managed to present the machinations of European powers and "interest groups" in the region and at the same time maintain the point of view of the Afro-Caribbean slave. His history, *The Black Jacobins,* is thus essentially a study of the dynamics of rebellion and revolution that subjects the rebellion of slaves to the same historical laws that governed the revolt of the French masses during the French Revolution. From James's perspective, the internal conflicts and contradictions which shattered the stability and prosperity of the island rested ultimately on the constantly shifting equilibrium between classes and between slaves and masters.

The revolt in San Domingue was therefore a process of definition that enabled illiterate slaves to assess their possibilities and reevaluate their place in the plantation structure, and every move and strategy propelled them closer to understanding and self-awareness. James explores the nature of their freedom, and his analysis of their transformation from slaves to free men presents the odds against them and the choices they were forced to make.

Although James grasps the paradoxes in the situation of the slaves, his historical analyses and judgments reveal a personal ambivalence as well as a surprising Eurocentrism in his perspective on history. While he sees the revolt as an aspect of self-awareness and reevaluation he is unable to characterize the real nature of the slave's freedom. Rather than analyze the actual nature and quality of the rebels' freedom, he perceives and demonstrates its contradictions in the personality of Toussaint L'Ouverture, in the ambivalence that committed him single-mindedly to the freedom of slaves and at the same time made him obsessively dependent on French culture in the consolidation of this freedom. "The leaders of a revolution are those who have been able to profit by the cultural advantage of the system they are attacking," James says at the very beginning of his analysis. Later, in his examination of Toussaint's consolidation of the revolution, he reveals the implications of the ex-slave's paradoxical relationship with his master's world. "Toussaint knew the backwardness of the laborers; he made them work, but he wanted to see them civilized and advanced in culture. He established such schools as he could . . . He was anxious to see the blacks acquire the social deportment of the better class whites with their Versailles manners. Struck by the carriage and bearing of a French officer, he said to those around him, 'my sons will be like that.'"[20]

In both comments, James uncovers the ambivalence in the ex-slave's exercise of freedom. But because he writes his history mostly from the point of view and perspective of Toussaint's impact and achievement, he is unable to investigate the meaning of this paradox. Evidently, the engagement with French culture had made Toussaint culturally dependent on the French. It had separated him from the masses of black people at a time when he should have been helping them to understand the responsibilities of freedom in terms of their own social and psychological situations and circumstances. Yet James's account of this phase of Toussaint's career glosses over the issues of freedom and appears to limit its responsibility only to the acquisition of culture, manner, and deportment. His historical perspective explains away Toussaint's failure too easily and as a result deflates the crucial issues of the ex-slave's psychological relation to his freedom.

Indeed, James's empathy with Toussaint seems so total that even where he draws contrasts between the personal vision of Toussaint and Dessalines, he fails to see the ideological implications of the contrast. "If Dessalines could see so clearly and simply, it was because the ties that bound this uneducated soldier to French civilization were of the slenderest. He saw what was under his nose so well because he saw the failure of enlightenment not of darkness."[21] Clearly James's premise in explaining Toussaint's action is that the consolidation of freedom also depends on a certain measure of cultural solidarity which the rebels lacked and which French culture could provide. But this premise is only partly true for the rebel slaves. A measure of cultural confidence is, of course, essential for freedom; but for the rebel slaves, so newly free, that culture did not have to be French. James himself appears to admit this twenty-five years later in his appendix to the second edition of *The Black Jacobins,* where he makes the connections between cultural freedom and true freedom in Haiti. "In 1913 the ceaseless battering from foreign pens was reinforced by the bayonets of American marines. Haiti had to find a national rallying point. They looked for it where it can only be found, in their own background. They discovered what is known today as Négritude."[22] This recognition of a new national identity in twentieth-century Haitian politics is therefore a reorientation of James's previous perspective and an acceptance that a certain measure of cultural identity is crucial for true political freedom, that this correlation was an important stage in Haiti's national development.

James's earlier perspective on the ex-slave's relation to his master is not really unique in West Indian historiography. Interpretations of the past in this century have also often tended to pursue a continuous wall in relation to time and have viewed historical activity in the region in terms of political and economic activities of European settlers and metropolitan interests. V. S. Naipaul's reinterpretation of Caribbean history in *The Loss of El Dorado*, for instance, is inspired both by a personal sense of dislocation and shipwreck and by a nineteenth-century vision of man as shaped by a given environment. Conceiving of contemporary West Indian society as permanently defined by the past, Naipaul perceives the history of oppressors and their victims as a story of the progressive debasement of a society by the exigencies of slavery and the plantation system. Caught in such a context, Naipaul develops no criteria for assessing other perspectives and offshoots of creation and activity that might have been evident in the drama of oppression, and his history merely tends to illustrate what his later novels have claimed: that "history" has permanently marred society and possibility in the region.

Other twentieth-century historians, such as Elsa Goveia, Eric Williams, Orlando Patterson, M. G. Smith, and Edward Brathwaite also reinterpret historical activity in the region, using more rigorous historical methodologies yet, ironically, often coming up with conclusions no less depressing.[23] Goveia's history of slave society in the Leeward Islands, for instance, accepts the premise that, in spite of being part of an oppressive system, slave and master were mutually engaged in relationships which shaped both their lives and created a coherent society. Yet even from such a premise, Goveia's analysis ultimately concludes that the fundamental principles of inequality and subordination embodying the necessities of the slave system kept groups apart and made slave society a fragmentary society of separate groups marked off by differences of legal and social status, by political and economic opportunity, and by racial origin and culture.

Patterson's analysis of slave society in *The Sociology of Slavery* presents an even more depressing pattern of fragmentation in which, more than the separations between sections of the society, there was also a total breakdown of values and morals. His study argues and attempts to prove that

within the segmented sections of society, understanding was possible between master and slave, but that these only led to the creation of stereo-
types, not to real mutual understanding. Indeed, the overall picture given
by both Goveia and Patterson is of a plural society without any real internal
cohesion except, as Goveia's analysis shows, the negative cohesion based
on a consensual acceptance of Negro inferiority.

The uniform pattern of fragmentation and breakdown depicted in this
twentieth-century "nationalist" historiography is not unexpected since the
method by which the analyses are made points to the inevitability of
the conclusions reached. Patterson and Goveia and Smith all concentrate on
analysis of the structure and development of political and social institutions
and base their conclusions on what they reveal themselves to be. Thus, although Goveia's study also reveals that a lack of real contact between field
slaves and the white population threw Negro slaves together into a community with a homogenous "culture" common to the majority of slaves, she
presents the community not in relation to the other segments of the society
but rather to that consensus on black backwardness and inferiority which
determined the ordering of all groups in plantation society.

In relation to these two studies and to other twentieth-century interpretations of the region's history, Edward Brathwaite's study of the development
of Creole society in Jamaica attempts something wider than an analysis of
European-derived institutions and segments of fragmented society. As such it
represents a new dimension in the general tenor of twentieth-century West
Indian historiography, a perspective based "upon the enigma of the Amer-
indians and involving immigrant cultures of essentially different paradigms
connected through violence, racism and colonialism yet producing something creative and new, a perspective that needs its particular surrealism to
express what it can of the extraordinary complexity of creolization." Brathwaite calls it a "prismatic" perspective, and its methodology, as spelled out
and applied by him, develops "a quadrilateral rather than a linear approach;
collage, metaphor, non-archival sources, which have their own shape, their
own pressure of outline."[24]

Within this framework Brathwaite argues from an opposite angle to the
concept of plural societies in the West Indies and presents the view that
plantation society was shaped not only by its structure and the nature of its
institutions but also by human interaction and attitudes of individuals and
groups to each other, the institutions of their society, and the entire culture
of the Americas. The process that gave birth to this entity is for Brathwaite
a complex phenomenon that involved Jamaica's reactions to external, metropolitan political pressures as well as internal adjustments necessitated by

the juxtaposition of master and slave in a culturally heterogeneous complex. In his study Brathwaite places the entire creolization process in the context of a wider New World culture shaped by European settlement and exploitation but influenced by revolutionary changes that created a new sense of identity and destiny. Indeed, he argues strongly that the American and humanitarian revolutions contributed to a certain integration of the society as a cultural unit separate from the larger metropolis, but that this was an opportunity which influential white planters failed to utilize for self-assertion and independence.

Brathwaite's whole perspective on the social ordering of Creole society stands in opposition to the assumption of cultural polarity behind the classic paradigm of a plural society.[25] He argues and tries to prove that in spite of being fragmented along lines of status and color, the separations of Creole society were not rigidly applied at the level of marriage and personal relationships;[26] that within this leeway the folk culture of the slaves managed to assert itself and contribute to the larger creolization process. Brathwaite is firm and forthright on the proposition that a cultural action based on the responses which individuals within the society summoned to their environment was the single most important factor in the development of Jamaican society. Thus, in his view, there were two cultures fighting to adapt themselves to a new environment and to each other and creating in their confrontations frictions that were both cruel and creative—cruel in the degradations of plantation culture and creative because of the slaves' adaptation of their African culture to the New World experience. The process as Brathwaite presents it in his historical accounts was not unproblematic. For "to be creole did not completely imply satisfaction, stabilization or completion of a process. To be creole in the changing world of the nineteenth century was to be in a state of constant bias from/towards the ancestral cultures," and within this framework even the rebellion of a "Caliban" or the split allegiance of an "Ariel" could be part of the crisis of creolization. For it was "the shape of the transport from the past, the fragmentations of impact and its consequences in death and resurrection, which slowly influenced what the various creole elements would define, essentially, as their future: their vision of continuation/fragment (the plural society) or wholeness (prismatic possibility)."[27]

By attempting to understand creolization from the point of view of each culture's subjective experience of the new environment and its relationship to other cultures in similar experiences, Brathwaite avoids a monolithic presentation in which Jamaican society is made up of one single sacred construction with other inferior and marginal cultures in polarity to it. By taking in more than the details on what actually happened, by concerning himself not only with events in time but also with the possibilities of situations and, in the case of slave history, with the paradoxes of plantation society, Brathwaite manages to present several contrasting visions that push history beyond a merely linear analysis of the documents of political and social institutions. His historical perspective, which has continued to inform his imaginative exploration of experience in the New World, represents a significant shift in the perception of slave society and the tenor of historical writing in the region: "[What] we have to keep in mind is that this social reality may be as much figment as fragment: result of our apprehension of reality; that the pessimistic/plantation view of Caribbean society, to put it another way, may very well not be the last word on Caribbean society."[28] His cautious observation here suggests a need for an assessment of Caribbean history from perspectives other than the economic and political institutions of the colonizer. It hints at the enlightening possibilities of those subtle presences and discontinuities which are also part of the region's history but not necessarily embraced in constitutional, political, or social histories.

Harris expresses a similar view when he urges Caribbean historiography to alter the dialectic of historical discourse by freeing itself from the dead end of fixed time and the domain of imperial history to evolve criteria for assessing other subtle presences in the area. The capacity to assess such presences depends however on a conception and methodology of history much beyond the scope of those nineteenth-century conceptions and methodologies which twentieth-century West Indian historiography appropriates. Yet Harris feels that only the assessment of such presences and such areas of history can break the uniform pattern of imperialism and point to the "originalities of man as a civilization-making animal who can alter the architectural complex of an age."[29] Such an alteration of dialects, he suggests, involves perceptions and transformations more suited to the arts of the imagination than the conventions of historiography. Perhaps the very nature of the historian's method is a constriction of the possibilities of his imagination. For history as has been developed in Western and West Indian historiography demands a particular context of space and time, a particular dating scheme as well as a way of separating moments of time, of measuring relations between cause and effect, and of reaching conclusions. Its conception of past time is of a single solid unit from which smaller units (epochs, centuries, decades) may be removed, described, and shaped.

Such conclusions as may be reached from these separations may have present relevance but still be of a static nature and limited only to particular moments of time. The imaginative artist's conception of past time is, in contrast, much more fluid, much more capable of transcending epochs, of appropriating other movements of time and incorporating them in a single movement by way of overcoming fixed self-conceptions and destinies. In terms of the capacity to possess and utilize history, the imaginative writer's freedom is boundless. Unlike the historian he has a freedom of emphasis and a freedom from conclusions. He is free to choose an emphasis which may not necessarily be the most salient, and his vision of existence and life may appear miles away from the vision of the historian.

It is this sense of the difference between the freedom of the artistic and "historical" imaginations that inspires Harris's confidence in the writer's ability to evolve the criteria he talks of: "I want to make it clear," he says in "History, Fable, and Myth," "that a cleavage exists in my opinion, between the historical convention in the Caribbean and Guianas and the arts of the imagination. I believe a philosophy of history may well lie buried in the arts of the imagination. My concern is with epic stratagems available to Caribbean man in the dilemmas of history which surround him."[30]

Harris argues that possibilities do exist in the Caribbean for perspectives on renaissance which could bring into play a figurative meaning beyond the real. Such multiple perceptions of the region and its history call for methodologies that move beyond the scope and ideological capacity of the Hegelian models which twentieth-century West Indian historiography appropriates. The fundamental principle of European historicism, one could argue, is an unfolding structure of self-realization in the historical process. This evolution, always Eurocentered and often incorporating the imperatives of imperialism, created its own perspectives and methodologies: a self-centered ideology of dominance and a context of space and time with its particular dating scheme and its way of separating moments of time, of measuring relations between cause and effect and reaching conclusions.

How then may the West Indian confront such a model of history except as object and victim? How may he/she find a place in it or wrest a vision from its lessons? Harris has consistently called for the deconstruction of this monolithic and linear history and argued for a perspective and methodology that would reconstitute the region's history to include larger spaces and forces: other landscapes, other pasts and mythologies which though seemingly "lifeless" may yet yield the essential degeneration and erosion of historical perspectives, the kind of erosion necessary for the deconstruction of patterns of imperial history. "When I speak of the West Indies I am thinking of overlapping contexts of Central and South America, as well . . . and I am thinking here of the European discovery of the New World and conquest of the ancient civilizations which were themselves related by earlier and obscure levels of conquest . . . The environment of the Caribbean is steeped . . . in such broken conceptions as well as misconceptions of the residue and meaning of conquest."[31]

What is needed in such renaissance perspectives is an imaginative effort that would reconcile the broken parts of the enormous pre- and post-Columbian heritage of the region. The smallest area of the region one sees (whether it is island, village, flatland, or buried valley), Harris argues, can be charged with an openness of imagination that may help to relate the existing pattern of each community to its variable past and create an independence of spirit that would liberate it from constricting history. Indeed, Harris considers this dilemma and strategy a peculiarly West Indian problem, which may nevertheless apply to "every phenomenal society where minorities (frail in historical origin and present purpose) may exist and where comparatively new immigrant and racial cells sometimes find themselves placed within a dangerous misconception and upon a reactionary treadmill."[32]

Such a strategy of perception and inscription may lie outside that realistic consolidation of history and reality that occurs in Western historiography and the modes of the realistic novel. For it is a methodology that creates visions of consciousness rather than consolidates fact and situation, and its vehicle for creation and transformation are an art of memory and an art of language. Here the meaning and implications of memory extend beyond events and experiences we can actually recall to include mythic and ancestral memory. Mythic memory, every man's birthright, recovered when its primordial origins are penetrated, can be retrieved from man's submerged consciousness and reintegrated into his psyche. In the same way ancestral memory, which Harris identifies as ancient sympathies lost through dis-continuities, can be retrieved not necessarily to bridge the discontinuities of the past but to be absorbed in a fluid future and into a continuous cycle of change and renewal.

Harris's theory of memory is linked to a theory of language that invests heavily in a radical and figurative extension of words which continuously transforms inner and outer formal categories of experience. "[The] peculiar reality of language provides a medium to *see* in consciousness the 'free' motion and to *hear* with consciousness the 'silent' flood of sound by a continuous inward revisionary and momentous logic of potent explosive images evoked in the mind."[33]

This view of language, linked to Harris's view of history and the representation of experience in fiction, invests in the capacity of language to transform inner and outer formal categories of experience in such a way as to permit other possible meanings within an experience. Structuralist poetics, distinguishing between metonymic and metaphorical use of language in texts, points to language's capacity to explore through metaphor whole new areas not necessarily continuous with the actual contexts of a text. In Harris such a transforming potential is a revolutionary one for bringing out what is unknown and hidden (the still life in the painting or sculpture, the music one has ceased to hear) and for expanding the outward and inward creative significance of the novel.

This deconstruction of historical space and heritage is complemented by a similar deconstruction of the historical event. Behind Harris's conception of "the event" in history is a rejection of the dead end and fixed conceptions of linear history, a rejection that also relates to his idea of how we must appropriate history in the present. To subjectively "alter" the historical event is then to explore alternative possibilities, to "rehearse" the implications of the event as a mode of understanding and as a way of creating a vision for the present and future. Thus the European exploration and conquest of the New World, subsumed in the El Dorado myth, may acquire a residual pattern of illuminating correspondences: "El Dorado, City of Gold, City of God, grotesque, unique coincidence, another window within, upon the Universe, another ocean, another river."[34] By extension the historical story of the conquistador may likewise present its illuminating paradoxes: conqueror, materialist, ruthless exploiter, inspired by greed; or adventurer, spiritualist, inspired by innocence and love. Such correspondences, while still validating the brutality and pain of "the event," move beyond them to understand the different circumstances and states of mind involved in the events of the past, so that history becomes new understanding, new knowledge, a preparation for the future. Such a conception of the event in history would be more accessible to the imaginative writer than the historian, since the conventions of historiography would tend to work against the appropriation of such fluidity.

Although Harris himself did not write an academic history, he did point to the cleavage in the two traditions when he noted the potential of the arts for radical transformations of conceptions of history. Other West Indian writers have operated in the two traditions as they have responded to and conceptualized the nature and impact of the region's history. C. L. R. James, V. S. Reid, V. S. Naipaul, Edward Brathwaite, and Derek Walcott have all constructed "histories" at the same time as they responded imaginatively to history's ramifications in the region. Thus the cohesion and

tension between the two types of history should reveal illuminating correspondences and at the same time test the limitations and potential that
Harris has pointed to.

Among West Indian writers confrontations with linear time have generated other dialectical arguments and creative alternatives. In Walcott linear
time is the nightmare that the poet's philosophical and creative writing
continually interrogates. The two modes of writing enhance each other,
and Walcott's analytical essays reflect and exemplify aspects of his poetry
and drama, especially in their groping for a vision of historicity not
bounded by a single historical moment. For the single moment in history is
that which explains and justifies yet remains circumscribed within the fixed
event of the past. The truly tough aesthetics of the New World, Walcott has
argued, should neither explain nor forgive "history" but refuse to recognize it as a creative or culpable force. Thus, for "history" Walcott substi-
tutes "myth," "the timeless yet habitable moment" which neutralizes biases and makes the lessons and possibilities of history accessible to all, and
in such a way that "violence is felt with the simultaneity of history. So the
death of a gaucho does not merely repeat, but is, the death of Caesar. Fact
evaporates into myth. This is not the jaded cynicism which sees nothing
new under the sun, it is an elation which sees everything as renewed."[35]

The New World poets whose sense of history Walcott venerates are precisely those who celebrate the timeless and creative potential of an elemental New World man, an Adamic man, outside history but capable of inhabiting any historical moment unencumbered by time. Walcott shares this
vision of timelessness because he too believes in an elemental Caribbean
man, an amnesiac slave who with the newness of a second Adam absolves
himself from the histories of the old world and creates a new and entire
order, from religion to the domestic rituals. It is this awe of the numinous,
Walcott argues, "this elemental privilege of naming the New World which
annihilates history in our great poets."[36]

Yet this relationship to history, while enlarging the domain of historical
time and emphasizing creativity, nevertheless coexists with Walcott's own
awareness of a historically determined disability in Caribbean people:
a feeling borne out of linear time and its legacies and consequences.
Throughout his writing Walcott accepts and works with the ambivalence of
the two contrasting views of history, recognizing the defining impact of
linear history and at the same time rejecting its deterministic impulse and its
ability to negate his creativity.

Such an ambivalence need not become problematic. For even within
academic historiography there is now a new interrogation of the whole

enterprise of historical analysis and its epistemological certainties. Post-modernist critiques of systems and totalization, structuralist critiques of signification, and the new poststructuralist distrust of the self-certain subject have fostered a healthy distrust of metanarratives, emphasizing the plurality of perception and text within subjects. Thus, though history is still largely conceived of in terms of the facts as they were, there are now several other variables and perspectives that question the sufficiency of the recorded fact and of objective interpretation as sufficient and complete explanations of history. The assumptions of historicism and the misleading symmetry of linear history are now being challenged by the diverse perceptions of anthropology and sociology. Alternative historiographies recognize more than ever before those biases within metahistories that deflate or subvert the histories of the powerless. Thus, in recent Caribbean discourse on history, objective interpretations coexist with what Glissant calls a sober, reflective, indirect treatment of lived reality, revealing the dynamic quality of history which, like the sea, is constantly changing and renewing itself.[37]

Such dual perceptions of history seem to come naturally to the Caribbean writer, since he more than most must contend with a largely negative and inhibiting past. The contrasts between history as "history" and history as fiction, drama, or poetry in the works of West Indian writers reflect both this duality and the limits of West Indian historiography itself. For they nearly always reveal the tensions between objective interpretations and the elusive irreducible reality that cannot be transformed into an all-encompassing system. More than this, they demonstrate a creative attempt to remake the future by remaking the past, a perspective borne out of a sense of the dynamic and constantly changing nature of history itself.

Thus C. L. R. James's history of Toussaint L'Ouverture and the black Jacobins of Haiti when creatively transformed into drama presents not only the facts as they are glimpsed from records and letters but a wider psychological understanding of the pressures and hidden conflicts which plagued ex-slaves in their efforts at self-assertion. In James's drama the tensions of Toussaint's frenchified consciousness and his vacillations between dependence and self-assertion reveal themselves. Whereas in the "history" the exigencies of confrontation between France and the revolutionaries set up clear-cut divisions which tended to present the rebels more as a block or single force, the play explores them as people and as characters, giving a wider range to the conflicts which separated them within the context of their rebellion. Conflicts between Moise and Toussaint, between Dessalines and Toussaint, are explored in the play as ideological conflicts, involving attitudes to freedom and to the relationship between independence and cultural freedom, ideas which not only relate to the particular history of the "black Jacobins" but also to the present and future of Caribbean man. In a similar imaginative variation, "vodum" becomes an elusive variable in the cultural contest between the Haitian peasants and French culture in general. Whereas in the "history" James was quick to explain Toussaint's "dependence" on France as his way of ensuring civilization and progress for ex-slaves in their new freedom, the play explores his attitude as part of the dramatists' interrogation of the relationship between political and cultural freedom.

In the same way the contrasting interpretations of history in the *Development of Creole Society* and *The Arrivants* reveal similar tensions and purposes, showing Brathwaite's analysis of institutions and records and his imaginative linking of the various spaces of African, Caribbean, and New World history. Perhaps it is only in an imaginative work like *The Arrivants* that the reconstruction of displacement and dispossession can at the same time be balanced with the poet's subjective view of the "rights" of passage and the paradoxes of history.

Interestingly, these contrasts in historical interpretation reveal the West Indian writer as a deconstructionist before "deconstruction." The tensions over history as system which led these writers to interpret "history" as fiction, drama, or poetry are the same tensions that surface in postmodernist challenges to the separations between history and literature. A new skepticism about historical writing as an empiricist and positivist endeavor is, for instance, evident in the writing of a historian like Hayden White, who has argued that historical narratives are manifestly verbal fictions, "the contents of which are as much *invented* as *found* and the forms of which have more in common with their counterparts in literature than they have with those in the sciences."[38] This conception of the historical text as a literary artifact molded by the imperatives of emplotment, point of view, and "mythos" suggests the possibility of a plurality of subjectively inscribed texts. It implies too that there is never one truth but rather "truths" in the plural. The rewritings of and engagements with "history" in the writings of West Indian authors problematize the nature of historical knowledge itself by demystifying its objectivity and making it serve the imperatives of self-definition. They are postmodernist rewritings in the sense that they re-present the past in fiction, poetry, or drama "to open it up to the present, to prevent it from being conclusive and teleological."[39]

Chapter Two

The Novel as History
Edgar Mittelholzer and V. S. Reid

There are various senses in which history and the novel cohere naturally as modes of apprehending and conveying the past. History records and re-creates past human experience by turning it into a particular picture or story. It becomes fiction when the historical imagination creates out of generalized memory a story with a definite place and moment as well as particular situations and relationships. Thus, as a re-creation of experience, history involves an almost parallel imaginative exercise to the art of the novel. The novel is similarly a kind of history that treats the past in a particular way, or rather, resurrects and fixes it into a picture through a synthesis of the imagination. Both modes share an active awareness of people in society as well as a sensitivity to their ceaseless interaction with nature and with other social conditions and forces. Indeed, as a genre, the novel itself emerged in Europe at a time when social relations between individual and class had developed and crystallized, and its basic character as a genre springs from a central concern with the individual and society. From its very emergence, then, its manner of portrayal was closer to empirical reality than, for instance, a genre like drama.[1] For even where it is limited to only a section of reality it is still aimed at evoking a full span of life as well as the intricate processes of social interaction and development.

Significantly, the novel also emerged at a time when historians had crystallized a new vision of history as the relationship between people and the circumstances which condition their actions. The new historicist perspective focused on human life and its processes of growth and transformation as the essence of history. Abandoning the conceptual approach of eighteenth-century histories with their basis in general historical laws and principles, historicism emphasized the infinite varieties of historical manifesta-tions at different ages and in different cultures, thus revolutionizing histori-cal writing by presenting it as an empathetic re-creation of the character and spirit of the past.

Thus, both in its subject matter and its methodology, historical writing in Europe came to function almost in the same way as the art of the novel. The novel creates a particular social and fictional reality, shows its various facets, and delineates particular trends within it, while history re-creates the atmosphere and feel of a specific period with imaginative sympathy; and both modes of writing are intrinsically linked as gateways to the past and present. Indeed, Lukàcs's emphasis on the common roots of the novel and history derive from the common philosophical and social thrust of their focus. His argument as to why the new historicism in art produced the historical novel and not the historical drama centers on the relationship between the novel and history as we have outlined here.

As a fusion of the traditions of history and the novel, the historical novel has also come to be conditioned by the various implications of the two modes. It has grown with them, widening both its meaning and scope as both history and the novel have developed in concept and perspective. The historical novel that developed in the early nineteenth century, in which a concrete and realistic portrayal of a historical period also incorporates a keen awareness of when and how a particular world has evolved, has un-dergone various transformations in the course of time. The obligation to stick to historical truth, the need to demonstrate artistically that historical circumstances and characters existed in a particular way, allowed certain modifications, especially as perceptions of history and the novel's own boundaries continued to change.[2] The historical novel itself as it was con-ceived in the early nineteenth century has crossed the boundaries of the past with the contemporary novelist's consciously "historical" presentation of the present.

Indeed, over the years the novel's own relation to history has also changed, and a novelist may now not only confront history as the nineteenth century did but also invest it with subjective, figurative meanings that have signifi-cant implications for a vision of the future. A "historical" novelist may now exploit the imaginative leeway of artistic construction to explore not only exact details or events of history but also their imagined possibilities. The historical novel in the West Indies has begun to move towards such figurative conceptions and representations of history not only as a way of breaking the usual polarization of European "subject" and West Indian "other" but also to reconstruct a wider sense of the region's history and create new self-conceptions and sensibilities. An imaginative relation to this history that explores even its apparently irrelevant footnotes in radical ways, can, as Harris has argued, create a new corpus of sensibility "wherein the function of character within the interior of the novel will begin to displace a helpless and hopeless consolidation of powers."[3]

The consolidation of character and situation in the novel would be much less suited to a West Indies where discontinuities and heterogeneity defied the kind of stabilization of reality and values characteristic of nineteenth-century European realism. In a region which for centuries was perceived and defined through other eyes and which is now being continuously redefined, what may be pertinent is a representation which mediates the given reality to produce other possible meanings and interpretations from a subjective engagement with history and experience.

Such perspectives and representations of history have made breakthroughs in the imaginative literature of the region even though, in its beginnings in the early twentieth century, West Indian historical novels had taken only a straightforward and literal view of the region's history. The early historical novels of De Lisser and Mittelholzer consist mainly of realistic delineation of past society. Their objective worlds reflect various aspects of plantation society, but neither novelist seemed able to move beyond this surface world even to understand the "whence" and "how" of its evolution. De Lisser particularly had failed to correlate the moral degeneracy of his created world and the deficiencies of its historical past. Regarding the social scene simply as a given world, he had proceeded in *The White Witch of Rosehall* to record it faithfully, measuring it in relation to the world and values of metropolitan England. His history was thus really only a chain of happenings, an accumulation of incidents reflecting the surface character and atmosphere of a particular age, and his novels, in the end, had no historical message beyond the obvious one that the Jamaican society of the time was rotten and degenerate.

Mittelholzer moved a step beyond De Lisser in his conception and understanding of the objective world. The idea of a continuity embodied in the Kaywana trilogy[4] was, for instance, an affirmation of a Caribbean experience of history, and his reconstruction of this experience in the Guianese slave and colonial societies of his novels did show a certain understanding of the social forces at work, even though he did not always sustain such an understanding. His portrayal of the colonial society suggested that it was in its beginnings, at least, a fairly promising world which inspired in the early settlers a Nietzschean idea of strength and daring—a feeling is perverted in the course of the trilogy by greed, lust, and personal egoism. Although he does not relate this corruption explicitly to the exigencies of plantation society we can confidently infer from the maze of his moral ambivalence and faint ironies that the reality of plantation society generates a new and corrupting philosophy of survival among settlers; that more than just inner strength and daring, survival comes to mean oppression, brute force, and self-interest.

The entire ethos of the plantation society which informs Mittelholzer's trilogy is a fictionalized reconstruction, depicting his personal view of the ways in which the social structures and institutions of the plantation shaped people's images of themselves and regulated relations between them. Throughout the trilogy the novelist's faint ironies suggest persistent conflicts between the planter's view of his slave as chattel and demonstrations of the slave's humanness. Such ironies could be crucial pointers to the ways in which personal relations between slave and master shaped and modified their social relations. But most of these, often unconscious, are never really utilized by Mittelholzer in the interest of social insight.

Yet it is precisely this understanding of the relationship between the psychology of people and their economic and moral circumstances within the framework of historicism that reveals a novelist's historical awareness of his material. Mittelholzer appears to lack such a sustained historical focus and vision. His handling of historical material, even of real historical events, evinces a literal and often unhistorical perception of social reality and motivation. In his trilogy an upheaval like the Berbice slave rebellion is re-created almost without a historical vision or focus, so that its interest remains mostly on the level of action and story instead of social awareness and insight. The details of the rebellion stretch over several pages, but its origins remain obscure, because in spite of the general historical framework from which he presents it, he shows no real interest in its social or psychological significance. The rebel slaves, unperceptive, dazed, almost without motivation, come on the scene suddenly, and Cuffy, the rebel leader whose consciousness the novelist never really attempts to penetrate, comes across only as a man struggling over negative forces. Although very little documentary information could have been available on Cuffy's motives, Mittelholzer (if he had sympathetically focused on Cuffy) could have followed the broad outlines of the rebellion as far as was possible and supplied his own psychological insight into Cuffy's motives as a rebel. But he had no such interest in either Cuffy or the rebels. The entire Berbice rebellion is merely a necessary backdrop and prop for his real interest in and engagement with the Van Groenwengels and their fortunes, with their consolidation as a ruling power, with their strange mixture of bloods and their heritage of strong and weak personality traits.

This is indeed history written from the point of view of the conqueror and master, one in which the rebellion of the slave is handled as a disturbance the master must confront and surmount. Thus, in order that the master may appear strong and resilient, the rebel slave must be shown as a slave through and through, as a baffled puppy groveling before the white master even at the height of his self-assertion. Indeed, Cuffy's suicide, which could have been an important denouement had psychological insight been sustained, becomes merely a distraction, described in detached and theatrical terms and perceived only as part of the strength and triumph of the ruling power. Mittelholzer, throughout his re-creations of Guianese history, links himself rather uncreatively with the ruling power, thus missing out on other aspects of the region's history which could have liberated him from fixations on power and identity.

Evidently, the kinds of perspective and the vision of history which Harris looked for in the arts of the imagination do not really appear in De Lisser and Mittelholzer. Harris's kind of West Indian perspective does not really emerge in the West Indian novel until the publication in 1949 of V. S. Reid's *New Day*. The West Indian perspective and the sense of history that emerge in Reid's novel can be traced to the emergence of a national consciousness during this period. For without doubt, the nationalist political agitation for change in the West Indies also facilitated an important historical awareness that became part of a growing sense of a West Indian people distinct from other groups. The idea was not really new in West Indian thought. As far back as the eighteenth century, Edward Long, Bryan Edwards, and other Jamaicans thought in these terms and vigorously argued the distinctiveness and separateness of a Jamaican society.[5] But their idea of a free and separate Jamaica did not really envisage the freedom of slaves or even of ex-slaves as free and component members of a developing society. Reid's conception of a West Indian people was thus a radical advance over the view of the early Jamaicans and over the vision of Mittelholzer, whose trilogy had affirmed the dominance and continuity of the planter class even though his novels had dealt with miscegenation and the mixing of bloods as a significant phenomenon in the history of the Caribbean.

Reid's historical perspective in *New Day* claims and dramatizes a solid place for the ex-slave as a component member of a developing society, and it is such a vision of West Indian development that informs his historical attitudes throughout the novel. It explains his major decision to link the Morant Bay rebellion with earlier slave rebellions and with the granting of a new Jamaican constitution, and the sense of continuity that these links imply also affirms his view of the ex-slave's progress and development in the West Indies.[6] He had already taken for granted the facts of migration and displacement and was instead seeking to give the ex-slave roots in his new landscape. Thus the novel does not celebrate loss but rather dramatizes the emergence of a people. Its meticulously created world affirms the ex-slave's rootedness and identification with his new world and presents this world as important evidence of the adjustment of vision and consciousness which slaves had to make in a new landscape.

Reid focuses on postemancipation Jamaican society as the background for this development and proceeds to create the social and physical geography of that world. Because of the underlying sense of Jamaican identity, his picture of the economic barriers, social stratification, and color divisions is balanced with a pervading sense of a distinctly peasant sensibility borne out of an involvement with the soil and symbolized by a powerfully evoked landscape linked to the consciousness of the people. Soil, sea, rock, forest, scents and sea smells, plant and animal life—the world that physically surrounds Jamaica—make up the imagery and rhythms of Reid's created world, coloring the very idioms and modulations of people's speech. Such distinctive speech patterns are so central to the novel's historical perspective that they operate consistently throughout the work, as can be glimpsed from these two widely separated passages:

> Cool and sweet is the water, and you take off your pantaloons and swim from bank to bank and the water hugs you close. Like say when you dream at night that duppy-ghost is a-chase you and you cry out and mother hugs you and you wake up and her breasts are a-kiss your face and there is peace on you . . .

> . . . When men make songs on contented bellies, there is depth and roundness in their throats. Wet earth and full trees bring quiet and content. But Stoney Gut men are a-dirge through three years o' dry earth and Humphrey's tithes, so aloes ha' come to their throats.[7]

This is the organic world that encloses, interacts with, and determines the nature and quality of people's lives in Reid's world. It is thus naturally the authentic background of the Morant Bay rebellion. For Reid perceived it not just as physical rage and violence but as an aspect of the self-awareness and sense of identity of the people. Throughout the excitement and agitation, the conch shells blow to signify the movement and modulations of people's feelings: the pain and helplessness, the wildness and anger that characterize the depth and confusion of feelings generated by economic and social frustration and underlying the entire process of Negro emergence in this region. Reid appears to accept at this time that the ex-slave has found a place in the existing order; that having become a Jamaican, he has also acquired a distinct sensibility and evolved a particular language, and his rebellion, rather than overthrow this order, should become a form of creative resistance within it.

This is the view that colors Reid's treatment of historical characters, explains his modification of historical facts, and ultimately determines the nature of the novel's conflicts. For though *New Day* is based on two major historical events, its other details are heavily fictionalized, as indeed are some of its historical facts. The Campbells, for instance, represent a typical social class in postemancipation Jamaica but are entirely fictional. In the novel the entire direction of Deacon Bogle's protest is changed so that Bogle does not only protest against poor conditions and injustice but also demands secession and total freedom. The actual historical facts in Bogle's case are remarkably different. He never preached secession. His movement rallied the peasants against the injustices of the local magistracy but all the time affirmed loyalty to the Crown. Indeed, in a later novelette written eleven years after *New Day* and dealing specifically with the events of 1865, Reid is more true to historical facts than he is in *New Day*. The Bogle of *Sixty-Five* is clear about the nature of his resistance. "We do not fight against the Queen . . . What do we fight against? The injustice that makes the planter judges fine the poor people more than they can pay, for wrongs they did not commit; the injustice that keeps us from Crown lands, where with better rainfall and better soil we could grow more food for our children."[8] In *Sixty-Five* Bogle's only mistake is that, untrained and unprepared for war, he resorts to violence and pushes his followers into a needless and violent confrontation with the authorities. In *New Day* his error is that he not only preaches violence but also secession and total freedom.

Whenever a historical novelist modifies the facts of history, he inevitably implies a moral judgment and indicates an intention to produce something more satisfying to his sense of right than the real events of the past. Why then does Reid shift the direction of Bogle's protest? What is the moral behind his historical modification? The preface of the novel clarifies his intentions: "I have not by any means attempted a history of the period from 1865–1944. What I have attempted is to transfer to paper some of the beauty, kindliness and humor of my people, weaving characters into the wider framework of these eighty years and creating a tale that will offer as true an impression as fiction can of the way by which Jamaica and its people came today."[9]

Such an emplotment of Jamaica's historical evolution introduces new themes and tensions. The Morant Bay rebellion is, for instance, envisaged not as a rebellion against an entire structure but as a local uprising that seeks to redefine the ex-slave's position within a colonial and creolized system. The exigencies of plot and theme necessitate that the drama of secession and complete independence become a sterile link in Jamaica's progress. Bogle's stubborn and separatist action precipitates violence and self-destruction; Davie's independent settlement becomes a dogmatic, static, and unconnected venture that must be destroyed to make room for a new ethos, just as his son, conceived and born on the isolated Zion, must die to make room for the hybridized grandson, Garth. The novel's resolution consists in the reorganization of the economic and political relations between ex-slave and ex-planter. Master and slave, capital and labor rearrange their relationships for a common purpose, and the new arrangement becomes the basis for a new, equitable political order.

Such a rearrangement may be neat and satisfying, but it involves subtle forms of dependence and a largely unproblematic relationship to an imperial ethos, and its various ramifications are never fully explored, even in the fictional construction. The responsibility for reorganizing new relationships rests too much with the planter and depends too heavily on his pliability. Besides, the union of labor and capital may present a good basis for a new political order, but the old relationships, as the story of rebellion exemplifies in part 1, represented an entire sociocultural fabric which a superficial linking of capitalists and trade unions may not necessarily dismantle. Roy Augier has argued that the "predominant values transmitted by the plantation to the slave reinforced the subordination to power inherent in his status,"[10] and his point of view hints at those complexities that remain subsumed in Reid's optimistic representation.

The entire thrust of the second section of the novel may indeed appear contradictory to the theme of rebellion and identity that dominates the first section. Kenneth Ramchand has pointed to the inconsistencies between the two sections and blamed them on Reid's well-meaning but uncomplicated wish to link the events of 1865 and 1944. "If wishing to run his history from 1865 to 1944, the novelist had stuck to his ground, allowing the condition of the people to continue to be the substance of the novel after the Morant Bay section, the novel thus produced would have been a serious challenge to the historian."[11] Yet it is difficult to imagine how Reid could have linked the two sections in this way when the first section had already revealed the tension between his view of rebellion as self-expression and his suspicion of spontaneity and violence. What seems like a contradiction between the two sections is really a deliberate ambiguity that points to a striving for a much larger vision of Afro-Caribbean continuity and progress. For in spite of being entangled in the web of fictionalized constitutional and economic history, Reid is also interested in another and different aspect of history in the West Indies. There is a major sense in which the fictional story within the drama of rebellion and constitutional history is also an enactment of the hybrid nature of the West Indian legacy, a thematic thrust which necessitates the containment of rebellion within a fundamentally Creole and hybrid framework.

In the text the evolution of the Campbell family with its mixture of bloods and personality traits cuts across the divisiveness of the economic and political order to suggest a more subtle aspect of the human relations between black slave and white master. The Campbells may well be half-white and far up in the social ladder, but their relation to the land and their consciousness of their surroundings are distinctly Creole and peasant, and their relations with people cut across the color and economic divisions of the stratified society. For instance, Davie's sense of his own and his family's identity takes in the entire world and background of his Afro-Caribbean roots: "Where my family once locked their door everybody except for the wealthy buckras, hungered. Everybody around me were my people and when they hungered, hungered me too."[12]

This conception of family, people, and identity is well reflected in that self-perception which enables Davie to link himself with the struggles of slaves and ex-slaves throughout the history of Jamaica; it is the same self-apprehension that leads him to identify with Bogle and the Stony Gut rebels. Reid, quite self-consciously, uses the Campbell family to formulate a history of blood mixtures and relationships that suggests the idea of growth and development within a new milieu. The family appears to contain within itself not just the West Indian heritage of mixed races but also the cross-cultural and human experiences which sum up the hybrid character of the West Indian experience. Thus the elder Campbell inherits Scottish blood but his sensibilities are the peasant sensibilities of the slave/ex-slave world, and although his religious and political conservatism detaches him from the rebels, he is ironically implicated in the rebellion through the commitment of his son, Davie. Davie's son, James Creary, conceived and born in the isolated Zion, loses his roots in the West Indian world of his father and marries into the empire. His son Garth, redeemed, inherits English blood afresh and is reintegrated into his grandfather's Creole world and traditions. Thus, although Garth is relatively better off than the bulk of the people he leads, he has a natural concern for the welfare of the poor and, like his grandfather, is informed with a spirit of national unity that cuts across skin color and class. As a family, then, the Campbells may symbolize an aspect of that process of coming to being which underlies Reid's vision of history in *New Day*. History in this sense moves beyond the precise details of what happened to incorporate an imaginative exploration of what is possible.

Such a possibility is lodged in the implications of the racial and cultural heritage of the Campbells. The successive shifts and variations in their blood denote this aspect of inheritance, although the idea is suggested without an exploration of its implications. It seems that the particular space and time of the historical novel as well as the actual historical events Reid deals with deflate this other focus. For the novelist neither appears to be in conflict with the mulatto condition nor even to present it with a suggestion of paradox. Neither Pa Campbell nor Davie nor Garth seems to experience any major personal crisis in connection with a dual heritage. James Creary, who cuts himself off from his Afro-Caribbean base and marries into "Empire," could conceivably have suffered a personal crisis, but he is quickly dispatched from the scene in order to make way for Garth.

The uncomplicated nature of the continuities established in *New Day* are partly the result of the nature of historical construction itself. Hayden White has observed that "history writing thrives on the discovery of all the possible plot structures that might be invoked to endow sets of events with different meanings . . . By suggesting alternative emplotments of a given sequence of historical events, historians provide [them] with all of the possible meanings with which the literary art of their culture is capable of endowing them."[13] In presenting the hybrid nature of a fictional family and linking it to real events in history, Reid employs the historian's method of emplotment and structuring, highlighting those elements of plot that give meaning to his historical theme. In *New Day* a central idea is the dual legacy of the Caribbean experience, and the reconstruction of history highlights this view at the expense of several subtle nuances of psychology and relationships which a purely fictional work might have grasped and explored.

The phenomenon of miscegenation and its repercussions on the mulatto heritage of the Campbells is hardly a problematic issue in *New Day*. Yet as a historical fact of the Caribbean experience, it is fraught with cultural, psychological, and other conflicts which need to be explored as part of any reassessment of the Caribbean experience. The Guyanese scholar and painter Denis Williams long ago pointed to the questions it raises and to its creative function as a unique cultural phenomenon, even though organically it could also be socially divisive in a society of emigrants standing in filial relationships to various racial ancestors of the old world.

The first fact of the Caribbean situation is the fact of miscegenation, of mongrelism. What are the cultural implications of this mongrel condition? . . . the imperatives of a contemporary culture are predominantly those of our relationship to this past. Yet in the Caribbean and in Guyana we think and behave as though we have no past, no history, no culture. And where we do come to take notice of our history it is often in the light of biases adopted from one thoroughbred culture or another . . . In the light of what we are this is a destructive thing to do, since at best it perpetuates what we might call a filialistic dependence on the cultures of our several racial origins while simultaneously inhibiting us from facing up to the facts of what we uniquely are.[14]

Williams's essay throws a revealing light on the New World response to miscegenation, especially in its inherited concepts of "pure blood" and "pure culture." As he argues, a filial relationship to the ancestor often perpetuates the idea of the half-breed as inherently impure and morally contaminated, a perception which deflates his/her unique possibilities as someone both racially and culturally transformed through centuries of separation, adjustment, and creolization. Thus, in light of Williams's argument, Mittelholzer's obsession with racial purity and family strength in the Kaywana trilogy, for instance, presents a limited New World philosophy by applying the distorted bias of pure-blood ancestors to the reality of a New World situation which is essentially unique.

In contrast, Reid's perspective in both *New Day* and *The Leopard* presents a more open and complex exploration of miscegenation in the mulatto's relationship to the ancestor. From an uncomplicated relationship in *New Day* we move towards a deeper probing of the conscious and subconscious ramifications of the ancestor complex in *The Leopard*. The various nuances in the tortuous relationship between the half-white Toto and his African father, Nebu, explore both the stresses and possibilities of this relationship. The historical perspective and the mythical framework provide leeway for making inferences that cut across the immediate context of rebellion and violent confrontation which form the subject matter of his novel. The landscape of the novel is thus both the particularized landscape of Kenya and the imagined landscape of the New World. Its quality of beyondness and timelessness creates a context for those generalized truths explored in relation to the Mau Mau struggle and their repercussions in the birth of the mulatto.

The major characters in *The Leopard* are also equally subsumed in this myth: Nebu is at once *kikuyu* man, archetypal African, and West Indian slave ancestor, coping with both the paradoxes of rebellion and the burdens of fathering a mulatto. Toto becomes in the same context the archetypal mulatto: half white and half bwana, showing the peculiar psychic complexes that are part of the heritage of West Indian man. Placed in such a thematic relationship to the exploration of rebellion, freedom, and identity, the relationship between Nebu and Toto becomes one aspect of the human factor, the paradox which qualifies the clear-cut polarities of the violent racial confrontation. On one hand, hatred and violence may be justified, may even be natural and cleansing in a situation of oppression. Yet on the other, they may be qualified by considerations that put other meanings on the confrontation between oppressor and oppressed. When Nebu trails the unknown white man in the bush, he believes he is pursuing an enemy, a murderer, a dangerous man-animal whom he would be justified in killing. Yet the white man he trails turns out to be no other than Bwana Gibson, the man he has wronged and whom his morality forbids him to harm, a man who also brings him face to face with "Toto," the human product and factor in the confrontation of violence with violence.

It is within this paradoxical context that Reid presents the relationship between Nebu and Toto. Toto becomes the child of paradox, the product of a brief moment of human recognition and communication between oppressor and oppressed, a moment that may well hold the multiple interpretations of the colonial encounter. Within this context the journey which Nebu and Toto make through the forest becomes symbolically a charting of the nuances of this relationship, a gradual and slow movement towards an understanding of its meaning and possibilities. Both Nebu and Toto must overcome not only their personal insecurities and prejudices but also the generalized evils and hatred spawned by the situation of conquest and oppression and symbolized by the leopard and the white man's gun. Both are at some points associated with the symbolic implications of the leopard and the gun, images of the evil, hatred, and destruction which foul and bastardize the gorgeous Edenic quality of the landscape.

Reid appears to begin his exploration from an idea of the half-white as physically, emotionally, and culturally crippled by the negative circumstances of miscegenation. The half-white child inherits all the suspicions, hatred, and animosities generated on both sides of the color line. More than this, his self-contempt and basic insecurities show up in his rejection of the

African ancestor, just as his constant clinging to a "white-bwana" status reveals a distorted self-perception. The mulatto stands out as psychologically maimed, even as racially tainted: "The half-bwana was a thin coin. Making recompense through such a boy would be cheating his way of a debt. A son from the Masai girl would have been ample payment. She had limbs that made her sweet-moving as a slow river, a proud river. She broke like a queen, and at that time you knew that a son of hers would be coin from the mint, firm, unhandled."[15]

Nebu's disappointed and despairing view of Toto is inspired both by the extent of Toto's self-hatred and by his own prejudiced feeling that a certain weakness and unwholesomeness occur in the process of miscegenation. The Masai woman's son would be "pure mint, unhandled, firm," identified with the natural world, with the very landscape of his soil, while, in contrast, Toto loses this sense of sureness and identity through the division in his physical makeup and his consciousness.

Yet this idea of taint and unwholesomeness is precisely what both Toto and Nebu must surmount. In Reid the mongrel condition does not spell irrevocable doom, as it does in Mittelholzer. Taint does not occur simply through the physical mixing of bloods; rather, it occurs because of the circumstances of humiliation, dehumanization, and mutual hatred that surrounds the domination of one race by another. Thus, whereas in Mittelholzer's trilogy mongrelism and the mixing of bloods represent an inherently disruptive and degenerate force, that same force becomes for Reid the hidden possibility beneath the negative emotions unleashed by the meeting of races in a colonial and oppressive relationship. Nebu's and Toto's journey through the forest becomes an inner journey that leads to reassessment and a new understanding, one that is facilitated by the relatively neutral ground of the forest, freed by its primeval character from the social and racial constraints that ordinarily determine relationships between people and races. Nebu learns to find something of value in Toto, learns to love and accept him in spite of who he is. Through his evaluations and reassessments, he acquires valuable human knowledge about the irrelevance of skin and status in the real instinctual and spiritual relationships between people.

"Loins," Nebu demanded, "speak then. Which did you love most? The girl or the Msabu?" "*But I was blind!*" his loins protested "*my eyes were closed when I sang.*" "But was there any difference in your singing?" Nebu persisted "Was your singing more splendid for the black woman or for the white woman?" "*Is today's rain different from yesterday?*" retorted his loins. "*Does it rain lead today and gold yesterday?" "Will the moon at next harvest be larger or smaller than the last?"*

... Nebu laughed, floating along on waves of agony "I may not be here to tell you." *Then leave the question with your nearest kinsman.*[16]

Nebu reaches out towards the closed doors of the "half-bwana," offering his newly gained illumination on the complex flow of feelings on both sides of the confrontation, originally obscured by the clear-cut polarization between the two races. Toto, with the divided sensibilities of a cross-cultural breed, responds with ambivalence, opening up to Nebu at some points and at others closing tight behind his perverted consciousness. Unable totally to free himself from "a debt of history" to the white man, he cannot achieve Nebu's exhilaration of self-knowledge and freedom: "[His] skin and bones were bondservants to the presence of the leopard. He sat still as the print in a book."[17] On the contrary, Nebu's final act in slaying the Englishman (more a conception of the leopard than an Englishman per se) represents an assertion of self and confidence which are continually asserted as the lessons the "half-bwana" must learn.

In this treatment of the feelings involved in violent confrontations between oppressor and oppressed, Reid not only moves some way but actually deepens the complex forces and impulses inherent in what may appear as a straightforward opposition. In *New Day* such deeper nuances are subsumed in the demands of a specific time and space of history and in Reid's own anxiety to create an optimistic sense of progress by consolidating the span of a particular family. Within this consolidation the dilemmas of mulatto identities in an ex-slave and racially stratified society may be suggested in the ironical presentation of the older Campbell, but this presentation does not involve as deep a probing of their inner conflicts and subconscious ramifications as is possible in *The Leopard.* For though the general contexts of the meeting of races in a situation of conquest may be similar in the two novels, *New Day* is in a representational sense a "history," while *The Leopard* is essentially a dialectic that brings out the nuances and contradictory impulses inherent in the dual identities of Caribbean people and attempts to reconcile them. As a representation it invests more in imagination, inner dialogue, and psychic ramifications than in the classification and consolidation of things and people. The Kenyan landscape and the dilemmas of the novel are thus more archetypal than real, and characterization more a visualization of what could be possible than a consolidation of what is.

With such a framework Reid is able to suggest more possibilities than he could with the historical medium in *New Day*. He can present contrasting interpretations of the place of violence in the confrontation between oppression and liberation and can grapple more deeply with the moral and psychological challenges of the West Indian's relation to the white ancestor instead of accepting the mulatto condition as an unproblematic situation. The contrasting modes of representation in the two novels differentiate the varying possibilities not only of history and fiction but also within fiction itself, of fiction that consolidates and that which invests in dialectics and imaginative possibilities. In the West Indian context of redefinition, where perceptions of self, society, and history require revolutionary reassessments, fiction that mediates a given reality to produce other possible meanings can transcend fixed conceptions of Caribbean history. Both of Reid's novels attempt this transcendence by endowing given events with figurative meanings. But the different forms of their representations interestingly reveal the limits of the "historical" form and the expansive scope of the imaginary and the dialogic.

Chapter Three

History as Loss

Determinism as Vision and Form in V. S. Naipaul

The medieval mind which saw only continuity seemed so unassailable. It existed in a world which, with all its ups and downs, remained harmoniously ordered and could be taken for granted. It had not developed a sense of history, which is a sense of loss; it had developed no true sense of beauty, which is a gift of assessment. While it was enclosed, this made it secure. Exposed, its world became a fairyland, exceedingly fragile.

V. S. Naipaul, *An Area of Darkness*

In West Indian writing a tradition of historical fiction has continued to grow and extend beyond the frontiers of past time into the very contemporary present. The novelist's consciously historical conception of the present is itself part of a nineteenth-century European relation to history, an offshoot of that interplay between historicism and fiction which gave rise to the European realistic novel of the late nineteenth century. The century's belief that man was the agent of activity in history, its idea of human progress as developing out of the inner conflicts of social forces meant that human existence and social activity could be interpreted and conceptualized as history. "Society from being a framework could be seen now as an agency even an actor, a character. It could be seen and valued in and through persons. [It was] now not just a code to measure, an institution to control, a standard to define or to change. It was a process that entered lives to shape or to deform."[1]

Thus rather than contend in restricted ways with the facts and truths of the historical event per se, the novelist could interpret the conditions of his/her characters' lives, their states of mind, and the assumptions that governed their lives; and the historicity of the novel would then be embodied in his/her conceptualizations about their present existence as it is touched by the past.

For a novelist like V. S. Naipaul, such a narrative of society answers to a desire to explore contemporary man's relation to history and to a fundamental understanding of that interplay between man and history which has been characteristic of the European mind since the Renaissance. "History tries to analyze those circumstances and forces, those subtle forms of necessity which condition human action and constrict the operation of the human will in the world."[2] Herbert Butterfield's echoing of nineteenth-century historical thinking resonates in every premise from which Naipaul has perceived and interpreted contemporary society. The ability to wrench freedom from necessity is itself linked to a belief in the rationality of the historical process and its dialectic of man's evolutionary progress towards perfection.

In Naipaul such a dialectic inspires a vision of history as loss and of a historical sense as a constant correlation and assessment of past and present. It is also fundamentally an appreciation of the relationship between man's existence and his creativity through time and, in *An Area of Darkness*, becomes the principle that marks the difference between what Naipaul regards as the unconnectedness and pointlessness of Indian ruins and the history of Europe, "where monuments of sun kings are part of the development of a country's spirit, expressing the refining of a nation's sensibility, adding up to the common growing stock."[3] The basis of this distinction is the difference between what Naipaul calls a positive and negative principle and what Camus describes as the capacity and incapacity for rebellion.

> The problem of rebellion . . . has no meaning except within our western society . . . Thanks to the theory of political freedom, there is, in the very heart of our society, an increasing awareness in man of the idea of man and, thanks to the application of this theory of freedom, a corresponding dissatisfaction. In fact, for the Inca and the [Hindu] pariah the problem never arises, because for them it had been solved by a tradition even before they had time to raise it. If in a world where things are held sacred the problem of rebellion does not arise, it is because no real problems are to be found in such a world, all the answers having been given simultaneously. Metaphysics is replaced by myth. There are no more questions, only eternal answers and commentaries, which may be metaphysical.[4]

In *An Area of Darkness*, it is the separations that Naipaul makes between his own and Indian attitudes to myths and legends that best exemplify Camus's distinctions and the ramifications of his own sense of history as loss. His argument is that to assess relationships between the ruins of the past and to accept the loss of the god of legend is not only to experience a sense of loss but also to establish a continuity in history since the very awareness of loss and the sense of regret at the disintegration of culture can sharpen an understanding of creativity in the present and establish an imaginative order for a writer.

It is from the perspectives of such a conceptualization that Naipaul constructs his visionary "history" of Trinidad in *The Loss of El Dorado*. The relationship he builds up between the European document and his own fictional text provides the leeway for a "created" text in which his own biases and personal history converge. Thus, with the underlying idea of connecting the little island of Trinidad to great names and great events, he creates a governing vision, a determinist theme of perverted ideals and a diminished society: "From the undiscovered continent, to the fraudulence and chaos of revolution . . . from the discovery by Columbus, a man of medieval Europe, to the disappearance of the Spanish Empire in the nineteenth century."[5] By the end of the actual process of interpreting and creating, the governing vision itself has become part of a structured order which determines the judgmental tone and the values from which Naipaul interprets and assesses the documents. The synthesis he talks of is thus also a thematic continuity that links events in a repetitive pattern of promise and failure: the promise of El Dorado contrasted with the greed, brutality, and incompetence of conquistadors; the liberalism of the metropolis juxtaposed to its mediocre equivalent in the slave society and the bogus revolution in Spanish America.

The recurring patterns fit together neatly to present the history of Trinidad as essentially a history of oppressors and their victims, with Europe cast as the oppressor and subject and Indians and Negroes cast as the victims and objects. Thus Trinidad's history from 1633 to 1776 appears in *The Loss of El Dorado* as a Spanish story, featuring Indians only as they illuminate Spanish brutality and incompetence. Similarly, the making of Trinidadian society between 1803 and 1813, a period of social flux and adjustment, becomes a principally British drama, featuring the conflict between the colonial simplicities of settler planters and the complex moral drive of metropolitan radicals. Naipaul's main bias, of course, is to pit metropolitan idealism against colonial debasement and demonstrate that radical humanitarian opposition to colonial values was finally ineffective because its substance contradicted the slave-based society of the island. In presenting this perspective, he features slaves, free Negroes, and mulattos, but these appear only as instruments in the more important fortunes of British history-makers, and they disappear almost as soon as they outlive their usefulness.

Yet this was a period of flux and change, especially in the composition of the original slave society. Slaves had already made adjustments and transformations in their relations with plantation culture, and even in 1800 the mulatto represented something. What was his life? How did he see himself? How did his situation affect relationships between sections of the society? Naipaul offers no insights in this area. Indeed, as far as he could gather, the Trinidadian Negro slave perceived the world of property and labor (of which he himself was such a significant part!) only on the level of fantasy. He was incapable of the self-awareness and self-assessments necessary for rebellion. He had no history, no story. "The slave was never real. Like the extinct aboriginal he had to be reconstructed from his daily routine. So he remains existing like Vallot's jail (of which no plan survives) only in the imagination. In the records the slave is faceless, silent, with an identification rather than a name. He has no story."[6]

In Naipaul's history the failure of idealism is matched by a systematic debasement and diminishment, an irretrievable taint in which all endeavor and political assertion are paralyzed. The South American revolutionaries in *El Dorado* are caught in the same trap as the politicians in *The Mimic Men* and fit logically into the picture of failure and taint. Vulnerable, susceptible to various delusions and corruptions, their failure becomes not just in part but wholly a colonial and predictable failure: "They saw their disabilities as economic and political alone . . . they could not conceive the deeper colonial deprivation, the sense of the missing real world that Miranda had spent a lifetime making good."[7]

And behind this judgment of the revolutionaries, there is more than a judgment of society; there is a hint of inevitability spurred by a sense of absence, of an irretrievable loss the deprivations of which would trap them and their people forever. People are only what societies make them, Naipaul insists, and the revolutionaries will remain colonial, dependent, insecure, striving for the missing real world, over-compensating their deprivations, looking at their society with the borrowed eyes of the metropolis and getting lost in fantasies. And it is as if we have made a turn back to *The Mimic Men,* to those feelings that bridge the years and link unlikely places; it is as if we can recognize Singh's sense of captivity and lurking external threat as well as his regret and pain at the thought of a rich world destroyed and rendered null. Yet these are personal feelings that had arisen out of a strange complexity of sources, from a sense of displacement, from feelings of shipwreck, from delusions about order, even from personal disassociation. History as response to displacement and homelessness; history as catharsis. In Naipaul there is not much differentiation between history and personal situation. The two are inseparable, and the insights of history provide an understanding that leads to a catharsis and a calm.

The impulses that reveal themselves in *The Loss of El Dorado* reappear in all Naipaul's fictional writing. For him, the necessity that governs Caribbean man is what history demonstrates in *El Dorado* just as the freedom that can come out of the knowledge of necessity is the understanding and order which his own writing continually strives for. The determinist idea that man is fashioned by heredity and environment has helped the formulation of a vision of history which has developed and deepened as Naipaul has moved from novel to novel. History in *A House for Mr. Biswas* is thus basically an exploration of the ways in which the past shapes the lives and consciousness of characters in fiction. The account of Biswas's life, of East Indian response to the New World, of the nature and impact of the colonial society itself, represent the present as it has been molded by the past. For Naipaul, the experience is one of displacement, disorientation, and void, and Biswas, the symbolic colonial, has to find his way through a confused Indian world and a chaotic, slave-based colonial world. His precarious progress through these and his association with other colonials making similar adjustments constitute the background of the novel's scrutiny of West Indian man's relationship to the past.

The relentless delineation of the degeneration and decline of Tulsi values and the parallel drama of Biswas's quest for place enact scenarios of colonial disorientation, loss, and ambiguities which are differentiated only in degree and emphasis from character to character. Biswas's loss and confusion may be differentiated from the situation of the Tulsis only in his level of struggle and awareness of his condition. For whereas he spends a lifetime struggling to come to terms with displacement and the new society, the Tulsis seem unable even to be aware of their particular situation as displaced people in an amorphous society. Biswas's search is therefore an act of personal definition, a growth in sensibility, and a source of all that is possible in his response to the New World. The house he finally acquires becomes an all-embracing symbol of his struggle, of the ambiguous place he has managed to create, and of the compromises he has had to make with history.

But curiously, it is such a vision of growth and possibility that is deflated by the novel's vitiated ending and by the suggestion that Biswas's house is only a fragile retreat that brings him love and personal contentment but also the threat of disaster, lethargy, and the dullness of a life purged of ambition and drive. Indeed, the threat of disaster that hangs over Biswas, the slow corruption of his aging body, the madness that seems inexplicable, become part of a cycle of darkness and destruction outside that suggests an inevitability about Biswas's condition as colonial.

Yet his acuteness and insight, one feels, should amount to much more than they do and should lead to the kind of positive ordering that Naipaul's own assumptions and techniques lead us to expect. Such positiveness is definitely part of the assumption behind a capacity for awareness, a quality which in *An Area of Darkness* Naipaul defines and likens to Camus's concept of the rebel. But whereas in Camus the rebel attacks his shattered world in order to demand a unity from it; whereas his freedom consists in his insight into his condition and his rejection of it, Naipaul's Biswas is limited by a situation of displacement which his author now sees as unalterable.

Homi Bhabha argues that the themes of castration and loss that lurk behind the foregrounded values of individualism and progressiveness in Biswas's confrontation with Haunuman House should produce an alternative evaluation that is not merely the result of another form of mimetic reading; that the disturbance in narrative enunciation that produces the contradictions identified here enact rather the gap in coherence, the shifting and unsettling of the otherwise unitary space of narrative enunciation that announces "the impending crisis in a myth of narrative based on linear progression and closure."[8] This gap in narration, Bhabha argues further, is the logical outcome of the problematic nature of Biswas's colonial fantasies on which the authoritative markings of identity and individuality are based. "Colonial fantasy raises questions about the link between self-consciousness and moral conduct which has become the Western norm for the individuation of the 'person' and the basis of its social designation . . . [It] presents scenarios that make problematic both Authority and Intention. It registers a crisis in the assumption of the narrative priority of the 'first person' and the *natural* ascendancy of the First World."[9] Quoting Foucault, Bhabha suggests that this specific historical formation of the subject demands another kind of reading, one that is capable of "liberating divergence and marginal elements, the kind of dissociating view that is capable of decomposing itself, capable of shattering the unity of man's being through which it was thought that he could extend his sovereignty to the events of the past."[10] Bhabha sees the narrative disturbance in *A House for Mr. Biswas* as shattering Western bourgeois social and psychic assumptions about representation in ways that are both familiar and terrifying to Western readers.

But Bhabha's argument is based solely on a narrative disturbance arising out of a scenario of colonial fantasy that still keeps Biswas within an orbit of marginality: "a spectacle of colonial fantasy that sets itself up as an uncanny 'double' to reveal things so profoundly familiar to the West that it cannot bear to remember them."[11] Behind Biswas's fantasies, however, there is still the sinister assumption that the inexplicable darkness outside is an inevitable fact of the workings of his world. There is still an apprehension of a fundamentally unalterable loss against which he would always be paralyzed. Such a vision of loss is really what enacts the gap in coherence that Bhabha identifies. It persists in *A House for Mr. Biswas* as a restricted and deterministic vision of Biswas's world and as an aspect of a personal mythology which Naipaul constructs as he moves away from a preoccupation with history as "the past" towards a concept in which the missed coherence and continuities of the displaced become a major disequilibrium that can be bridged only on an imaginative level. Thus Harris's view that *A House for Mr. Biswas* consolidates one's preconception of humanity without erupting into a revolutionary or alien question of spirit is a valid observation on the restricted historical perception that makes comparison with Harris's own transforming visions of history pertinent and rewarding.[12]

On a thematic level, therefore, the shift from the central image of the void in *A House for Mr. Biswas* to the image of shipwreck in *The Mimic Men* denotes a shift in Naipaul's view of the relationship between the West Indian and his/her past. The void is an image of the present and future, representing the fears and uncertainties of the displaced in an unformed society. It is a challenge that requires confrontation, one that needs to be met with a vision of possibility and achievement. In *The Mimic Men* the image of shipwreck, symbol of displacement, is of a past from which there can be no escape. Its real and frightening symptoms are presented as existing inside the protagonist and as persisting wherever he is. The image, a Crusoe archetype, is appropriated and enlarged to include all the psychological disorders which Caribbean people inherit from their condition of displacement and their status as colonials. In *The Mimic Men* and in Naipaul's subsequent novels it is characterized as a situation of disorder, and its major connotations are presented in the beach house drama in *The Mimic Men* when Singh records two visions of his landscape, the man-made and the deserted and natural:

> The sea broke out on us almost without warning. Only a height of sky and a quality of openness behind the tops of trees suggested that

a little way beyond there was no more land. And then, at the end of the coconut trees, was the living destroying element, almost colorless at this distance. The trees swayed and rustled and crackled. Among the trees, the two storeyed timber house. No garden, no yard, no fence: just sand and the unnatural plants and vines glittering green, that grew in hot salt sand. Not my element, I preferred land, mountains and snow. Night came, moonlit or black, spectral or empty; and nothing could be heard except the wind and the trees.[13]

So much is suggested about the man-made landscape that the image can be said to dramatize both the isolation and the disequilibrium that Singh sees as the consequences of displacement. Apart from the desolation of the scene there is a precarious feeling of danger here, a sense of wrongness and, more terrifying, a suggestion of an antipathy between man and landscape. The violent predatory elements seem to work against man. The sea has a masterly presence which is unsympathetic and destructive, and beside it men and their puny dwellings seem defenseless and vulnerable. In the midst of this unnatural violence and dislocation Singh sees a drifting tree on the desolate beach as an image and a reminder of his own shipwreck, one that provokes alarming thoughts of uncertainty and threat in his mind. The vision of dislocation glimpsed here is worked out in the nature of relationships between people. First, Singh flays the man-made island, seeing its hot stale sand and its darkness as evidence of its corruption and taint. Secondly, he interprets activity on the beach as reflecting the island's situation and character. Nothing seems to draw people together on this beach, neither the monstrous spectacle of the drownings with their stark reminder of human vulnerability, nor the sight of the dead bodies stretched side by side on the sand. Over and above this vision of the disconnection between man and landscape and between man and man, Singh also has a vision of the natural, unviolated, pre-Columbian landscape, the neatness of which suggests a quality of purity in direct contrast to the depletion, ruggedness, and taint of the man-made island. Here in this natural landscape the continuous cyclic movement of the tide suggests a flow and order not tampered with, and in this natural, fresh, untainted landscape the great tree is not adrift, not stranded, but lies fast and rooted in the sand.

In his recapitulation of the island's society and relationships Singh explores the symbolism of order and disorder which he glimpses here in the two beach images. He traces the chaos of cultural, economic, and religious relationships on the island as well as the decay of culture and ritual back to this central disorder. Accordingly, the Isabella he presents has no center, no tradition, no rituals that can unite the fragmented society.[14] Each group he evokes seems trapped in its private fantasy and its rituals of private actions. Even his childhood memory of house and school present the same images of fragmentation and disconnection in which both house and school appear as private hemispheres that hardly meet. These images of separation and disconnection reflect that dislocation in relationships which Naipaul now sees as unalterable consequences of displacement.

Singh's memoirs explore this phenomenon as the commonest psychological expression of "shipwreck" and characterize it as that general feeling of abandonment and irrelevance that leads the shipwrecked to long for other landscapes. It is in this light that he identifies all the characters as "shipwrecks" and exposes even the apparently rooted Deschampneufs as a victim. For Deschampneufs, descendant of French Creoles and the only character who articulates a concept of rootedness in the novel, is also a man apart, secure and imprisoned in his race and class. The vision of rootedness which he holds out to the alienated Singh is exposed then as impressive but only partially satisfying: "You are born in a place and you grow up there. You get to know the trees and the plants. You will never know any other trees and plants like that. You grow up watching a guava tree, say. You know that browny-green bark peeling like old paint . . . Nobody has to teach you what the guava is . . . where you born, man, you born. And this island is a paradise, you will discover."[15]

In *The Mimic Men* the idea of rootedness is conceived of in more complex terms than in *A House for Mr. Biswas* and extends beyond a simple identification of man and landscape. Here rootedness means a coming to terms with the facts of history, however squalid; it means a coming to terms with the facts of several migrations and the creation of that link between men which is nonexistent in society and which Singh thinks impossible anyway. It is in this respect that Naipaul feels that Deschampneuf's vision of rootedness can be seen as inadequate. For it is a vision which rejects a relationship with the Indian and unconsciously sees the "paradise" of Isabella as a principally French Creole creation. It is also a vision that does not quite escape the fantasizing which Singh identifies as the commonest reaction of the shipwrecked. For it hangs on to a myth that links his little island with the great world outside (with Stendhal's writing, with Europe) and saves him from that feeling of abandonment and personal irrelevance which plagues and corrupts people like Singh. Thus, if Deschampneufs is saved from corruption it is only because in the imagined security of his rootedness he does not attempt to impose an order on the existing colonial order, and for Naipaul, corruption only comes from such an attempt.

In the logic of Singh's analysis, corruption is conceived of as the self-deception which leads the shipwrecked to believe he can impose order on the disorder of his society, and this is the corruption traced in the two political movements in the novel, which are explored both as extensions of the fantasy world of their leaders and as an aspect of their "shipwreck." Gurudeva's political movement becomes a purely personal creation, an answer to his frustrations and a return to the private fantasies of his younger days when, as the "aboriginal" young man discovered by the missionary lady, he had imagined himself in a larger world and involved in bigger events. The presentation concentrates on the apparently popular and political nature of his movement and the purely personal needs that inspire and sustain it. Every personal detail is built into the progress of events leading to the climax of rebellion to allow us to separate the personal from the apparently political.

Eventually the personal motivation overshadows the political, and the movement becomes a purely personal creation in which Gurudeva sees himself only as a man attempting the good life as laid down by his Aryan ancestors and overcoming at last the feelings of irrelevance generated by his shipwreck. In the context of this personal commitment, the symbolic killing of Tamango, which may appear as the climax of the movement's act of rebellion and anger, is then in reality only Gurudeva's own sacrificial tribute to his life. "An ancient sacrifice, . . . a thing of beauty, speaking of the youth of the world, of untrodden forests and unsullied streams, of horses and warrior-youths in morning light."[16]

For here, at last, is the escape from darkness, the link with the glorious past that had seemed to elude him after his missionary years. His new vision of himself in relation to the island is indeed a denial of it and a romantic re-creation of its reality. And because his movement is no more than this personal vision, it cannot have a purpose and cannot be revolutionary, and drama and disorder are the only ways the despair it creates can be expressed.

In contrast to the benign disturbance of Gurudeva's movement, the larger political movement, though equally a response to shipwreck, creates illusions of order by actually abolishing the external colonial order; and in the logic of the novel's delineations it is this illusion of creation and order that simplifies political action, reduces it to mere "drama," and leads eventually to fraudulence. "Detachment alone would have shown us that in the very success of our movement lay the pointlessness of our situation. In our very success lay that disorder which, daily, we feared more."[17]

In *The Mimic Men* the central drama of political action is structured from this perspective of detachment and reappraisal, and the novel be-

comes a piecing together of the background of history and historical repercussions from which the politicians should have made their assessments in
the first place. The novel is therefore in theme and structure, Singh's recapitulation and assessment of the larger political movement. From a perspective of his own and other childhood, adolescent, and adult backgrounds, he reveals the history of disorder, of personal insecurities and
racial separations which become the real barriers to true political action
and freedom. The reshaping and analysis presents a detached and critical
view of the movement, of Browne's personality and delusions, and of his
own fraudulent belief that he could be linked to the slave island in a political action.

From this perspective of Singh and his theory of disorder, we are led to
conclude that the attempts of the shipwrecked to impose order on disorder
are not creative, that the would-be politician has really only two equally
noncreative choices: to acquire a limited outlet for benevolence and service
within the colonial pattern of dependence, or to abolish the colonial order
and descend into controlled chaos. In Singh's mind the chaos seems at first
to be linked to the movement's deficiencies, to that "secretion of bitterness"
which becomes its only appeal and truth and which pushes untalented,
noncreative men to the helm of affairs; but later we identify it as a pervasive
and lasting disability existing within and linked to the unalterable historical situation.

Considered solely from Singh's point of view as deduced here, *The
Mimic Men* presents both critical and thematic difficulties. The central
character from whose sole point of view the drama and reassessments are
presented is also a victim of the disorder, and this situation calls for an
authorial irony that can separate Singh the victim of displacement from
Singh the critical appraiser. In the novel this irony is occasionally inconsis-
tent and confused. We are not always able to separate Singh's appraisal
from his personal crisis, and especially in his assessments of Browne, this
presents a critical difficulty. We note, for instance, that the earlier Singh had
been a deeply neurotic person whose vision of New World disorder had
coexisted with fantasies about distant and larger landscapes; he was a man
who had experienced alienation and despair so compelling that only the
decision to abandon his island had saved him from possible suicide, a man
who had deliberately simplified his relationships because his imminent
flight had rendered these temporary and unimportant; a man whose terror
of external threat had driven him to incest as the only secure relationship
possible amid the ethnic and class chaos of the island society.

Yet it is solely from the point of view of Singh and often in the light of his personal crisis that the relationship between him and Browne is examined. Singh's first visit to Browne's house is, for instance, deliberately poised to establish the nature of Browne's denial of the New World and to illustrate the fumbling and failures that come with the ritual simplifications which Singh has opted for. Indeed, the entire background of their separate "shipwrecks" is meant to expose the fraudulence of their political alliance and the delusions of order which their movement implies. In his mature analysis, Singh does admit his own dishonesty in drifting into a union with Browne, knowing he has not come to terms with the fragmented society, knowing that a deep racial and class gulf separated him from Browne. Yet in spite of evidence that he has not overcome his personal crisis, Naipaul still retains him as the sole point of view and source of analysis of the movement, creating an inconsistency between Singh the critic and Singh the neurotic with a personal crisis. The entire theory of disorder from which Singh makes his connection between Isabella's past and its possibilities presents other thematic and critical problems. For Singh's vision of Isabella's disorder and doomed political future also coexists with a broad authorial irony in which his own delusions about order and purity (delusions against which he has always measured New World disorder) are exposed and mocked. It is possible, for instance, to trace a consistent irony against Singh from his early fantasies about Asiatic and Persian Aryans and "snow men" of the Himalayan mountains through his idyllic picture of the ordered plantation estate, through the imagined order of his Roman house, to the time in England when he seeks the city's order and longs for a "limpid direct vision of the world."[18]

I suggest that the images of Aryan horsemen and snowy landscapes should be linked to all Singh's other delusions about order and seen as the beginning of a progressive movement towards that total desolation when he realizes that all to which man links himself flatters only to deceive. By way of tracing this movement, we are able to link this image to Singh's repeated confrontations with the metropolitan city and the revelation of the city's order as an illusion. We should see this as a mockery of Singh's wish to link himself to a larger order and recognize the self-deception and fraudulence of his attempts to counteract this discovery about the city. His attempts to create a city personality, his marriage to Sandra, and his fascination with Lady Stella would, in this case, all be acts of delusion and fraudulence that gravitate towards those two pathetic experiences of total placelessness and desolation, experiences which reflect the dreaded picture of shipwreck he had spent almost a lifetime trying to make good. We must consider as well the picture of disequilibrium, the sense of being adrift, of being without a center, the total vision of homelessness which Singh experiences when, for the second time, he discovers the city to be a city of fantasy presenting no order to which he can be linked.

The panic and restlessness engendered by this feeling should be regarded as a link to Singh's repeated disillusionment, culminating in his nightmarish encounter with an unnamed woman in an unnamed city, that moment linked to nothing during which he loses all sense of self and diminishes into what he had always feared: "a cell of perception, indifferent to pleasure or pain."[19]

For these are the two climactic experiences which push Singh towards a resolution and towards the chastening vision of placelessness as an attitude of mind, a secretion from within: "Certain emotions bridge the years and link unlikely places. Sometimes by this linking the sense of place is destroyed, and we are ourselves alone: the young man, the boy, the child. The physical world which we yet continue to prove, is then like a private fabrication we have always known."[20]

This realization, which comes to Singh as he writes his memoirs, should have led him to reassess the theory of New World disorder which had all along been maintained in relation to his vision of the larger world's order; and the reassessment should have illuminated his reappraisal of the political movement better, especially as the process of writing, the order of recreating and ordering are supposed to uncover all self-deceptions and fraudulence. Singh's admission that the impulse behind all his actions in the novel had been the denial of his landscape and his delusions about order does, after all, affect his manner of writing. It leads him to avoid a chronological order and to reshape his material around the two crucial incidents of denial: his first snow and his discovery of the young girl's photograph in the attic. Yet there is no similar rethinking of his vision of Isabella's disorder. His mature assessment of political change is still based on an image of disorder grasped from a deluded vision of order which has now been mocked and rejected. Indeed, the novel's final resolution does not leave Singh with an understanding that leads to renewal and further action. It is a personal illumination which saves him from madness by revealing that action is irrelevant because displacement is real, and the order and purity he had always sought would be unattainable. "We are a people who for one reason or another have withdrawn from our respective countries, from our families. We have withdrawn, from unnecessary responsibility and attachment. We have simplified our lives. I cannot believe that our establishment is unique. It comforts me to think that in this city alone there must be hundreds and thousands like ourselves."[21]

Singh's illumination appears in the end not an admission of defeat but a triumph of assessment, a personal sense of history which overcomes the illusion of order and continuity and transcends the disintegration of defeat and failure. To recognize failure, defeat, and loss in this way is also in Naipaul's view to refuse to succumb to them, and such an understanding is in the end only an individual responsibility. *The Mimic Men* thus appears in this sense an individual solution to a personal sense of "shipwreck," a solution which insists that illumination, reconciliation, and some kind of order are possible only for characters who make connections between present action and the historical necessity that conditions or restrains it.

This reconciliation, though coming at the end of Singh's analysis, is really only a form of inaction and withdrawal, a simplification which reveals to us that the act of writing while abolishing disturbance may indeed bring on further delusions; that the calm and order which analysis provides may confirm rather than alter the reality and neurosis of displacement. Singh's ridiculous posture at the end of the novel as a fawning overseas student is, for instance, still a return to a colonial syndrome and to the insecurities of displacement. In the same way his belief that his ultimate withdrawal is a fulfillment of Aryan precepts suggests a measure of delusion and returns him to that denial which has plagued him throughout the novel. By the end of the novel, Naipaul himself has still not resolved this problem of representation and its significance for the reality that Singh has structured in his memoir. Irony, which should be the chief source of meaning in a first-person narrative, has been unclear, and our understanding of a particular reality has been forced through the totalizing vision of an unreliable narrator.

In the novels after *The Mimic Men* Naipaul suggests that the kind of illumination and imaginative order which Singh achieves are possible only for characters who make connections between their present action and the historical necessity that conditions or restrains it, and in *Guerrillas*, in which no character appears to possess such a capacity, the omniscient narrator becomes the principal interpreter among other interpreters in a reconstruction of the "Michael X" story within a Trinidad social and political context.[22] As with *The Loss of El Dorado*, there is a re-creation of history from records and documents, though this time in reverse representation, from history to fiction. The difference between the documented history in "The Killings in Trinidad" and the fictional reconstruction in *Guerrillas* should therefore illuminate Naipaul's art of creation as well as reveal the ways in which a fundamentally determinist vision can impact on a novelist's representation of reality.

In various commentaries and critical writing Naipaul himself has given several insights into his fictional methods and his relationship to the European novel. In a critical reading of Conrad's "The Truth of Karian" he expresses reservations about what Conrad calls his need to present a conscientious rendering of truth in thought and fact in his fiction. "He didn't seem able to go beyond his first simple conception of a story; his invention seemed to fail so quickly . . . he had refined away, as commonplace, those qualities of imagination, fantasy and invention that I went to novels for."[23] But the correlation between fact and invention within an essentially determinist perspective is what creates problems of representation as well as the nihilism that has continually surrounded Naipaul's vision of the Caribbean. The invention also takes its source from an ideal which the determinism cannot allow in the long run.

Yet the ideal vision is always the point of reference, the crucial image which heightens the protagonist's special quest or neurosis. In *A House for Mr. Biswas*, it belongs somewhere in the vague past and encapsulates certainties and coherence lost through displacement; in *An Area of Darkness* it is evoked in the awesome beauty and orderliness of the Himalayas, once better known and more closely related to people's lives; in *The Mimic Men* it is symbolized by the order of the medieval world, the world before Columbus, and by the image of Aryan horsemen riding to the very end of the world (an image of open spaces and larger possibilities); in "The Circus at Luxor" it is embodied in an ancient painting, "the special vision of men who knew no other land and saw what they had as rich and complete."[24] Even in *The Loss of El Dorado,* which is a reconstruction of history, there is an aspect of invention which pits history against an ideal prelapsarian world.

In *Guerrillas,* in which Naipaul constructs fiction out of "history," the same correlation exists between fact and invention, and the ideal vision is here lodged in the novelist's own consciousness, since no character possesses an untainted personal vision. Naipaul wrote *Guerrillas* after *The Loss of El Dorado,* and, with the publication of *The Enigma of Arrival* and the autobiographical material now available, it is easy to make connections between the history in *El Dorado* and the fiction in *Guerrillas.* Naipaul lets us into the process through which his reconstruction of history gave him a new relation to his island's past. "Through writing—knowledge and curiosity feeding off one another—I had arrived at a new idea of myself and my world . . . I wanted to see the island where I had been living in a new way in my imagination for the last two years, the island I had restored, as it were, to the globe and for which now I felt a deep romance."[25]

But in *El Dorado* the romance of the island and its relation to antiquity also coexist with a squalid reality which Naipaul delineates with relentless determinism. I suggest that the contrast between the landscape of the novelist's imagination and the reality of the landscape in Trinidad has a lot to do with the hysteria with which Naipaul constructs landscape as a backdrop to the Michael X story in *Guerrillas*. Whereas in the documented story he builds up the linear details of Malik's past, linking his life in England to his life in Trinidad, in the fiction he fits him in a landscape in which his particular fantasy and sense of disorder are paralleled with several other fantasies and disorders. Thus in correlating fact and invention Naipaul creates a new theme in which the ideal is an old order now in the midst of disintegration; an order in which a man could be himself without having to create a false personality. Bryant's tears at the cinema appear to be shed for all who had lost this ideal, that innocence and naturalness in which he became what he truly was, "not a man with a gun, a big profession or big talk, but himself, and himself, was loved and readmitted to the house, and to the people in the house. He began to sob, and other people were sobbing with him."[26]

Yet there are contradictions in the ways in which Ahmed's story is continually linked with Trinidad's future and with a dereliction and taint often apprehended by European characters who are themselves flawed. The orchestration of narrative and perception suggests from the beginning that the focus of delineation is Ahmed's relationship with the two visitors, Roche and Jane. The ironies that come out in those first sections of the book are ironies that expose the various egoisms and contradictions in their relationship. Indeed, from the very beginning, the erotic fantasies of Jane and Ahmed are what engage and preoccupy the novelist. Yet at the same time, every aspect of landscape comes under microscopic examination as the narrator and the two foreign characters flay sea, beach, forest, and city, recording an impression of dereliction and desolation, which are continually contrasted with visions of the ancient landscape: aboriginal sites, separate and unconnected to the lives of people. There are historical connotations implied in these parallel representations, and the dereliction is linked to a history of spoliation and diminishment, suggesting that the world is lost forever, that revolution would always become a pose, part of a role to confront the larger disorder.

But there is a certain pointlessness about these evocations, since they are merely given impressions unconnected to the people's active relationship with their landscape, impressions shared by characters whose own delusions about the security and order of their worlds are continually flayed in the novel. Indeed, the apparent order and safety of the larger world suggested through the smug assumptions of Jane and Roche are equally exposed as the safety of a decaying world, a world as fragile and capable of manipulation and dereliction as the New World depicted in the novel.

It seems that in most of his writing after *A House for Mr. Biswas* Naipaul has been writing the history of the New World into that of the larger world and seeing global correspondences in the paradigms of displacement he has explored. Indeed, the sense of loss which has all along underlain his vision of history becomes the burden and pain of modern man as Naipaul confronts the worlds of migration and transformation in *A Bend in the River.* Though the idea of loss in *A Bend* suggests the loss of tradition and culture, it also implies in a broad and major sense a perception of man's creations, developments, and losses through time and of their interrelationships and significance. Such an awareness involves an effort of assessment and is in the end a vision of man's progress through time, a measure of his identity and a base from which he can confront, change, and regulate actions within it. Disintegration in the past is therefore counterbalanced by feelings of regret and pain, indicating an understanding of the processes of change. History itself becomes a continuous story of movement, and past time a single unit separated from the present yet defining its quality.

This is the interplay between past and present that governs the idea of loss and its delineation in *A Bend in the River.* Thus, more than a novel about Africa, *A Bend in the River* is a modern novel that explores all the ramifications of modern man's relationship to his past. Its explorations proceed against a framework of a conception of history which insists that man only understands his present and future from an assessment of himself in relation to events that happen to him, and accordingly the novel dramatizes various relations to history and their impact on the ways in which men order and regulate their lives. Those regions in Africa which Naipaul evokes become, therefore, points in a meeting of peoples, backgrounds for enacting that interplay between present and past which is for Naipaul the domain of history. The novelist widens his canvas considerably in this novel so that in contrast to Singh, the central narrator in *The Mimic Men*, Salim, through whose point of view the different attitudes unfold, demonstrates a different relation to the writing and presentation of history. Singh's history had been a reordering of the events of his life as a means of understanding his historical condition and of fashioning order out of a personal chaos. Salim's history records instead the movement of time, presenting a chronology of events in which description and analysis are accompanied by personal response and deductions about the meaning of life, a method of historical discourse which demonstrates Naipaul's engagement both with personal and other histories.

Thus from the very beginning Salim establishes a relationship to history which in Naipaulian logic vindicates his position as the novel's central intelligence. For unlike others in the novel he has learned to make connections between events in history and assess their significance, acquiring a sense of history very much in contrast with his community's unexamined sense of continuity. More than this necessary detachment his rejection of the fatalism of his people sets him apart as someone interested in knowing the past and assessing its connections to the present, and it is from his developed historical consciousness that we ourselves perceive the relations between people and history in this region. For Salim continually draws out correspondences between people's perception of history and their fortunes, between their historical awareness and their capacity to deal with change; and it is basically from such assessments that he judges the fortunes of Africa and of the communities of people living on its fringes. "Once the Arabs had ruled here, then the Europeans had come; now the Europeans were about to go away. But little had changed in the manners or minds of men . . . People lived as they had always done; there was no break between past and present. All that had happened in the past was washed away, there was always only the present."[27]

The capacity to separate past from present, the ability to recognize it as a distinct territory from the present, a distinguishing feature of Western historical thought, becomes for Salim all of the meaning of history.[28] To possess such an understanding is in his view to visualize the past as located in a particular space and time. It is to see experience within this context, to see things as standing in certain relations to each other and to monitor these relationships in the movement and progress of time. It is also, above all, to benefit from hindsight, to be able to assess the consequences of the past with an eye on future action and thinking. The African mind, according to Salim's thesis, never achieves this historical sense of itself because it never makes the necessary separation between past and present. Its vision of the world, "in which the ancestor was living in a higher world but part of the presences of the forest, watching, providing security,"[29] gave only a limited tribal concept of self and security insufficient to cope with relationships beyond both tribe and continent. Salim interprets this absence as a significant factor in Africa's lack of development, its incapacity for rebellion, its susceptibility to plunder. As he argues, the security of the tribal world, when exposed as in the novel, leads only to a disordered present and future incongruous with the new creation of the domain which gives an impression of possibility and development but is really without assurance and direction.

The basis of this argument, derived from an essentially intellectual and Western conception of the meaning of history, is principally also a reflection of the communities of people in Africa and about their loss of place and identity. Indeed, as both Salim and Indar admit secretly to themselves, "Between our discussion about Africa lay some dishonesty or an omission, some blank around which we both had to walk carefully . . . That omission was our past . . . the smashed life of our community."[30]

It is these communities in Africa that had suffered displacement and confusion from their inability either to cultivate their own past or merge more intimately with the world around them. They were the ones who had maintained a sense of continuity without really examining the connecting links between their past in Arabia and India and their present in Africa. Like the African in the town (displaced from the forest) these communities also suffer a sense of disorientation from loss of place and identity. Thus, if Ferdinand, the up-and-coming African, possesses no sense of his own link with history; if the present is all he knows and he cannot understand the incongruity of the new Africa (the Africa of the domain, of words and ideas), Salim, Indar, and Shoba and the rest of the "alien" community are equally disoriented, equally incapable of dealing with change. Salim assesses their fortunes from this perspective and in relation to a European historical awareness and sense of identity: "But the Europeans could do one thing and say something quite different; and they could act in this way because they had an idea of what they owed to their civilization . . . Because they could assess themselves, [they] were better equipped to cope with changes than we were."[31]

Yet for all the obsession about the past and its connections with the present, there is a certain ambivalence implied in Salim's relation to history. He appears ironically unaware of the manipulation involved in European constructions of history and seems ignorant of the principle that can be derived from his own observation that those who write histories are the people with power and can manipulate history in the interest of "what they owed to their civilization." There is in addition a certain ambivalence implied in Salim's own relation to history. His desire to cultivate the past, his pain at the thought of its disintegration, are in some measure objects of satire in the novel. For the past, never positively asserted, is only inferred negatively from the suggestion of dispossession, and the inference is itself shrouded in ambiguity. Thus Salim may regret his community's inability to cultivate the past but the vision of the past, never coherently visualized in the novel, remains only a figment of his imagination, just as the lost Africa, the Africa of simplicity and truth, remains a romance and mirage in his mind.

Indeed, more than the mirage of home and the past, there is also the very ambiguity of the past itself and of the way its appearance of solidity and protectiveness are paradoxically balanced with its weakness and vulnerability. Thus Indar can rage at the destruction of two generations of a community's creation and also lament the deficiencies of a community that provided energy without a solid base of tradition. Salim himself can record his regret at the loss of home but also recognize the constraints and rigidities of its rules and methods as revealed in the lives of his community. Equally, the African river may fascinate him as primeval, as the very source of life, as something familiar "you had known at some time but had forgotten or ignored, but which was always there."[32] Yet it is also in the reality of the novel merely a secluded world doomed by its safe isolation.

From these ambiguities the loss of home itself becomes something less concrete and more of a vision, a dream of purity which is in the end also a vision of isolation. Indar's vision of home as he responds to the forbidding image of England is ironically not a vision of the stretch of the African coast which has been his family's home for two generations; it is rather a visualization of a country road lined with tall, shady trees, "fields, cattle, a village below trees . . . the fresh flowers, the shade of the trees in the middle of the day, fires in the evening," an Arcadian vision of safety and security which is also in the end a wishful dream of isolation. Indeed, it looks as if in the final analysis the idea of place and home and the unity of experience are given a new realistic qualification as Naipaul realizes that there is really nothing to go back to; that people like Salim and Indar have to live with the world as it is, without home, without place. "Trample on the past. Get rid of the idea of the past, and make the dreamlike scenes of loss ordinary."[33] And it is really this exaggerated sense of loss, this illusion of pain at the loss of the past that appears to be exorcised here, evidently with immense reverberations on all the delineations of displacement in earlier Naipaul works.

In the earlier novels the vision of loss was always the point of reference, the crucial image which heightened the protagonist's sense of history. With its apparent exorcism in *A Bend in the River* comes Salim's final acceptance of the condition of placelessness as wholly the sum of his real experiences. It is an acceptance of the reality of his condition and the novelist's own realization that the idea of the past as he had conceived it did not exist and that in reality he and all his community were made by the world as it existed, by the simple world at the bend and on the coast.

The deficiencies of personality that link Salim with this world become clearer from then on. For he is himself revealed as a man of safe compromises, unfit to act in the circumstances thrown upon him. Indeed, the evidence that he lays bare during his account of the atrocities of the rebels ironically surface in his own life, in his violent attack on his mistress, an event that links him with both the corruption and violence of the "Bend." His stark and depressing realization is thus ultimately the only resolution possible in the novel. For the image of the rebels and the measure of their rebellion confirm only what has been suggested about the repetitive nature of Africa's history, just as the final picture of Salim as alone and placeless confirms dispossession and placelessness as the most conspicuous features of modern man's relationship with his past.

The bleakness of vision which permeates Naipaul's later novels is really an aspect of the inevitability and determinism that govern his conception of history. The idea of the present as rigidly conditioned by the past, of history itself as a progressive movement through time, are nineteenth-century conceptions which continually prove themselves inadequate as descriptions of cataclysmic change in the modern world. For continuity and development are, after all, not the most important features of history as it has been manifested in the modern world. Indeed, the entire notion of history as development and progress is subject to questioning and argument, because it is not always that we can understand the nature of things solely from their development, and even in a novel as explicitly clear in its conception of development as *A Bend in the River,* the historicist idea of development is ironically undermined in the fortunes of the protagonist and his friend. Both Salim and Indar had, for instance, considered the civilization of Europe as singularly able to cope with change because of the continuity of its development and its capacity for assessment. In England Indar looks at English artifacts, contemplates the effort of creation and the impression of development, and sees this stability as what he himself needs, as what could wipe out his own sense of insecurity. Yet ultimately the England he encounters and which Salim also confronts is a shrunken, mean, and forbidding England, incongruous both with its imperial image as conqueror and maker and with the image established of its history as a continuous progress towards beauty and perfection. Although Naipaul does not pursue these ambiguities to their conclusions, the ironies themselves create unease at the idea of continuity and development as the most conspicuous features of history. They undermine as well the novel's obsessive preoccupation with continuity and loss and indeed hint that if both history and the historical novel would overcome the frustration and nightmare of a vision of man as chained to his past, they would have to develop criteria to measure aspects of history outside the domain of continuity and development.

It is in *The Enigma of Arrival,* Naipaul's autobiographical novel, that the contradictions and subtle ironies reappear as offshoots of the novelist's own vision and private fantasies; it is here, where the novelist confronts, explores, and reorients these fantasies, that we find a more rigorous interrogation of the historical positions he has held, positions from which he had made repeated and relentless onslaughts on the worlds that had made him. As in all his writing, the fundamental sense of history as loss underlies the microscopic observation of his Wiltshire surroundings. The idea of antiquity as at once diminishing and enabling the current activity of men, the sense of the link between man's creativity in the past and present, the wonder at the sheer oldness of the world and of man's activity and creativity—these are the pure moods and feelings Naipaul had looked for years before in the India of *An Area of Darkness* and now looks for again in the Wiltshire neighborhood of *The Enigma of Arrival.*

But the idea that history is understood and possessed in this way by all people becomes in the end only Naipaul's own romance. For nothing much in people's attitudes to the past and its ruins suggests the "pure feelings" and sense of historical continuity which he looks for. If in India he had found a lack of history and an unexamined sense of continuity, he finds in the restorations and renovations of his Wiltshire neighborhood a sense of history as egoism, as religion, as what one owed to one's own self, one's own religion. Jack's garden, which Naipaul sees (at first) as a remnant of the past, continuing the medieval life handed over by generations of English peasantry, turns out to be a personal creation, a specially chosen lifestyle through which Jack had sought fulfillment. History even in the old historical English countryside has not been perceived as continuous, as a linking of the impulses behind man's creativity in the past. This becomes part of Naipaul's shattering recognition and disappointment in the novel.

The recognition and disappointment have their paradoxes, however, and, though these are curiously never envisaged for Africa, they distinguish Naipaul from Salim and Indar in *A Bend in the River* and create ironic reverberations on their attitudes. For even in the midst of disintegration and flux, there still remains the wonder and appreciation of man and his continuing creativity: "the ways of glory dead, and held on to the idea of a world in flux: the drama of creation in the god's right hand, the flame of destruction in his left."[34]

Thus even the history of an old and historical village in Wiltshire may reveal not continuity but "plateaux of light, with intervening troughs or disappearances into darkness,"[35] and within this paradox people can remake themselves, remake the world. It is in this sense of being able to remake the world and themselves that the characters in *A Bend in the River* are flawed. For to accept simply to trample on the past is to accept defeat; to accept the paradoxes of history as revealed in *The Enigma of Arrival* is to admit that history may reveal the impermanence of men's work as well as its continuing creativity.

It seems that within his subjective interpretation and ordering of his own personal feelings Naipaul moves away from the romance of historical continuity which had plagued his attitudes to history throughout his writing career. His fiction after *The Enigma of Arrival* moves towards personal experience, personal history, even anthropological history. In the travel book *A Turn in the South,* he looks for other histories: the kinds of bonds and communities, for instance, which African Americans created from various sources, religion, custom, shared history. For these too are aspects of history, ways of understanding and knowing built from different kinds and shades of ruins.

Chapter Four

Lamming and the Mythic Imagination
Meaning and Dimensions of Freedom

It is that natural experience of separation from their original ground which
makes both master and slave colonial. To be colonial is to be in a state of
exile. And the exile is always colonial by circumstances; a man colonized by
his incestuous love of a past whose glory is not worth our total human
suicide; colonized by a popular whoredom of talents whose dividends he
knows he does not deserve; colonized by an abstract conscience which must
identify its needs with justice; . . . colonized, if black in skin, by the eye
whose meanings are based on a way of seeing he vainly tries to alter; and
ultimately colonized by some absent vision which, for want of another faith,
he hopefully calls the Future . . .
 But the mystery of the colonial is this: while he remains alive, his instinct,
always and for ever creative, must choose a way to change the meaning of
this ancient tyranny.
Lamming, *The Pleasures of Exile*

There is a general but fundamental way in which Lamming is linked to both
Naipaul and Reid in his relation to history. Like the two novelists, he
grapples with dimensions of historical experience within a fictional framework of space and time. Reid fictionalizes two historical events in Jamaican
history to create a narrative of continuity which rehearses other possibilities in the historical experience; Naipaul imaginatively re-creates a period
in the colonial history of Trinidad, focusing on one individual's experience
of it. As with Reid in *Sixty-Five* and *New Day*, he writes the "history" of
Michael X and the Trinidad killings and at the same time fictionalizes it in
a novel. Lamming, while not focusing on the historical event per se, weaves
a narrative in which it becomes an aspect of the historical reality within
which characters operate. Since all three novelists conceptualize attitudes

to history and write within a realist framework, their transformations within this mode should reveal subtle links and differences in the Caribbean historical imagination and its representation in fiction. Why, for instance, would Reid rework personal and racial themes unexplored in *New Day* in new, "mythical" constructions in *The Leopard;* why would Naipaul, crystallizing a vision of the world's "half-made societies," find the realism of the novel of manners corrupting and constricting; why do certain characters in Lamming's fiction occasionally break the surface of conscious reality to descend into the farthest regions of consciousness and memory?

As would appear from our comparative delineations, the sense of constriction within the realist mode has different meanings and ramifications for each writer. When Naipaul talks of his dissatisfaction with the novel of manners, he talks mostly from the point of view of style, of the writer's impulse to exercise his art and push his imagination in various directions in realizing a story. In his view the realist's mimetic impulse to offer an illusion of reality in which the reader can share may remain circumscribed within an unoriginal representation unless the novelist exercises his imagination to invent, fantasize, and re-create life anew. "In the experience of most writing the imaginative realizing of a story constantly modifies the writer's original concept of it. Out of experience, fantasy and all kinds of impulses, a story suggests itself. But the story has to be tested by, and its various parts survive, the writer's dramatic imagination. And the writer trying to make his fiction work, making accommodations with his or her imagination, can say more than he knows. With Conrad the story seems to be fixed; it is something given."[1]

Naipaul's dissatisfaction with Conrad's realism illuminates his ideas on the art of writing and reveals that his problem with the novel of manners is an essentially stylistic one. In a philosophical sense, the subject from which the original idea of a story springs hardly changes. His historical subject, "the histories of half-made societies that seemed doomed to remain half-made,"[2] is always the starting point of the idea, and it is through the rewriting and transformation of the idea within this subject that he wants to move beyond the realism of the novel of manners. So, consistently in his writing after *A House for Mr. Biswas,* a romance of purity, a notion of the ideal becomes a fantasy of expectation while it is at the same time rejected as an impossibility in a fallen and tainted world. This paradox is played out in his characters as they experience and conceptualize the aftermath of history in a contemporary setting, and because the subject itself does not change the determinist idea that men are shaped by heredity, environment, and history remains a fundamental and shaping principle, even in the romantic transformations. Constructed against a vision of one unattainable ideal after another, the sordid and tainted histories become as predictable and fixed in their ideas as Conrad's morality that Naipaul criticizes.

The constriction of the novel of manners is in Lamming's case fundamentally a constriction both of subject and method. What Lamming presents as the real is not always the realist novelist's perception of what is known and certain but also the "not obvious," the unknown. His historical conception of reality thus occasionally strays from linear objective representation and its conversational mode into mythic descents and revelation, bringing to light subterranean dimensions that cannot be contained within the framework of realism. Edouard Glissant has argued that "the implosion of Caribbean history (of the converging histories of our peoples) relieves us of the linear, hierarchical vision of a single History that would run its unique course. It is not this History that has roared around the edge of the Caribbean, but actually a question of the subterranean convergence of our histories."[3]

Such convergence implies that representations do not always assume the order and coherence of historicism, that, rather, they open avenues for mediation and transformation instead of being accepted as a given progressive order. In Naipaul the representation of the colonial suggests that the themes of displacement, cultural heterogeneity, and historical anomie which are the content of the colonial text preclude that realistic progress towards culmination and transcendence which is the central assumption of literary realism. Working from this assumption and in relation to Naipaul's *A House for Mr. Biswas,* Homi Bhabha argues that the colonial implications of Biswas's status work against that idea of cultural cohesiveness suggested in conceptions such as "character" and "mimetic irony" as applied to Biswas. *A House for Mr. Biswas,* he argues, resists these implications and instead enacts a disturbance in narrative in which narrative authority and control are lost, because "the very objective of narrative—its plenitude, its signification of a unitary real—is jeopardized in the articulation of the scenarios of colonial fantasy." Bhabha argues further that the conflict between Biswas's individualist and progressive values and the totalitarianism of the Tulsis (the two discourses within which narrative control has to be maintained initially) may satisfy the ideological and formal demands of realist narrative but cannot contain the more somber subject of Biswas's madness, illness, and loss within the same realist narrative without a disturbance. "For it faces the traditions of realist discourse with a spectacle of loss and failure unparalleled in its social and generic history."[4]

In Lamming such contradictions in the representation of the colonial are approached within the realist novel in other ways. A deterministic sense of the colonial's situation is, for instance, countered with the representation of two visions of history: the actual historical reality and the possibilities inherent within it. A Lamming novel is thus always a multidimensional representation of reality, offering possibilities for alternative interpretations and meanings. Within it the past becomes a challenge, "a soil from which other gifts, or the same gifts endowed with different meanings, may grow towards a future which is colonized by our acts in this moment."[5] History, conceived in Lamming's novels as both the lived experience and a consciousness at work, is thus re-created as a series of antagonistic situations in which several levels of interpretation and possibility are rehearsed. The present becomes a reflection of the negative and inhibiting past, as if to suggest a continuing and unbreakable correlation. But invariably several levels of meaning suggest themselves as possibilities both for personal and public freedom and a reconfigured sense of history.

The microcosmic world of *In the Castle of My Skin* presents us with several instances of such quality. A pattern of poverty, dereliction, and dependence may reflect the unchanging aftermath of plantation slavery as well as a colonial structure of awareness which defines "history" as the achievements of conquerors and colonists. Yet behind this unchanging scenario is the inscription and affirmation of a West Indian world and people in daily communion with their world and with each other. The organic world of women, steeped in legend, song, and shared rituals, and the inner world of children, a world of dream, mystery, curiosity, and personal identity, represent other historical texts written into the colonial structures of the village; and within its context it is possible to envisage the possibility of political action as a source of freedom.

The failure of the novel's political movement is in this sense less important than the possibilities it reveals for assessing the quality of freedom. For failure is here mediated by its own paradoxes. Slime's movement fails to change colonial relations and instead brings about the disintegration of the old economic order, giving rise to an exploitative class contemptuous of the village's past and its social reverences. Yet instead of a linear movement and development of incident and story suggesting rigid inextricable links between cause and effect, the drama of political action is contexualized within a series of overlapping perspectives which rehearse other meanings and possibilities of freedom. Thus, on one hand, the idea of a sense of history as a prerequisite for political definition is demonstrated in the perceptions of Boy "G" and others, which together with the novel's omniscient intelligence act as centers of vision, correlating past and present, drawing out the significance of situations, and challenging the villages' unexamined sense of continuity. As a perspective this relation to history insists on a dual historical vision, linking slavery with the pattern of wreckage and dereliction in the village and at the same time highlighting those shared rituals through which the community creates a sense of itself and makes its own history.

The perspective of the old man, Pa, introduces a mythic dimension that enacts another overlapping level of meaning and possibility. First, his emergence as a bearer of mythical history affirms the revelatory and illuminating possibilities of the collective unconscious and challenges the historical void in which Slime's movement defines its freedom. His trance-like descent into the innermost subconscious actually retrieves aspects of submerged history that illuminate not only the link between past and present but also the significance of the link to the meaning of West Indian freedom. His shamanistic speech thus encapsulates more than the cumulative experience of the village and provides a crucial understanding that explains both Slime's failure and the seemingly repetitive nature of history in the region. Although its recapitulation of dispossession bemoans the loss of an "Eden" of cosmic wholeness, its emphasis is rather a challenge of transformation. The vision of the New World as a world without links, as despoiled by the silver of exchange, is balanced by an awareness of new combinations, new relationships, and a whole new consciousness in which the fates of the islands are solidly intertwined. The possibilities of this evocation perch precariously between stasis and fruitful transformation yet provide a contrasting historical perspective that liberates both history and narrative from a confining naturalistic rendering into alternative allegories of possibility.

In another sense, the layer of consciousness represented by Trumper, the entire episode in which his views are balanced against the actions of Slime, the attitudes of the village and the perceptions of Boy G present an opportunity for exploring other possibilities in the political drama. Trumper's wider sense of history, his understanding of the connections between public and private worlds, and his affirmation of a larger racial identity repeatedly clash with Boy G's veneration of individual separateness, introducing a conflict of perspectives that surfaces in all of Lamming's novels. Trumper's views are sure and confident, especially in their understanding of the possibilities of a larger racial identity. Yet the separate inner world of self, the world of individual identity and creativity treasured by G, is given equal validity in the text. The exchange between Trumper and G in which their two perspectives are contrasted is carefully manipulated in G's favor and indeed, partially reported from his point of view. G's bewilderment and alienation, his sense of loss at the breakup of a meaningful world, and his emotionally crippled psyche all present themselves as deeply relevant personal issues that are stridently deflated in Trumper's all-encompassing racial prescription. Indeed the drama of alienation at the end focuses sympathetically on G, upholding his personal crisis as a valid inner disequilibrium that may not be resolved through Trumper's definitive vision of race.

Gordon Rohlehr has observed that "Lamming [does] not rule out social responsibility for the artist, but redefines it in such a way that it [coincides] with the artist's private quest for self-knowledge and self-definition."[6] The observation sums up a dual commitment on Lamming's part to both personal and public freedom. Yet such a duality has often proved problematic in some Lamming novels, and what Brathwaite identifies as Lamming's privileging "of the introspective, self-regarding artist"[7] is a real and major problem, a conflict of the individual and collective pulls which continually plague the conflation of myth and history in his novels.

Yet such a conflation is crucial for Lamming since his fiction constructs historical meanings instead of engaging futilely with a given and deterministic past. "Myth *coils* meaning around the image itself: which means that it is as distant from pure realism as it is from scrupulous and in-depth analysis."[8] Glissant's definition clarifies precisely that point of divergence between myth and history which makes their conflation ideal in a fiction in which history is an imaginative construction as well as the lived experience. Myth by its nature also objectifies collective rather than personal experience and is in this sense quite foreign to individualism. Thus the personal and artistic need to protect the inner life becomes problematic with the necessary collective thrust of myth and legend. In *Of Age and Innocence* such a problem surfaces in the cleavage within Mark Kennedy, in the conflicting claims of the inner private self predisposing him to separation and silence and the public collective world of myth and legend which promise self-understanding and a wider vision of the Caribbean past.

As in *In the Castle,* the mythic dimension provides alternative avenues of understanding, a contrasting perspective to the material, linear history in which political action is a failure. The linear drama moves beyond the ineffectual rebellion of the emerging middle class in *In the Castle* to explore politics as a mass movement within a nationalist context and ideology. Here, there is a more deliberate dialectical relationship between the lived experience and its imaginative and mythic possibilities. The linear realist action explores a straightforward correlation between past and present, delineating the various ways in which the colonial's wresting of freedom may be disadvantaged. As in *The Mimic Men* the colonial's freedom is inextricably linked with the meaning of history, and in both novels he is unable to transcend the consequences of personal and public history.

Yet the meaning of history and its ramifications both in the conception and representation of the colonial works in different ways and towards different conclusions in the two novels. There is in both the intimidating presence of a colonial order perceived as the only alternative to the chaos of decolonization. In *The Mimic Men* this contrasting vision of order and chaos is actually endorsed and internalized by the colonial himself; in *Of Age and Innocence* it is enacted and implied in the linear action but continuously contested throughout the novel. The future of San Cristobal, glimpsed in the vision of freedom and in the alternative history available through myth and legend, becomes another possibility that challenges the idea of a monolithic colonial world as the only center of value and order. This fundamental difference in the perception of the region's history explains not only the representation of political action in the two novels but also the kinds of ideals against which the linear action is constructed in each novel.

Behind the idea of violation and taint in *The Mimic Men* is an ideal of purity and order which is unachievable within the novel's context and which may be grasped only on an imaginative level. The order of the Himalayas and the vision of central Asian horsemen riding to the very end of the world may present a symbolic contrast to the disorder around, signifying an imaginative longing that accentuates the novel's crisis of dislocation and disorder. But these myths of order are themselves so far removed from the actual histories delineated that they remain unachievable fantasies which only serve to fortify the deterministic view of an orderly world lost forever. The vision of disorder curiously does not spring only from the particular landscape and history of the Caribbean but from a generalized vision of disorder, "the shock of the first historian's vision," a larger philosophical sense of disorder and constriction that encompasses "this man, this room, this city, this story, this language, this form"[9] and which ironically inspires an unrealizable fantasy for those larger spaces and limitless worlds already dismissed as illusionary possibilities in a tainted world.

"To use myth as an energizing or ordering principle, and to appeal to the imagination through it, is to suggest a validity which is in large measure controlled by the context which a work of art provides."[10] The implications of William Righter's argument do not apply in *The Mimic Men*. The context of unalterable violation and disorder rule out all the possibilities of order implied in the myth of the Himalayas and central Asian horsemen, so that a political action that moves beyond mere "disturbance" to attempt a new order becomes only an illusory act, unrelated to the real import of history in the region. There is thus an unbridgable gap between myth and the historical realities it may energize, and myth is here not a curative power but a contrasting symbol, an imaginative play that only confirms the novel's general thesis about history as loss.

In *Of Age and Innocence* the mythic dimension is more actively contextualized in the historical theme and is in fact an alternative construction to the linear history. It operates at the level of legend, ritual, and revelation as other sources of historical knowledge that counteract what in *The Mimic Men* is the disorder of shipwreck. Within the novel's nationalistic framework and ideology, myth also achieves an immediacy that energizes and inspires a dynamic vision of land and community, evoking entirely new dimensions of space and time through the aura of timelessness and beyond ness with which it surrounds the landscape. Here landscape and its symbolic connotations create a framework in which it is possible to conjure the primordial past of aboriginal Indians as a link with the present. On an even more numinous level, the land becomes a force in itself, invested with a divine power that inspires myths and rituals of propitiation and enacts spiritual relationships between men and the cosmic to suggest a cultural base for a history of resistance. Accordingly, legends and rituals link the resistance of the "Tribe Boys" with the rebellion of the Haitians to reflect a consistent choice on the side of freedom and to indicate a dimension of history that subverts the broken history of conquest symbolized by statues of European historical figures.

Of Age and Innocence thus begins its political drama in ritual and from a point of identification with land and nature which differentiates it from the context of *The Mimic Men,* in which the land is continually envisioned as violated and an object of denial. In *The Mimic Men* the sea defines the limit of island space and is at the same time a lonely, desolate, empty world, a living, destroying element, sullied and tainted. Here the landscape holds no mythology, and its legend, small in scale and time, tells only of the rise and fall and extinction of people: "Slaves and runaways, hunters and hunted, rulers and ruled."[11]

The historical text even in formal historiography is always also a literary text, and, as Hayden White argues, "How a given historical situation is to be configured depends on the historian's subtlety in making up a specific plot situation with the set of historical events that he wishes to endow with meaning of a particular kind."[12] In the novelist's consciously historical conception of the present, the leeway for literary construction is even wider, and the novelist has only to shift his/her figurative discourse or point of view to put a different meaning and emphasis to a situation in history. Thus, in the constructed history of Lamming's *Of Age and Innocence* the sea is imaged rather as a timeless symbol of myth that continuously enacts the cyclical movement of time and offers a lesson in the possibilities of renewal, pointing not to a static, one-dimensional view of history but to a sense of history as continuously renewed. Here the Caribbean Sea may well be in a literal sense the gateway to a history of conquest and violation, but it is its ambivalence that is stressed: its preternatural power to sink the island underneath its waters and its ability at the same time to transform, to test a man's character in the "challenge and the battle for catching an escape,"[13] and to reveal the many sources hidden within the individual self.

Such mythic dimensions are what frame the alternative construction in *Of Age and Innocence,* and the dialectical relationship between these and the political drama suggests that the past that resides in landscape and legend can release its meaning and create new sensibilities and feelings if imaginatively and empathetically encountered. Yet the linear drama of political struggle in the novel is unable to utilize these possibilities to inspire a collective understanding that would construct a "new" history of the region and translate it into the ever-changing present. The movement affirms the motions of the rituals but is never able to move beyond frenzy and a high pitch of religious feeling to make a choice for freedom. Shephard's lyrical affirmation of the myth of San Cristobal remains merely euphoric, inseparable from his personal neurosis. Though he chooses political action as a means of defining a new self outside the definition imposed by the colonizer, this need is itself inspired by deeper impulses and neuroses which he is never able to conquer. The past still encircles and creates a disturbing continuity with his present. Thus, even in political action he shows the same obsession with personal power, the same confusion between self-assertion and self-abnegation which he had exhibited as a boy, revealing a deep-seated, fractured sensibility which remains in permanent crisis. He regresses (according to his plan) into the old image (becomes Shephard, in spite of) but never really emerges, as he hopes, with a new self, and because he achieves no personal freedom he is unable to translate myth into a new understanding, unable to move politics beyond anger, promise, and the rearrangement of privileges.

The urgency of the search for myth in Lamming's works proceeds from the need to imaginatively transform a history in which the Caribbean man or woman is inevitably a victim. Its concern is with the future; with the creation of new meanings from the past. The function of myth in such an enterprise is not only to exist as a natural inheritance in the consciousness of characters but to move them beyond knowledge of the myth towards its imaginative translation into a fluid present and future, and in this conflation of history and myth characters and situations are continually tested for a capacity for mythic translation. The old man's descent and revelation in *In the Castle* is, for instance, a possibility that is never grasped imaginatively by the people with power. Shephard's appropriation of San Cristobal's myths remains only at the level of rhetoric and euphoria, and Ma Shephard, the cosmic figure and repository of history, is equally incapable of establishing a dynamic link between the immaterial time of myth and the changing world of the present. Her relationship to the material of myth is defined by factors which imprison her in a dependence on prayer and divine intervention, leaving her with a powerful but static mythic vision.

It is perhaps only in Mark Kennedy that the possibilities of myth as illumination and revelation find momentary enactment. Mark's view of choice and action as the meaningful expression of freedom places him on the opposite pole of Ma Shephard as able (in thought at least) to move beyond the knowledge of history which myth and legend provide. His sudden eloquence and momentary hallucination reveal to both him and us the possibilities of myth as an initiator of vision. Indeed the processes of such a possibility are actually enacted before us: childhood memories of legend and ritual move the alienated intellectual to a pitch of feeling and emotional empathy with the crowd, whose faith makes possible the certainty he has lost. "The crowd had become his anchor. They formed a center vital and still as a root whence he could report on what he had seen. He had entered into some agreement with them . . . It was an act of pure participation in this vision which he was trying to describe."[14] What Mark provides in interpretation and extension of the legend reveals inferences capable of exploring the meaning of the movement, of pushing it beyond struggle and frenzy, beyond even the crowd's hypnotized faith in the certainty of freedom. It is his empathy with the legend and the crowd's communal response to his interpretation and inferences that trigger his hallucinatory and prophetic vision, achieved in a momentary descent into subconscious self, an experience which like Pa's visionary dream in *In the Castle* provides a vision that explains, interprets, and illuminates past and present.

Here then is another level of relation to myth, a psychosomatic level which utilizes its ancient connotations as possession and prophecy, demonstrating the belief that myth can touch on the innermost regions of the unconscious and generate images that may illuminate the past in a nonrational way and offer flashes of understanding, even of prophecy. Thus a conscious grappling with the meaning and implications of the movement glides imperceptibly into a subconscious vision that predicts the confusions, division, and turbulence which could surround the birth of nationhood. It moves further than a vision of turbulence to clarify the meaning of freedom and the essence of that action which the Tribe Boys chose in an affirmation of it. It is such an interpretation of the legend that inspires the crowd to make connections between their human will and the national spirit underlying the movement.

This sharing of understanding about the illuminating possibilities of myth represents that ideal translation of myth into purpose which the political movement never achieves. The momentary flash of its possibilities becomes a pointer nevertheless to what even Mark is unable to sustain. The problem that Mark faces is in effect also the problem of the artist's relation to myth and may reflect the tension between commitment to social responsibility and the inner individual self which Rohlehr identifies in Lamming's writing.

The nonrational nature of mythic descent, its roots in the collective unconscious, and its emphasis on collective experience may work against self-consciousness, self-possession, and the privileging of personal experience. It is such a tension that underlies the artist's relation to myth both in *Of Age and Innocence* and *Season of Adventure*. It sparks a major question: are the surrendering impulses and collective pulls of myth necessarily a conspiracy against the individual self? This is a question Mark grapples with even as he recognizes the potentialities of his act of pure participation. He found no "way of uniting his personal fear with the collective hope of the voices which acclaimed his words,"[15] and the moment and its possibilities are left hanging in his consciousness, stalled by his fear of compromising his private inner self and by his deliberate deflation of the spiritual impact of the experience.

The problem is posed as an exploratory one at this stage, and the representation of the tensions within Mark Kennedy reveals a more sympathetic perception of the artist's conflicting yearnings than the categorical affirmation of the supremacy of the inner vision which Lamming had made in 1956.[16] Its contextualization within the politics of decolonization and within a historical theme in which the text constructs an alternative history points rather to the possibilities and pitfalls of the inner life in its relation to myth and national freedom. Indeed the contrasting experience of the young boys of the secret society confirms this exploratory thrust in the dialectical relationship set up between the young group and the adult characters in the political drama. What the boys of the secret society achieve (and which the adult players fail to do) is a oneness of feeling born out of a single-minded commitment to the group, one that surpasses fragmentation, alienation, and the isolating tendencies of individualism.

Wilson Harris has remarked that *Of Age and Innocence* fails as a novel because it loses sight of a genuine tendency for a tragic feeling of dispossession.[17] Yet it is not so much the tragedy of dispossession as the possibilities of mythic enlightenment and translation that are the novel's genuine and ultimate thrust. There is a mythic center in the novel that continuously holds out an alternative and reconstructive vision against the story of dispossession, and its thrust is embedded (as argued) in the dialectical relationship between the adult players and the young boys. The fundamental human needs that define their interpersonal relationships, their commitment to the group, and their significance as the only group that can be transformed by the legend of the Tribe Boys is both an ironic comment and an assertion of those illuminating and curative possibilities of myth that can offset the tragedy of dispossession.

Unlike the politicians, intellectuals, and liberals, crippled by history and by past systems of alliances, the young boys are catapulted into an accident of time exploding from the whole accumulated muddle of their past, opening "the earth under their feet to honor their fantasy and their hope."[18] Their descent into legend and history becomes a magical experience which, far from being escapist, binds them to the historical experience of the island, banishes their fears and insecurities, and renews them with new perception and strength. Their strange and magical experience achieves its climax and catharsis in such a way that when the moment of descent works its magic and returns them to an ordinary commonsense awareness of the night, they appear transfigured, possessed of a new and invulnerable self-awareness and confidence that shut out the physical power of the ruling authority and which alone give them the strength to defy the curfew.

In contemplating and internalizing the legend they are in turn imaginatively transformed by it and are able to achieve an insight into the past which they would have been unable to acquire in a linear grappling with history. These possibilities of myth and legend are crucial aspects of the mythic imagination that provide vital sources of reconnection to legend and history, offering alternative psychic sensibilities which deflate a commonsense perception of dispossession as an unalterably tragic history.

It is this undercurrent of myth and its imaginative and psychic possibilities that the novel moves towards in the final analysis. The possibilities include not only myth's ability to illuminate the meaning of freedom and nationalism but also its subterranean power to possess and empower, to pit itself against void, negation, and the consolidation of the self-sufficient individual. In this sense myth works towards the same end that Harris claims for the "tragic feeling of dispossession." For when he argues that it is "within the suffering and enduring mental capacity of the obscure person (which capacity one shares with both 'collective' slave and 'separate' individual in the past and in the future) . . . that a scale emerges . . . which makes it possible for *one* (whoever that *one* may be today or tomorrow) to measure and abolish each given situation,"[19] he is pointing to similar possibilities in the mythic imagination and their capacity equally to measure and abolish the given situation. The contrasting perspectives of linear and mythic histories in *Of Age and Innocence* work to counter a circumscribed and deterministic view of the colonial's freedom as irretrievably mortgaged to the consequences of history.

Thus, even though the text of *Of Age and Innocence* may work within a realist framework that fosters the consolidation and overelaboration of character and situation the mythic dimension works against this thrust. Lamming's restlessness within his framework stems from such a tension and may represent an ironic undermining (unconscious or deliberate) of the commonsense realism within which he has explored the colonial's freedom so far.

Such a restlessness is apparent in the deepening mythic focus of the historical theme in *Season of Adventure,* in which myth is a medium for enacting possession, descent, catharsis, and vision. The illuminating and transforming possibilities of legend and myth which remain largely unutilized in the politics of *Of Age and Innocence* become a fundamental theme and structure in *Season of Adventure.* What Lamming calls the "backward glance" of the ritual descent is not just a reconnection to the unconscious or mythic past in which, in Jungian terms, the individual psyche participates through ritual or dream; it is a drama of understanding and redemption, "the drama of returning, the drama of cleansing for a commitment to the future."[20] The ritual ceremony of souls is in its functional sense a mode of dialogue between the living and the dead. In *Season of Adventure* it becomes a dialogue both with history and with suppressed fear and shame about origins. The ritual descent is thus also the beginning of dialogue with self, and the protagonist's experience awakens several levels of awareness. On one hand the ritual tickles a memory of the past, which emerges not as a chronology of events in time but as a series of images threaded together through recollection, intuition, and memory; on the other, it generates a crisis of dislocation, a sense of terrible separation from the world the protagonist knows, and a natural kinship with the world she has long suppressed and rejected. The passionate intensity and turmoil of the crisis erupt in violent physical changes within her: fevers, disjointed visions, hallucinations, all of which suggest disorientation and madness but provide vision and awareness in the end.

What the "backward glance" generates then is a new way of seeing, a quality of perception which the protagonist grafts on to her old self to become "other than." Unlike the "dead" of the ritual, resurrected only to move on to eternity and rest, Fola remains alive and free to choose a future, free to destroy what has gone before, to alter the effect of the past by constructing new meanings above it. The mystery of the colonial, Lamming has argued, is that "while he remains alive, his instinct, always and forever creative, must choose a way to change the meaning of this ancient [colonial] tyranny."[21]

This idea of history as a construction is indeed a fundamental aspect of the West Indian writer's relation to the past and is the inevitable outcome of the tension between a one-dimensional linear perception of history and a commitment to a future which seeks transformative meanings instead of progression. The problem is not limited to history; it relates to the whole notion of artistic representation, and it is easy to see how the engagement with history indirectly addresses the conceptual ground of artistic representation in the colonial text. Homi Bhabha has posed the problem with clarity: "There is . . . another way of raising the issue of the representation of the colonial subject which questions the collusion between historicism and realism. It proposes that the category of literature, as of its history, is necessary and thoroughly mediated; that its reality is not given but produced; its meanings transformative, historical, and relational rather than revelatory; its continuity and coherence underscored by division and difference. This other view demands quite another notion of the historical inscription of literature and entails a critique of representation as simply given."[22] Even in Naipaul, whose works are continually framed within realism and historicism, there is still an element of construction in the rejection of the necessary unfolding consciousness. The absence of the transcendental consciousness that achieves fruition within a continuous and coherent world is alone a statement on the colonial context of dislocation and difference that undermines realist assumptions on representation.

In Lamming the construction of history is predicated rather on a belief in the future, and new meanings are derived not only from the cause and effect of the event in history but from their possibilities as well. In *Season of Adventure* the individual vision acquired through dialogue with self and history is translated into a public vision through political action. The relationship between the individual's inner truth and the collective thrust of myth and ritual is again reexamined within politics and its possibilities. Where Mark Kennedy had been paralyzed by an obsessive fear of encroachments on the individual self, Fola charts out a public dimension to her personal vision. Her reconstruction of the mythical ancestor in the murderer's portrait is itself a political statement, an interpretation of the dual and enigmatic nature of West Indian origins. It is such a dimension of the town's forgotten self that the portrait resurrects and channels into political action. On another symbolic level the portrait reveals the subtle implications of this duality, especially the two different ways of seeing implied in black and white ancestry. "The left eye seemed more nervous, more reluctant to open up as though it were afraid of what it saw glancing backward from the corner of its socket. But the right eye was wide and fierce, a triumphant glare of certainty dazzling its surface. The eyes seemed to compete for an exclusive vision of what confronted them, fixed, hard and determined, as though they were in private agreement about two different ways of seeing." It is the implications of these competing ways of seeing that Fola confronts in her joint and reconciliatory action with the Forest Reserve. "The artist's work," Lamming suggests, should be an attempt "to show the individual situation illuminated by all the possibilities which keep pushing it always towards a destiny which remains open."[23]

Fola's acquisition of "otherness" and her entire political action become such a possibility, asserted in the text in contradistinction to the Houngan's perverted vision, to Chiki's exaltation of the creative force at the expense of community, and to Powell's obsession with personal freedom. The dilemma of the artist's individual and collective pulls seems somewhat resolved at this point. For it is the combined perceptions of Fola and Gort rather than the obsessive visions of Chiki and Powell which remain the novel's ultimate statement. Gort's belief that the origin and end of all work lies in the artist's own hands gives the artist absolute centrality and presents him as both the source of vision and the arbiter of its extension. Thus, while in Chiki the creative will is external to the artist and needs to be constantly justified through work, it is in Gort's vision the very embodiment of all the artist's own energies, needs, and desires. Gort's integrated personality therefore contrasts him with the divided selves of Chiki, Powell, and Shephard and presents him as the character most capable of complementing Fola's new sense of community and translating personal vision into various possibilities.

Season of Adventure explores a much deeper relationship between personal and political freedom. It defines freedom itself in a much wider context and insists through its treatment of Fola's adventure that it is not enough simply to destroy those forces which condemn Caribbean people to the status of colonial, to be men "in spite of." Here the backward glance moves beyond the meaning of "colonial" and becomes a revaluation of the West Indian's place in history. It is neither romantic nor escapist. For the drums which are resurrected in the celebration of freedom do not have the rhythms of the old drums. Nervous, insecure, and melancholy, they reflect the people's uncertainty, the break in continuity and the inevitable loss involved in all change and transformation.

In Naipaul political action within the limitations of a colonial context becomes merely an illusion of freedom; in *Season of Adventure* the notion of freedom in political action is symbolic, contained mostly in the consciousness of the people and the awakening of the drums. The emphasis is on renaissance and on an activation of memory made possible through mythic apprehension. The construction of unrecorded and forgotten histories breaks through the empirical layer of realistic construction, just as the penetration of the deep divisions within the West Indian psyche create possibilities for that integration of personality crucial for true freedom and authority. Glissant has remarked that a "reality that was long concealed from itself and that took shape in some way along with the consciousness that the people had of it, has as much to do with the problematics of investigation as with a historical organization of things."[24] *Season of Adventure's* imaginative and psychic link to history through myth signifies an aspect of the literary investigation that orients historical thought in West Indian writing. The imaginative ordering it achieves and the possibilities it unearths are themselves the biggest contradiction of the determinism of a linear history.

If Lamming's fiction up to *Season of Adventure* appears to work towards a climatic vision of collective history and public action, his later novels revert to previously unexplored areas of colonial relations, revisiting themes of personal history and individuation in Caliban and Prospero. Unlike Brathwaite, who establishes the possibility of rebirth in *Rights of Passage* and moves towards a deeper exploration of submerged history in *Islands,* virtually taking on a shamanistic function as a poet, Lamming seems to contract from considering further ramifications of the backward glance. In *Water with Berries* and *Natives of My Person,* he returns to the beginnings of colonial history and to an imaginative evocation of the triangular voyage as if seeking, like Harris, to reconstruct and rehearse motives, impulses, and violations in the colonial encounter which may point the way forward in self-understanding and personal relations. Although on the face of it he may appear to be merely returning to a literature of recrimination in his pictures of horrors and intrigues, his explorations are symbolically a generous and empathetic rehearsal of the human possibilities that could have saved the past and may yet save the future. Within its delineations Lamming moves the colonial encounter beyond irreversible history into a timelessness in which a future purged of fear and retribution may be possible. In *The Pleasures of Exile*, he states, "For I am a direct descendant of slaves, too near to the actual enterprise to believe that its echoes are over with the reign of emancipation. Moreover, I am a direct descendant of Prospero worshipping in the same temple of endeavor, using his legacy of language—not to curse our meeting—but to push it further, reminding the descendants of both sides that what's done is done, and can only be seen as a soil from which other gifts, endowed with different meanings, may grow towards a future which is colonized by our acts in this moment, but which must always remain open."[25]

It is with such a vision of mutual complicity that Lamming constructs a dialogue between Caliban and Prospero, both of whom he defines as colonial in different ways. In choosing to work with the framework, assumptions, and interpretive possibilities of *The Tempest*, Lamming attempts a deconstructive exploration in which paradigms from the play become frameworks for argument and metaphorical extension, uncovering certain presences and links not easily apparent in critical readings of the text. Thus, in various subtle ways *Water with Berries* and *Natives of My Person* take up and extend the plot of *The Tempest*, hinting (as the play itself hints) that in the history of colonization there might be as many contrasting, even opposing, ways of perceiving given events and moments of time. Lamming's reading extends the suggestion offered throughout *The Tempest* that the past of the island has different connotations and possibilities for Caliban and Prospero. If Prospero's sense of the island's past begins with his own arrival and historical continuity, Caliban's begins with his mother's possession of the island, with his sense of Prospero's betrayal and with his personal understanding and rootedness in the island. In another dramatic situation, two such opposing perceptions might present a collision necessitating certain resolutions, but in the play, Prospero's perceptions stand dominant. His power and authority remain unchallenged, and Caliban's rebellion, lacking in self-assessment and futilely circumscribed within Prospero's control, leads only to comic futility.

In his paradigmatic exploration of the play as a drama of colonial relations, it is these unexplored and largely ambiguous areas of relationship that Lamming reconstructs and interprets. Working from the premise that the encounter of Caliban and Prospero entailed in all its brutality reciprocal relationships that stamped and shaped them both, he argues that Caliban's redefinition must not only include a dialogue with self and history but with Prospero's consciousness, as well. For Lamming the basis of such a dialogue lies in the constantly erupting contradictions between Prospero's view of Caliban as monster and slave and Caliban's frequent demonstrations of his humanness, even his humanity. Lamming works with the implications of this contradiction to suggest the idea of a common humanity and shared vulnerability as the basis for dialogue. His interpretation of the national spirit as a universal human instinct in *Of Age and Innocence* invests it with a potential for creating a common ground, a kind of rapport between colonizer and colonized. For even in the ancient legend of the Tribe Boys and the Bandit Kings, which is the inspiration behind the new freedom movement, the national spirit embodies such a potential. It was, after all, the momentary awareness of an equal humanity in the Tribe Boys that made the Bandit Kings retreat, recognizing and respecting an equal instinct for freedom among their opponents.

In the drama of the novel this instinct and common ground reside in the motives and desires that link Bill, Penelope, and Marcia to the possibilities of freedom and new beginnings in San Cristobal. It reverberates as well in the empathetic understanding which Penelope acquires for Shephard as he recognizes a common situation of alienation and vulnerability between the Negro and the lesbian. It appears then that as Lamming moves beyond fractured history to explore other perspectives and meanings of the Caribbean past, he identifies the Negro's sense of separation and alienation from self as equally the problem of modern man. "To speak of the situation of the Negro writer is to speak therefore of a problem of man and more precisely of a contemporary situation which surrounds us with an urgency that is probably unprecedented. It is to speak in a sense, of the universal sense of separation and abandonment, frustration and loss, and above all else, of some direct experience of something missing."[26]

From this universalist perspective Lamming hopes that the empathy between Shephard and Penelope, between the British liberals and the returned exiles, will bridge the gap in their personal histories and return them to new relationships. Yet curiously, even with such intentions, the new relationships between the Prosperos and Calibans remain fragile, battered on both sides by those scars of history which continue to linger in their consciousness and their personalities. Thus, whether in relationships with Shephard or Mark, the vision of a common humanity and goal which had driven the British visitors finally falters, revealing (especially in Bill Butterfield) a submerged, fixed, and superior self-conception as well as attitudes of revulsion towards the Calibans. "He wanted to forget San Cristobal. He felt a sudden revulsion of feeling when Thief mentioned this service to Shephard. Already he had lost his desire for any share in the future of people like Thief. The future had arrived with Penelope's death, and he could not forgive it."[27]

Indeed, as he learns of Shephard's complicity in Penelope's death, this revulsion magnifies itself in Butterfield's consciousness until it assumes an ever-present and permanent attitude, and Shephard's image becomes fixed in his mind, "consistent, unmoved, impervious . . . as though the image had always been there, a shadow in the dark, brought suddenly to light by an event which had ruined his love." Thus, by the time Butterfield finally escapes from San Cristobal, he has regressed in attitude, to the extent of even affirming the point of view of the colonial status quo: "He was no longer averse to Crabbe and those who made the official alliance. He thought he understood Crabbe's fear."[28]

These failures in relationships reveal the future to be even more dependent on circumstances and relationships of the past. They suggest that the new meanings and changed relationships that Lamming envisages would be possible only after a ruthless exorcism of the branding cages of personal history on both sides, and it is perhaps for this reason that Lamming returns to the details and implications of the colonial encounter in *Water with Berries*. His reenactment of the encounter, elaborated with myth and ritual, extends the encounters of the emigrant Calibans in *The Emigrants* in order finally to exorcise the hold of the colonial past and push for new meanings in the future.

Although in Lamming's stated intentions, the focus in *Water with Berries* is on the present, on Caliban's choice of the terms on which future relations with Prospero would be based, his explorations take their cue from those myths and archetypal relationships based on the first colonial encounter in *The Tempest*. The explorations scrutinize and challenge the assumptions of this relationship, investing it with new meanings to bring it in line with the future he claims for Caliban.

What is happening here is that I am in a way attempting to reverse the journeys. In Shakespeare's *Tempest*, it was Prospero in the role of visitor to Caliban's island. In *Water with Berries*, it is reversed. The three characters really represent three aspects of Caliban making his journey which was at the beginning a logical kind of development because of the relationship to Prospero's language. Then they discovered the reality of Prospero's home—not from a distance, not filtered through Prospero's explanation or record of his home, but through their own immediate and direct experience.[29]

This relationship to Prospero's language becomes the single most significant effect of the encounter, the area in which all Caliban's future possibilities can be located. Far from merely denoting speech and utterance, language is also the seed of dialects, of a process of perceiving and reasoning
which makes possible an emergence from nature, from pure instinct. Lamming argues that the circumstances of Caliban's acquisition of the Word
compromise his choices, actions, and possibilities.

> I pitied thee,
> Took pains to make thee speak, taught thee each
> hour
> One thing or other. When thou didst not, savage,
> Know thine own meaning, but wouldst gabble
> Like a thing most brutish, I endow'd thy purposes
> With words that made them known.[30]

For in these circumstances surrounding Caliban's acquisition of language in *The Tempest,* word and concept do not become a way of registering personality since they are no more than a means of serving Prospero, a
way of measuring the distance which separated him from Caliban. Yet in
his explorations in *Water with Berries,* Lamming reveals that such a relationship to Prospero's language need not be permanent because Caliban
can explode Prospero's myth by christening the word anew and making it
the product of human endeavor. The very ability to use the word in an act
that registers a distinct personality and consciousness in itself undermines
Prospero's enterprise and breaks the cloying powers of his words. Here,
then, is an important reexamination of the myth of Caliban and Prospero;
one that not only explores its historical, moral, and personal implications
but also grapples with ways of breaking and destroying its dominant
myths. It is significant that all the exiles are artists. Art is also a form of
endeavor which, like the revolution in San Domingue, contains the potential for altering colonial relations.

Lamming places the roots of Caliban's relationship with Prospero solidly within the historical conditions that create a slave-based colonial society, generating all manner of social and cultural deprivations and at the
same time nurturing insecurity and dependence by holding the metropolis
up as the real world. Thus, for the colonial exiles, the ramifications of their
careers as artists without a supporting community and their delusional
assumptions that England should be the logical consumer of their talents
raise and at the same time attempt to resolve major issues in their relationship with Prospero. First, the diminution and eventual death of their cre-

ative expression reveal their irrelevance in a society clearly unable to nurture and sustain their creativity. As all three artists experience in their different ways, the very context and functions of their artistic skill must contend with the menace of Prospero's attitude. In a more crucial way, the fact that their personal histories of dislocation, disconnection, and insecurity follow them into England reveals them as a people created and shaped by particular personal histories which they must confront and resolve before rearranging their relationship with Prospero.

Such personal histories reveal themselves in different ways among the three exiles. Roger's unreconciled sense of displacement as well as his rejection of landscape and history render him desolate and unanchored, a ranting, cursing Caliban until Nicole appears in his life. Indeed, as a symbolic vision in the novel, Nicole, along with other Miranda figures (Myra/Randa), becomes a powerful embodiment of that sensitivity and compassion which Lamming sees as a healing force in the perilous encounter between master and slave. When through his blindness and his obsessions with racial purity Roger loses Nicole, he loses his only connection to this possibility, and the total disintegration of his personality afterwards dramatizes the disconnection and desolation that can engulf the exile in an environment in which he can neither find his present nor his future. Roger's acts of arson, his rebellion against rejection by England, might have remained merely on the level of drama if it had not been preceded by his understanding of the possibility that Nicole symbolized. Although this recognition is only an understanding, its ramifications are linked with the vision of rapport and reconciliation implied in the Teeton/Myra scenes on the heath. For Nicole too represents an aspect of the new meanings that can be put on history in the future relationship between Caliban and Prospero.

In the consciousness of other Caliban figures, purgation and awareness move to even higher levels, becoming not just acts of rebellion and exorcism but also affirmations of destinies and futures distinct from that deluded sense of connection with Prospero's future which continually plagues the colonial Calibans. For a character like Derek, for instance, it is significant that the ritual of confrontation with his past as well as the moment of purgation should be enacted through the metaphor of possession, that powerful ritual of descent into self which his childhood Pentecostal religion had long inculcated in him. Although prior to his possession and descent Derek goes through several illuminations in which he reassesses his entire artistic career and personal history, it is not until his moment of possession that he actually rejects his colonial status. It is really that moment of discovery which both inspires and initiates his decisive choice against a corpse-like existence in England. "It was like the silence which would happen in his childhood when they waited on their knees; and stayed there, wordless and waiting until the pastor had at last found his voice. There was always the moment of dreadful silence; a beautiful silence as though the clouds had spread out, and come down like the hands of God to gather up every echo and build a barricade of silence over and around the chapel . . . It was such a rich and solemn hush which now hung over the auditorium."[31]

Within this charged atmosphere, Derek's anger against the entire terms of his relation with Prospero assumes a distinct and ungodly aura that claims the pride of Lucifer and the revolt of the beast and rejects the simplistic holiness of the pastor transmitted through Prospero. That such a moment of self-confrontation and choice should be inspired by the fervor and rituals of his Pentecostal childhood is significant, especially as Derek also rejects the pastor's simplistic virtue, regarding it as the source of his warped personality and corpse-like career in England. It seems that for Lamming such an ambiguity is a valid statement about Derek's relationship to his island's past, to those aspects of it that suffocate and those that inspire, and it is as if even the paradox of this relationship is an affirmation of a distinct consciousness separate from Prospero's "Bigger Light," capable of helping him to order history.

In the novel's exploration of the pitfalls and possibilities of exile, Tee-ton's story is perhaps the most significant, since it is the only one which unearths the paradoxes inherent in a revolutionary commitment to self-determination and an emotional involvement with the colonial country. Its dilemmas may reflect aspects of Lamming's own situation in the early 1950s as an "exile" in Britain, writing novels that explored the politics of decolonization in the West Indies, a paradoxical personal situation which he articulates more directly in his nonfiction: "When the exile is a man of colonial orientation and his chosen residence is the country which colonised his own history, then there are certain complications."[32]

The most subtle complication in this case is of a form of colonization through love which neutralizes the sense of separateness crucial for independence. The drama of Teeton and the Dowager explores its psychological burdens and the tortuous, almost brutal modes through which the colonized extricates himself from its cloying hold. And it is here in this drama that the Caliban/Prospero paradigm is most extended and radicalized.

When thou camest first
Thou strok'dst me, and mad'st much of me; wouldst give me
Water with berries in 't; and teach me how
To name the bigger light, and how the less,

That burn by day and night: and then I lov'd thee,
And shew'd thee all the qualities o' the isle,
the fresh springs, brine pits, barren place, and fertile;
Cursed be I that did so![33]

The drama of Teeton and the old Dowager moves beyond the two extremes of emotion that characterize Caliban's feelings towards Prospero. His docile unexamined love is here transformed into the cautious, subtly ritualized relationship between Teeton and the Dowager, which survives sentimentally yet precariously above the subterranean antagonisms of Teeton's political movement. The drama works by symbolically shedding the social masks that support the smooth domesticity between them and creates neutral ground on the scraggy island where unmediated undercurrents of feeling are unleashed. Here Dowager's control of the very roots of Teeton's emotion can become a brutal, menacing power, and Teeton recognizes for the first time the paralyzing sense of guilt and shame that has always characterized his relationship with her.

In a confrontation that works towards a ritual exorcism of negative history, the entire history of plantation slavery is relived not only to expose the hatreds of the pilot and the protective love of the Dowager as two sides of the same Prospero syndrome but also to historicize Teeton's own rebellion as part of a continuum of resistance in colonial relations. Earlier rebels had burned down plantations and violated planters' daughters. Would Teeton's endeavor be a movement forward in the quality of Caliban's rebellion?

The structuring of the last stages of Teeton's rebellion becomes in itself a comment on the nature and quality of rebellion and something of a concluding statement on the explorations of exile begun in earlier novels like *The Emigrants* and *Of Age and Innocence*. By placing this final act of ritual exorcism between Derek's rebellion in the Circle Theater and the final meeting of the "Gathering," the novel connects it both to the rituals or purgation and the self-assertion and definition symbolized by the Gathering, the group of West Indian artists in exile. For Teeton in particular, burning the old Dowager's body becomes symbolic: choice and endeavor redeem him from the past, redeem him even from his old obsession with personal safety, that fear of death which had earlier on led him to betray the cause by accepting the compromising terms of his escape from prison.

Yet, as the text indicates, the future and freedom that Teeton chooses may be as dangerous and ruinous as the past he has exorcised. For the profile-like horizon of the mainland, which he spots from the seas "shivers like the fangs of a jaw where the houses rose behind the ragged mouth of the bay. But Teeton had come to the end of his safety . . . he was calm; no pulse of his blood; no whisper of a beat from the cage of steel that covered his heart." Having now conquered his instinct for safety, he is ready to begin anew, and it is to this redeemed Teeton that the novel's final apocalyptic vision is addressed: "He was gazing where a cave of fire began to open the sky . . . A trinity of voices came up from the floor of the ocean. Teeton was ready to move; and he was so calm."[34]

But personal redemption is not the novel's ultimate vision. For its ending is open-ended enough to suggest that freedom itself may be open to other meanings and interpretations. In *Water with Berries* such meanings are suggested in the possibilities of dialogue between the Caliban and Miranda figures. Lamming himself hints at the paradigmatic importance of Shakespeare's Miranda: "In some real, though extraordinary way Caliban and Miranda are seen side by side: opposite and contiguous at the same time. They share an ignorance that is also the source of some vision. It is, as it were, a kind of creative blindness. In different circumstances, they could be together in a way that Miranda and her father could not."[35]

The special relation with which these figures stand to the Calibans through their selfless giving and compassion represent the only empathetic relationships in the novel. Yet even these can only be fully claimed at the level of ritual and myth. The ceremony of souls becomes their kind of inner confrontation and dialogue that pushes both Teeton and Myra towards an understanding of their individual histories and the history they share with each other. Their dual exchanges enact each character's insights into the personal history of the other and links them further in a common history and consequence. Thus, as Myra narrates her island history Teeton begins to find his way easily through the familiar names of her childhood: "His recent knowledge of his past enriches his interest so that her face becomes part of the rivers and mountains which his maps had kept alive."[36]

Teeton's symbolic map of rivers and mountains, the inspiration behind a nationalist and revolutionary commitment, expands now to incorporate the opposing history of slave/master and plantation owner, thus pushing history beyond oppositions into an understanding and compassion which liberate Myra from the prison of memory, paving the way for renewal and new beginnings. The dialogue is finally inconclusive, but its open-endedness suggests further exploration, and Lamming leaves its implications as another possibility in the continuous search for new meanings of the past.

As in *Water with Berries,* Lamming's focus on the European contact with the New World in *Natives of My Person* rehearses similar possibilities in the colonial relationships of the past. The imaginative evocation of the triangular European voyage leads Lamming to explore the motives, impulses, and corruptions behind the European involvement with the New World. The conception behind the Commandant's enterprise, the idea of rectification and amelioration of the past, becomes a "ceremony of souls," a confrontation with the past which allows the crew of the *Reconnaissance* not only to come to terms with weaknesses and failures but also affords them the chance to extract new meanings for new relationships in the future. It is for this reason that, like Harris's crew in *Palace of the Peacock,* most of the crew are known to have made the triangular voyage in the past. Indeed, the correlation between the Commandant's own past voyage of greed and his present journey of expiation and altruism gives Lamming the leeway to explore the paradoxical impulses of greed and achievement, of ambition and promise which characterized European motives in the New World.

The vision of El Dorado, the honorable vision of empire, Lamming feels, was as much a possibility in the New World as the mediocre reality which actually evolved. Thus, in *Natives of My Person* the interplay between the noble dream and the perverted reality does not, as in Naipaul, enact a debased idea locked in a deterministic past. Rather, it rehearses several versions of history as important in determining the meanings we put on the past and the kinds of futures we may claim. The very idea of constructing other versions of history and making them a fundamental part of the narrative is itself an elaborate enactment of the complex motives and impulses that interfere with historical knowledge and interpretation. It is a demonstration of the relationship between fact and interpretation, between historical understanding and personal bias, between recorded history and unwritten history, and between "history" as such and the historical knowledge gleaned from the intuitions of myth and legend. So many histories crisscross in the novel, and so much of everything is so crucial to understanding, that it is the reader who becomes the ultimate historian, unraveling biases, locating sites of power, and deconstructing totalizing historical visions.

The dialogic representation becomes an interrogation of monolithic historical constructs and the tradition of European historiography which has appeared to monopolize the documentation and dissemination of historical knowledge about the Caribbean. In the novel it is enacted as a series of texts within the main text of the journey, and it is within the interrelationships of these texts that discourses on colonization, history, colonial relations, and freedom are embodied. The two versions of exploration and conquest (the earlier voyage of greed and pillage and the new journey of settlement and empire) play upon each other to reveal the repetitive prison of history in which the entire crew appears to be locked. Although several crew members have made the triangular journey before, none seems truly chastened by the experience, and the European idea of "the other" which had informed the ideology of conquest and subjugation in the sixteenth century is still operative, even in the Commandant's grandiloquent enunciation of the enterprise. The extracts from travel journals, part of the discourse on colonization, parody some of the extravagant representations of "the other" which made up the text of several travel books in the seventeenth century. Indeed, within the main text of the journey other representations of earlier voyages surface, crisscross, and interrogate each other, not only to question the meaning of the enterprise but also to decenter European ideas on what constitutes history. Thus extracts from the diaries function as insight into the writing of history itself, one which presents it, in Pinteados's words, as "personal witness," as a subjective presentation tempered as much by the recorder's biases as by the events themselves.[37]

Several contrasting perspectives of people, land, and events leave the reader free to characterize each representation and determine the relationship to others in Lamming's multivisioned narrative. There is, for instance, the typical travel-book account of the slave raids in Guinea, contained in the extract from the voyages of Pierre, where the usual rationalizations for enslavement are spelled out, and there is within this text the unorthodox revelation: the unspoken unrecorded "text" experienced by Ivan, the only far-seeing and visionary member of the crew. As a source of the unknown presence that encompasses other levels of the known, Ivan registers another history in his experience of the fury of the land, giving a different and tragic view of the aberration that has occurred and which has been so glibly explained away in Pierre's records.

On other occasions the very foundations of the conquistador's ethic, the idea that to overpower by strength and force is to acquire and rule, are shaken when Indian tribesmen present other versions of resistance and freedom. The Commandant calls upon the tribes to yield to his exploits in the cause of imperial glory, "giving his warning to the stones and the trees and the fresh river water that flowed with gold,"[38] but the same stones and trees unravel a separate story of resistance in the nuances of his own dreaming memory, just as later Ivan the seer would reveal the separate history of the tribes in his visionary reading of the moon. Throughout the novel the landscape of the Caribbean assumes an obsessive presence, becoming another text in itself and enacting a paradoxical blend of beauty and mystery desired by the crew but eventually ignored and subsumed in their personal ambitions. As in Harris's *Palace of the Peacock,* this elaborate characterization of landscape attempts to erase a historical limbo by creating a depth of space and continuity which would supply another text to the text of European activity and history.

Naipaul has said in *The Loss of El Dorado* that it is the absence of the Indian that distorts the time scale in the Caribbean. *Natives of My Person* corrects this distortion imaginatively in a reconstruction and valorization of Caribbean legend and myth related to the Indians. The legend of the Tribe Boys is, for instance, a parallel and equally valid historical text the reconstruction of which highlights and validates those modes of knowing which written histories often disregard; modes like the signs of nature, the subterranean levels of mythic recall, and the implications of elemental images. Ivan's visionary reading of the moon can, for instance, coalesce both past and future in a perception of history that draws out significance from past and present. Its power to probe and disturb becomes in itself an acknowledgment of its validity as another mode of knowing the past.

In another sense the resistance of the Tribe Boys becomes a parallel and equally valid demonstration of that universal need for freedom which inspires all major struggles in the novel. Here the issue of freedom is linked to the crucial question of who should possess San Cristobal, and though the question seems already resolved in Ivan's futuristic vision, the crisscrossing of past and present in the narrative enacts the personal crisis of each officer as if to suggest that he is unfit to complete the enterprise. For instance, the Commandant's idealistic pronouncements on empire-building are subverted both by their own contradictory rhetoric and by their disconnection from the facts of conquest and the hierarchies that separate members of the crew from each other. The personal histories and struggles of Baptiste, Ivan, and the common hands represent other ironical relations to freedom which shatter the noble and magnanimous facade of a common imperial enterprise. Certainly, the possibility of common people breaking centuries of exploitation to take action for their freedom and destiny is linked not to the story of the imperial enterprise but rather to the story of resistance and freedom embodied in the "otherness" of San Cristobal itself. Thus, as with Harris's crew in *Palace of the Peacock,* there appears to be a linking of personal histories and inner disturbance which implicates the characters incestuously in each other's situation and destiny, though the characters are not as metaphorically "in the same boat" as the characters in *Palace of the Peacock.* In that novel the interchange of personal weakness works towards a grasp and understanding of a common mythic destiny, while in *Natives of My Person* it creates only suspicion and further separation as each officer uses his knowledge of the other's vulnerability as a way of exercising power over him. The merging of personalities is thus not for redemption but for the eradication of the order and paradigms they represent. The entire patriarchal/imperial order, it is suggested, must crumble to give way to other possibilities, and the scenario in which all the officers have been eliminated by the end of the novel actually enacts such a collapse.

In the structural logic of the ending the novel appears to move beyond this collapse by locating the "future" in the values and perceptions of women (the wives of the officers). The matriarchal paradigm revealed in their perceptions and sensibilities answers to the needs and common weaknesses of the men, which Pinteados identifies as a sickness of the spine that makes them incapable of accepting both the power and responsibility of authority. "To be within the orbit of power was their total ambition . . . To feel authority over the women! That was enough for them. But to commit themselves fully to what they felt authority over. That they could never master. Such power they were afraid of."[39] The women's unshakable commitment to the future of a new world, their willingness to sacrifice, to recognize their husbands' weaknesses as native to their persons, are represented as the future the men must learn.

Yet such a future appears too simplistic to ameliorate the monumental loopholes in the patriarchal order so relentlessly delineated in the novel. Indeed the common experiences of the women reveal them in another light as women who had given up their right to choose in order to save their men from pride. Their symbolic link with the elemental, with "the red veins of the soil in the ceiling of rock"[40] and with the wide open skull of the earth in the cave enacts only their ability to transcend their husbands' familiar absences. The future they represent interestingly excludes or deflates the futures of characters like Baptiste, Ivan, and the common hands, who also stake a future, however precariously, by breaking away from the hierarchical structures of the past to seize the special moment of empowerment.

The text itself suggests a much wider future, one that Pinteados sees as his own, a future of multiple dimensions that may be fraught with paradox and ambiguity. For if, as Priest confesses, the world itself is broken into fragments and every necessary foundation of belief crumbled, then the future that emerges should move beyond the ruler/ruled dominance of a class-ridden world to encompass Pinteados's vision of multiple choices. It is the presence of such choices that unlocks "history" from the determinism of history as fact and invests in a future in which the lessons of the past are themselves forms of knowledge and understanding, "a soil from which other gifts, or the same gift endowed with different meanings, may grow towards a future which is colonized by our acts in this moment."[41]

In *Natives of My Person* the "different meanings" that may grow towards a future can be grasped from the ramifications of the various personal histories that unravel and crisscross in the claustrophobic world of the *Reconnaissance.* Boatswain's story in some respects enacts part of Lamming's own discourse on history. The revelation that history is written by the people with power, that the powerless can be coerced into distorting historical situations to serve a dubious honor, is not unrelated to Lamming's own enterprise in deconstructing European representation of the colonial encounter. Equally, Baptiste's larger revolutionary vision and his perspectives on freedom become the largest potential for empowerment in the novel, as it seizes the special moment and becomes the "quiet and terrible conscience of each common mariner down below,"[42] converting even Ivan the visionary into a man of action.

The return to the beginnings of Caribbean colonization in *Natives of My Person* is thus not a contraction out of the implication of the "backward glance" but a further exploration of its ramifications in terms of Caribbean historical links. It is a means of establishing an even larger framework of historical space and an attempt to look beyond the past into the future of these links. By dissecting so intricately the minds, motives, and personal struggles that intersect the colonizing ambitions of the empire-builders, *Natives of My Person* deflates the historical dichotomies of conqueror/conquered, civilized/savage, moral/immoral that have dominated the discourse on colonial history. The colonizing enterprise emerges not just as one driven by greed and brutality but also as a regenerative effort which fails because its players cannot transcend the emptiness at heart which prompts the ameliorating mission in the first place. More significantly, the discourse on freedom offers insights for a modern Caribbean in which the end of empire still conceals subtle continuities in the power relations between "empire" and "colony."

Chapter Five

Beyond Realism

Wilson Harris and the Immateriality of Freedom

To be a truth-seeking mythographer is therefore a high and serious calling, for what a group of people knows and believes about the past channels expectations and affects the decisions on which their lives, their fortunes and their sacred honor all depend. Formal written histories are not the only shapers of a people's notions about the past.

William H. McNeill, *Mythistory and Other Essays*

I am convinced that there is a tradition in depth *which returns, which nourishes us even though it appears to have vanished,* and that it creates a fiction in the ways in which the creative imagination comes into dialogue with clues of revisionary moment. The spectral burden of vanishing and reappearing is at the heart of the writer's task.

Wilson Harris, "Literacy and the Imagination"

Seven days it had taken to finish the original veil of creation that shaped and ordered all things to be solid in the beginning. So the oldest fable ran. Perhaps seven, too, were needed to strip and subtilize everything. Seven days which would run in logical succession in time, but nevertheless, would be appointed or chosen from the manuscript of all the spiritual seasons that had ever been.

Harris, *The Secret Ladder*

In Caribbean thought and literature, engagements with history often involve interrogations and reworkings of European master-texts in history and literature, and to move from Naipaul through Lamming to Harris is to confront related but varying discourses on history and modes of representation. As previous chapters have demonstrated, the history of European exploration and settlement in the New World has been reconstructed in

Naipaul's *The Loss of El Dorado,* in Lamming's *Natives of My Person* and in Harris's *Palace of the Peacock,* and a reading of Harris that connects itself to these other texts is bound to yield insights on his own unique perspective and on the multiplicity of complementary responses to history in West Indian imaginative writing.

In connection with such related readings, it is significant that Naipaul's *The Loss of El Dorado,* in spite of its fictionalized narration, is a "history." For even as a literary reconstruction of human history, distinguished from the historian's method of extracting historical principles, it remains a history confined within the truth of records and documents. Naipaul's artist's mind could, of course, create a story, capture the wonder of a new landscape and represent the fantasy and idealism inspired by the romance of new virgin lands. It could expose the glaring ironies, the perverted ideals, and the mediocre reality of empire and slavery. But basically his story is no more than its historical truth. Conquistadors are still conquistadors: idealistic, amateurish, brutal, egotistic. Indeed, as an explanation of the present *The Loss of El Dorado* has a particular theme:

> The idea behind the book, the narrative line, was to attach the island, the little place in the mouth of the Orinoco river, to great names and great events: Columbus, the search for El Dorado, Sir Walter Raleigh. Two hundred years after that, the growth of the slave plantations. And then the revolutions: the American revolution, the French revolution and its Caribbean by-product, the black Haitian revolution . . . From the undiscovered continent, to the fraudulence and chaos of revolution; from the discovery and Columbus and those lush aboriginal Indian "gardens" he had seen . . . from the discovery by Columbus, a man of medieval Europe, to the disappearance of the Spanish Empire in the nineteenth century.[1]

Invariably this theme informs the human story, colors interpretation, and explains the ease with which Naipaul links the failure of endeavor and revolution in the region to the perversions of this period.

Lamming and Harris work with the same basic material about the beginnings of the New World. Yet for them the leeway of the imagination provides the open possibilities of other texts. For Naipaul's history there are only the documents and records of empire-builders and slave masters. "I could see, in the documents of this later period, the lineaments of the world I had grown up in. Asian-Indian immigrants had come in the period of nineteenth-century torpor. As a schoolboy I had assumed that torpor to be a constant, something connected with the geographical location of the island, the climate, the quality of the light. It had never occurred to me that the drabness I knew had been man-made, that it had causes, that there had been other visions, and indeed other landscapes there."[2]

For Lamming and Harris "other texts" connote spaces, presences, and lives before conquistadors. They involve an imaginative "reading" of landscape and a novel relationship to myth as another way of knowing and understanding history. Thus, whereas in *The Loss of El Dorado* Naipaul glimpses Indian responses and rebellions only from official Spanish and Capuchin records, Lamming constructs from legend the mythical story of San Cristobal[3] to present other versions of Indian response that create a different dimension of freedom and a new way of viewing the "victims" of history. Indeed, by juxtaposing such texts with other texts of oppression and struggle at different moments in time, Lamming's novel dislocates the fixed "time" and "history" of each journey of conquest, enabling meanings to reverberate through the present and creating psychical parallels in our own relation to oppression and freedom. Harris, on the other hand, appropriates the open myth of El Dorado, drawing out several illuminating correspondences for an imaginative interpretation of that collision of peoples and cultures which he sees as fundamental to the present New World reality.

The fact that Harris approaches El Dorado as open myth and Naipaul views it as a vision of the New World at a particular period in time is a significant pointer to the kinds of illumination which the history of exploration offers both writers. El Dorado as a description of a New World condition is, for instance, specific and limited in Naipaul's history: "The mystery of the final adventure lies in Raleigh's book about his first Guiana journey, *The Discovery of the Large, Rich and Beautiful Empire of Guiana*. This is a book about the discovery of Arcadia; it suggests mines and gold, spaciousness, enameled forests, a world in which the senses, needs, life itself, can be extended. The book is part of the world's romance. But its details are precise and true. It catches part of the New World at that moment between the unseeing brutality of the discovery and conquest and the later brutality of colonization."[4]

The Arcadian vision of possibility exists here as a moment that was lost and which will never be regained. It draws attention to itself mostly to suggest the destruction of beauty, romance, and possibility, and its historicist perception of a given moment in history conceives of history itself as a phenomenon that is linear and coherent. In Harris's appropriation of the myth, El Dorado draws larger patterns and suggestions:

> Let us apply our scale, for example, to the open myth of El Dorado. The religious and economic thirst for exploration was true of the

Spanish conquistador, of the Portuguese, French, Dutch and English, of Raleigh, of Fawcett, as it is true of the black modern pork-knocker and the pork-knocker of all races. An instinctive idealism associated with this adventure was overpowered within individual and collective by enormous greed, cruelty and exploitation . . . nevertheless the substance of this adventure, involving men of all races, past and present conditions, has begun to acquire a residual pattern of illuminating correspondences. El Dorado, City of Gold, City of God, grotesque, unique coincidence, another window within upon the Universe, another drunken boat, another ocean, another river; in terms of the novel the distribution of a frail moment of illuminating adjustments within a long succession and grotesque series of adventures, past and present, capable *now* of discovering themselves so that in one sense one relives and reverses the "given" conditions of the past, freeing oneself from catastrophic idolatry and blindness to one's own historical and philosophical conceptions and misconception which may blind one within a statuesque present or a false future.[5]

What Harris calls here a scale of reflection is a drama of "living consciousness" within which a writer responds not only to the salient features of a realistic plane of existence but also to the "instinctive grains of life which continue striving and working in the imagination for fulfillment." The distinction that he draws between Dante and modern poets in the body of his essay is thus a distinction between Dante's association with timeless moments of reality and fulfillment and the modern poet's perception only of "odds and ends of still life and stage properties," a distinction which in the final analysis Harris sees as a difference between "the historical self-sufficient individual as such, and a living open tradition which realizes itself in an enduring capacity associated with the obscure human person."[6]

A living, open tradition is, for Harris, the intuitive inner world of traditions and myths buried in the world's unconscious and therefore within ourselves; it is a world which in all Harris's writing is held in interrelationship with a material world glimpsed through conscious perception and depicted in realistic representations in fiction. To go deep into the unconscious and the past in this way is to inhabit cross-cultural traditions and myths that nourished writing and bore upon the great pre-Columbian sculptors. It is in effect to construct a world that penetrates the beginnings of language, sculpture, and painting, a multitextured background of known and unknown presences within which economic and political bonds of material time are deflated. Thus, in place of the static polarization occasioned by our conscious perception of colonizer and colonized, oppressor and victim, we have an amalgam of several manifestations of the dislocated personality, as well as an interaction of different states of consciousness among characters in fiction.

Harris's perception, interpretation, and representation of Caribbean history in fiction must be seen in the context of the relationships between such material and immaterial constitutions. For this context is the basis of his mythic construction of history, especially in *Palace of the Peacock*. Unlike the "historian" in Naipaul's *El Dorado* or the omniscient author in Lamming's *Natives of My Person*, Harris's historian is a mythmaker, and his history, dreamed from various historical stories mythologized in conscious and unconscious memory, enacts its paradoxes almost from the very beginning. The wider myth, strung from all the sovereign epochs and ages of the world, embodies contrasting motives which Harris exploits for a subjective reworking and transformation of a story of conquest.

Within this framework we are presented with two contrasting journeys: a journey of conquest inspired by greed and a search for perfection inspired by innocence and love. The clue to this paradoxical construction seems to me to reside in the character of Harris's mythmaker-narrator and his mode of creating his story. The fact that he has a double perspective and combines "one dead seeing eye" with "one living closed eye" means that he presents two levels of history that operate upon each other and upon himself. There is, for instance, the level of conscious linear history, the "curious stone" upon which he stands, the unchanging, uniform reality of colonial conquest, and there is the level of mythic history, the blind, dreaming recall of the unconscious myth of El Dorado.

The drama played out in the opening section of *Palace of the Peacock* indicates that the narrator's inspiration for the transforming journey is the conventional story of conquest in which struggles and polarizing tendencies are enacted in the conflicts between Donne and Mariella. The narrator's mediation in this conflict, his ability to inhabit Donne's conquistador mind and at the same time empathize with Mariella and the unnamed presences that surround her, casts him as the right medium for Harris's dual representation.

Yet throughout *Palace of the Peacock*, there is continual tension between the two levels of representation, which suggests a mode of dialectical argument about the limits of mimetic representation and the necessity for mythic construction. Thus the beginning of the journey finds the dreaming narrator clinging to his symbolic map "as to a curious necessary stone and footing, the ground [he] knew he must not relinquish . . . They were an actual stage, a presence, however mythical they seemed to the universal and the spiritual eye."[7]

Even as he suggests the mythic aura of the journey (by presenting the crew as the ghosts of other mythic explorers and indicating that the possibilities of El Dorado were a "fleshly shadow" in their unconscious), the narrator still struggles between mimetic and mythic representations. There are moments when he abandons the process of unconscious dreaming and recall and attempts to participate realistically in the material story. But each moment's struggle works out an argument which validates the mythic mode, until on occasions he himself becomes a participant in the mythic story and is created by it. Thus, at the beginning of the boat journey he is forced to mediate between a static linear history of cruelty and revenge apprehended realistically from Donne's perspective and a mythic, timeless one which creates correspondences for the present and future. At Mariella he again struggles to overcome a material urge and fantasy to relive the realistic history enacted before the journey. His dream at dawn is a hallucination that interrupts his unconscious recall to experience the Donne-Mariella story at a personal level.

On other occasions he is petrified by the breakdown of sequential time which the mythic mode imposes. He is, for instance, made uneasy by his own futuristic vision and by the realization that the Arawak woman Donne has arrested is the woman he has dreamt about. "Had we made a new problematical start—a pure and imaginary game, I told myself in despair—only to strip ourselves of all logical sequence and development and time? And to fasten vividly on our material life as if it were a passing fragment and fantasy while the curious nebulosity of ourselves stood stubborn and permanent? and as if every solid force and reason and distraction were the cruel stream that mirrored our everlastingness? I felt I was caught in a principle of never-ending anxiety and fear, and it was impossible to turn back."[8]

These conflicts enact a tension which Harris purposely creates between the two types of historical representations. It is a dialectic that is rooted in the brutalities and cruel repercussions of material history but moves beyond them and is finally resolved at the last stages of the journey, when the narrator unconditionally accepts the mythic mode.

The action of Harris's novel, however, continually enacts the interpenetration of the two types of history. Both in his description of the crew members and in his account of their relationships with each other the narrator reveals aspects of personality and psychic dislocation which are the consequences of the history of conquest. The self-complacent, exploitative, and cruel psyche of the conqueror/slave-master Donne and the insecurities and alienation of his subordinates are all aspects of material history which Harris counters in his own way within the larger myth. For instance, in rehearsing contrasting states of consciousness among his crew and in creating a common mythic womb and destiny for them, he breaks down the rigid material situations that polarize them, so that victim grasps and understands the mind of conqueror and conqueror experiences the insecurities and alienation of the conquered. Indeed, more than the common grave and womb that binds the crew, Harris suggests another unifying bond in the hybridity of their ancestry, in the paradoxical, bittersweet "web of slave and concubine and free" which, together with an intuitive relation to mythic presences and an immaterial vision, can create new sensibilities and a new sense of community for West Indian people.

The point of the mythic mode is precisely the creation of dimensions that would deflate the inevitability and stasis of the colonial convention, and the imaginative leeway provided by the unconscious recall inscribes a new, potent relationship to landscape, creating new depths in space and new metaphors of self-apprehension. The narrator's particular encounter with the dense interior, significantly placed at the beginning of the boat journey, stirs a consciousness and self-awareness which touch similar chords in old Schomburgh: "His expression grew animal-sharp and strained to attention. Every word froze on his lips with the uncanny silence and patience of a fisherman whose obsession has grown into something more than a normal catch. He glared into my eye as if he peered into a stream and mirror, and he grumbled his oldest need and desire for reassurance and life."[9]

In an essay on the subjective imagination, Harris laments modern technological man's lack of imaginative daring to probe the function of roots as a criterion of creativity and as a capacity to digest and liberate contrasting space. He intimates that an apparently homogenous and fixed boundary may, for instance, conceal from us the heterogeneous roots of community. Thus, moving away from the coast of Guyana into the interior may bring one in touch with a fantastic density of place that may reveal eclipsed perspectives of place and community. He describes an experience in the interior where a canvas of phantoms revealed hidden depths and past accretions that stirred his own consciousness. "I had forgotten some of my own antecedents—the Amerindian/Arawak ones—but now their faces were on the canvas. One could see them in the long march into the twentieth century out of the pre-Columbian mists of time. One could also sense the lost expeditions, the people who had gone down in these South American rivers. One could sense a whole range of things, all sorts of faces—angelic, terrifying, demonic—all sorts of contrasting faces, all sorts of figures. There was a sudden eruption of consciousness."[10]

Part of Harris's purpose in *Palace of the Peacock,* then, is to transform relationships with Caribbean landscapes and with the aboriginal folk who inhabit them, and he seems to me to situate such transformations within the framework and mythic implications of Carroll's music. Carroll's music at the beginning of the journey, while paradoxically startling away every imagined misery, fear, and guile and anticipating the creative ecstasy and renewal of his final music also intimates an uncanny link between the confused motives of the crew and those of earlier journeys in memory. "He saw that the omens and engines of grace and salvation were so easily turned again into doom. He felt—without clearly understanding why—that the entire crew had been drawn together almost against their will. It seemed now that their living desire was as ambivalent and confused as the origin of the first command they dimly recalled and knew in the grave of memory."[11]

In contrast, his music at the end of the novel is a summation of the reversals that have occurred, indicating not only the self-awareness and individuation of the crew members but also the transformation of El Dorado from a vision of gold to a vision of depth in space, of creative renewal, a vision of God.

In *Palace of the Peacock,* such transformations are mirrored in the confrontations, struggles, sacrifices, deaths, and changed relationships that occur throughout the journey to Mariella. Harris presents the folk not only as a foil to the crew but also as a value and possibility that have always existed. Thus, on one hand, he can suggest that the undivided consciousness of the folk and their grasp of the possibilities of their landscape give them a substance that separates them from the crew and their death-in-life state. On the other hand, he can present the crew's individuation as a gradual breaking down of the barriers within themselves that separate them from the folk. For instance, the possibilities of El Dorado which they had pursued in their earlier voyage present themselves in the form of the old Arawak woman's transformation into an object of desire which is at the same time lodged in their own consciousness.

The entire drama of transformation in *Palace of the Peacock* becomes a breaking down of barriers, masks, shells, fixed self-conceptions, and dead reality, and Harris orchestrates it by first presenting it in dialectical terms as contrasting perceptions in Donne and the narrator. In this dialectic he seems to ask the questions: What is the right and redeeming relationship to the folk and how may the crew achieve it? Donne perceives this relationship in purely material terms and from his own need to survive as a landlord and exploiter of the folk. "After all I've earned a right here as well. I'm as native as they, ain't I? . . . The only way to survive of course is to wed oneself into the family. In fact I belong already."[12]

But the narrator insists on the inadequacy of such a relationship:

"We're all outside of the folk," I said musingly.

"Nobody belongs yet . . ."

"Is it a mystery of language and address?" Donne asked quickly and mockingly.

"Language, address?" I found it hard to comprehend what he meant. "There is only one dreaming language I know of . . ." I rebuked him . . . , "which is the same for every man . . . No it's not language. It's . . . it's . . ." I searched for words with a sudden terrible rage at the difficulty I experienced . . . "it's an inapprehension of substance . . . an actual fear . . . fear of life . . . fear of the substance of life, fear of the substance of the folk, a cannibal blind fear in oneself . . . the haunting sense of fear that poisons us and hangs us and murders us. And somebody . . . must demonstrate the unity of being, and show . . . that fear is nothing but a dream and an appearance . . . even death."[13]

In revealing the corrosive fear within that keeps the crew bound to the material world of appearances, the narrator at the same time defines another form of relationship and communication: the misapprehension of substance, the living immaterial reality of unconscious myth whose "dreaming language is the same for everyone." Thus, when he talks of the unity of being he talks in terms of the necessary interpenetration of conscious and unconscious reality as the two levels at which the crew can relate to history, myth, and culture. Harris believes in the collective unconscious as a repository of myths which can nourish the conscious imagination and create illuminating perceptions of landscape and history. The drama of the crew's encounter with the nameless rapids enacts these processes and possibilities as a way of demonstrating the various ways in which unconscious myth can energize conscious reality. Because the recourse to unconscious reality is not a mere visionary escape from the brutalities and pain of material history, the drama also delineates the insufficiencies of personality and weaknesses of apprehension which are then exorcised as a preliminary to unconscious perception.

The crew's contact with each other, their revelations about the past, and their responses to tragedy, while traumatizing their material identities, also expose and exorcise the exploitative, domineering, and murderous impulses of the conquering ego as well as the self-abasing and insecure tendencies of the laboring "other." As with Lamming's crew in *Natives of My Person,* Harris's presentation of the crew as a microcosm of Caribbean social and class alliances enables him to solidify the social thrust of his drama of consciousness, so that even while the crew purges its selfish exploitative relation to the folk, it can react as well against Donne's capitalist tendencies. "Donne was the only one in their midst who carried on his sleeve the affectation of a rich first name. Rich, it seemed, because none of his servants appeared at first to have the power to address him other than obsequiously. The manner of the crew could change, however, one sensed, into familiarity and contempt. It was on their lips already to declare that their laboring distress and dream was the sole tradition of living men."[14]

The confrontation with unconscious reality, while ushering in the possibilities of rebirth and the immaterial vision, is nevertheless a slow and gradual process which in Harris departs from conventional ways of enacting and communicating reality in fiction. The collective unconscious does not understand the language of the conscious mind, and the unconscious can therefore be reached only through the suspension of material identities and material conventions in fiction. As Jung has pointed out, "the union of opposites on a higher level of consciousness is not a rational thing, nor is it a matter of will; it is a process of psychic development that expresses itself in symbols."[15] Thus in *Palace of the Peacock,* the crew's individuation is expressed and communicated in symbols which at the same time correspond to the highest intuitions of the conscious mind. Harris lays down the condition for unconscious perception as the unconditional surrender to the immaterial vision. "Call it spirit, call it life, call it the end of all they had once treasured and embraced in blindness and ignorance and obstinacy they knew."[16]

It is against this condition that we witness the blind dream of creation crumble as it is reenacted by the crew on the third day of creation. For none of the crew members except Vigilance can discern the possibilities of creation and rebirth suggested in the symbols they confront. For instance, the high walls and precipice that hang over their heads and which they stare at helplessly are "the ancient familiar house and structure," the repository of ancient myths and traditions; the river, which is as smooth and clear "as a child's mirror and newborn countenance,"[17] is a mirror of the heaven they can achieve; the parrot with a ring on its foot, which Cameron sees as a vulture and which da Silva confuses with an earthly lover, is, as Vigilance discerns, "the blue ring and pentecostal fire in God's eye."[18]

As with the crew, Donne's psychic development and remolding involves similar patterns of revelation, self-surrender, and understanding. His ascent, flooded with a multiplicity of symbols, demands a new perception of the monolithic structures he has built as well as a humble, liberating, and unifying vision of that divine essence in the universe that binds all creation together. The last image he confronts is perhaps deliberately the image of the Arawak woman, symbol of the folk. It is the nearest he and the crew actually get to Mariella. Harris circumvents an easy physical reconciliation by choosing to keep his resolution an artist's harmonizing vision. For instance, it is over Vigilance's dreaming shoulder that the narrator's artist mind finally sees the savanna as reaching far away and everywhere; it is the artist's ubiquitous metaphysical outline that fills in blocks where spaces stood, not only populating space and harmonizing contrasting spaces but actually supporting the life of nature and giving it a full, invisible meaning and perfection.

Carroll's music, which is a complementary projection of the creative imagination as a medium of illumination and harmony, is a further enactment of the artist's capacity to move beyond the limits of memory and beyond outward sense and sensibility to create depth in space, initiate self-understanding, and actually reenvision the quest for El Dorado as a desire for heaven and perfection. That desire, which had "once been turned by the captain of the crew into a compulsive design and a blind engine of war,"[19] can now be seen in another light, not as a rejection of the reality of the past but as a projection of possible future relationships.

It seems, then, that while the raison d'être for Harris's exploration is rooted in social and political imperatives, its thrust is relentlessly imaginative and visionary. *Palace of the Peacock's* final vision is unconditionally a spiritual one, since its essence, as embodied in Carroll's music, cannot admit of the "limits and apprehensions in the listening mind of men and their wish and need in the world to provide a material nexus to bind the spirit of the universe."[20] This seeming incongruity between sociopolitical imperatives and a spiritual resolution can cause discomfiture. But Harris's concern is perhaps with what Sandra Drake has called "the immanent moment," that moment when truth—reality—becomes a state of consciousness, of perspective, when "thought rectifies itself, in which the mind, suddenly drawing back and including itself in its new and widened apprehension, doubly restores and regrounds its earlier notions in a new glimpse of reality."[21] Certainly this altered apprehension is what Harris himself meant when he advocated a drama of living consciousness which responds to the "instinctive grains of life which continue striving and working in the imagination."[22] Harris's *Guiana Quartet* is a related whole, and it is significant that from *Palace of the Peacock* onward, Harris's characters move from awakening towards the acquisition of authority and vision. It is as if, aware of the immense possibilities of the resurrected consciousness, he begins now to explore other dimensions of history, moving away from fixed spaces, time, and events towards presences in the landscape, towards gateways between civilizations in the New World:

> Such a gateway complex between pre-Columbian primitive and ornamental Latin symbolism carries within it, nevertheless, a new latent capacity, a caveat or warning we need to ponder upon deeply and to unravel in our age. If we succumb to a black hearted stasis—to enclosures of fear—we may destroy ourselves; on the other hand, if we begin to immerse ourselves in a new capacity or treaty of sensibility between alien cultures—we will bring into play a new variable imagination or renaissance of sensibility steeped in caveats of the necessary diversity and necessary unity of man.[23]

Harris's statement is exemplified in various ways in *The Whole Armour,* in which he is concerned with providing an answer to what he sees as the enigma of vision. Vision is enigmatic for Harris at this stage because it has to be explored in the midst of a system of values established by a history of conquest and already in danger of becoming a fixed, all-consuming bias. It is the bias and stasis of these values that Harris urges the New World imagination to confront and transform. The artist has to alter the accepted textures of naturalism not only to resensitize them and free himself from their narrowness but also to rediscover new spaces and new scales of community.

In *The Whole Armour* the thematic and structural emphasis is on the enlargement of scale and the discovery of community, a process which takes place within the physical and psychological landscapes of Guiana, saturated by the traumas of conquest, by Arawak/Carib pre-Columbian vestiges, by the natural primeval life of the jungle, and by a colonial psychological worldview, the accumulation of perceptions and values from centuries of conquest and its orientation. Such a process requires a revolution in sensibility, and Harris's characters have to break through the fixed order of values that imprison them with narrow conceptions of themselves and relate afresh to other spaces, other beings, and other scales of community.

The process requires a revolution in sensibility, and in the novel the ritual of the "wake" provides a context and becomes a potent symbolism for such a revolution. Its very essence reveals that polarization between settlement and jungle that has led to narrowness and stasis in the personalities of people, and because its ritual seeks to repair a weak link in the people's defenses against the jungle, it becomes an appropriate medium for Harris's delineation. His rendering holds up a canvas of dogmatic and fixed relation ships and a complacent self-conception which he attempts to penetrate and surprise into new awareness. As he argues in "The Native Phenomenon," "The force of ritual beauty [ritual beauty as the victor's assets or hoards of conquest] lies in the stasis of conquest within which the victorious side apparently succeeds in pressing the face or faces of the vanquished into the dust of uniform conviction so that the reality or play of contrasts is eclipsed within an order or self-deception."[24]

In *The Whole Armour* this stasis is revealed through an ironic play of contrasts: the people of the Pomeroon rally all their forces into an incestuous persona to resist surrender to the encroaching jungle, yet this resistance is the very antithesis of their dark truth and history, "written in the violent mixture of races that had bred them as though their true mother was a wanton on the face of the earth and their true father a vagrant and a rogue from every continent";[25] they maintain narrow and rigid kingships and relationships, yet the reality of their history reveals several turbulent adjustments in relationships: "superior landlord redeemed by inferior slave, proud indigenous folk married to the economic emancipation of tyrants . . . an archaic sanction that constantly sought to reassert itself and bless every flood of enormity in a present and past life."[26]

In *The Whole Armour* it is these rigid kingships and relationships which have to crumble along with the fixed personalities they inhabit, and the wake provides the appropriate context for revelation and self-perception. Most characters perceive and come to terms with an extra force of reality that resides ironically in their own consciousness. In his helpless sensation of being manacled to the floor of Madga's room, Peet is, for instance, confronted with a vision similar to Abrams's dream of love and innocence in Jigsaw Bay. The sounds of the wake intermingle in his memory with "a braking sea on a jagged coast at Abram's doorstep," and on the floor where the void holds him in its frightful jaws the ground is crisscrossed by dead memory: "the floor of an ancient jigsaw, stylized furrows and mats belonging to a temple, naked roots on a fantastic farm, ditches of alabaster in the jungle. The shadows were frozen and white as Abram's blood on tropical moonlight-snow. They ran between a dim wave of crested sea and a dark forest of cultivated night, the sensational corpse of the medium of man borne swiftly by the living tiger of death."[27]

These transformations are symbolic portrayals of the flow of memory from fixed orders of self-deception into new spaces of community, and they provide characters with new conceptions of themselves. In Peet they give a sense beyond his narrow function as an incestuous persona and force against the world out there into what Harris has called the "heterogeneous ground-work of authentic community"; they retrieve from his innermost conscious-ness perceptions that link him with the vision of Abram and Cristo, so that "however much he tried to mend a carnival conceit and glory it remained a basket and a sieve—crippled by the compulsive perception of the bizarre womb of Abram—out of which Cristo had been reborn and split."[28]

The "bizarre womb of Abram" is a major thematic symbol in the novel, and it relates not only to Harris's idea of widening the historical canvas of the Caribbean region but also to his creative attempts at uniting contrasting spaces in the area. The creative imagination, Harris believes, should digest and liberate contrasting elements in the region; it should retrieve the mon-ster of the jungle back into itself as native to its psyche before it can pen-etrate the mystery of origins and transform Caribbean beginnings.

The tiger/monster is part of the fable of the land and of everybody's memory. It is Abram, the outcast and hermit, who first visualizes its savage presence in his dream, and in his death and rebirth are reflected all the deaths, rebirths, and transformations in the novel. Thus the uncanny resemblance between dead and living characters and the ease with which the dead reap-pear among the living dramatize the symbolic flow of memory from con-sciousness to consciousness, confirming its timeless and mythic qualities and corroborating Harris's suggestion that the "derelict premises Abram ruled had no true geographic location (and was) a region of absurd displacements and primitive boredom, the ground of dreams, long-dead ghosts and still-living sailors, ancient masters and mariners and new slaves, approaching the poor unchartered Guiana Coast and beckoning the aboriginal mummy for whom all trespass beyond the sculpture of death was an act of brutal unimag-inable faith."[29]

The primordial origins of such a memory, it seems, reside in the depths of the interior. The swamp into which the tiger's trail leads Peet and the search party is the navel of the womb, a vision of buried fertility whose head lies under Peet's feet "while its feet lay far away from Peet's own, far across the continent in the midst of buried time."[30] Peet is unable to explore its possibili-ties because he cannot at that stage of his life move beyond his material consciousness and dogmatic self-conception. It is Cristo, the novel's protago-nist, whose contact with Abram and with the interior awakens him to a knowledge of his affinity with the earliest grassroots and oldest native and who at the end of the novel stands poised to redeem his drought-stricken land with a new conception of Caribbean beginnings and a Caribbean scale of community.

Like Cristo, Harris's protagonist in *The Secret Ladder* must acquire a new sense of Caribbean space and community but has to move further than Cristo to digest and transform his awareness of origin. For in this last novel of the *Guiana Quartet* the emphasis is on transformation and the acquisition of the authority and psyche of freedom. The drama of consciousness centers on the protagonist, Fenwick, but the sense of a purely personal individuation is countered through the visible economic and political realities which surround the drama and in the various ways in which Fenwick's own personality is mirrored in members of his crew to suggest their participation in the transformation of consciousness. Unlike *Palace of the Peacock*, in which the concern with mythic consciousness necessitates that sociopolitical realities are inferred in a general sense rather than explored specifically in a realist delineation, *The Secret Ladder* is rooted realistically in the economics and politics of a particular period. What is involved here is rather the stripping and subtilization of what is consolidated and the dismantling of a prison of appearance. It is a process which may run in logical succession in time but nevertheless has been appointed or chosen from the manuscript of all the spiritual seasons that have ever been, "Each choice drawn from its claustrophobic epoch and all strung together like a new immaterial genesis and condition."[31]

The political and economic facts behind the drama of consciousness relate to the political emergence of East Indian workers and farmers and to an economic situation in which a government irrigation project would link the "primitive snake" of the Canje River to the "wavering disposition of the coast."[32] Can these farmers and workers reconcile their emergence with the liberal germs of the past? What would be the import of the old runaway Negro, Poseidon, and his buried community in a project that would benefit East Indian rice and sugarcane farmers but leave him and his community exposed and vulnerable? Though it is within these material issues that the symbolic implications of Poseidon and the questions of African origins are explored, the dialectical argument moves beyond the material realm to encompass visions of consciousness in which historical events are subjectively altered in a rehearsal of alternative possibilities that would create a new vision for the present and future. Within this rehearsal Poseidon is presented with an ambivalence that reflects the paradoxes of Caribbean history itself, paradoxes of space, time, and consciousness in which he is at once the grand old man of African history, the runaway slave and initiator of a certain tradition of freedom, and a symbol of a multiple heritage, of dimensions of space, and of the buried unconscious.

The dialectical argument about the meaning of freedom and authority is set up within the context of these ambivalent associations, and the crux of the argument rests on the attitude which both Fenwick and Bryant adopt towards Poseidon and on the claims each makes upon him. Bryant becomes in this argument a projection of Fenwick's other self, the self with which he is in constant struggle and debate. His unproblematized view of Poseidon as the long lost ancestor whom he must reinstate in his consciousness struggles continually with Fenwick's more questioning and exploratory relation to the possibilities Poseidon holds for Caribbean transformations. Thus, in the dialectical argument it is Fenwick's view that is posited as the problematic of the Caribbean man's relation to the ancestor: "I feel I have stumbled here in the Canje on an abortive movement, the emotional and political germ of which has been abused in two centuries of history."[33] Within this initial recognition Fenwick perceives the runaway's own movement as abortive, fraught with paradoxes, and unable in the end to achieve true freedom and authority. He surmises on its possible misconceptions and locates its failures in a blinding and overemotional self-conception, which in the past disregarded his paradoxical situation in a landscape he shared with other people, other combinations of races: "Something was misunderstood and frustrated . . . Maybe it was all too emotional, too blinding, this freedom that has turned cruel, abortive, evasive, woolly and wild everywhere almost. And yet the affair is still fresh in our mind, and so it is not really finished. Maybe it has only now began."[34]

In arguing his relation to this notion of freedom Fenwick points to the incongruity between the exclusiveness implied in Poseidon's notion of freedom and the all-inclusive image of his house with its evidence of a multiple heritage. "To what and whose spirit did the house belong? Had it been grafted from above, unconscious of itself?"[35] These questions, suggesting paradoxes of space and heritage, are what move Fenwick beyond Bryant's simple view of Poseidon's freedom into a quest for understanding and authority. "You shout of freedom," he says to Bryant, "but with every word you ignore the inescapable problem of authority. And without understanding the depth of authority you can't begin to understand the depth of freedom."[36]

Brathwaite has argued that this view of the maroon's freedom may itself be a misconception of the runaway African and an indication of Harris's own ambivalence towards him: "[The] cruel abortion of freedom [Fenwick] speaks about, the over-'emotional' negritude [he accuses Poseidon of], was and is not only a function of maroonage, it was and is even more certainly the consequence of opposition to the plantation. How else can we interpret the fate and history of Haiti, the greatest and most successful maroon polity of them all."[37]

Brathwaite writes, most validly, with the "historian's" perception of the actual history of Poseidon. Yet the conception of Poseidon's freedom which determines Harris's delineation becomes meaningful when linked to the ecumenical vision that translates freedom itself into immateriality. The deconstruction of the historical event rehearses alternative possibilities not to consolidate the facts of history but to move beyond them towards a vision of the future, and in this rehearsal Poseidon is not only the maroon but the African with the Greek name, the privileged son or grandson of a slave, indissolubly linked to the landscape and the inheritor of a multiple Caribbean heritage. It is within these various contexts of "rehearsal" that Poseidon can symbolize more than the maroon and be linked also with the buried unconscious of Caribbean people to the extent that Fenwick, seeing him for the first time, "could not help fastening his eyes greedily upon him as if he saw down a bottomless gauge and river of reflection."[38]

In the dialectical argument on history and origin the crucial word is transformation, and Fenwick's confrontation with the multiple symbolism of Poseidon permits an exploration of the argument as a process, a reconciliation of opposing propensities within Fenwick himself; in this sense, Poseidon holds a divine promise of ultimate freedom but also the viable possibility of "inexhaustible self-oppression."[39] Fenwick is linked to the promise and is an appropriate vessel for the drama of consciousness because his own personality is made up of just such a paradox. He has kept a false appearance of harmony in himself and with his crew by using the hard-hearted and calculating Jordan as a protective shield that stops him from confronting the self within. Yet at the same time he possesses a waking dream, an inward flowing truth that keeps him spiritually alive and makes him create an image of all the rivers of Guyana as the "curious rungs in a ladder on which one sets one's musing foot again and again, to climb into both the past and the future of the continent of mystery."[40] It is this spiritual potentiality that leads him in his dream to slay the cruel muse (Jordan), deflating that sovereign petty side of him which Jordan represents, the trait which must die if he is to integrate Poseidon into his consciousness and into a fluid, immaterial future.

Fenwick's drama of consciousness begins, then, as a surrender to this immaterial thread of awareness he possessed of his own nature and of other creatures, and with his surrender comes a new resolution, a closer affinity with the land and forest and a new empathetic relation with people that extends from his crew to even a stranger like Catalena. It is a spiritual climax that dismantles the intense self-preoccupation and prison of appearance demonstrated by Jordan, his other self. Its possibilities and potential as an immaterial self-conception are paralleled by the natural world itself, which provides salutary reminders of the displacement of the past and "the basic untrustworthiness in every material image as well as in the conception of a supporting canvas."[41] The fluidity of the immaterial is here asserted against the consolidation of the material, and in the contrast is located a view of how Poseidon might be integrated in the Caribbean consciousness for the creation of true freedom and authority.

In this sense the story of Van Brock's grandmother and the story of the death of Poseidon have an ironic link that is significant to the implications both of Caribbean origins and a memory of the past. Michael Gilkes emphasizes the symbolic meaning of the Van Brock story and sees the gold ring he retrieves and replaces on his dead grandmother's finger as the buried past, "the ideal of a living organic community of spirit which Van Brock must establish links with."[42] But it seems to me there is an ambiguous link with the story of Poseidon's death that permits another interpretation more thematically linked to the implications of memory and the meaning of freedom and authority. For the story is as critical of the mode of reconnection to the past as it is of Bryant's simplistic reconnection to Poseidon. Indeed the ague that confuses the generally self-indulgent and self-satisfied Van Brock has by the time of Fenwick's questioning of him penetrated inward, shaking "every conception of duty and existence."[43] In addition, the passage that describes and validates his conception of duty as the restoration of memory raises several questions and ironies. "[He] descended into the grave pit even before she did, searched for the ring and restored it to her finger as a dutiful high priest at the wedding of memory." Yet there are questions raised about this almost religious conception of duty to memory. "Was it an ancestor of life or of death he had created at that moment? He was obsessed with the self-indulgence and ordure of love as with the ghost of glory."[44] Van Brock's grandmother cannot bear the decapitation of memory signified by the loss of her ancient ring, and in recovering and restoring the ring, her grandson restores the bond of love and memory which she craves. Yet, as Harris implies throughout the novel, it is not "the ordure of love" nor the "ghost of glory"[45] that would liberate Caribbean man and encapsulate him out of a material future and helpless function, but the freedom and authority that envision an immaterial consciousness.

It is in this sense that the Van Brock story is ironically linked with the story of Poseidon's death, and from the way his death is delineated we are made to feel that it is a similar desire for static continuity and the simple perpetuation of memory that leads him to strike out against all peril. ("He knew he would live for ever in the minds of his people.")[46] His death at the hands of Bryant, the grandson he had conceived in the "dreadful apotheosis of history," is thus literally willed by Fenwick in his imaginative dreaming inquisition of dead gods and heroes. Poseidon is struck dead almost at the same time that Catalena is animated even in her unconscious state, and in contrast to this death, the love between Catalena and Bryant, for all the uneasiness of its truce, is perceived as the beginning of a vision that transcends both the insecurity of pleasure and the stasis of a certain conception of the past, a vision that permits Bryant to look through her to the end of a "blind trail" of static history, beginning an individuation that is to transform his perception of Poseidon. It is, for instance, with a transformed perception of Poseidon that he pleads with his (Poseidon's) followers to transcend the eternal and broken cage in themselves and look upon the survival of Catalena and her links with him as the last tribute to an ancestor "whose uplifted stroke should be transformed into the nerve of progeny in their imagination."[47]

Bryant, Poseidon, and most of the characters of *The Secret Ladder* appear eventually to be rescued from the "prison-house" of ancient memory into a fluid future. Even Poseidon's followers, who dramatize their bitterness and void to the end, eventually succumb to the phantoms that move involuntarily in their minds with new visions, and Fenwick himself, who has dreamed this transformation by descending into the innermost unconscious, has by the end of the novel overcome the temptation to fix himself in the material universe and its conception of time.

Harris's psychoanalytical model for refiguring and transforming history in the Caribbean is an original and carefully worked out philosophy that demands a great deal of confidence in the visionary and spiritual capabilities of the Caribbean person. The imperatives that inspire it are valid, and Harris is convincing when he argues that the Caribbean historical convention should free itself from fixed time and the biases of imperial history by altering the boundaries of reality and naturalism to explore the psychic as a domain of possibility. Yet the metamorphosis within the unconscious may sometimes appear decontextualized, removed from the flux of historical interaction. In *The Secret Ladder* the political, social, and economic facts of a particular period in Guyanese history contextualize the drama of consciousness within Fenwick, so that the implications of the new psychic construction are understood within that context. The questions posed at the beginning about relations between the coast and the hinterland, about East Indian political emergence and its ability to connect itself to the liberal germs of the past symbolized in Poseidon, are answered in the transformation of Poseidon's own history and freedom.

Indeed, Poseidon and his maroon community touch on the large question of social and racial interaction in modern Guyanese society, and Poseidon's symbolic import as the force that unearths conflicting responses to race in the subconscious minds of the crew may succeed in dismantling fears, repression, and alienation (in the case of Fenwick and the crew) as well as a static response to the ancestor (in the case of Bryant). But the symbolic import is one-sided, confined mostly to the internalization and psychic projection of Fenwick and the crew. Poseidon's own thinking and articulation do not occupy a place in the transformation except as symbols manipulated by Fenwick's dreaming consciousness.

In Fenwick's consciousness the necessity of Poseidon's death is justified by the fact that he insists on perpetuating a self-conception, authority, and freedom which are no longer tenable. Every representation projects his fight to perpetuate his memory as a race of "unequal body and spirit," and in the ironical circumstances of his death he himself appears on the brim of a realization of the folly of static self-perpetuation. Yet all these ramifications are dramatized solely from Fenwick's consciousness, and Poseidon appears not to be a subjective agent of the historical transformation. It is difficult to surmise what part he plays or what input he contributes to the kind of integration envisaged in modern Guyanese society.

But Harris's major preoccupation, it seems, is with how Poseidon is understood and integrated in the ambivalent consciousness of the modern Guyanese. "To *misconceive* the African . . . is to misunderstand and exploit him mercilessly and oneself as well,"[48] and the process towards this understanding is embedded in Fenwick's psychic growth on the secret ladder of conscience, which, as Harris has consistently argued, is a more fluid source of transformation than a material context with its relationships of cause and effect. Yet the possibility of misunderstanding is still imminent even at the conclusion of Fenwick's dreaming. For the moment when it seems an inquisition of dead gods and heroes has ended in the sacrificial death of Poseidon, "[the] one chosen from amongst them to descend [Poseidon himself] was crying something Fenwick was unable to fathom, [breaking through the] echoes of annunciation [that] grew on every hand and became resonant with life."[49] The problem in relation to Poseidon appears not to be completely resolved at this point, and the process of understanding is probably a continuing one, even though the drama of consciousness has opened up the immaterial consciousness as capable of revolutionizing our thoughts on history.

The problems raised by the relationship between the drama of consciousness and its sociopolitical context make us uncomfortably aware of the generally linear and material character of our experience of life and therefore the validity of the material vision expressed by writers like Lamming, Reid, Naipaul, Walcott, and Brathwaite. Indeed, Harris's idea that the Caribbean man can retrieve a mythic consciousness, extend the dimensions of space and community in the region, and create a new sensibility from such spaces is challenged by Walcott's vision (certainly in his early poetry) of the amnesia of the displaced. His sense of the possibilities of "memory" in the Caribbean may link him with Walcott's interpretation of "memory" and with Brathwaite's idea of tribal memory, but its ramifications are often so different that they challenge and are in turn tested by Walcott's vision and by Brathwaite's aesthetics of renaissance. Such correspondences and differences, however, confirm Harris's centrality as a Caribbean thinker and distinguish his perceptions on history and the arts of the imagination.

Chapter Six

Transcending Linear Time
History and Style in Derek Walcott's Poetry

The vision of progress is the rational madness of history seen
as sequential time.
Derek Walcott, "The Muse of History"

No horsemen here, no cuirasses
crashing, no fork-bearded Castilians,
only the narrow, silvery creeks of sadness
like the snail's trail,
only the historian deciphering, in invisible ink,
its patient slime,
no cataracts abounding down gorges
like bolts of lace,
while the lizards are taking a million years to change,
and the lopped head of the coconut rolls to gasp on the sand,
its mouth open at the very moment
of forgetting its name.
Walcott, *Another Life*

Although as works of art all literary forms are close enough to each other
to allow relational and comparative readings, especially in the context of
ideology, there are enough differences in the internal organization and
structure of genres to affect the nature of discourse in each genre. To move
from a discourse on history in fiction to poetry's engagement with history
is therefore to encounter different conceptualizations and representations.
For unlike fiction, which represents experience in ways that approximate
our ordinary experience of life, poetry captures experience as a whole, depending mostly on tight verbal organizations in which words are signifiers

of things as well as projections of feelings and associations. The poet does not set out consciously to construct ideas in a poem. It is the critic who constructs meaning and creates a coherence in ideas through the relationships the poet creates between words. The following chapters on poetry attempt such a construction, and their approach, though slightly different from the explorations of fiction, is ideologically continuous with the arguments developed so far.

To compare Walcott's relation to history with perspectives in Naipaul and Lamming is thus perfectly valid, since in engaging with Caribbean reality and with his own situation as an artist within that milieu Walcott automatically explores the consequences of history in the region. In several essays and critical writings he has also grappled dialectically with the meaning of history and created an illuminating and coherent line of thought against which his poetry may be fruitfully explored. His major essay, "The Muse of History," is, for instance, an argument about the ways in which the linear structures of history and fiction may confine and limit experience and create an inevitability which may leave West Indian people chained to the particular time and space of a negative history.

Although the poetic mode freed him from the constraining linearity of fiction and history Walcott's own philosophical understanding of the meaning of history had pushed him towards the despair of determinism before his later realization that "the vision of progress is the rational madness of history seen as sequential time."[1] For a writer who began with a sense of history as heroism and achievement and who had once felt that landscape and history had failed him,[2] Walcott comes a long way in the views of history he articulates in "The Muse of History" and *Another Life*.

The evolution of such a vision has been gradual in Walcott's work, beginning with a widening sense of the meaning of history in the Caribbean and an appreciation of the human history of suffering, endurance, and possibility in the region. Walcott's distrust of linear time, his vision of the past as timeless, and his conception of history as myth can be seen as the climax of his groping and exploration in the early stages of his poetic career. The vision of history which he eventually articulates in "The Muse of History" frees him from the restrictions of time and allows his historical and artistic imagination the freedom to move through the ruins of great civilizations unencumbered, seeing everything as renewed.

In Walcott this freedom from the restrictions of time has been facilitated by the medium of poetry, the genre within which he has generally operated. For unlike realist fiction, which must describe and narrate events, giving the illusion of life lived in a certain time and space, poetry can extricate itself from linearity to portray only the moment, only the particular intuition and illumination. This freedom from "realistic" portrayal which the poetic mode allows has enabled Walcott to explore varied relationships to the history of the Caribbean as he has struggled to transcend its linearity and inevitability. The nature and form of his poetry have been greatly influenced by the twists and turns of his relationship to history, though paradoxically he has also tried throughout his work to minimize the relevance of "history" in the Caribbean, preferring to see the region's problem as essentially a creative one: "What would deliver (the New World Negro) from servitude was the forging of a language that went beyond mimicry, a dialect which had the force of revelation as it invented names for things . . . one which began to create an oral culture of chants, jokes, folk-songs and fables; this, not merely the debt of history, was his [the Caribbean man's] proper claim to the New World."[3]

The "debt of history" is what Walcott sees as the uncreative "rage for revenge," which in its veneration of and servitude to historical time sees history only in terms of subject and object, of the oppressor and the oppressed. In rejecting such a relation to history Walcott favors a tougher aesthetic which would neither explain nor forgive history and which would in fact refuse to recognize it as a creative or culpable force in the region, an aesthetic that would invent the New World anew and acquire the faith to use the old names anew. To do this, he had to rid himself of the "debt of history," to "return through a darkness whose terminus is amnesia . . . [make] the journey back from man to ape . . . to articulate his origin, but for those who have been called not men but mimics, the darkness must be total, and should not contain a single man-made mnemonic object. Its noises should be elemental, the roar of rain, ocean, wind and fire. Their first sound should be like the last, the cry. The voice must grovel in search of itself, until gesture and sound fuse and the blaze of their flesh astonishes them."[4]

For Walcott the "debt to history" and the deterministic view of it as time are countered by the potential of the elemental man, a man outside history yet capable of inhabiting various historical moments without reference to time. In this affirmation of the elemental, Walcott links himself to the historical perspective of a New World tradition rooted in nineteenth-century American perceptions of history: the sense of a break with the past, the belief in the possibility of new beginnings, and the whole Edenic metaphor of the elemental mark an intellectual repudiation of a deterministic past. The philosophy beyond such perceptions, Walcott argues, is not a regression into the innocence of a noble savage but a tough and deliberate act of creation inspired by the faith to name and possess the landscape anew, a creative effort that Walcott believes has the force of revelation and can generate a sensibility strong enough to overcome the ravages and negations of the past.

Yet in spite of this sense of the New World's "Adamic" potential, Walcott is also aware of the imprint of "history," of a historically determined disability peculiar to Caribbean man. He is aware, for instance, of the sense of insecurity caused by a brutalizing and crippling slave and colonial past as well as an absence of tradition and historical continuity. His problem then has been to reconcile a vision that annihilates history with one that is determined by history. The entire course of his creativity and poetic development has progressed towards such a reconciliation; and though the process has been gradual, tortuous, and occasionally even despairing, it has enabled him to engage creatively with history and create a poetic language beyond mimicry.

In Walcott this struggle with "history" and an elemental vision has covered several phases, and, like most West Indian perceptions of the subject, began with a sense of loss. Behind the images of isolation, poverty, and dereliction; behind the empty rituals of religion and the imitative habits of the people in "Laventville" lies Walcott's sense of coherence and certainty lost through the aberration of the Middle Passage:

> Something inside is laid wide like a wound,
> some open passage that has cleft the brain,
> some deep, amnesiac blow. We left
> somewhere a life we never found,
> customs and gods that are not born again.[5]

Walcott does not necessarily particularize what is lost, nor does he dramatize, as Brathwaite does in *Rights of Passage,* the image of a receding past and consciousness. For him the loss of place, self, and identity is subsumed in the all-encompassing image of the "amnesiac blow" which strips and denudes the New World man of his past but also leaves him with the possibility of new creation. Thus in Walcott's "Laventville" the survivor of the Middle Passage is caught in a limbo between two worlds, neither of which he truly possesses. The ironic juxtaposition of images of death and birth, especially in the suggestion implied in "swaddling cerements," projects not just the finality of the break and the amnesia of the race but also the absence of a new birth:

> some crib, some grille of light
> clanged shut on us in bondage, and withheld

us from that world below us and beyond,
and in its swaddling cerements we're still bound.[6]

This sense of the past both in "Laventville" and the rest of *The Castaway* does not begin and end in the vacuum of amnesia but rather looks forward to a birth which may still be trapped in the ravaged history of the islands. It is this dual sense of void and possibility that underlies Walcott's evocation of the Caribbean landscape and becomes the basis of his delineation of the "castaway" persona in the anthology. Thus the physical ravages evoked in "The Swamp," the sense of destitution and chaos which the landscape reflects, symbolize on one level the amnesiac history of the region. The swamp begins nothing and is linked to nothing. "Limbo of cracker convicts, Negroes,"[7] it represents not just the chaos of the landscape but the cultural absence and the void of the castaway's condition. In a similar evocation of absence in the poem "Air" he blames this destitution on the blankness of a landscape without memory or mythology:

> Long, long before us,
> those hot jaws like an oven
> steaming, were open
> to genocide; they devoured
> two minor yellow races and
> half of a black.

Like the "Fearful original sinuosities" of the swamp, the forest evoked in "Air" is a devourer, a force that obliterates all traces of the indigenous American tribes. Its

> shell-like noise
> which roars like silence, or
> ocean's surpliced choirs
> entering its nave, to a censer
> of swung mist, is not
> the rustling of prayer
> but nothing; milling air.[8]

For Walcott the barrenness of a landscape without a mythology, as well as the negative destructive effects of an imposed religion and culture, add up to a "blankness" which is the inheritance of Caribbean man, that from which he should create a new birth. It is for this reason that even in a negative poem like "The Swamp" the mangrove sapling with its obscene roots has in all its chaos, perversion, and negation a potential for birth, concealing

within its clutch, the mossbacked toad,
Toadstools, the potent ginger-lily,
Petals of blood.[9]

This vision of amnesia and possibility counteracts Brathwaite's and Lamming's view of a tribal memory and rejects as well Harris's notion of a primal cosmic memory. Its implications challenge Harris's view that a primal consciousness exists outside the material consciousness of space and time, which can become a source of Caribbean consciousness and identity. Walcott denies the possibilities of such a memory. His poem "The Voyage Up River," ironically dedicated to Harris, separates the experience of Harris's crew from the "real" situation of Caribbean man:

On that vague expedition did their souls
Spawn, vaporous as butterflies, in resurrection,

Or the small terrors multiply like tadpoles
Below a mangrove root or a headstone?

Stillborn in death, their memory is not ours,
In whom the spasm of birth

Gendered oblivion.[10]

Here, the confrontation with the primordial enacts no rebirth, reveals no mythic memory, only chaos, "an aboriginal fear" which is the "nothing" from which the Caribbean must create.

Like Harris, Walcott does confront the elemental, but he does so not to seek a mythical memory but to generate a rebirth and a new consciousness through a personal effort of creation. A great deal of his poetry in *The Castaway* explores this attempt at a genesis, revealing just how individual and personal the effort can be.

If I listen I can hear the polyp build,
The silence twanged by two waves of the sea,
Cracking a sea-louse, I make thunder split.[11]

The "castaway" figure, alone in the vast seascape, confronts the elemental not to inhabit an original mythic memory but to observe and imitate the creative principle in the cosmic. Witnessing the minutely slow process of the coral's growth, he is moved to imitate its creative force, moved to become his own god.

In "A Tropical Bestiary," the poet, seeking similar creative powers, looks to the natural world for a principle which could help him order the chaos of his landscape. His unraveling of the order and pattern of natural law as it operates in animal functions leads him to similar conclusions about human nature and its potentialities. The balance he discovers between potency and impotence, between plenitude and depletion; the coexistence he notices in the natural scheme of complexity and plainness, of terror and innocence, reconcile him to a natural law of existence and to the chaos and perversity that exist with the "greenness" of the landscape. From these perceptions, the poet as "Adam," "Crusoe," and "Friday" attempts to interpret his green world, to invent a language and forge a mythology through an individual act of the mind; and his isolation in the "mind's dark cave"[12] engenders an inner probing and self-discovery which inspire his perceptions and insights. Behind this mode of creativity is, of course, the assumption that amnesia leaves the Caribbean poet with no models, that the colonial past may offer only the dead metaphors of an imposed tradition.

Yet even in these early stages Walcott's dependence on the elemental reveals its particular problems. Creating new symbols, myths, and metaphors through the individual act of imagination is a struggle that can be undertaken by only a few special minds. The attainment of godhood and the imitation of elemental creative forces dramatized so hopefully in "The Castaway" is, after all, only possible in fleeting, isolated instances. For man cannot achieve complete godhood without discarding the material world in which he lives. So Walcott, even in these early "Castaway" poems, probes his way towards an enlargement of his conception of history and begins to look to other kinds of experience as evidence of history and sources for metaphor.

It seems all too obvious from the poems in Walcott's first two anthologies that from the beginning he had, as he himself confesses in *Another Life,* seen "history" through the sea-washed eyes "of his choleric, ginger-haired headmaster"[13] as an account of battles, conquests, and heroic deeds. This rather juvenile and limited understanding of history broadens into a larger vision in *The Castaway* and progresses into a fully fledged concept by the end of *Another Life.* It is possible, for instance, to trace a development in Walcott's understanding of history from *In a Green Night* through *The Castaway* to *The Gulf* and *Another Life.* His despondency at the failures of New World history, his disappointment with its lack of heroism and significant ruins are revealed in a poem like "Ruins of a Great House," in which he not only laments the failure of potential but also expresses a sense of waste and regret at the absence of nobility, heroism, and achievement.

Stones only, the *disjecta membra* of this Great House,

. . . .

Remain to file the lizard's dragonish claws;
. . . .
A smell of dead lines quickens in the nose
The leprosy of Empire.[14]

Behind the anger and bitterness which Walcott finally resolves at the end of the poem is a lurking sense of history as heroic achievement, measured in artifacts and bequeathed to generations through time. There is an interesting paradox, for instance, in the comparison with Greece and America and in the contrast drawn between "Marble as Greece, like Faulkner's south in stone" and "Deciduous beauty prospered and is gone."[15] The poem's subtle changes in tone and its final resolution are not only movements from bitterness to compassion but also an enlargement of perspective on what constitutes history in the Caribbean. The poet's recognition that the leprosy of empire and the humanistic traditions of its conquerors represent ambiguous strands of a historical heritage which he must reconcile is an admission of the different and uniquely paradoxical nature of his heritage.

In another confrontation in the same anthology, Walcott grapples with a similar relation to history. His evocation of the Vigie landscape in "Roots" assumes a tone of epic grandeur as he imagines himself the St. Lucian Homer, uncovering the glory and beauty behind historic ruins. The style of narration and the allusions used surround Vigie with epic proportions that transform it into Aegean mythology, a grandeur compared to which the racial quarrels alluded to in "Ruins" are "blown like smoke to sea."[16]

This idea of history as heroism and achievement is never entirely obliterated from Walcott's works, and it is possible even as late as *Another Life* to find him caught in the fever of heroic example. Thus in the midst of his own sarcasm against "A history of ennui, defense, disease,"[17] he can still render the epic leap to death of the Caribs at Sauteurs, that act of defiance by which these aborigines chose death and annihilation over submission and slavery. The transition in *Another Life* from "Nostalgia! Hymns of battles not our own"[18] to the "epic" evocation in the same poem of the heroism of the Caribs which he can at least appropriate reveals a waning of the poet's fascination with imperial history but at the same time suggests a continuing interest in heroic feats and epic achievements as important marks of history. Indeed, Walcott finds himself driven in this poem to the same elevation that had transformed the Vigie landscape to classical mythology in "Roots":

I am pounding the faces of gods back into the red clay they
leapt from with the mattock of heel after heel as if heel
after heel were my thumbs that once gouged out as sacred

vessels for women the sockets of eyes, the deaf howl
of their mouths and I have wept less for them dead than I did
when they leapt from my thumbs into birth . . .
. . . .
    I am one
with the thousand runners who will break on loud sand
at Thermopylae, one wave that now cresting must bear
down the torch of this race, . . .[19]

Yet in the long run even this kind of mythologizing which the poet can
appropriate becomes only a cold comfort. "The classics can console. But
not enough,"[20] and traditional European mythologies and forms cannot
save the islands from their historical scars. It is thus a mark of Walcott's
maturing vision that he can move beyond heroism, beyond a conventional
and restricted concept of history into a larger all-encompassing vision. In
"The Almond Trees" the tension between history as achievement and history as ordinary living seems momentarily resolved as Walcott defies conventional history to assert the ordeal and survival of the twisted, coppery
sea-almond trees as history. The "nothingness" that echoes Naipaul and
denotes the absence of ruins is by the end of the poem mythologized and
transformed into a human history of endurance and creation. The sea-
almond trees, like the poet's slave ancestors, survive a curing as worthy of
recording in history as the heroism of the Caribs on Sauteurs.

A sense of the relationship between the West Indian's present and past
progresses in the course of the poem into an evocation of the nature of that
past, a mythical evocation in which landscape and setting combine with
image to suggest the quality of West Indian inheritance. Seascape and physical nature define the boundaries of the Caribbean, separating it from the
Atlantic and from Africa. The configuration of sand and ocean—

    cold sand
    cold churning ocean, the Atlantic,
    no visible history.[21]

—returns us to the setting of "The Castaway" and "Crusoe's Journal," in
which the poet, perched between "ocean" and "green, churning forest,"[22]
takes on the roles of Adam, Crusoe, and Friday in an attempt to invent a
new mythology and language. In "The Almond Trees" the poet's conception of the basis of the new myth and language is widened and made to
extend the imperial past, beyond even the self-creative efforts of the "Castaway," to encompass a sense of the slave past. Here memory of the past
does not, as in "Laventville," stop at the horrors of the "hot corrugated
iron sea" and the poet's sense of anguish and loss; it becomes a central

positive vision, opening up possibilities for exploration and self-discovery. The symbolic linking of the coppery sea-almond trees, the slave ancestors, and the suntanned flesh of the girls, mythologized and enhanced by the Daphne myth,[23] establishes a less anguished and more positive identity between the present and the slave past. The experience of slavery itself, mirrored in the crucial images of "the furnace" and "the smithy," is conceived as a process that burns but shapes and toughens, as well:

> The fierce acetylene air
> has singed
> their writhing trunks with rust,
>
> . . . .
> but their aged limbs have got their brazen sheen
> from fire. Their bodies fiercely shine!
> They are cured,
> They endured their furnace.[24]

Walcott's emphasis here, even as he uses the slave past as a positive beginning, is on transformation and re-creation. The totality of the slave's uprooting, imaged in words like "naked," "stripped," and "lashed raw," combines with the setting to emphasize the separation from Africa and the new and unique metamorphoses. This experience of "The Almond Trees," which Walcott offers in place of "Ruins" and "visible history" as a base for consciousness and identity, originates in the experience of slavery and colonialism but has the potential to become the basis of a new, redefined Caribbean consciousness. This is the potential which he explores in "Crusoe's Journal," in which he dramatizes the gradual process by which Friday, the descendant of the slave, appropriates his master's language and forges new names and new associations for the old words of his master. The poet, in his role as Friday and Crusoe, enacts this process, combining the hermetic skill of the "Castaway" with this new sense of origin and identity to reinterpret his experience:

> parroting our master's
> style and voice, we make his language ours,
> converted cannibals,
> we learn with him to eat the Flesh of Christ.[25]

Izevbaye has pointed to an interesting use of irony in "The Castaway" poems as the "telescoping of a double consciousness"; the technique can be linked not only to the poet's hermetic skills but also to the new consciousness created by his widening vision of Caribbean history.[26] The double meanings implied in old concepts like "conversion" and "cannibal" reflect the poet's movement from the condition of slave and parrot to a new sense of himself as the African, "stripped of [his] name, tagged with Greek and Roman names," "washed out with salt," "fire-dried," and now appropriating the master's hermetic skill

> . . . to shape . . . where nothing was
> the language of a race.[27]

It is from such a consciousness that words like "conversion," "cannibal," and "flesh" acquire double meanings; it is from this perspective, for instance, that conversion comes to mean not just the molding into a different faith but also a personal development that perceives the contradictions and failures in the new faith itself. The associations which Walcott introduces to link cannibalism and the Christian practice of communion convey a judgment and a criticism that present Friday as a separate personality. They demonstrate his new modes of perception and his willingness to remain on his master's ground from the angle of his new identity.

This sense of identity, I suggest, is the basis of Walcott's new consciousness and the spur to the development in vision and form which permeates his poetry from *The Gulf* to *Another Life*. From now on, the new consciousness progresses at the same time as the poet's fascination with the "moon" decreases, until by *Another Life*, Walcott, settling for the "resinous" smell of country sweat, attempts to

> shake off the cerecloths,
> to stride from the magnetic sphere of legends,
> from the gigantic myth
> . . . .
> for a future without heroes,
> to make out of these foresters and fishermen
> heraldic men![28]

Correspondingly, in *The Gulf* there is a definite shift from or rather an added dimension to the isolated position of the "castaway" poet, a movement from the "mind's dark cave"[29] and the hermetic world of pure poetry into a sociocultural setting and towards familiar, everyday experience. There is in addition a marked waning of a fascination with the moon, symbolic in the poet's mind of the mesmerizing power of whiteness. For Walcott not only enacts a symbolic journey from sea to land, asserting the poetic potentialities of the familiar world—

there's terror enough in the habitual,
miracle enough in the familiar. Sure . . .[30]

—but also attempts to shake off the mesmerizing power of the moon and
the "lolling Orphic head," symbol of the introspective poet, of self-sufficient creation.

> I watch the moonstruck image of the moon burn,
> a candle mesmerized by its own aura,
> and turn
> my hot, congealing face, towards that forked mountain
> which wedges the drowned singer.
>
> That frozen glare,
> that morsured, classic petrification.
> Haven't you sworn off such poems for this year,
> and no more on the moon?[31]

By extension, the moon also becomes for Walcott a physical, concrete
image of the power of whiteness, the gripping power that engenders the
mixture of yearning and resentment which perpetually plagues the black
West Indian. The poet's confrontation with its power, especially in *The
Gulf, Another Life,* and *Dream on Monkey Mountain,* is, I suggest, the
direct result of the sense of origin grasped from the vision of history developed in "The Almond Trees." From his new appreciation of the human
history of the Caribbean, Walcott can see the moon as the source of the
cultural and psychological confusions of the colonial mind. In the three
different passages quoted from *Another Life* the emphasis is on the monumental power of the moon and its capacity to mesmerize and confuse the
colonial:

> The last hill burned
> the sea crinkled like foil,
> a moon ballooned up from the Wireless Station. O
> mirror, where a generation yearned
> for whiteness, for candor, unreturned.
>
> Above the cemetery where
> the airstrip's tarmac ended
> her slow disc magnified
> The life beneath her like a reading-glass.

Well, everything whitens
all the town's characters, its cast of thousands
arrested in one still
As if a sudden flashbulb showed their deaths.
. . . .
They have soaked too long in the basin of the mind,
they have drunk the moon-milk
that X-rays their bodies.[32]

All three quotes concretize the moon's power and emphasize its capacity to define, hypnotize, and petrify. Its enormous white disc is in all the stanzas the attraction that turns the island on its axle, plunging it into unreality, inducing feelings that can never be reciprocated and ultimately generating the self-contempt that is the curse of the island's black population. The poet's own movement from the moon's hypnotic clutches (he was her subject, changing when she changed) towards his recognition of its deadly powers and to the symbolic obliteration of its lure in *Dream on Monkey Mountain* runs parallel to his widening vision of history in the Caribbean. This acceptance of the past and its metamorphosis becomes part of the confidence from which he allows his dreamer/protagonist in *Dream* to destroy the moon's image.

The distance which Walcott puts between himself and the moon's power is paralleled by a new closeness to the banal and commonplace rhythms of actual experience. No longer, it seems, would the poet declare, even with a qualification, as he does in "Crusoe's Island":

Fanned by the furnace blast
Of heaven, may the mind
Catch fire till it cleaves
its mold of clay at last.[33]

For Walcott no longer seeks a private heaven in poetry:

Convinced of the power of provincialism,
I yielded quietly my knowledge of the world
. . . .
commoner than water I sank to lose my name,
This was my second birth.[34]

This new attitude towards poetry, with its assumptions about the poet's function and role in society, is born out of a sense of history. The poet's awareness of the valid human history of the Caribbean opens up several possibilities for exploration and self-discovery, and *The Gulf* thus becomes the collection in which Walcott examines himself as a poet in society. The world of *The Gulf*, whether in the Americas, England, or the West Indies, is a frayed and decaying world aptly symbolized in the beginning poem by the frayed tide, fretted with mud and by the

> shoreline littered
> with rainbow muck, the afterbirth
> of industry . . .[35]

It is a world marked by widening and alienating gulfs in human relationships, by separations between societies, landscapes, and people, and within individual psyches. Walcott presents these separations as decidedly more sinister than the "dangerous currents of dividing grief"[36] which separate regions and societies in an early poem, "A Map of the Antilles." Here in *The Gulf* divisions and alienation are brought on by hatreds and violence and by the entrenchment of fixed, narrow identities which reject the promise of a humanistic and federated world. The poet's feeling of isolation and rejection in *The Gulf* are, for instance, undercut by the New World's ideals of humanism and expansiveness to which both America and the Caribbean are historically linked. The American South feels like home to the poet:

> But fear
> thickened my voice, that strange, familiar soil
> pricked and barbed the texture of my hair
> my status as a secondary soul
> The Gulf, your gulf, is daily widening.[37]

The same sense of alienation is revealed in "Exile," in which the Caribbean emigrant claims cultural kingship and historical affinity with England yet suffers rejection from the closed doorways of British worlds. These alienating shadows in human relations are corroborated in the landscapes of history. The framework of absence and destitution which they represent reflects that failure of history and ideal which the poet laments throughout the collection. The forest in "Air" is not only devoid of pantheon and mythology but is like "The Swamp," linked to nothing, having devoured the Carib "petal by golden petal" and left the Arawak without.

> . . . the lightest fern-trace
> of his fossil to be cultured
> by black rock,
> but only the rusting cries

of a rainbird, like a hoarse
warrior summoning his race
from vaporous air
between this mountain ridge
and the vague sea.[38]

It is within such absences and failures of history that Walcott explores
the transcendent possibilities of the artistic imagination as he examines his
own poetry in relation to a redefined view of history:

if the shoreline longs sadly for spires,
there is nothing left for us
but to make these coarse lilies lotuses,
for filth to contemplate its own reflection.[39]

Walcott's recognition of the social dimensions of poetry and of the poet's
capacity to transform and shape the image of his generation leads him to
explore such possibilities and examine both the impact and the purpose of his
own poetry. Even within the despondent moods of a poem like "Exile," in
which he laments the artist's isolation and alienation from Britain in spite of
his indenture to her words, he is at the same time aware of his ability to
transcend the gulf through the potent transforming power of his imagination. The artist in "Exile" transforms isolation and void into visions of identity, uncurling prose that validates a separate identifiable self and world.

. . . earth began to look
as you remembered her,
. . . .
a world began to pass
through your pen's eye,
between bent grasses and one word
for the bent rice.
. . . .
the bullock's strenuous ease is mirrored
in a clear page of prose,
a forest is compressed in a blue coal,
or burns in graphite fire,
invisibly your ink nourishes
leaf after leaf the furrowed villages.[40]

In other sections of *The Gulf* Walcott moves beyond the poet's ability to
imagine his world, to explore his particular reaction to it as an artist. The
engagement is crucial, because in certain sections of *The Gulf* Walcott does

question the social impact of his style of poetry and wonders whether it could transform his people's anger as well as give them an image of themselves. The depressing tones of "Homecoming: Anse la Raye" and the self-doubts in "Nearing Forty" address this aspect of the poet's relation to his people and express misgivings about the import of his style of poetry. The metaphors and style of "Homecoming" enact the alienating shadows between poet, landscape, and people, distancing poet from people in the arrangement of words and images. Here, the absence of rapport is enacted as a problem of style. For even within the social and historical perspectives of *The Gulf* the poet seems too anxious about the modulations of his own voice, by the rhythmic flow of his lines and the accuracy of his rhyme, and these anxieties demonstrate an overindulgence of art and threaten to stall his hope to provide a vision for his people.

> You give them nothing.
> Their curses melt in air,
> The black cliffs scowl,
> the ocean sucks its teeth,
> like that dugout canoe
> a drifting petal fallen in a cup,
> with nothing but its image,
> you sway, reflecting nothing.[41]

The kind of failure which Walcott identifies here relates to his self-doubts in "Nearing Forty" and to the perspectives of those poems in which he explores his relation to the people and his own function as a poet in society. Thus the poems "Hawk" and "Mass Man" grapple with the nature of his relationship to the collective experience of the people, in this case, the folk expressions of "parang" and "carnival." In both poems Walcott presents two visions of the ceremonies: the vision enacted by the general mass of revelers (a gloating euphoric projection of hedonism, fantasy, and blind, often cruel abandon) and the tough, discriminating vision forced into this projection by the meditative poet.

Indeed, the poet's attitudes and conclusions differ from one poem to the other, for in his working out of these attitudes to history, "Mass Man" seems to be a development of his position in "Hawk." The mass enactment of "parang" in "Hawk" remains on the level of hysteria, exultation, and hedonism, a totally undiscriminating vision which the poet re-creates in order to reject and destroy. Walcott uncovers the fantastical world of the revelers to reveal the wreckage of their lives as well as the reality of their historical relationship with the old masters:

the negroes, bastards, mestizos,
proud of their Spanish blood,
of the flesh, dripping like wires,
praising your hook, gabilan.
Above their slack mouths the hawk
floats tautly out of the cedars,
leaves the limbs shaking.[42]

In "Mass Man" the poet's attitude is slightly different. The subtle network of associations in the poem reveals his double vision of carnival, and
the implied dialogue between him and the revelers suggests both involvement and withdrawal, pointing to a personal working out of a relationship
to this aspect of Caribbean expression. There is on one hand a vision of
carnival as a "creative" self-expression, and on the other as an excess of
fantasy:

What metaphors!
what coruscating, mincing fantasies!

The association of carnival with "metaphors" and with the brilliant, dazzling, and witty implications of "coruscating" and "mincing" define it as a
"creative" self-expression, not perhaps unlike the poet's own art of painting and writing.

"Join us," they shout, "O God, child, you can't dance?"
. . . .
But I am dancing, look, from an old gibbet
my bull-whipped body swings, a metronome!
Like a fruit-bat dropped in the silk cotton's shade
my mania, my mania is a terrible calm.[43]

Walcott's manipulation of words like "dancing" and "mania" and his
successful incorporation of carnival/folk language into his poem may suggest a personal participation, but he is in many respects separated from the
dancers and is sufficiently in control of himself to transcend their blind
abandon and their excess of fantasy. Although this stanza and the poem's
last have often been quoted to illustrate Walcott's rejection of a philistine
carnival mentality, they seem to me to represent a more subtle definition of
his relationship to "history" and of his role as a poet in society than a
mere contemptuous condemnation. Patricia Ismond has observed that "As
[Walcott] watches the frenetic gaiety behind the carnival extravaganza, he
is conscious of the emptiness behind it all; and the sensuality, devoid of any

significance beyond the most philistine type of self-indulgence, assumes
sinister resonances. So that the child 'rigged like a bat,' far from experienc-
ing any genuine merriment, is aware of the absurd scene of its isolation."[44]

Ismond's argument may well reveal an aspect of Walcott's view of carnival, but it does not in my view exhaust all the metaphorical implications of
the last two stanzas and consequently fails to grasp the poet's more significant dialogue with himself about his relationship to history and his role
in the development of an "aesthetic." His image of himself as the "bull-
whipped" body of a slave, swinging from an old gibbet and registering time
like a "metronome," the image which he summons as evidence of his "participation" in carnival, is a contrast to the "frenetic gaiety" of the revelers
and a reminder of the bitter historical truths which their fantastical masks
conceal. The intrusive image is thus a deliberate reference to the poet's role
as watchful assessor and recorder of significance. It links logically with the
second image he offers of himself: the image of the fruit bat dropped in the
silk cotton's shade. The bat image, a development from the second stanza,
presents the poet as a survivor, in contrast perhaps to the child rigged like
a bat, who collapses. The poet survives by virtue of his removal from
the glare of the "whirlwind's radiance" into the calm of the 'silk cotton's
shade," and the separation is the distance required by the meditative poet in
the midst of the mass hysteria. It does not represent an outright and total
separation. Indeed, the last stanza "involves" the poet even more closely in
the expression, portraying him not just as the assessor and recorder but also
as the sacrificial conscience of his society:

Upon your penitential morning,
some skull must rub its memory with ashes,
some mind must squat down howling in your dust,
some hand must crawl and recollect your rubbish,
someone must write your poems.[45]

The figurative reference to Ash Wednesday may thus not only suggest, as
Ismond argues, the humanistic poet's outrage at the violation and self-des-
ecration behind the frenzied jollity but also point to the poet's role as at
once the assessor, conscience, and "victim" of his society's innocence.

Walcott's position in "Mass Man" seems a progression, a development
of the situation of the isolated artist in *The Castaway.* The isolation and
separateness that shape his perceptions and give him an insight into society
in the "Castaway" poems are evident here in "Mass Man," as well. What
is novel and significant is the poet's new relationship to his society and its
expression. Whereas the isolated poet in "The Castaway" often remained

and "triumphed" in his separateness and noncommunication, the poet of "Mass Man" is separate yet peculiarly involved in the society's destiny. There is quite a difference, for instance, between the point of view of the observing artist in a poem like "The Wedding of an Actress" and the point of view of the artist, recorder, assessor, and victim in "Mass Man":

Through the illusion of another life,
I can observe this custom like a ghost,
Watching the incense snaking overhead
Dissolving like the water laid
In wine along the tongue,
Hearing their promise buried in this vault,
Their lines drawn in the surges of a song.[46]

Here in "The Wedding of an Actress" the poet is separate from the group by virtue of his greater awareness and perceptiveness, but because the larger group itself appears hypnotized, overpowered and smothered by an alien and destructive religion, his noncommunication becomes a triumph of his isolation. In "Mass Man" he is also separated from the crowd by virtue of his greater perception, but he is neither the "ghostly" observer nor the wry ironist, "safe" in his other life of art and loneliness. He is recorder, assessor, victim all at once, and his position is influenced by the overall point of view of *The Gulf* with its new sense of the potentialities of the Caribbean's human history and its new appreciation of the "miracle" in the familiar and the "terror" in the habitual.

But in the context of the historical insights gained in "The Almond Trees" and extended throughout *The Gulf*, both "Hawk" and "Mass Man" represent a somewhat negative awareness. The undiscerning revelers remain unconscious of the complex historical and human factors that have forged the Creole personality and soul. In spite of their wit, color, and "creativity," the mass players appear untouched by the depths of history and unaware of the

    . . . something rooted, unwritten
    that gave us its benediction,
    its particular pain . . .[47]

Only the poet seems to relate the expression of carnival to the past and the future; only he appears to bear the burden of this necessary correlation. Does Walcott then resign himself to the "gulf" that separates him from the people, and does the acceptance propel him to forge the uncreated conscience of his race in terms of his own perspective? This seems to me the burden that he takes on in *The Gulf* and *Another Life*, a burden which in both anthologies involves him in an inescapable confrontation with history.

Thus in the "Guyana sequence" of *The Gulf,* for instance, history assumes wider, more complex proportions for the poet, becoming a confrontation not only with historical, cultural presences but also with mythic presences inherent in the aboriginal landscape. His symbolic journey into the Guianese interior reveals not the milling vaporous air between the mountain ridge

> and the vague sea
> where the lost exodus
> of corials sunk without trace.[48]

It reveals all the possibilities inherent in the landscape which could quicken his own consciousness and by extension the consciousness of his people. His lexicographer in "A Map of the Continent," like the naked buck, traverses an unexplored world the interior of which, like the aboriginal world of Carpentier's *The Lost Steps,* harbors traces of myth and traditions which the New World persona can claim and appropriate. This, for Walcott, is part of the mythohistorical legacy of the New World, the creative basis of a new naming of things and a historical consciousness.

> The lexicographer in his cell records the life and death of books;
> the naked buck waits at the edge of the world,
>
> One hefts a pen, the other a bone spear;
> between them curls a map.
> between them curl the vigorous, rotting leaves,
>
> shelves forested with titles, trunks that wait for names—
> . . . .
> Between the Rupunini and Borges,
> between the fallen pen-tip and the spear-head
> thunders, thickens and shimmers the one age of the world.[49]

In *Another Life* the satisfaction and exhilaration which Walcott and Gregorias feel in their work come out of their attempts to respond to and possess the landscape. There is a sense of wonder and surprise at the realization that the landscape could hold such possibilities.

> For no one had yet written of this landscape
> that it was possible, though there were sounds

given to its varieties of wood;
. . . .
whole generations died, unchristened,
growths hidden in green darkness, forests
of history thickening with amnesia . . .[50]

Here was vegetation with a discernible history which could be reclaimed and
which could become a source of fulfillment and a medium of rootedness:

here was a life older than geography,
as the leaves of edible roots opened their pages
at the child's last lesson, Africa, heart-shaped,

and the lost Arawak hieroglyphs and signs
were razed from slates by sponges of the rain,
their symbols mixed with lichen,

the archipelago like a broken root,
divided among tribes, while trees and men
labored assiduously, silently to become

whatever their given sounds resembled . . .[51]

Here, localized and concretized at last, is the progression of Walcott's call in
"The Muse of History" for a return to the elemental. Here, the elemental is
extended and impregnated with meaning to include landscapes of history
and mythic presence which may become the sources of a Caribbean historical consciousness. This affirmative vision of the landscape as embedded
with history; this sense that a feeling for the land and a responsiveness to its
history can become a meaningful way of rooting oneself, of acquiring an
identity, is also shared by Brathwaite and demonstrated in several poems in
Islands. It is also, interestingly, a point of contention in Naipaul's later
novels and the crucial problem, I think, behind his protagonist's neurosis in
The Mimic Men.

In Brathwaite's "Coral," the first poem in the section in *Islands* entitled
"Possession," the historical landscape is beautifully enacted. The land and
its history rise and take shape before us in the same way as Walcott's landscape does in chapter 8 of *Another Life*. The landscape grows as the coral
dies and adds to it. The "snapped necks" and the medley of dead bodies
metamorphose into new life, and the process continues through time, revealing its moments of bloom—

rain unhooks flowers,
green stars
of the soil stare up from the stalks,

—as well as its periods of pain and gloom—

the sky glints in the wet mud
streaked with trees,
hedges, darker
ponds. I hear the boom
of the mango bursting its sweetness, spectacular
cloud riders through the tall
pouis: walls of white,
walls of red, stations
of blooms, wells
of bottomless
gloom.[52]

And Brathwaite, like Walcott, like Césaire in *Return to My Native Land,*
accepts all, accepts the cyclical process of this historical movement:

And slowly slowly
uncurling embryo
leaf's courses sucking grain's armor
my yellow pain swims into the polyp's eye.[53]

In "The Castaway," Walcott, in direct confrontation with the elemental,
grasps other lessons from the polyp's growth:

If I listen I can hear the polyp build,
The silence twanged by two waves of the sea.
Cracking a sea-louse, I make thunder split.[54]

In these early stages of his development, when he had sought a self-
generative creativity to counter the dead metaphors of an inherited "alien"
tradition, he identified only with such powers within the polyp and strove
to imitate its principle. But his widening vision of Caribbean history, his
appreciation, for instance, of the human history of the Caribbean and of its
possibilities for self-exploration and discovery, gives him a broader vision
of the landscape, so that in "The Almond Trees" his conception of the
elemental extends itself and the landscape reveals its history and its possibilities as

one sunburnt body now acknowledges
that past and its own metamorphosis.[55]

The same acknowledgment is enacted in *Another Life* as Walcott unreservedly embraces landscape, history, and myth in the same wholehearted way that Brathwaite accepts the coral's growth.

In Naipaul's *The Mimic Men* the historical landscape is also a crucial image of identification and rootedness. The possibilities of this identification, romanticized almost, are offered by both Browne and Deschampneufs, two characters differentiated from each other by race and history, for whom the Caribbean landscape has different meanings and connotations. Their conception of history and rootedness appear at first to be possibilities that may cure the protagonist of his alienation from the land. Browne offers a vision of the land that appropriates its slave past and its mythic and elemental associations:

> In the heart of the city Browne showed me a clump of old fruit trees: the site of a slave provision ground. From this point look above the roofs of the city and imagine! Our landscape was manufactured as that of any French or English park. But we walked in a garden of hell, among trees, some still without popular names, whose seeds had sometimes been brought to our island in the intestines of slaves . . . this was what Browne taught. This was the subject of his own secret reading.

Deschampneufs, on the other hand, offers a vision of the land that stresses its unique fauna and its capacity to cushion and define:

> you are born in a place and you grow up there [says the elder Deschampneufs to Singh]. You get to know the trees and plants like that. You grow up watching a guava tree . . . you know that browny-green bark peeling like old paint. You try to climb that tree. You know that after you climb it a few times the bark gets smooth-smooth and so slippery you can't get a grip on it. You get that ticklish feeling in your foot. Nobody has to teach you what the guava is.[56]

But Singh rejects both perspectives of the land, and though his rejection appears at first as a self-condemnation, it is later made explicable by Naipaul's own projection of the landscape as incapable of inspiring this kind of rootedness. For in his evocation of landscape and delineation of people's response to it, Naipaul reveals the whole idea of rootedness as far more complicated and dependent on historical continuity than both Deschampneufs and Browne are prepared to see. In his portrayal, the incongruity between the original and man-made landscape, between the new landscape and the people it holds, is perceived as the aftermath of an original violation which can never be overcome. Indeed, the text demonstrates that it is part of Deschampneuf's innocence that he cannot see the contradiction, for instance, between his slightly sentimentalized concept of rootedness and the reality of "history" that lurks beneath his refusal to shake the hand of the Indian Singh.

The vision that Browne offers is somewhat similar to the perspectives of both Walcott and Brathwaite. The idea that the landscape has mythical presence, historical associations, and elemental connotations which can become part of a Caribbean consciousness and the basis for definition is the same idea explored by both Walcott and Brathwaite. In the same way, the landscape of slavery which Browne tries to differentiate from the manufactured landscape presents opportunities for exploration and definition. Yet in the text Browne is unable to move beyond identification to definition and vision and cannot interpret his own displacement or offer a meaningful vision to the neurotic Singh. Singh's own displaced consciousness rejects such a vision of landscape anyway, because for him, as for Naipaul, the incongruity between the original landscape and the manufactured landscape is more evidence of the shipwreck and violation that are permanent symbols of the reality in *The Mimic Men.*

The vision of the land, of the New World as perpetually tied to historical time, is what Walcott attempts to overcome in *Another Life* and what he categorically rejects in "The Muse of History." "But to most writers of the archipelago who contemplate only the shipwreck, the New World offers not elation but cynicism, a despair at the vices of the Old which they feel must be repeated. Their malaise is an oceanic nostalgia for the older culture and a melancholy at the new . . . a rejection of the untamed landscape, a yearning for ruins."[57] Yet, as Walcott argues in the same essay, the New World should signify something different and new, the beginning not the end of history.

The raison d'être behind this vision of man in the New World is derived from a developing concept of history, which is of special importance to Walcott's progress as a West Indian poet: "The Muse of History," which is an amplification and development of ideas in the earlier essay "What the Twilight Says," crystallizes a view of history which offers a revealing judgment on Walcott's own earlier work as well as the works of his contemporaries and other New World poets. The concept first takes shape as a rejection of the idea of history as time, around the implications of which Walcott himself has operated in his early works: "the method by which we are taught the past, the progress from motive to event, is the same by which we read narrative fiction. In time every event becomes an exertion of memory and is thus subject to invention . . . Thus, as we grow older as a race, we grow aware that history is written, that it is a kind of literature without morality, that in its actuaries the ego of the race is indissoluble and that everything depends on whether we write this fiction through the memory of hero or victim."[58]

This vision of Caribbean man as tied to his past becomes a dead end: this new perspective, an unnecessarily limiting vision, confines the New World artist to a literature of remorse or revenge, depending on whether he/she is the descendant of the master or the victim. The literature of revenge, in Walcott's view, is the greatest threat to the creative potential of the New World person, because by presenting him/her as a creature chained to the past, and perhaps with a future already determined by that past, it condemns him/her to the status of object and deprives him/her of the potential of the elemental person, a creature full of presence and capable of elation and wonder in a New World. In the two essays, Walcott details all the uncreative pitfalls of this vision of history: its tendency, for instance, to see language also as history and to limit expression only to the groan of suffering and the curse of revenge, unable to separate the rage of Caliban from the beauty of his speech when it comes to equal the elemental power of his tutor.

Indeed, with the hindsight of maturity and self-criticism, Walcott parodies and holds in irony that aspect of his own work that had reflected this vision of history and its traps:

[Gregorias] had his madness
mine was history.
. . . I prayed . . .
for the clods to break
in epochs, crumbling Albion
in each unshelving scarp,
. . . .
I saw in the glazed, rocking shallows
the sea-wrack of submerged Byzantium,
as the eddies pushed their garbage to this shore.[59]

Another Life, his long poem of remembrance and personal history, moves beyond that tiered concept of the past which defines history only in terms of monuments and cultural artifacts. Here a sense of history as loss is continually balanced against the identification that derives from elation in a new landscape. In a major sense then the poem marks the climax of Walcott's most decisive engagement with history and style and reflects as well some of its ramifications and problems. Often, ideas on history raised and argued in the essays "What the Twilight Says" and "The Muse of History" are reflected not only in the themes but also in the art of composition and styling. The poet's old vision of history as amnesia, his rejection of historical time, and his new vision of man in the New World as elemental all have repercussions on the discourse on history and the language of poetry in *Another Life*. Gregorias and Walcott, the two young artists in the poem, are portrayed as being without history, beginning again like Adam to "name" the landscape and, in the sheer elation and exhilaration of discovery, lighting their world, penning prose, and painting canvasses rooted in the landscape. Theirs, Walcott implies, is the "style past metaphor,"[60] plain, simple craftsmanship rooted in the environment:

> I watched the vowels curl from the tongue of the carpenter's plane,
> resinous, fragrant
> labials of our forests,
> over the plain wood
> the back crouched,
> the vine-muscled wrist,
> like a man rowing,
> sweat-fleck on blond cedar.[61]

Although as Walcott suggests, the two poets create out of a personality shaped by history ("Sunset and dawn like manacles chafed his wrist, / no day broken without chains"), the actual substance of their creation rejects the defining and deterministic power of history. Their evocation of the island in its original state is thus like an attempt to leap across history, to evade the dead ghosts of the past, not by futilely reckoning with them but by recognizing their irrelevance to their creativity:

> Where else to row, but backward?
> Beyond origins, to the whale's wash,
> to the epicanthic Arawak's Hewanora,
> back to the impeachable pastoral,
> praying the salt scales would flake from our eyes
> for a horned, sea-snoring island
> barnacled with madrepore,
> without the shafts of palms stuck in her side.[62]

This is Walcott's ideal vision of the island. "Barnacled with madrepore" (in a natural process) instead of pincers and manacles, the island is without "history," the salt-crusted mythological whale before the harpooner reduced him "from majesty to pygmy size."[63]

On another level, this vision of the land as the first inhabitants may have seen it is an image, a metaphor for the poet's desire to begin again, to create without being hampered by those moments of history which could fix him in a particular mold. These moments and their degradation, Walcott argues, have already been endured to the point of irrelevancy. History is irrelevant, "not because it is not being created, or because it was sordid; but because it has never mattered, what has mattered is the loss of history, the amnesia of the races, what has become necessary is imagination—imagination as necessity, as invention."[64]

The irrelevance of history and the necessity for imagination and invention are indeed the crucial issues in chapter 22 of *Another Life*, although in the development of these ideas Walcott qualifies his statement by making a distinction between the "history" he rejects and the "history" he affirms. This section of *Another Life*, originally published separately as "The Muse of History at Rampanalgas,"[65] crystallizes, develops, and concludes Walcott's ideas on these two issues. The significance of Rampanalgas as the poem's setting has already been commented upon by Edward Baugh,[66] but it is interesting to add that although Rampanalgas returns to the "cold sand and the cold churning ocean,"[67] which in "The Almond Trees" define the boundaries of the island world, it also recalls through its historically unimpressive setting and its images of unwholesome vegetation the atmosphere and mood of "The Swamp." In Walcott's working out of ideas on history in this section of *Another Life*, images are deliberately evoked to confound the historian, worshipper of time and artifacts (there is no sense of continuity and no artifact of history), and to suggest the darkness and nothingness which hold possibilities for imagination and invention.

Here, enacted in poetry, are the basic arguments of Walcott's "The Muse of History." The poet, at his most strident and dismissing, devotes five entire stanzas to parodying the absurd pitfalls of a vision of Caribbean man based on a veneration of historical time. The parodies, some rather exaggerated and others interestingly reflecting certain tendencies of Walcott's own early poetry, magnify the tedium and the uncreativeness of the conventional and linear view of history: the frantic search for primordial presence and mythical memories; the self-defeating longing for artifacts, for the grandeur of a golden age, even with all its cruelties; the tedious recounting and reconstruction of the past; the desire for grandiose landscapes and heroic connections. Walcott opposes these tendencies of the historical preoccupation in the Caribbean to the starkly evoked reality of Rampanalgas, symbol of the New World, and the contrast defines the special and particular situation of the Caribbean and castigates the tendency to relate it to the situation of the old world.

After this release, Walcott's more positive energies are spent on a relentless effort to establish that potential which makes history irrelevant in the New World. He works with the ambivalent symbol of the child without history, without knowledge of its prior world, whose only history and knowledge is the elemental landscape of the Caribbean:

That child who puts the shell's howl to his ear,
hears nothing, hears everything
that the historian cannot hear, the howls
of all the races that crossed the water.[68]

The ambivalence of nothing and everything is the difference between history as the historian sees it and as Walcott knows it to be: a history of human endurance and survival within the boundaries of the Caribbean. To accept this without reference to or longing for ancestral connections is to make amends with history and to possess the New World. Thus, the paradox of nothing and everything is also the paradox of dispossession and possession: "there was such a moment for every individual American, and that moment was both surrender and claim, both possession and dispossession. The issue is the claim."[69]

The poet's commitment in the end is to the lessons of endurance and renewal in the human history of the Caribbean and to the symbols which enact them.

I sit in the roar of that sun.
like a lotus yogi folded on his bed of coals,
my head is circled with a ring of fire.

O sun, on that morning,
did I not mutter towards your
holy, repetitive resurrection, "Hare,
hare Krishna" and then politely,
"Thank you, life?"[70]

The sun, the afternoon light that finally emerges as the truth, the light to which the older, renewed poet dedicates himself at the end of the poem, is the same blare noon which gives the poet its benediction in chapter 7. It is "the fierce acetylene" air that singes the almond trees in *The Castaway* and in a similar connotation, relates to the sunburned body of the girl acknowledging the past and its metamorphosis in "The Almond Trees." This sun, symbol of the truth, source of the poet's creativity and element of his imagination, now becomes an all-embracing symbol of history, not of linear history or of a tiered and ordered history in a conventional sense but the human history of endurance and survival which is the poet's inheritance.

In some respects, though not explicitly stated, the symbol's life-asserting quality establishes it in opposition to the mesmerizing and petrifying power of the moon, the dominant symbol in the early sections of *Another Life* and in Walcott's early poetry. The sun that ripens the valley, whose image characterizes the epiphanic moment of the poet's transfiguration, can now be seen in opposition to the moon that arrests the village in one still.

As if a sudden flashbulb showed their deaths

or to the

. . . moon-milk,
that X-rays their bodies,
the bone tree show(ing)
through the starved skins . . .[71]

As an image of contrast and opposition, the symbol's reverberations also stretch to *The Gulf,* to the poem "Moon" and to the qualities of imagination and creativity which must now separate it from the connotations of the moon's creativity. "[The] lolling Orphic head silently howling / [its] own head [rising] from its surf of cloud / . . . a candle mesmerized by its own aura"[72] would no longer represent a source of ambivalence in the poet's resolution in *Another Life.* The commitment to the sun is more than a commitment to life; it is also a commitment to a certain kind of poetic style, the style past metaphor

. . . that finds its parallels, however wretched
in simple, shining
lines, in pages stretched plain as
a bleaching bedsheet under a guttering rainspout.[73]

The ramifications of Walcott's ambivalent relationship to this style represents a great deal of the drama of *Another Life.* For the social basis of its perspective and its commitment to realistic representation appear to clash with the poet's imaginative need to heighten, re-create, and extend life through metaphor and paradox. A great deal of Walcott's exploration here is therefore geared towards a balancing of opposites, towards a reconciliation of the two stylistic impulses:

> . . . I rendered
> the visible world that I saw
> exactly, yet it hindered me, for
> in every surface I sought
> the paradoxical flash of an instant
> in which every facet was caught
> in a crystal of ambiguities.[74]

Walcott had hoped that the realistic and metaphorical impulses might "by painful accretion cohere / and painfully ignite," but the cohesion had been impossible in painting, and he had finally accepted "failure," recognizing that he "lived in a different gift, / its element metaphor."[75]

The complexities of these tensions and Walcott's attempts at reconciliation are not just limited to the problems of the artist's apprehension and translation of reality; they also involve his conception of time and ultimately his ideas of history. The pull between representing reality as it is and re-creating it in other reflections is also the pull between arresting the moment, the particular time, and seeing the moment represented in all time. The tensions of these oppositions represent the drama of "A Simple Flame," and Walcott's dilemma here hinges on the "truth" of the reality represented. If the poet enlarges, heightens, and idealizes reality, has he betrayed landscape and people? If he sees the moment repeated and renewed in other moments, in all time, does he negate the connotations of that moment?

Walcott's presentation of this dilemma is dramatized in his relationship with his first love, Anna, the sixteen-year-old girl who is also an embodiment of his island. First, he identifies a certain concept of Anna and a particular attitude towards her which is balanced by another conception and attitude:

> when dusk had softened the first bulb
> the color of the first weak star,
> I asked her, "Choose,"
> the amazed dusk held its breath,
> the earth's pulse staggered,
> she nodded, and that nod
> married earth with lightning.[76]

Reflected in the images of these lines is the vision of Anna as the embodiment both of the landscape and of the kind of poetry that is a natural
twinning of environment and language. Against this vision of Anna is the
vision inspired by the poet's need to extend and re-create, to see several
facets embodied in a particular reality. The need, for instance, to perceive
both the calm of the shallop rowing in measured strokes towards Anna's
house and the disturbing bray of the "donkey's rusty winch, / . . . a herring
gull's one creak" renders the bay too heavy for reflection.[77]

The tensions arising out of these opposites are reflected in the ambivalence of the poet's own attitude: his desire on one hand to arrest the moment, to preserve the uniqueness of Anna, and his tendency on the other to
see her as a reflection of other situations, as an embodiment of all love, all
passion:

> The first flush will pass,
> But there will always be morning
> and I shall have this fever waken me
> Whoever I lie to, lying close to, sleeping
> like a ribbed boat in the last shallows of
> night.[78]

The ambivalence of the poet's attitude represents a debate with himself. One part of him rejects this re-creation, rejects the reflection of other
lights and the transcendence of the moment, seeing it as a negation of the
specialness of Anna:

> all that pursuing generality,
> that vengeful conspiracy with nature,
> all that sly informing of objects
> and behind every line, your laugh
> frozen into a lifeless photograph.

But the poet's other voice counteracts this suggestion in the next stanza,
demonstrating that it is possible to see a particular reality or moment renewed and repeated in other situations and at other times.

> In that hair I could walk through the wheatfields
> of Russia,
> Your arms were downed and ripening pears
> for you became, in fact, another country,
>
> You are Anna of the wheatfield and the weir,

You are Anna of the solid winter rain,
Anna of the smoky platform and cold train.[79]

To Anna's accusation that he had made her into a metaphor, represented her as other than she really was ("I became a metaphor, but / believe me I was unsubtle as salt"), the poet presents another view, explaining the relationship between memory and reality and pointing to the imagination's capacity to repeat experiences, to re-create them in other moments: "a man lives half of life, / the second half is memory."[80]

In "A Simple Flame," the ambivalence of these positions is deepened by the poet's realization that the moment itself could be vulnerable and that sometimes preserving it would only mean watching the visionary glare:

tarnish to tin . . . (walking) the kelp-piled beach
and hearing the waves arriving with stale news.[81]

Thus, the poet's desire to be linked to his island even in his absence, his plea to be "doubled by memory," to see his island experience repeated in other ways and at other times, is undercut by reminders of his own past betrayals. When he prays to the Earth-heart—

uproot me, yet
let what I have sworn to love not feel betrayed
when I must go, and if I must go,
make of my heart an ark
let my ribs bear
all, doubled by
memory, down to the emerald fly
marrying this hand, and be
the image of a young man on a pier
his heart a ship within a
ship within a ship, a bottle
where this wharf, these
rotting roofs, this sea
sail, sealed in glass

—the poem's omniscient voice intrudes, reminding him of past rejections and betrayals that must qualify his new commitment:

How often didn't you hesitate
between rose-flesh and sepia
your blood like a serpent whispering
of a race incapable of subtler shadow
of music, architecture and a complex thought.[82]

Yet in the end the poem's resolution seems to me to rest on these very ambiguities. For the poet points to a depth of feeling and empathy with the people that cuts across this ambivalence and which can be repeated and renewed through memory. For this empathy is a quality that can redeem, and the poet, for all his ambivalence, can free his people by returning them unto themselves through the act of "naming" them, of capturing their lives, their grief, their landscape, and their language.

> I knelt because I was my mother
> I was the well of the world
> I wore the stars on my skin
> I endured no reflections.
> My sign was water
> tears and the sea.[83]

Walcott's description of his vocation in these symbols of redemption remind us of his images on another occasion and indeed complete this encircling vision of the nature and function of the creative imagination, giving centrality to the poet as both the mirror and conscience of his society. Yet Walcott's poetry as it has developed in *Another Life* appears to struggle with an ambiguous relationship between the artist's words and the people's consciousness. In some sense his poetry dramatizes the poet's difficulty in activating the consciousness of the people in spite of his elation and his rooted language. The problem as it reveals itself in *Another Life* seems to rest on the artist's own ambivalence towards the people as well as on the tension between his conception of the imagination both as a reflection of the people's life and as a transcendental and self-igniting phenomenon. Although such an ambiguity may appear to question the sufficiency of a philosophy of elation as a historical vision of the West Indies, Walcott seems to me to accept it as a valid enough basis for his function as a poet. In his poetry, the poet is not a priest, as he often appears to be in Brathwaite's poetry; nor is the imagination purged entirely of ego, as it appears to be in Brathwaite's trilogy. In *Islands,* Brathwaite's poet has the character of a shaman, with the burden both of recovering the Word and of moving the people to self-awareness and revolution. In Walcott's poetry the poet carries both the burden of the Word and the burden of the imagination, which by its very nature also carries the poet's ego, the sheer joy and exhilaration in the mind's power to stretch itself and transform reality.

Throughout his poetry after *Another Life* this tension emerges, even as Walcott moves towards a coalition of the two strains through vigorous self-exploration. There is thus on one hand the acknowledgment of rootedness and creative indebtedness to place and on the other an ambiguous relationship to its negative and corrupting ethos. If in *Another Life* the poet had desired to be "doubled by memory," in *The Star-Apple Kingdom* rootedness and memory are themselves complicated by deep disaffection and by feelings of exclusion and impotence. It may appear then that the thrust of the anthology, as the first poem suggests, is towards escape, abandonment, journey. Yet the flight from place in the "The Schooner *Flight*" is actually a movement towards a more intimate grasp of its grief and dilemmas. The protagonist of the poem may well say "I had no nation now but the imagination,"[84] but in the anthology the poetic imagination is itself inspired and energized by response to land, people, and language, and the idea of poetry as solely the personal odyssey of a distanced, introspective poet is offset by the choice of personae whose personal histories embody some of the corruption, contradictions, and paradoxes of the Caribbean itself.

The poet persona in "The Schooner *Flight*" is not only a man of multiple heritage whose ancestry may define a heterogeneous concept of nation more correctly descriptive of the region's history; he also mirrors some of its corruption and evasions. The protagonist of the title poem is similarly a man of self-doubt and inaction whose impotence mirrors the poet's own feelings in most of the poems of the anthology. Such composite representations enlarge the poet's individual dilemmas and widen the dialectic on history, making poetry not solely the "flash of an instant" that catches all facets in ambiguity but the multiple experiences of a region which the poet links together in metaphors to give voice to a people's grief.

The poet in *The Star-Apple Kingdom* is thus both within and out there. Shabine is a common man and a poet who before his journey of insight has evaded confrontation with the ghosts of history, panicking before those images of the past which he encounters at the bottom of the sea. Yet it is his imagination and insight that link and metaphorize the various scenes and experiences during the schooner's journey. His anguished desire for a "rest-place" or "harbor," "the window I can look from that frames my life,"[85] becomes the underlying motif of the journey, as if to suggest that the ground and space needed to make meaning of reality are the islands themselves.

The poet weaves memories, experiences, and insights into metaphors as his imagination attempts to make sense of history and human actions. The failure of transformation (the reason for Shabine's flight) not only haunts the poems but also defines the mood of the anthology. Shabine's memory of corruption in Trinidad, his evocation of isolation and decline in "Sabbaths, WI," and the history of poverty and degeneration in the Jamaica of "The Star-Apple Kingdom" demonstrate the need for transformation, just as other poems enact the dream of transformation. Shabine's hallucinatory vision of poetry's transformative powers finds echoes in the protagonist's hopes of healing the malarial island in "The Star-Apple Kingdom."

Yet revolutionary transformation is never a reality in the anthology. Rather, it is its ambiguities and loopholes that are enacted. In "The Schooner *Flight*" revolution is either the politics of blackness and tribal memory or the powerlessness of young revolutionaries whose

> noise ceased as foam sinks into sand.
> [who] sank in the bright hills like rain,
> . . . leaving shirts in the street,
> and the echo of power at the end of the street.[86]

In "The Star-Apple Kingdom" it is the ambivalent symbols embodied in the female figure who haunts the male figure's remembrance that proffer a vision of revolution. An ambiguous, even contradictory symbol, she is perceived both as a victim and a destroyer whose vision of revolution and history is both a lure and a death trap:

> a black rose of sorrow, a black mine of silence,
> raped wife, empty mother, Aztec Virgin
> transfixed by arrows from a thousand guitars,
> a stone full of silence . . .

Her raped condition sanctions the protagonist's political vision of transformation but at the same time contradicts its ideal as he perceives them: "[Her] voice had the gutturals of machine guns / across khaki deserts where the cactus flower / detonates like grenades."

> . . . Now she stroked his hair
> until it turned white, but she would not understand
> that he wanted no other power but peace,
> that he wanted a revolution without any bloodshed,
> he wanted a history without any memory,
> streets without statues,
> and a geography without myth. . . .[87]

The protagonist's fear of "memory" is a fear of a self-created mythology of Africa that he thinks may have little bearing on present transformations. His vision of the islands as "turtles" in a bobbing trek for the open Atlantic ("they yearned for Africa / they were lemmings drawn by magnetic memory / to an older death, to broader beaches / where the coughing of lions was dumbed by breakers")[88] argues the implications of a Caribbean identity within the Caribbean itself and within the open Atlantic (Africa). Indeed, the protagonist's only act of boldness in the poem is when he cries out against the suicidal yearning for memory, for Africa, with that scream

> which, in his childhood, had reversed an epoch
> that had bent back the leaves of his star-apple kingdom,
> made streams race uphill, pulled the water wheels backwards
> like the wheels in a film . . .[89]

The politician protagonist resists the understanding of history implied in the revolution, just as Walcott resists it in "The Sea Is History" when he defines the boundaries of Caribbean history within the context of the Caribbean itself:

> First, there was the heaving oil,
> heavy as chaos;
> then, like a light at the end of a tunnel,
>
> the lantern of a caravel,
> and that was Genesis.
> Then there were the packed cries,
> the shit, the moaning:
>
> Exodus.
> Bone soldered by coral to bone,
> mosaics
> mantled by the benediction of the shark's shadow.[90]

But the irony here is that within "The Star-Apple Kingdom" there looms a reality the gloom of which pervades the entire anthology, pointing to a crisis both of nationhood and personhood and crying out for radical ways of conceiving self, history, and transformation. The "seashell silence, resounding / with silence"[91] that ends the poem is the silence of an unchanging situation mirrored in the noise of a "government groaning uphill" and in the impotence of the poetic imagination in some of the poems in the anthology.

Lloyd Brown has remarked that the nervousness about sexuality and the pervading aura of impotence in *The Star-Apple Kingdom* are a reflection of the social and political malaise that is the reality of the Caribbean. Citing the sense of insecurity and vulnerability evident in the poem "Egypt, Tobago," he argues that there is an aura of impotence about the love and tenderness that is affirmed as the poem's resolution—"as if it is a mere compensation for the loss of a certain power, the decline of a daring and creative will."[92] Yet there is also ironically some feeling of confidence about poetry's resilience, a deeper understanding of history and a modest perception of the value of poetry within the turmoil of politics and systems. Shabine's earlier self-dramatizing sense of his mission as a poet ("I shall scatter your lives like a handful of sand, / I who have no weapon but poetry and / the lances of palms and the sea's shining shield!")[93] gives way to the quiet benediction at the end and to a sober renewed faith in the value of poetry as that which will not lose sight of the human in the cause. His metaphysical search for the window that frames a life has by the end of the poem defined itself not only as a search for the individual or particularly Caribbean experience but also for the wider and general experience within "archipelagoes of stars."[94]

The flight of the imagination in *The Star-Apple Kingdom* may move towards "a target whose aim we'll never know," but in its context Walcott defines a purpose for his poetry: "I am satisfied / If my hand gave voice to one people's grief."[95] And the idea has implications beyond mere mirroring and recording. It touches on the ramifications of history and contemporary experience and signifies explorations in which questions and dilemmas confronted in the anthology are reexamined and grappled with again and again in other contexts.

Walcott's recent long poem *Omeros* is in this sense significantly linked to *The Star-Apple Kingdom*. For it too is a further exploration of human action in a continuum of space and time. In *Omeros*, however, the ground and space for defining reality are considerably widened, and definition includes an enlarged perception of the possibilities of the poet's imagination and craft. The commitment to give voice to a people's grief acquires wider connotations here as the poet's craft becomes an integrating medium for the multiple experiences of "history." The final sections of *Omeros* thus enact and affirm these functions and are significantly the sections in which Homer, Seven Seas, and the narrator appear together. It is here that Walcott clarifies the multiple thrusts of the poet's act—his ability to play tricks with time, to roam around differing worlds, and, like the sea-swift's hyphen, to stitch the seams of the text and sew "the Atlantic rift with a needle's line, / the rift in the soul."[96]

Thus in *Omeros* experience and perceptions are spread out between a set of narrators who are yet linked by a network of images and metaphors, signifying the multiple experiences which make up the "window" of the poet. The image of the ubiquitous "swift," symbolizing the integrative thrust of the poet's imagination and craft, connects all the stories of departure, just as the image of the wounded cedar links all conditions of displacement and uprootedness. All the five stories delineated are also thematically or dialectically linked to each other, and their interaction in the poem not only demonstrates the multiplicity of experiences within the "window" that frames a life but also reveals ironies and ambiguities, some of which are still unresolved at the end of the poem.

The dialectic on history may appear at first to center on two main historical commitments in the poem: Plunkett's anxiety to give St. Lucia a worthy history and myth and the narrator's commitment to give a voice to the "voiceless" people of the region. Yet in the poem the two commitments intersect with other aspects that not only debate their assumptions but also widen them to encompass other ramifications of history.

Plunkett's mythical hallucinations about St. Lucia prove futile eventually because his relation to history is continually undermined and ironized. The history he sets out to create would make St. Lucia itself the prize fought over by colonial powers.

[It was] for her that *cedars* fell in green sunrise to the axe.[97]

Yet in the cleverly maneuvered interrelationship of images in the poem, the felled cedars are also associated with the decimation of the indigenous Aruacs and with the metaphorical implications of Philoctete's wound, thus juxtaposing an ironic dimension to the justification of plunder in Plunkett's history. In a delineation that reveals a novelistic rather than a poetic technique, Plunkett's dry and passionless history of facts and artifacts are made (in one brief epiphanic moment) to confront the reality of his own emotions and needs and to question both the sufficiency and motive of the history he creates. The real and instinctual contact with Helen that surprises him with his own passions also uncovers other dimensions of the history of battles and imperial settlements which make up his historical research:

> all History's appeal
> lies in this Judith from a different people,
> whose long arm is a sword, who has turned your head,
> back to her past, her tribe; you live in the terror
>
> of age before beauty, the way that an elder
> longed for Helen on the parapets, or that bed.[98]

The dimension of the island's history that touches on the senses—the smells, sights, and the intimacies of emotional and sexual relations between master and slave—were fundamental to the foundations of Creole society in most of the islands,[99] and Plunkett's obsessive history of sea battles and artifacts deflates a historical reality which his own emotions ultimately affirm. Despite the snake-like images he uses to cast Helen as temptress and seductress, an irony has already been established and another historical reality of St. Lucia has forced itself into his imperial mythology.

> Black maid or blackmail, her presence in the stone house was oblique
> but magnetic . . .[100]

Indeed, the entire perspective of Plunkett's history falsifies several of his own private dilemmas and needs as a person: his alienation from his place of birth, his search for a home, for a place whose landscape he can relate to, all the hopes and dreams that inspired his migration in the first place. The ironies that multiply around his historical project reveal the motives and biases that often surround the historical text and demonstrate that in the rewording of time there may be as many texts as there are biases.

Within the contrasting perspectives and ironic juxtapositions of the poem, the narrator's commitment to give voice to his people, to let his art circle the islands, introduces that other unwritten and unrecorded history whose ruins are only seen in the lives of ordinary folk. Yet it is not only the narrator's voice but the composite voices and lives of ordinary folk that carry the dialectic on history further by revealing its ramifications in their own dramas. Thus the narrator's voice may draw attention to the sorry ruins of imperial history, delineate the madness of color and class divisions in Castries, and reveal confusions and illusions in relations to Africa; but the import and connotations of uprootedness and displacement can only be fully grasped and explored in the implications of Philoctete's wound, just as the debate on origin and African roots may be fully appreciated only in the context of Achille's dream visit to Africa.

The metaphor of Philoctete's wound thus embraces most of the conditions of existence delineated in the poem. Indeed, within the poem's design, the implications of Achille's dream visit to Africa, the narrator's wanderings in America and Europe, and the medicine that finally cures Philoctete's wound are all composite points of a dialectic on history. The narrator emphasizes this interrelatedness in a deliberate linking of consciousness that leaps over time and space to suggest a common historical situation and pursuit. Thus Philoctete, Seven Seas, and the narrator all appear in Achille's dream visit to Africa, and the explorations reverberate not only on the meaning of Philoctete's wound and the broader multidimensional history of the general Caribbean but also on the illusions of islanders whose paradise "is a phantom Africa. Elephants. Trumpets."[101] The confrontation here is with history, the relation with which Africa stands to Afro-Caribbean history and definition, and it is in this sense linked to themes in Walcott's earlier work, *Dream on Monkey Mountain*. But whereas in *Dream* the emphasis is on the satire that exposes the self-rejection behind Makak's dream of kingship in Africa, Achille's dream vision is from the start geared towards self-understanding and definition.

Yet even here the enactment reveals the complex web of feelings that govern West Indian relations with Africa. Achille himself is caught between conflicting pulls. The images of Africa relayed in his dream vision are those of the African movies he had yelped at in childhood. His terror in Africa is real and related to his insistence on seeing his relation to the continent in the two dichotomies symbolized in the images of the "mud without shadow" and the "clear sand," "the snaking river" and "the open sea." But although the dichotomies (and other dualities) are played out as a source of irony and a reminder that Time and History stand between Africa and the Caribbean to invest each with a different future, Africa's own future is constricted into a one-dimensional image as it facilitates a Caribbean sense of separate history.

As in Brathwaite's *Masks*, two sets of consciousness operate ironically in Achille's dream: the consciousness that crouches at the edge of the spindly pierhead, homesick for the history ahead, and the consciousness that is drowned under the pierhead "featureless in mien." Thus, as one pull draws Achille into a sense of home in Africa, another intrudes with the dualities of his own wider history and at the same time enacts that history of disintegration which had led to his own displacement and to a different history symbolized in the

> vast meadows of coral,
> over barnacled cannons whose hulks sprouted anemones
> like Philoctete's shin . . .[102]

The real history and the "epical wonder" becomes then for Achille the history of the crossing and the survival of slaves in the New World; it is the creation of a new sense of "nation" based not on tribe but on the sense of oneness in the sea wind that tied them into one nation "of eyes and shadows and groans; in the one pain / that is inconsolable, the loss of one's shore."[103]

In spite of the sense of a separate future and destiny from Africa, Achille's dream journey achieves other insights that make this section of *Omeros* different from earlier perspectives in poems like "The Almond

Trees," "The Sea Is History," and "The Star-Apple Kingdom." In reliving the history of strife and disintegration that led to the enslavement of his ancestors Achille not only recognizes his historical beginnings in the larger history of Africa but becomes emotionally linked to the tragedies of this history. The text makes this link almost unobtrusively when the griot's recounting of the community's history focuses not as before on "who was swift with the arrow, / who mated with a crocodile, / who entered a river-horse / and lived in its belly . . ."[104] but the song of sorrow, acknowledging an aberration as it narrates the departure of slaves. The consciousness of the African griot appears to merge with the West Indian griot, Seven Seas, who appears in Africa after the raid, foaming with grief. The tragedy becomes then a West Indian tragedy as well, and Achille integrates it into his consciousness in much the same way as Shabine internalizes the decimation of Aruaks in "The Schooner *Flight.*"

In addition, the dream visit uncovers cultural recognition and connections between the West Indies and Africa which complicate any suggestion of total loss and amnesia and which become particularly relevant in the later sections in which Philoctete's symbolic wound is finally cured. For the weed whose power is rooted in its bitterness is also the vehicle which contains within itself all the power, roots, and rituals of the unburied gods

> for three deep centuries dead,
> but from whose lineage, as if her veins were their roots,
> her arms ululated, uplifting the branches
> of a tree carried across the Atlantic that shoots
> fresh leaves as its dead trunk wallows on our beaches.[105]

What the weed cures through the connection and continuities it acknowledges is the sense of shame, the self-hate and the fear of ancestral memory that had for centuries weighed down "the head of the swamp-lily," arched "the sea-almond's spine," and festered Philoctete's wound.[106] The cure encircles both the island and the narrator ("I felt the wrong love leaving me . . . / . . . I felt her voice draining / from mine. / . . . I felt an elation / opening and closing the valves of my paneled heart")[107] and is experienced as a self-acceptance and a release that ushers in new self-perceptions and beginnings.

Yet in the poem's remarkable network of related images the "swift" and the weed are also connected to the "cedar" and the "lizard" and to the two instances of dispossession in the history of the New World, so that the implications of the images move even further than the connections with

Africa to encompass the wider world of the poet's imagination. The sea swift ". . . aimed to carry the cure / that precedes every wound; / . . . her target [was] the ringed haze / of a circling horizon."[108]

There is a difficulty in *Omeros,* however, that relates to the connections made between the narrator's travels in America and Europe and the consciousness of Achille, Philoctete, and others. In terms of the poem's design these sections relate to that other part of the West Indian multiplicity which figures throughout the poem in the presence and implications of Plunkett and Maud and in the narrator's own constant intervening reminders of the archipelago's centuries of history. But these explorations are not so intimately integrated into the consciousness of the ordinary characters; what they establish is a parallel narrative that sheds light on the other stories in the poem. The perceptions they offer on the history of conquest, on the rise and decline of empires, and on the correlation between progress and plunder have moral and analogical implications for all the stories and characters.

Yet there is a sense in which the section also represents the narrator's own private craft and the conflicts he experiences in relation to it. There are occasions when he censures his own tendency to represent the island and its people in metaphors of Greek literature, sensing in the metaphors the same patronage he perceives in Plunkett's "remorseful" history. By reconciling himself to the differing and wider directions of his craft, the narrator also reconciles himself to its distancing tendency, seeing no conflict with his sworn commitment to give voice to his people's grief. Thus the ambiguity between the ego of the poet's imagination and his desire to give voice to his people's lives remains throughout *Omeros* as part of the poem's power but also as the source of structural tension in its integrationist thrust.

Chapter Seven

From Myth to Dialectic
History in Derek Walcott's Drama

To move from Walcott's poetry to his drama is to encounter not so much a
new set of ideas as another dimension of discourse and a different mode
of expression and communication. As a genre drama itself asserts a completely different context from poetry. Its pluralistic and cultural nature enacts
insights, truths, and emphases from a much wider range of signifying practices, incorporating within its mode backgrounds and perspectives on history, sociology, and anthropology. Poetry's flashes of insight may only occasionally reveal paradoxes and ambiguities that suggest other texts beyond the
reality of a poet's structured intuitions, but a play is always automatically a
"two-text" script encompassing a play text and a performance text which act
on each other in the communication and experience of meaning. In Walcott's
drama the difference between the two modes has meant that the poet-dramatist has engaged with history in different ways, asked other questions, and
enacted different aspects of the discourse on history.

The introspective and subjective pulls of poetry and the plural, communal direction of drama constantly enact schizophrenic tensions, which Walcott appears to accept as an energizing force in his work. The imaginative
urge towards paradox, metaphor, and ambiguity, for instance, may give
poetic pleasure by heightening, re-creating, and extending life, but it may
clash with a poet's other need to be truthful to the inner life of a people for
whom metaphor simply means conversation. Walcott's own articulation of
the distance between language and life in his poetry is a revealing pointer to
this tension and may perhaps explain his particular orientation in theater
and the changed relationship between writer and text in his drama. "Years
ago, watching them, and suffering as you watched, you proffered silently

the charity of a language which they could not speak, until your suffering like the language felt superior, estranged. The dusk was a raucous chaos of curses, gossip and laughter; everything performed in public, but the voice of the inner language was reflective and mannered, as far above its subjects as that sun which would never set."[1]

It seems that it was Walcott's awareness of this distance and his personal and artistic need to bridge its gap that influenced his desire to create "not merely a play but a theater, not merely a theater but its environment."[2] The necessity and implications of such an orientation have already been well argued in Walcott's own blueprint on his drama in "What the Twilight Says." For instance, in describing the background of colonial deprivation and self-doubt within which he founded a theater group in Trinidad he intimates that the function of drama in an environment like the Caribbean is not only to present the encoded truths of a dramatist's subjective vision but really to create a theater as a medium of self-discovery and exploration, a theater that would exorcise his "actors'" colonial hallucinations about other landscapes and other selves, one that would record the anguish of the race and some-times even startle the individual actor's domesticated voice into a scream, into the unknown within. For this kind of theater Walcott envisaged an en-gagement not with ancient gods and ancestors but with the elemental: "the roar of rain, ocean, wind and fire," the voice that must grovel within itself "until gesture and sound fuse and the blaze of the flesh astonishes." "We, the actors and poets, would strut like new Adams in a nakedness where sets, costumes, dimmers, all the 'dirty devices' of the theater were unnecessary or inaccessible. Poverty seemed a gift to the imagination, necessity was truly a virtue, so we set our plays in the open, in natural, unphased light and our subject was bare, 'unaccommodated man.'"[3]

The engagement with the elemental as part of the process of self-discov-ery and exploration has taken various forms in Walcott's drama, moving from the situation of unaccommodated man to the creation of Caribbean myths and to a dialectic whose performance text takes its medium from a folk form. The Sea at Dauphin, one of Walcott's earliest plays, begins this process of exploration, presenting a drama in which the precarious and frail existence of islanders becomes the theater itself. Walcott locates the Caribbean person in a cosmic context, as if to suggest that accommodation and history begin from the configuration of the sea. For there are no an-cient memories, no history except the memory of cane fields and cycles of drownings which bear witness to the people's confrontations and struggles with nature. In this theater land, sea, life, ritual, language, and character merge to suggest their interrelationship and to intimate that people's expectations and their kind of resignations are determined by this link. Indeed, in the people's mind (and especially in Afa's), sea, God, priest, and white man are linked in a relentless battering of the folk, so that Afa's curses of the sea are also rather ineffectually curses of God and priest and colonial master. Yet Afa, hard-hearted and cynical as he is, cannot move beyond the range of his curses, and his protest, like all other protests in Dauphine, is in the end circumscribed within a general resignation. Thus, after the deaths, the protests, and Afa's symbolic tearing of his scapular, the cycles of fisher-men's lives continue, beginning another generation's confrontation with the sea and enacting finally that stoic doggedness that hardens the fisher-man but teaches him courage. Walcott's presentation of these lives and tragedies in the dignifying proportions of Greek tragedy seems to over-shadow several other texts which are suggested but then subsumed in the focus and depth of emotion given to Hounakin's death. But Walcott, it seems, did have a purpose in deflating these other texts. For, as he says in "What the Twilight Says," the fishermen's lives smelled strong and true, and its truth was

> that in the "New Aegean" the race, of which these fishermen were the stoics, had grown a fatal adaptability. As black absorbs without reflec-tion they had rooted themselves with a voracious, unreflecting calm. By all arguments they should have felt displaced, seeing this ocean as an-other Canaan, but that image was the hallucination of professional ro-mantics, writer and politician. Instead, the New World Negro was disap-pointingly ordinary. He needed to be stirred into bitterness, hence, per-haps to action, which means that he was as avaricious and as banal as those who had enslaved him.[4]

While the bold and generalized claim may contradict the history of resis-tance in the Caribbean and in Walcott's own tragic drama of Haitian resis-tance, the conclusion Walcott elicits, that the creation of an oral culture of songs, fables, and myths would deliver the New World man from servitude and mimicry, is wholly valid.

Indeed, Walcott himself in three separate plays attempts either to ex-plore the theatrical possibilities and extensions of St. Lucian myths or works to create new myths through drama and theater. His very first play, *Henry Christophe* (1950), constructs a Caribbean mythology out of the rise and tragic fall of two Haitian kings, Dessalines and Christophe. The Elizabethan undertones with which Walcott surrounds the play as well as an allusion to *Hamlet* ("The cease of majesty / Dies not alone but like a gulf doth draw / What's near it with it")[5] announces the mythic import of the play and at once implicates the Caribbean person in the fortunes of the characters. For the burden of slavery, the "nigger smell that even kings must wear"[6] which confuses the ex-slave's self-apprehension, has parallels in the contemporary Caribbean. Walcott expresses it later as "a self-disgust [that] foreshadowed ours, that wrestling contradiction of being white in mind and black in body, as if the flesh were coal from which the spirit like tormented smoke writhed to escape."[7]

Although his delineations explore this division relentlessly in both Dessalines and Christophe, his explanation of the mythic implications of Christophe's tragedy seems to go against the suggestions in the actual drama. For throughout the play's action Christophe's qualities as a soldier, his understanding of what is required to build Haiti, are continually balanced against his ambitions and his self-contempt, so that when he claims later that "the nigger smell, that even kings must wear / is bread and wine to life, / I am proud, I have worked and grown / This country to its stature,"[8] the implications are more than what Walcott calls "one race's quarrel with another's God" and have a lot to do with the compensations that Christophe must make for being always a slave and always black. If such criticism is implied, then it seems rather strange for Walcott to conclude that "even if the slave had surrendered one Egyptian darkness for another, that darkness was his will, that structure an image of the inaccessible achieved. To put it plainer, it was something we could look up to . . . It was all we had."[9]

Walcott did intend to give his historical vision of Christophe the force of myth, but the play is the first and last in which he creates a mythology around a historical figure. The leeway for imaginative extension in such cases is too narrow, and in the 1950s Walcott was already considering other mythic possibilities in the elemental landscapes of the Caribbean forests.

And there were vampires, witches, gardeurs, masseurs, not to mention the country where the night withheld a whole, unstarred mythology of flaming shed skins. Best of all, in the lamplit doorway at the creaking hour, the stories sung by old Sidone, a strange croaking of Christian and African songs . . . they sung of children lost in the middle of a forest, where the leaves' ears pricked at the rustling of devils, and one did not know if to weep for the first two brothers of every legend, one strong, the other foolish. All these sank like a stain and taught us symmetry. The true folk tale concealed a structure as universal as the skeleton, the one armature from Br'er Anancy to King Lear.[10]

In using this background as a source of the drama in *Ti-Jean and His Brothers,* Walcott not only minimizes the "debt to history" but actually creates an entire theater within which the story of the three brothers is performed as myth, with the general structure of all myths and within the particular condition of St. Lucia and the Caribbean. As poet-dramatist he moves now from a hermetic world of allusive representation and flashes of ambiguity into a wider dramatization of human action and its reverberations in society; and within the public medium metaphor becomes not merely an image of the poet's subjective imagination but also conversation: the tones and inflections of speech, the implications and associations of images and myths. The actual performance of the play, the merging of landscape, people, and consciousness in celebration or purgation, integrates the old myth into consciousness and at the same time creates new ones.

Walcott's appropriation of the myth is not just an appropriation of its story, structure, and symbol; it is an appropriation of its incantatory force as an enactment and purgation of a community's fears and anxieties. His play links itself to the universal, immaterial time of the myth, situates itself within its space and takes on its characters and rituals. Thus, aside from the stylized but lyrical language (which Walcott achieved by breaking the iambic line in half to accommodate the lilt of dialect speech), aside from the inner structure and the three moral revelations, there is also the "performance text," which presents the play as an elaborate performance of the story of the three brothers. Here the mythic space becomes a character in the drama, embodying an arena of the unspoken to which characters and audience are continually invited to relate. It is an enclosed world of forests, men, and the elements, an area of wet, melancholy mountains, of rain falling hard on leaves or caught in dripping branches; a primordial world in continual metamorphosis, where animals eat animals as nature's law demands and where the earth becomes a womb that swallows man. As a source of myth this arena is the site of a metaphysical and political contest (all the brothers have to pass through the bamboo forest, over the black rocks, out of the enclosed forest, and into the open valley to meet the devil/planter) and throughout the performances the actors within the play, the audience within the play, and the play's own audience are continually invited to integrate this space into consciousness as a link with the past and as a source of other myths.

In addition and in keeping with the mobilization of emotions and energies involved in performance, the play makes direct links at various points with actors, players and audience, inviting them to participate in the struggle over inimical forces and contradictions as well as the final resolutions of Ti-Jean's contest. In ordinary drama elements of conflict crisscross and move relentlessly towards a dramatic concentration and resolution which are presented as spectacle for the aesthetic enjoyment of an audience. In *Ti-Jean* the rituals of myth are part of the inner structure of the play as well as its performance. The frog tells the story as an incantation to persuade the moon to light the evil dark and take away the rain. But the animals who are his listeners and audience are continually involved in the dangers, threats, and fears experienced by the actors in the story. The old man is at once within and outside the enactment, projected as part of the unheard and unspoken life of the community and with a stake in the resolutions of the contest. Thus his song of disappointment at Gro Jean's certain defeat is also a song in anticipation of the mythic hero who can defeat the forces of evil. On those occasions when he becomes part of the enactment, he seems to me to function as a part of a built-in control that enacts the multifaceted nature of evil. His many disguises appear as mechanisms through which the community initiates the mythical hero into the enigmatic nature of evil, whether it resides in the forest or is embodied in the planter. Indeed, there are elements of play, suggestion, and gentle persuasion in the old man's various disguises (old man of the forest, planter, devil, God) to indicate a paradoxical function and suggest he has as much stake in Ti-Jean's victory as the animals.

Laurence Breiner has suggested that *Ti-Jean* is a play that selects its own hero,[11] and it seems to me that this is a suggestion about the various emotional involvements enacted as part of Ti-Jean's contest with evil. The final contest between Ti-Jean and the devil is indeed an elaboration in which all the players are implicated. First, the drama and the 'Bolom's song and dance announce the urgency of the journey and what is at stake for the unborn possibility; then the metaphysical and political arena are focused upon: the evil dark of the forest, where sun and rain contend for mastery, simulating Ti-Jean's own contest and leaving the question in balance as to whether he will win with the sun or perish with the rain; and later, the political battleground of the sugar estates, the arena of new myths central to the modern audience.

Every stage in the performance then becomes a celebration in which emotions are shared by actors and audience. The challenge that Ti-Jean poses, his refusal to accept old categories and definitions, the disturbance he causes in the devil/planter and the revolutionary burning of the estates, all release energies which reverberate among the actors, animals, and audience and which the narrator of the myth extols by deliberately returning into the story to recount the event in epical tones ("And all night the night burned / Turning on its spit / Until in the valley, the gird / Of the canefield glowed like coals").[12] On the other hand, the final confrontation, during which it is uncertain whether Ti-Jean will succeed, becomes another performance in which all characters with stakes in the victory are part of the anxiety and suspense: the "Bloom" casting himself between Ti-Jean and the devil to outline the contest and stake a claim to life; the mother's song and prayer suggesting victory by hinting at Ti-Jean's Christlike and redemptive destiny; and the animals entering the contest as inspirers, as a chorus that with Ti-Jean and the natural world affirms renewal and continuity in the face of evil.

The performance achieves a collective purgation on two fronts. The incarnation works, the rain stops, the sun appears, and some reunification is restored, suggesting possibilities for renewal. In the modern myth a certain paralyzing fear of the devil/planter is exorcised. The mythic hero has caused a disturbance, forced him to confront his own tortured, two-faced personality: his evil nature, his still divine essence, and his longing for human feeling and mortality. The liberation of consciousness involved in the purgation, it is suggested, must change self-perception, distill fear, and share understanding, and it is perhaps only in theater that such empathy and purgation can work to exorcise the demons of the past.

The Caribbean writer and critic Edouard Glissant has noted that as in the unfolding of myth, what theater expresses in its early stages is not the psychology of a people but its shared destiny through the investigations of why it acts and how its forward movement unfolds.[13] In this unfolding, which has its source in the past, it is the dispersal and linking of emotions achieved through performance rather than the nuances and ambiguities of the constructed text that afford a suitable medium. Glissant's statement may apply in slightly different ways to Walcott's continued myth-making in the plays after *Ti-Jean*, even though the forest and its space is still the source of myth and the demons of the past still the sites of confrontation and exorcism. The folklore material of *Ti-Jean* dramatizes a different spiritual journey, inspired by different threats and fears. Walcott's modern myths are prompted by other anxieties. Where in *Ti-Jean* actors, players, and audience are continually invited to share in the trials, suspense, and catharsis of the confrontational journey, as in all myths, we have in *Dream on Monkey Mountain* individual manifestations of the journey inspired by the same disturbance but internalized and resolved in separate ways. It is as if in the modern myth Walcott suggests that purgation from the psychic disturbance of the past is an individual effort.

For this reason the epilogue of *Dream* hints not at communal purgation but at Makak's messianic and mythic function, a role he acquires because he contends with and exorcises the demons of his own disturbance. His execution of the apparition is his way of coming to terms not only with the failure of his dream but also with the psychic confusion and personal crisis that had inspired his assumed African and European identities. Other characters never achieve this catharsis, though they are involved in the rituals of the spiritual journey performed in the play. Because purgation in *Dream on Monkey Mountain* is private, myth functions as performance in other ways. The dream itself becomes a large metaphor of disturbance with its source in the alienated and schizophrenic psyche that brings on Makak's hallucination, and through its disjointedness and open-endedness Walcott explores the Caribbean subconscious, incorporating all other characters in the exploration.

Thus, even before we plunge into the nature of Makak's dream, Walcott demonstrates fragments of the Caribbean psyche in the mime, in the associations of the African drum, in the moon and the sun, and in the two figures who act out a relationship to these symbols of the past. The connection between the mime and the jail scene becomes a reflection of the psyche as it has been acted upon by the differing symbols, just as the enactment of the dream in the jail scene becomes a performance, a "mask"[14] in which all players act out different roles and rituals. Here the carnival songs and dances, the masks and symbols combine to present an atmosphere of spectacle within the similar and contrasting performances of which the play's statements and epiphanies arise. Yet within this general mimicry the empowering dream remains a reference against which may be measured the perverted parodies of other characters. Makak's genuine ritual of empowerment and healing is, for instance, savagely parodied in Moustique's and Tigre's selfish impersonations, just as Lestrade's sudden and simplistic conversion from "white" to "black" becomes a foil to Makak's true purgation and liberation. We have moved away, it seems, from the communal catharsis of the old myth, and Walcott's modern myth is the myth of the lone visionary.

It is therefore on the processes of Makak's confrontation, struggles, and purgation that the performance now concentrates. For Makak must confront the contradictions of the Africa of his mind, especially as the dream and the myth continually interchange with reality and history to drive him to despondency and doubt:

I was a king among shadows. Either the shadows
were real, and I was no king, or it is my own

kingliness that created the shadows. Either way,
I am lonely, lost, an old man again.[15]

Beyond such doubt and despondency Makak's performance must also take him through the processes by which his dream degenerates into a vision of power and revenge and into the vengeful politics that push him to reverse the white exclusionist policies that had generated his own condition of alienation and self-contempt.

It is such enactments that give credibility to Makak's final exorcism of the dream, since they also epitomize moments of struggle, discovery, and illumination which make his beheading of the apparition a genuine coming to terms with the impulses which had given rise to the dream in the first place. Indeed, Walcott heightens the truth of this illumination when he separates Makak's understanding of the apparition's significance from Lestrade's. For contrary to Lestrade's insistence that the apparition is a mere illusion of Makak's longing, Makak himself knows she is the source of his dream, that the new identity the dream confers springs from feelings of negation inspired by whiteness.

In giving this liberating experience the aura of myth, Walcott isolates the elemental beginnings of the Caribbean landscape as the source of origin and the cradle of community. Makak returns there as an old hermit to "the green beginning of the world," his final words hinting at a messianic role. "Let me be swallowed up in mist again, and let me be forgotten, so that when the mist open, men can look up, at some small clearing with a hut, a small signal smoke, and say, 'Makak lives there. Makak lives where he has always lived, in the dream of his people.'"[16] But it is the ambiguities surrounding the return and Makak's own seemingly uncertain feelings about the mythic significance of his experience that raise questions about the nature of Walcott's mythic import. The entire drama of purgation, of course, dramatizes the basic ideas of his approach to drama as argued in "What the Twilight Says." As he has argued, "To record the anguish of the race . . . they must return through a darkness whose terminus is amnesia. [Make] the journey from man to ape . . . the darkness must be total, and the cave should not contain a single man-made, mnemonic object."[17]

Yet Makak's return to the elemental is a return to further isolation in a society that remains basically unchanged. His own place in relation to the mulatto Lestrade and to the rest of society is so well mapped in the course of the play that it is easy to imagine the implications of the return. What, then, is the import of the mythic conception? Is it simply to make the experience archetypal and accessible to correspondences in human experience in the Caribbean? But then the insistence on the amnesia of the race and the suggestion that hallucination and romanticism are the only modes of the West Indian's relation to Africa are arguable, especially in the face of what Walcott himself reveals in other ways about myth, tale, song, and expressions which have their sources, however remote, in African continuities in the Caribbean.

In Walcott's drama after *Dream*, myth making gives way to other explorations, though the play text still concentrates on the communicative event. If the texts in *Ti-Jean* and *Dream* are subsumed in performance, the text in *Pantomime* (1980) becomes the performance itself, providing a vehicle for language as an enactment of song and an expression of a Caribbean (Creole) linguistic mode. The performance within the play becomes an elaborate metaphor for exploring creative responses to imperial history, a vehicle also of the dramatist's subjective rewriting and gradual deconstruction of the "Crusoe" myth. It raises several issues about historical perception and interpretation, about art and literature, and about the imagination's capacity to relive and reinvent history by re-creating it as myth.

Thus the drama of *Pantomime* deliberately "commits" art by transforming the static history in Harry's simpleminded pantomime into a re-created mythology. Far from remaining merely a light entertainment, the play within a play engages with internal dilemmas and personal psychology and progressively enacts the squalor and violence which surround the experience. Walcott creates a problem for the actors in the reversed roles which Harry proposes. Such reversals merely re-create moments in history without necessarily transcending their defining cages. Indeed the action that enacts these reversals works towards an expected dead end of revenge and defensiveness until a reordering of relationships carries both characters beyond static historical relationships.

The process itself enacts several of Walcott's dissatisfactions with static history, and the two interpretations of the "Crusoe" myth—Harry's and Jackson's—highlight this stasis as each writer's script unfolds to reveal the impact of personal neurosis and bias. Harry's vision of Crusoe as a lonely man on a desolate island is as much influenced by his personal history as Jackson's view of him as a Creole is colored by his own Creole origins. It is these uncertain relations between the historical situation and its interpretation that in Walcott's view renders servitude to history dangerous and futile, for "[in] time every event becomes an exertion of memory and is thus subject to invention. The further the facts, the more history petrifies into myth."[18]

In *Pantomime,* the entire action of act 2 concentrates on moving the two actors' relationship to history beyond the historical moment and its categories of relationships. For it is only when the actors reach towards each other, touching chords of human needs and bonds, that they achieve an understanding beyond the defined roles of master and servant, so that eventually it is neither the reversal of roles nor the renaming of things that is creative and productive in this play but the careful and progressive breaking down and demythologization of the master-servant ethos that has dictated the terms of their relationship all along. Thus, contrary to what the movement of action suggests in act 1, act 2 does not return the actors to the colonial status quo from which they began. Rather, it moves to purge what comes between their human relationships as man to man, as actor to actor, and, as Jackson says, beginning this process of deconstruction and refashioning: "It go have to be man to man, and none of this boss-and-Jackson business . . . two of we both acting a role here we ain't really believe in . . . I ain't think you strong enough to give people orders, and I know I ain't the kind who like taking them . . . but man to man . . . that could be something else."[19] It is, then, as man to man that the two characters intuit, grasp, and accept each other's vulnerabilities, and in the process Walcott creates a medium of perceiving and communicating that is native to the Caribbean.

The differentiation made between classical and Creole acting creates an idiomatic distinctiveness for Creole as it is pitted against Harry's classical language and classical interpretation of the "Crusoe" text. In using Creole as a medium for revision, Walcott's Jackson makes the text native to the Caribbean. Crusoe's Creole idiom is, for instance, convincingly intertwined with the New World environment and consciousness of Jackson in such a way that it sounds sharply different from the idiom of the classical Crusoe. Walcott suggests that this kind of appropriation involves a great deal of creative perception and interpretation and is not necessarily a form of mimicry, so that in the end it is possible to "creolize" the classical "Crusoe" text and, by extension, the very history ingrained in it.

In addition to the Creole language, the calypso form, with its impromptu elements, improvisation, and invention, presents another medium of perception and communication which revises and finally creolizes the classical text, giving both actors and audience a personal, distinctive, and, finally, creative relation to history. Such a process is finally enacted at the end of *Pantomime,* when the two actors, now emotionally and spiritually attuned and coordinating their intuitions and expressions, create impromptu their panto/caiso.

It is only in drama, perhaps, that such an enactment may be possible and convincing; only within such a medium that a writer can share in the articulation and purification of the people's speech. So whereas in poetry language encapsulates the poet's individual thoughts and linguistic manipulations, in drama the very immediacy of communication demands different relations to language. Our experience of metaphor in Walcott's poetry is, for instance, different from our experience of it in his drama. In the context of speech in his drama metaphor is not the elaboration of image but the substance and tone of conversation. Walcott strives to create the precise inflections of speech, keeping as close to its tone and strengths as possible and in the process making the language and the oral traditions subsumed in it visible.

In engaging with drama, Walcott arrives at other conceptions of art and the writer's role in creating it. The pluralist nature of drama itself fosters a liberating interplay with other areas of thought and action: with customs, beliefs, rituals, and popular culture, all of which exercise exciting influences on his work to create a sense of art not only as that which an artist gives to his community but as that which he shares with it. It is perhaps this sense of being part of a shaping culture and tradition that Walcott had in mind when he saw the workshop's production of *Ti-Jean* and *Dream on Monkey Mountain*. "Our culture needs both preservation and resurgence, our cries need an epiphany, a spiritual definition, and an art can emerge from our poverty, creating its own elation."[20]

Indeed, within such perceptions the discourse creates other arguments the explorations of which present us with other dimensions and texts and juxtapose ideas on landscape, history, and culture in Walcott's poetry to similar ideas in his plays. To move from Walcott's poetry to his drama is therefore to encounter different texts as well as wider reverberations of the same ideas expressed in his poetry. Thus the dreaded landscape of "The Swamp," for all the sense of chaos and nothingness it emanates and the hysteria it generates in the poet, is not a totalizing and definitive vision, since in *Ti-Jean* and *Dream on Monkey Mountain* the landscape of the forest becomes the source of elemental beginnings, the cradle of mythology, the site not only of inimical forces but also of confrontation and renewal. And the sea, which in "The Castaway" images the poet's isolation and craving for godhood, presents different images and connotations when Walcott envisions it in the unspectacular but stoic lives of the people of Dauphin as they confront it in different everyday situations. The "Crusoe" themes, when they reappear in drama in *Pantomine*, generate wider reverberations, concerned more with moving beyond history and exploring creative ways of transforming colonial relations. In the same way the poet's relationship to carnival and parang reappear in different explorations, re-worked within the performance text in *Dream on Monkey Moutain* and *Pantomine.*

Such changes in perspective and text across genres occur continually in West Indian literature. For instance, C. L. R. James converts history into drama; Brathwaite moves from history to poetry; Naipaul turns from history to fiction. These transformations reflect not just the separate pulls of different genres but also the extent to which the discourse on history has inspired and driven writers to seek multiple modes of perception and exploration, and how in the process they have created a literature shaping its own canons and traditions. As Walcott has said more succinctly: "In the Caribbean we do not pretend to exercise power in the historical sense. I think that what our politicians define as power, the need for it, should have another name; that like America, what energizes our society is the spiritual force of a culture shaping itself."[21]

Chapter Eight

Edward Brathwaite and Submerged History
The Aesthetics of Renaissance

For on this ground
trampled with the bull's swathe of whips
where the slave at the crossroad was a red anthill
eaten by moonbeams, by the holy ghost
of his wounds
the Word becomes
again a god and walks among us;
look, here are his rags,
here is his crutch and his satchel
of dreams; here is his hoe and his rude implements

on this ground
on this broken ground.
Edward Brathwaite, "Vèvè"

The school of Caribbean literary criticism that polarizes the poetry of Walcott and Brathwaite has long been proved misguided. Explorations of the works of the two major poets continue to reveal the similarity of their fundamental preoccupations and demonstrate how they both respond to the same reality, share similar burdens about history, and strive in their various and separate ways to engage with and redefine Caribbean realities. The previous chapter has shown the processes by which Walcott re-creates myth from folk tale in *Ti-Jean and His Brothers;* our examination of the relationship between history and poetry in Brathwaite's works may reveal a similar interplay and imaginative activity. If Walcott's imagination moves beyond his memory of the songs and folk figures of folk tale to the immaterial time of St. Lucian myth to explore relations to Caribbean space,

Brathwaite moves beyond his knowledge of history and folk life to reconstruct a poetic story of that life; both preoccupations are fundamentally acts of remembrance, reconnection, and identity.

In Brathwaite's poetry there is constant interaction between the poet's understanding of the history of creolization and the material, perspectives, and styles of poetry. His historical study of slave societies in the West Indies and his special researches into the development of Creole society in eighteenth- and nineteenth-century Jamaica gave him tremendous insights into the social and psychological processes involved in creolization. *The Development of Creole Society in Jamaica* not only unearths a British-American cultural link but also explains and describes the complex organization created around the planting of sugarcane and demonstrates its role in "integrating" separate classes of Jamaican society. Brathwaite's research reveals the slave's position in this structure. In delineating the various functional groups of slaves and their relation to other groups in the structure, he not only lifts the faceless mask of silence long placed on the slave's existence but also complicates the sociological paradigm of a plural society: "Here, in Jamaica, fixed within the dehumanizing institution of slavery, were two cultures of people, having to adapt themselves to a new environment and to each other. The friction created by this confrontation was cruel, but it was also creative. The white plantations and social institutions described in this study reflect one aspect of this. The slaves' adaptation of their African culture to a new world reflects another."[1]

Brathwaite is aware, nevertheless, of the submerged existence of slave culture and of the possibilities that might have been achieved for Creole society had Jamaica recognized these elements of its creativity and integrated them more fully into the creolizing process. Such an awareness is undoubtedly an underlying factor in his relation to his material in *The Arrivants* and explains his conception of the imagination and of the artist's role as a myth maker and recoverer of "history." Harris has argued that "[the] limbo imagination in the West Indies possesses no formal or collective sanction as in an old tribal world . . . and the gateway complex between cultures thus implies a new catholic unpredictable threshold which places a far greater emphasis on the integrity of the individual imagination."[2] Harris's statement throws some light on what I see as the impulse behind Brathwaite's almost shamanistic relation to his material. For in the absence of a collective sanction and in the midst of what the poet must see as a general social and intellectual suspicion, Brathwaite becomes identified with the "authority" of the submerged culture while at the same time elaborating a far-reaching order of the imagination. As a shaman figure he descends into the farthest reaches of memory, becoming the consciousness of his people at the same time as he unearths history and makes new myths. In such circumstances he does more than describe and illuminate: he appraises and draws out meaning; he bears witness and upholds. As his persona in "Eating the Dead" claims,

> . . . I
> can show
> you what it means to eat
> your god, drink his explosions of power
>
> and from the slow sinking mud of your plunder, grow.[3]

Brathwaite's move from history to art, from historical writing to poetry, must be seen in this context. History continually deals with the details and evidence of how things came to be. Its ordering impulse collates and structures available evidence to make an objective whole which it then encapsulates in a realistic narrative. Brathwaite's history of Creole society in Jamaica works within these structures, though it manages to transcend them. If his description and analysis of Jamaican institutions are systematically corroborated with data and evidence, his history of slave life and culture is necessarily anthropological, committed to uncovering what is concealed under the surface. Even as a historian, he writes with an artist's eye for possibility and the future, revealing a perspective that was to influence his mythical rearrangement of history in *The Arrivants*. Certainly only the imaginative leeway of the poet could have allowed him to link periods of African, Caribbean, and American history in the simultaneous presentations he achieves in sections of his trilogy. In poetry Brathwaite's purpose becomes more ambitious, intent on breaking the historical boundaries of space and time to offer West Indian man a wider conception of himself in history. The deliberate and epical arrangement of *The Arrivants* reflects this purpose, just as the multiplicity of points of view, moods, tone, and voice reflects the variety of historical experiences he draws upon.

   Its first section, "Rights of Passage," an exploration of African response to the New World, is enclosed by a prelude and epilogue, showing the point from which the poet begins his examination and portending the direction of his movement. *Masks*, its most unified section and therefore deliberately placed in the center, traces the evolution of the West African people simultaneously as it enacts the modern West Indian's personal and psychic return to his African origins. Such simultaneous perceptions of periods in time enable Brathwaite to make connections between past and present and to deduce historical lessons without being limited or circumscribed within the aberrations of particular periods. The trilogy's last section, *Islands,* is in the context of the first two sections a beginning. The poet's consciousness, widened by his encounter in *Masks* and by the trilogy's underlying perspective of circularity and continuity, reexplores his previous themes as he gropes towards wider dimensions of historical experience and their correlation in poetic form.

Thus, true to its thematic structure in the trilogy, *Rights of Passage* becomes a conjectural evocation of a New World historical experience, poised between a repetitive experience of loss and deprivation and a growing movement towards a mode of seeing defined (ironically) by the repetitive experience itself. Within this ambivalence Brathwaite himself seems straddled between a vision of sterility and a vision of possibility, and his poetry moves between the two visions, presenting varying and contrasting interpretations of an entire New World experience. Poetry in this case becomes an act of memory, and the poet's memory travels backward and forward, making connections between the various migrations and modes of thought which precede and follow the Middle Passage.

The bigger African migration from the North African desert southwards to the forest regions of Western Africa, which preceded the Middle Passage, becomes the point of origin and the beginning of consciousness for the poet. His drama of this movement reveals certain patterns which act as a framework for appraising all other experiences in *Rights of Passage.* Thus the patterns he dramatizes throughout the prelude reveal a cyclical movement from decay to regeneration, from disintegration to re-creation, so that we have after the dryness, decay, blight, and futility in the desert scene a communal call for resilience, rebuilding, and creation. And we have following this call the poetic voice's images of destruction, stunted growth, and decay, beginning again the movement towards disintegration and death. We have in the midst of decay and death the dream of birth and creation in the thought of further migration, enacting the cyclical patterns in the moving history of Africa and, by imaginative extension, the New World.

From the framework of this circular pattern Brathwaite presents the Middle Passage as on one hand a symbol of disruption and death and on the other a tenacious grip on life, a continual odyssey for new beginnings and a new creativity. Thus, in "New World A-coming" captivity and enslavement, like defeat and destruction in the desert, are symbolized by dumbness, just as the hope of possibility accompanying the cosmic vision of time is mildly hinted at in the paradox of the "chained" and "welcoming" port and deliberately celebrated in the incantations of the spiritual:

let my children
rise
In the path
of the morning
up and go forth
on the road
of the morning
. . . .
see the rainbow
of Heaven.[4]

The framework within which Brathwaite projects this experience is part
of a conscious technique not just to create organic links between Africa and
the New World but also to weave the interactions into a New World consciousness and ethos. His mode of apprehension is based on a belief, proven
by his research, that a definite affinity existed between the first generation
of slaves and their African homeland. "It is in the nature of the folk culture
of the ex-African slave, still persisting today in the life of the contemporary
'folk' that we can discern that the Middle Passage was not, as is popularly
assumed, a traumatic, destructive experience, separating the blacks from
Africa, disconnecting their sense of history and tradition, but a pathway or
channel between this tradition and what is being evolved, on new soil in the
Caribbean."[5] Brathwaite's assertion is amply demonstrated in the early sections of *Rights of Passage,* in which his poetry captures the gradually receding image of the homeland from the consciousness of the slaves and their
conscious effort to remember. The image of the homeland survives, for
instance, in the "salt dream" recalled by

something seen
on the wet grass
the cool pasture.[6]

And indeed, the dream itself becomes a source of strength and sustenance,
a projection of an old world consciousness in the new surroundings. On a
creative level the consciousness becomes a medium of adaptation. New
ways emerge, new forms are evolved, but the basic attitudes remain: the
cosmic sense of time, the ritual ordering of society, the communal faith in
the certainty of rebirth.

Brathwaite dramatizes this process of transmission and adaptation
through his selection of material and his handling of rhythm and meaning.
His archetypal New World slave, Tom, becomes an ambiguous symbol. On

one hand he is the outcome of the slave master's sexual and economic exploitation of the slave woman; on the other he is the new birth and survival suggested in the paradox of the "chained" and "welcoming" port. This aura of ambiguity surrounds the New World slave throughout, becoming part of the developing consciousness reflected in gospel music and the blues. The slow, mournful chanting of "so many seeds" in "Tom," recognizable as gospel music, glides easily into the rhythms of Akan poetry, suggesting an affinity. The repetitive forms, the incantations, the laments, and the exhortations suggest that mixture of despondency, world-weariness, and defiant hope characteristic of gospel music and the blues.

Indeed, in its variegated structure and its shifts of mood the poem enacts the actual circumstances and process of creation. The alternations between visions of homeland and visions of plantation set the two tones of nostalgia and pain against each other. Nostalgia tones down the lament and converts it into strength, so that when the persona sings—

Drown the screams, shore.
Cool the lashed sore
Keep the dream pure[7]

—we recognize not just despondency and sentimentality but the defiance and resilience that contribute to catharsis in the blues. Here is a medium for appraisal and self-analysis, a ritualistic procedure which has become a means of purging shame and containing pain. And these are the peculiar responses which for all their limitations ("no crack / in the chain / starts / no bitter / flame / marks / my wrath")[8] contribute to the self-control and strength of Tom, becoming the basis of a positive personality and consciousness: "Sharp thorn / against toe / hard rock / under heel / feet stretched into stride / made you a man / again."[9]

Brathwaite's acceptance of an African consciousness in these early stages of African experience in the New World separates him in perspective from some of Walcott's early poetry. While Walcott accepts the slave's response to slavery as part of the human history which should form an Afro-Caribbean consciousness, he is anxious to emphasize the uniquely Caribbean nature of the experience. The basis of Caribbean people's endurance and survival in "The Almond Trees" is for Walcott not a lingering African sense of resilience and possibility, "not the seeding of the great African pastoral," but the natural molding and toughening brought about by a particularly painful and chastening experience. For him, the creation of the spirituals, part of the epic poetry of the "tribe," originates rather from the tribe's identification with Hebraic suffering and its hope of deliverance from bondage: "The phenomenon is the zeal with which the slave accepted both the Christian and the Hebraic, resigned his gaze to the death of his pantheon, and yet deliberately began to invest a decaying faith with a political belief." What was captured from the captor, Walcott argues, was his god: "God was being taken away from merchant and missionary by a submerged force that rose at ritual gatherings, where the subconscious rhythm rose and took possession and where the Hebraic-European God was changing color." [10]

From Walcott's perspective the circumstances of the slave's conversion and the new religion it fostered provided the religious and spiritual basis for the elemental poetry of the tribe, and since no culture can really exist without a religion, the epic poetry of the tribe must be seen as inspired by and steeped in the new, transformed religion of the converted African: "No race is converted against its will. The slave-master now encountered a massive pliability. The slave converted himself, he changed weapons, spiritual weapons, and as he adapted his master's religion, he also adapted his language, and it is here that what we can look at as our poetic tradition begins. Now began the new naming of things." [11]

For Brathwaite, on the other hand, the actual source of inspiration for this new artistic creation was the "old world" consciousness of the African. The gospel song in "Tom" does have a thematic identification with the Judeo-Christian mythology of exile and deliverance, but it is also principally the projection of an existing belief onto a new situation. The Christian mythology, Brathwaite believes, only offered the Negro slave a ready metaphor for expressing his traditional cosmic sense, and the new "naming" which Walcott talks of would have been possible only with the background consciousness of the African slave. To accept "amnesia" as the true history of the Caribbean, therefore, is in Brathwaite's view to reject an entire crucial and historical mode of apprehension basic to a New World consciousness.

A great deal of Brathwaite's poetry in *Rights of Passage* is an exploration of the nature and quality of experience in the New World and their implications for the Western Negro's self-perception and artistic development. In juxtaposing dimensions and varieties of response Brathwaite's poetry reveals similarities and patterns that dramatize a progression in the Caribbean perceptual and artistic consciousness. The mode of adaptation symbolized in the male-centered experiences of the archetypal figure, Tom, becomes the context for a consideration of both the psychology of enslavement and the quality of African response, and though this mode of representation enables Brathwaite to explore the balance between discontinuity and the creative force of memory, the very privileging of Tom's male-centered experience renders him susceptible to accusations of incompleteness in the representation of a total Caribbean experience of adaptation.[12]

Yet it seems to me that in *The Arrivants* at least the seemingly privileged world of Tom's descendants is asserted and at the same time ironically flayed as a world of ambiguities in which the outward lure of male pursuits is negated by the pull of memory and the roots and folk consciousness of a female world.[13] Thus, if on one hand Tom's self-containment, resilience, diffidence, and self-abnegation represent a mode of apprehension marked in artistic expression by the gospel song and the blues, the militant, exhibitionist sexuality and rootless journeying of his descendants enact a pattern of discontinuity and loss which are continually balanced by a lingering memory of home embodied in a rooted female world.

As a reflection of this dual pattern, Brathwaite's method in this section of *Rights of Passage* has a parallel movement built up as a series of paradoxes, in which the ramifications of the old slave's dream of rootedness linger on, suggesting the possibility of some continuity of consciousness. For instance, Tom's sons reject both his "dream" and the continuity implied in an identification with his work songs and gospel songs.

> . . . keep them
> for Alan Lomax, man, for them
> swell
> folkways records, man,
> that does sell for two
> pounds ten. But get
> me out 'a this place, you hear, where my dreams are wet
> as hell.[14]

Yet the quiet intrusion of "dreams" in the last line, though ironically pointing to the illusion of heaven in escape, actually mocks the persona's cynicism about home, stressing the need for a more meaningful dream. More than this, there is an underlying sense in the "spade's" satiric reference to the cheapening and bastardization of black experience and suffering by the "swell" white record companies, a sense which ultimately reveals his awareness of the real meaning and relevance of the blues.

Similarly, the shortened lines and scurrying rhythms of the last section of "Folkways" deliberately simulate the hurried impatient journey out of what the "spades" regard as the southern "hell." Yet the "boogie woogie" rhythms built into the poem are associated with the railroad workers' blues, with the pain of separation from the South and therefore with the memory and continuity of a sense of home and self. Indeed, the last lines of the "boogie woogie" section do not enact the frenzied impatience of "come quick / bugle train" but rather suggest the anguish of parting, the fear of the unknown, and perhaps the possibility of a continuing ethnic consciousness:

> long long
> boogie woogie
> long long
> hooey long
> journey to town.[15]

Brathwaite plays on these paradoxes to suggest the tensions (developed more fully in *Islands*) that pull the spades emotionally towards home yet also lure them away from home, towards the deathly values of the urban world, and the very paradox embodied in the suggestion keeps alive the idea of home and identity as well as the possibility of continuity. In line with this underlining ambivalence, he reveals a similar paradox when he presents the strength and clarity of Brother Man's rooted vision as trapped in the labyrinths of religious ritual. The crucial paradox here lies in the difference between Brother Man's reality and his dream: the mice eyes transformed into "hot pumice pieces," his own lice-laden brain suddenly clear and overwhelmingly correct in its assessment of social reality, his weak eyes transformed to "hawk's eyes, hard with fear," and finally, the self-possession and air of authority in which he not only proclaims a prophetic role, but also asserts a superior sense of self in contrast to the borrowed selves of the spades.

> Down down
> white
> man, con
> man, brown
> man . . .
> Rise, rise
> locks-
> man, Solo
> man, wise
> man . . .
> leh we
> laugh
> dem, mock
> dem, stop
> dem, kill
> dem . . .[16]

Although stylistically the biblical tones and incantatory rhythms of "Wings of a Dove" suggest affinities with the gospel songs and spirituals of earlier generations, the distinct dialect of the Jamaican urban poor embodied in the Rastafarian language as well as the new insistent militancy of Brathwaite's tone represent a progression of consciousness, implying a strong self-assertion from Tom to the spades. Their serious ritualistic tones and prophetic sense of doom are later to contrast with the easygoing, singsong beat of the calypsonian's satiric mode, defining a new, confident assertiveness and "dread" in the Afro-Caribbean consciousness.

Brathwaite gives Brother Man's vision a certain stature and importance in *Rights of Passage* because he seems, I think, to recognize his paradoxical situation and his sense of apocalypse as quite similar to his own groping for a medium and a voice. In his delineation of New World experience, Brathwaite also assumes a separate and prophetic voice as well as a similar assessment of middle-class rootlessness. His judgment of Caribbean exile and dispossession, like Brother Man's, also stirs up a psychic vision of continuity which, like the vision of the poem "South," gives him the courage to accept the Caribbean's turbulent history not as a negation necessitating exile but as the base for self-assessment and definition.

Thus, from the rootless wanderings of exile, the poet summons a positive response to the reality of the New World in the poem "South," and for the first time the region's violent history is not masked and deflated by the soothing rhymes of the calypsonian's music but recognized as a possible source of strength. The ocean now becomes a symbol of turbulence and enormity, suggesting the widening of perspective that could come out of a response to the historical upheavals of the New World. The African river becomes in part a symbol of time and continuity, and the poet recognizes its continuous, purposeful movement to its destination in the sea as a contrast to the purposelessness, denial of history, and discontinuity which exile must signify for the Caribbean man.

But today I would join you, traveling river,
borne down the years of your patientest flowing,
past pains that would wreck us, sorrows arrest us,
hatred that washes us up on the flats;
and moving on through the plains that receive us,
processioned in tumult, come to the sea.[17]

The link that Brathwaite suggests between the two visions in "Wings of a Dove" and "South" seems central to the purpose of *Rights of Passage*. From now on the vision of continuity revealed in "South" pervades the rest of the section, becoming a perspective for the poet's assessment of Caribbean politics and offering possibilities for a reconnection with "history" in a sympathetic reappraisal of Tom, the slave survivor and the first line in the continuity of black history in the New World.[18]

There is a deliberate attempt on Brathwaite's part to squeeze the positives out of Tom's crushed world: the faith, the dream, the grit, even the identity he is supposed to have lost. He works on a series of contrasts which are so well arranged as to become in themselves enactments of Tom's experience, showing the ways in which he has both succumbed to and resisted the most violent inflictions of history. The contrasts are between defeat and resilience, darkness and light, and Tom appears against these as a folk persona who survives with an inner hidden life. Brathwaite links him with the resurrected voices of the folk in "The Dust," offering their rooted vision as proof of the possibility which he has harped on even in his delineation of loss.

Thus, linked to the poet's voice, these symbols of folk identity embody a vision of continuity against which all detractors can be viewed. Indeed, at this juncture the grounded vision of the folk characters appear to interchange with the poet's. Their awareness of the spiritual poverty of their society, their sense of the numinous, and the stoicism that comes out of their cosmic sense of time, though not conceptualized like the poet's, reflects the possibilities that the poet's own paradoxes hint at throughout the poem. The representation of their voices becomes both an assertion and an act of possession which transcend that sense of rootlessness foisted on the West Indies in colonial historiography. In Brathwaite's works the voice is not merely a depository of African values; it is also itself evidence of an adaptation and creolization through which "we become ourselves, truly our own creators, discovering word for object, image for the Word."[19]

The enactment of women's voices within a pattern of other voices, including the poet's, has therefore reverberations both within *Rights of Passage* and in West Indian literature generally. Within *Rights of Passage* the voices counter the self-conception of the spades by revealing themselves as dimensions of memory and vision which can be equally conceptualized as history. The common idea of history as tangible material creation is then given a new significant qualification in the poet's ironic rendering of the point of view of the spades:

The memories
are cold:

. . . .

What we
can't touch
will never
be enough
for us to shout
about, who live
with God-

less rock
the shock

of dis-
possession.[20]

These assumptions are echoes of those that have continually bogged Caribbean people ever since Froude and, later, Naipaul condemned the region
to a historical limbo. The spades wallow in negative, defeatist postures, as
though the history of displacement and violation condemns them to a fixed,
deterministic, and cyclical existence:

For we
who have cre-

ated nothing
must exist

on nothing;
cannot see

the soil:
good

earth, God's
earth, with-
out that fixed
locked mem-

ory of love-
less toil
strength des-
troyed, chained

to the sun
like a snail

to his shell . . .[21]

But the women's voices, together with the poet's contrasting consciousness in the "Epilogue," offer a corollary in which within the region's circular, moving history, the "nothing" of history, becomes a creative possibility, generating a new self-awareness and a positive sense of humanity.

In relation to West Indian literature generally, the voices also reveal a confidence in articulation which presents a different connotation of loss to the loss Walcott expresses in "Laventville." The sense of amnesia, of a severance from ancestral worlds ("customs and gods that are not born again")[22] is here counteracted by different implications of loss within which a sense of loss is ameliorated by the possibilities of reconnection to a Caribbean ethos that survives precariously in voices and perceptions like those enacted in "The Dust." Thus when Brathwaite laments that "the land has lost the memory of the most secret places,"[23] what he refers to is not ancient dead memory (which is static) but "memories trunked up in a dark attic"[24] and consciously suppressed through shame, embarrassment, and fear.

Indeed, for Brathwaite ancestral memory, identified as ancient sympathies and remembrances lost through discontinuity, must be absorbed into a fluid future to liberate and transform the past. It is in this sense, for instance, that aspects of Tom's memory may represent a static relation to the past in contrast both to the voices of women and to his own dogged willingness to confront life in the face of aberration. Thus deliberately in "Epilogue," the Arcadian aura surrounding this memory reveals a paradoxical blight at the same time as it contrasts with the creolized voices of the women and with Tom's strategies of survival in the West Indies:

> you
> followed where the
> bird called:
> remembering woods
>
> when it was yesterday:
> young, gay,
> unblighted
>
> by the mildew
> of the world;
> woods where
> clear water
> clinked; pra,
> Volta, Tano: soft
> sloping banks,
> a girl to

kiss and
tumble down
the banks.[25]

In an ironically balanced paradox, Tom survives his ordeal by clinging both to life and the memory of the past. Yet in this almost paradisal memory, the clear waters of the Pra and the Volta Rivers "clink," reminding us of the aberration which his own presence in the New World and his history of discontinuity represents. Is such a relation to the past sustainable?

The poet persona's commitment to a progression of New World consciousness, his rhetorical decision to be part of a new "rebirth," to exploit the green crack of possibility, commits him to a more revolutionary destiny than Tom's. His new reappraisal conceives of a harsher destiny ("no / blessing by water / chastising by fire / you knew"), a less nostalgic vision of time ("woods of today / would be / fire tomorrow"),[26] and a stronger will to break the cage of personal history. His subsequent explorations in the trilogy are therefore new questionings and explorations of the possibilities of the reawakened memory, which, as he now asserts, can enlarge our understanding of our origins but cannot be restored simply to bridge discontinuities of time, since all such memory should in the end liberate and transform the past.

The kind of liberation and transformation that Brathwaite seeks is related to personal and political freedom and the acquisition of community in a West Indian society which is in continual process. In this general sense his quest cannot be fundamentally different from Harris's, for whom transformation means the freedom and authority of immateriality: the ability to translate material history into a fluid future in which all the spiritual seasons that had ever been would be strung together in a new spiritual genesis and condition. In the actual details of transformation, however, Brathwaite's emphasis is considerably different from Harris's ecumenical vision. His material and explorations throughout the trilogy and in *Mother Poem* and *Sun Poem* reveal a primary concern with how an awareness and appraisal of an Afro-Caribbean heritage can liberate his people from fixed self-conceptions and propel them to a larger understanding of the sources of their identity.

It is in this context that the relations between the three sections of the trilogy may be viewed. For *Masks* is linked to both *Rights of Passage* and *Islands* in a dialectical sense as an argument on the implications of Africa in the historical imagination of West Indian people. The thematic link is immediately obvious in the way in which a multidimensional perception of time, facilitated by a symbolic use of the mask motif, enables a simultaneous perception of history that allows the poet to envisage Afro–West

Indian origins as part of the larger history of Africa and amenable to its historical lessons.

Within this framework fact evaporates into myth, and historical lessons extend beyond particular periods and events, linking history to larger spaces and time and breaking the prison of history in which the linear past confines Caribbean people. For instance, the enactment of the processes and interrelationships behind artistic activity in *Masks* emphasizes the close connections between art, community, and universe in Africa; and for the masked poet, involved yet detached, this emphasis has its special inferences. The symbolic import of the drum naturally makes a cultural link in the poet's consciousness between Africa and the New World. At the same time, the idea of creation as an unfolding of a consciousness well integrated with its environment parallels Brathwaite's own idea of the relationship between creativity and culture. It portends the unique style of his explorations in *Islands* and explains several of his images. The idea suggested in *Masks* of creation as pain, as a major sacrificial thrust which hurts the creator but gives him a vision and release, is to reappear in *Islands* and the later poems as metaphors for exploration, affirming the connections that memory and sensibility have made between Africa and the New World.

In *Masks* such connections encompass not only ritual and art but also the entire cyclical movement of history in Africa, and for Brathwaite the evocation becomes an act of memory, a deliberate expansion of a West Indian concept of space, a widening of the sources of Brathwaite's own identity as a West Indian. As part of this evocation he traces the progress of tribal evolution, and "Pathfinders" re-creates an earlier historical time to parallel the poet's reassessments in the present. Again, the simultaneous evocation of the past in the present consciousness of the poet enables him to relate it to a West Indian situation of dispossession and migration.

In spite of the conflation of time and the mythical framework that enables the poet to explore periods in history simultaneously, *Masks* still focuses on a particular point in historical time in its reference to the Arab kings of the desert and the medieval cities of western Sudan. The poet's decision, for instance, to give the Christian Ezana, king of Ethiopia, an Islamic identity and use his praise-poem as evidence of the Islamic decadence that led to conquest and disintegration, is part of the poet-historian's anxiety to give a precise focus to his historical canvass by suggesting the real historical links between African migrations and the traumatic dislocation which is his subject in *Masks*. For in this way the historical lessons reverberate with particular correlation to the New World and to the consciousness of its poet. The poet persona, wearing the mask of the past,

achieves sufficient detachment to suggest the paradoxes behind the heroics
and the pageant, and in "Pathfinders" images of victory coexist with images of defeat and death, so that the gusto and exaltation behind the rhythm of lines like

Summon now the kings of the forest,

Summon the Emirs, kings of the desert,

. . . .

Blow elephant
trumpet; summon the horses,

are deflated by the slow melancholic rhythm of lines like

. . . El Hassan dead in his tent,
the silks and brasses, the slow weary tent

of our journeys down slopes, dry river courses;

dead horses, our losses: the bent
slow bow of the Congo, the watering Niger . . .[27]

Such paradoxes of creativity and loss, revealed in the circular movement
of history in *Rights of Passage*, surface also in *Masks* as Brathwaite enacts
the human pull towards movement, settlement, and further movement. His
symbolism in "Chad" offers a view of history that explains the urge towards movement and opens up possibilities for a cyclic return to rootedness. The sacred lake, at once the source of serenity and restlessness, contains the paradox that enacts man's circular movement through history:

no peace in this world
till the soul
knows this dark water's

World

and around these shores
man whirls
in his dark rest-
less haste; searching
for hope; seek-
ing his fate.[28]

Brathwaite accepts this circularity as natural and is concerned rather
with deducing its creative lessons and integrating them in the West Indian

consciousness. His drama of evolution uncovers several processes and rhythms: the migrating tribes remember who they are and what their lives had been like; they assess their past lives and feel their way towards new relationships with new gods; the new environment ushers in new fears but also holds new possibilities for regeneration; communication with that environment exorcises fear and uncertainty and creates new confidence for life. The forest's womb, for instance, uncurls its creative potential, and a whole new world of certainties is born, beginning again the circular movement: birth, death, rebirth.

For the poet, wearing his mask of the past and sufficiently distanced in the present to assess it, this historical journey presents its lessons: in the movement and demands of migration itself lies a continuing search, a continuing creativity and discovery. The African migrations into the New World, Brathwaite feels, are a part of this process and should present similar challenges. Indeed, the final line of "White River" jolts us out of the security that journeys have ended. Time's river, symbol of the people's journey, appears to end its flow in the White River, the sea ("This was at last the last; / this was the limit of motion"). But the symbolism of "Chad" persists, and the circle continues, hinting at further movement, further disintegration and loss of pathway, leading, of course, to the traumatic aberration:

O new world of want, who will build the new ways,
the new whips?[29]

Brathwaite sees the slave trade not only as the culmination of the traumatic contact between Africa and Europe but also as the climax of tribal decadence and the disintegration of African civilization. The white ax of lightning that finally splits the tribal tree flickers its way through the slits in the hollow eyes of elders, and defeat, when it finally comes, is a cultural collapse marked by disarray, loss of confidence, the decay of ritual.

Yet for the masked poet, with an already crystallized sense of history as cyclical, the significance of this decline is also suggested in the hope of re-creation. The solemn cry with which he ends "The White River" portends both doom and hope: hope not just for the disintegrating African culture but also for the poet's own New World. His reference to "New Ships" means more than just an allusion to slavery and suggests as well the new creation that could spring up even from such an aberration. At this moment of epiphany it is possible to surmise that the poet may be contemplating his own vocation, perhaps predicting the building of his own "new ships," his rigorous explorations in *Islands*.

It is for this reason that Brathwaite's relation to history in the last two movements of *Masks* is so much more personal and anguished. His confrontation with the past at this point would predictably become the symbolic enactment the catharsis of which would release him from the ghosts of the past and reconcile him to meaningful relationships with it. Because his relationship to his material in this movement is also a way of reexamining Tom's nostalgic memory of the past, the entire section becomes a dramatization of other, more complex relationships to memory. The returning New World persona confronts the present but is also forced to contend simultaneously with the shadow of history that lurks in the present. His decision to enter the dead world of slave ancestors and to relive their journey towards the slave ships introduces another dimension of time and perspective.

There is first the consciousness which hopes that "the new dead / cannot know that / time was evil,"[30] and there is the contrasting consciousness which grasps that time had been evil and that the wounds of history are real and frightening. It is the later consciousness which grasps the frightening realities of history, and it is this point of view that the poet is ultimately identified with. The other consciousness asks of the river:

Can you hide me now

from the path's hope-
less dazzles, halts
meetings, leaves' sudden

betrayal of silence the sun's
long slant sloping
to danger?[31]

But what it hopes for is an escape from the painful realization of the betrayals, wrongs, and failures of the past. The only answer, the only protection it gets is the pervading sense of the river's invulnerability, of its continual flow through centuries of building and disintegration, a fact which serves to remind the poet of the movement of life itself and of its cycles of death and rebirth. The recognition changes his attitude towards himself and the past he has uncovered, creating a new sense of separateness which qualifies his vision of himself as an exile who has returned to Africa.

This new sense marks a growth in the other consciousness of the poet, and from now on the two sets of consciousness merge. The poet's perception of history now is markedly complex, showing up in the poems "Kumasi," "Tutu," and "The Golden Stool," the greatest sources of nostalgia in *Rights of Passage*. As a result, Brathwaite's explorations in these poems operate against the background of Tom's memories:

Atumpam talking and the harvest branches, all the tribes of Ashanti dreaming the dream
of Tutu, Anokye and the Golden Stool, built
in Heaven for our nation by the work
of lightning and the brilliant adze: and now nothing[32]

Throughout this section, memory of the dream lies behind the poet's discovery of its perversion, and in "Kumasi" especially, it is juxtaposed with the brewing disintegration, particularly in those stanzas in which the Ashanti war cry penetrates the poet's prayer for peace.

The poet's discovery of cultural failure, greed, and the lust for power, his stark vision of tribal decadence in the Ashanti empire is both cleansing and cathartic. The consciousness that emerges after this experience is one that accepts the movement of time and the inevitability of death yet commits itself to incessant creativity. For the poet protagonist, history is now no longer a static quantity, no longer the memory of "woods / when it was / yesterday: / young, gay, / unblighted / by the mildew / of the world,"[33] but a continuing process presenting challenges for renewal and creativity. The poem "Sunsum" is therefore the poet's anguished exploration of this new creative possibility. His images return to the images of birth and creation, and his "trapped," "curled" tongue is poised, ready to uncurl into song as he searches feverishly for that glimmer of a cultural link which he now sees as a crucial possibility.

> Some-
> where under gravel
> that black chord of birth
>
> still clings to the earth's
> warmth of glints, jewels' pressures, spin-
> ning songs of the spider.[34]

But the act of creation, as the poet has also learned, depends on a multiplicity of relationships between the creator and his environment, between him and the rest of creation. The intermingling of ties makes up the "leaven" of the underground, the material for creation, and creation in this sense is an uncurling, an explosion, a triumph over fear. It is this background to the poet's view of creation that explains his anguished disappointment in "Sunsum." For it is as if his "trapped," "curled" tongue cannot uncurl into song in an environment in which he has no present or future.

> But my spade's hope,
> shattering stone,
> receives dumbness back
>
> for its echo.
> Beginnings end here
> In this ghetto.[35]

"Dumbness" is the dumbness of the womb in a state of limbo (non-creativeness), and "stone," "spade," and "ghetto" return us to *Rights of Passage* and to the New World, hinting that the search for origin and source should end in the "ghetto" of the New World. The poet's confrontation with the cycles of history in Africa has enlarged his consciousness, but as he recognizes, he is not part of that history's continuity and he cannot ultimately create from it. For "Sunsum" is not just about the poet's failure to find his present and future in Africa; it is also about the relationship between art, history, and culture and about the poet's recognition of the limitations that a sense of homelessness and an absence of historical/cultural continuity must impose on the creative potential.

> The termites' dark teeth, three
>
> hundred years working,
> have patiently ruined my art.[36]

Yet the idea of "dumbness" and the consequent necessity to return to the New World do not imply a "negation," as Patricia Ismond has argued, because the confrontation in *Masks* is not, as she assumes, a "withdrawal" into a sacred world or an initiation into "the mysteries of the heart of darkness."[37] It is a less escapist and more vigorous effort to understand the past and how the New World can relate to it. If it begins in nostalgia it nevertheless ends in a purgation in which fear and shock are exorcised for a more realistic relationship to the past. In the encounter, history reveals itself not as a body of knowledge with ready answers to why things happen; not as a safe harbor from the terrifying fact of human corruptibility or even as a refuge for the poet unable to confront himself; it reveals itself as a flow, a movement whose lessons can be grasped and whose answers are not necessarily complete. When the New World persona is unmasked and brought face to face with himself, he screams in shock, fear, and outrage:

Why did our gold, the sun's
sunsum, safe against termites, crack

under the white gun
of plunder . . .[38]

The years remain silent, and the dust learns nothing from listening. This silence, like the "dumbness" of non-creativity, is not necessarily a negation. It is a silence that like the "dumbness" stirs up an awareness that is positive. What emerges after these encounters is a consciousness purged of nostalgia, sentimentality, and fear.

Thus the poet's overwhelming sense of loss at the end of this movement is a loss not so much of the past as of "continuity." It is not a permanent sense of loss, however, only the beginning of a new self-awareness. What is lost is the dream, the old consciousness that had tried to "dare the ships." The funeral dirge sings of this death and signals the poet's new realization:

Exiled from here

to seas
of bitter edges,

whips of white worlds,
stains of new

rivers,
I have returned

to you.
Not Chad,

the Niger's blood,
or Benin's

burning bronze
can save me now.

You I depend upon:
Onyame's eldest son.[39]

The poet's invocation to Tano instead of the images represented by Chad and Benin seems more appropriate in the circumstance of his new attitude. He cannot now take refuge in the pasts of Chad, Benin, or the Niger. His immediate world has been identified now as "the whips of white worlds / stains of new / rivers"; and Tano, eldest son of Onyame the creator, river of life and river of death, is what he needs for his new birth. Significantly, his awakening is accompanied not only by the rebirth of his own consciousness but also by the awakening of life and creativity around him.

The dance, the essence of creativity itself, is for the poet the most significantly recognizable form here. He identifies completely with it. His memory "bends," "curves," "nods head," and "crouches," "feeding the dust at the sole / of its feet as it dances."

Thus by the end of this movement and by the end of *Masks* Brathwaite's confrontation with history has been wholly cleansing. He has not only examined and explored the possibilities of memory in understanding his identity but has also purged his own fear and shame of the past. Visualized within the broader canvas of African history and explored simultaneously with its movements and processes, West Indian history acquires wider spatial and temporal dimensions, crystallizing itself in Brathwaite's memory as a recurring process of disintegration and renewal and presenting its own creative challenges. At the end of *Masks,* the inevitable fact of human corruptibility is still as inexplicable to him as it was at the beginning, since not even his dead ancestor can tell him why aberrations had occurred. Yet in *Masks,* the poet learns the courage to accept the flow of time and the certainty of death and at the same time commit himself to creativity. This commitment at the end of *Masks* is a commitment to the West Indies, and *Islands* is in this major sense an exploration of creativity and the creation of an aesthetic.

But if to live here
 is to die
clutching ashes

the fist tight
the skull dry
I will sing songs of the skeleton

I will return to the pebble
to the dumb seed
the unlighted faces of the fetish in the vegetable kingdom
"Eating the Dead," *Islands*

It is in the last section of his trilogy that Brathwaite consciously explores the dimensions of an Afro-Caribbean aesthetic, and *Islands* is in this sense an engagement with new self-conceptions and new perspectives on Caribbean creativity. In *Rights of Passage* he had dealt mostly with the processes of discontinuity and had explored these as well as the subtle continuities in the broad historical experience of the New World African. Concerned mostly with the taut surfaces of things, he had been preoccupied with evolving various forms and rhythms to express the experience; and it was indeed for this reason that his own poetic voice did not emerge as a dominant voice until the second movement and why even when it did was not sure and authoritative, as it later becomes in *Islands*. In the structural pattern of the trilogy he had still to crystallize his ideas on history and carry out his explorations in *Masks*.

The engagement with tradition and creativity in *Islands* and the various processes of reclamation are therefore related to the illuminations of Brathwaite's explorations in *Masks* and to his concern with the creation of a Caribbean aesthetic. There is a definite correlation between the encounter with history in *Rights of Passage* and *Masks* and the new concentration on the art of creation in *Islands*. It was part of the poet's mature realization in both these sections of the trilogy that history had its cycles of movement and that what man had to do to prevent entrapment and stasis was to create incessantly in the present. *Islands* is therefore an exploration of the peculiar historical and cultural situations that make creativity possible or impossible in the New World.

In *Islands* this general perspective on history and creativity is enlarged by the poet's contact with the "past" in Africa and by his exploration of what had seemed a problematic relationship to its history. As he is to discover in *Masks,* creativity in whatever form is the summation of the artist's relationship with all the environmental influences of his world; therefore, his relationship to the continent had to undergo a new, realistic qualification. Africa was his remote past but not his present, and if he would move forward, if he would create, his material had to be those African continuities that were shaped or transformed in the New World. In *Islands* the exploration of creativity or attempts at creativity becomes a major preoccupation.

Yet in the West Indies an engagement with aesthetics may have its special difficulties. Aesthetics, after all, stems from the criteria of values and the corpus of sensibility from which we perceive, create, and judge works of art, and in the West Indies the idea of an aesthetic may become problematic because values and sensibilities have also been shaped by an absence and barrenness of "history," which has appeared to diminish both the frontiers and quality of experience and values. Harris identifies a further limitation: "(The West Indian artist) lives in a comparatively bare world—mountains, jungles, rivers—where the monumental architecture of the old world is the exception rather than the rule. Yet the values of that very old world have still imposed themselves most evidently on his culture patterns and economic way of life."[40] The imposed values that Harris talks of are the values of conquerors, well defined and unequivocal about the subject/object, superior/inferior dichotomies in colonial relations. Can the West Indian writer create an aesthetic from these?

Brathwaite had raised a similar question in 1960[41] and explored its ramifications in the paradoxical framework in which he presented the New World experience in *The Arrivants*. He believes with Harris that a history of subjugation and diminishment can be counteracted not by denying its truth but by negating its deterministic hold and investing it with contrasting visions of possibility. Harris has further clarified the implications of this paradoxical vision:

> What sort of art is the outcome of this environment? The art of the skeleton or cell, the lonely, diminished structure of man. In the old world that cell is the very mass under which the passer-by is squeezed. So that he is locked away in an eternal negative position. In the West Indies that cell is a paradox . . . the very barrenness of the West Indian world reveals the necessity to examine closely the starting point of human societies. The diminution of man is not entirely accomplished and a relationship between man and the paradoxes of his world becomes evident as a relationship which can still have momentous consequences.[42]

Harris's plea for the recognition and dynamic exploration of the diminished man has reverberations on Brathwaite's engagement with submerged history and with his paradoxical song of the skeleton. For Brathwaite shows a similar preoccupation with the validation of the diminished West Indian person, and in his works diminished person and diminished history are presented in so many vital and dynamic perspectives that they yield possibilities from which an aesthetic can emerge. Whether in *Rights of Passage, Masks,* or *Islands,* the losses of history are continuously and simultaneously measured against visions of new possibilities for creation, and it is from this commitment that Brathwaite derives the paradoxical framework and the complementary and contrasting visions of *Islands.*

Thus, as in Lamming and Harris, the dialectic in *The Arrivants* is based on perspectives of historical experience, an engagement that is nowhere more pronounced than in *Islands,* in which Brathwaite is also concerned with squeezing out an aesthetic from the totality of black experience in the New World. The ambiguities and paradoxes of this experience are deliberately enacted in the variety of moods and styles and in the balances which Brathwaite creates between them. Structured between opposite poles of sterility and growth, the experience of history moves beyond loss and stasis to become the basis of an aesthetic in *Islands*.

In this deliberate structuring of poems, the idea of creativity in all its forms dominates the sequences, suggesting a relationship between creativity and history, recovering the spirit of the past and creating new symbols and words for the present and future. The first two poems, functioning almost like a prelude to the entire collection, enact Brathwaite's paradoxical perception of historical experience in the New World. "Jah" reveals within its nuances and paradoxes the alienation and paralysis of slave and colonial history as well as the faint traces of tradition and self-perception which form the "root-blood," the source of West Indian creativity. The musician in "Jah" may well be confused and disoriented from a cultural dependence on his slave master, but he is revealed as still retaining a measure of authentic selfhood which presents a contrasting world of perception and vision. Indeed, the seemingly unrelated forest images which Brathwaite thrusts into the eighth stanza as emblematic of the jazz man's root-blood set up oppositions between it and the Western God's "bright bubbled heaven," depicting the distortions of creativity that must result from such conflicts.

> With my blue note, my cracked note, full flatten-
> ed fifth, my ten bebop fingers, my black bottom'd strut, Panama
> worksong, my cabin, my hut,
> my new frigged-up soul and God's heaven,
> heaven, gonna walk all over God's heaven . . .[43]

The jarring images differentiating the black artist's distinctively "blue" and "cracked" notes from his "new frigged-up soul" in "God's heaven" demonstrate the confusion of values from which he operates as a creator. For the God to whom he now uncurls his "leaven" is an exploiter, high up in his heaven, ungrounded and unrelated to his root life. In such circumstances, Brathwaite suggests, creativity achieves nothing; no self-realization, no growth, but simply the futility which the images suggest:

> eyes without bait, snout
> without words, teeth with nothing to kill,
> skill of fin for a child's wonder,
> pale scales for collectors to sell . . .[44]

Yet the nothingness that signifies a failure of creativity is not the total and permanent fact of this world. The god in "Jah" may be a soulless god whose clutches separate the New World creator from the most sacred things of his world, but in "Ananse" the creator's own cultural god is alive, a paradoxical symbol of obscurity and presence. The poet's image of his brain as a "green chrysalis / storing leaves," surrounded by glass, is indeed a summation of the way in which Brathwaite's images operate throughout this section. For in the paradox of the image itself lies the possibility of recognition, and in "Ananse" the god, symbol of heritage, clings to the edge of people's consciousness with a "black snake's unwinking eye"[45] and remains the only heartbeat of sound and the only potential for change in the New World.

Throughout *Islands* it is this potential for continuity and with it the hope of creativity that underlies Brathwaite's explorations of the ambiguities of history. In *Rights of Passage* he had hinted at possibilities for continuity, but his emphasis on discontinuity and his artistic interest in the "taut surfaces of things" had precluded any deeper probing of surface. He had suggested paradoxes in his image of the exile as the "sick stalk, torn / of its tugging hope,"[46] but he had not explored the tugging hope, and in his delineations the islands had remained "stones":

. . . bare
bones: powder-
ing spirit-
less stones
of this cold
and alien morning . . .[47]

Such images, placed beside the shifting and reverberating connotations of the limbo, womb, and coral images in *Islands*, show themselves as images of surface. In *Islands* the reverberation of image, its extension and transformation, is part of the surface and inner probing which Brathwaite carries out to suggest other dimensions of historical experience. It is part of his technique rather than a contradiction or confusion that his vision of the *Islands* should be extended and transformed throughout the poem. In his exploration of history he is poised between a vision of sterility and a vision of growth, an ambivalence that allows him to move beyond a one-dimensional linear vision towards contrasting perceptions that take in the possibilities of diminished history.

The consistently explored symbols of growth in *Islands* are therefore part of Brathwaite's conception of history as movement and part of his perception of the multilayered progression of black experience in the New World. The accumulation of history as he perceives it may well be as imperceptible as the gradual building of the coral, but the entire experience could conceivably become the base for a tradition and an aesthetic. Thus in the poem "Coral" the gradual and continual growth of the coral parallels the region's accumulated experience, so that each generation of coral that dies adds to it in a process which persists even in times of conflict, turbulence, and pain.[48] For here, ironically, it is the coral's soil of conflict, its medley of dead bodies, snapped necks, and leaden tongues that give birth to new life. The process is continuously recurring, and in the midst of the bloom of life the new pain begins:

walls of white,
walls of red, stations
of bloom, wells
of bottomless
gloom.[49]

Brathwaite enacts this cyclical process and links himself to it when in the final vision he makes the uncurling embryo swim into the polyp's eye, signifying the recurrent patterns, paradoxes, and ambiguous possibilities of Caribbean history.

This acceptance is not without qualification. The poem also suggests that whether or not "growth" would be creative depends on how honestly we confront and settle the past. The "embryo" images are therefore originally images of natural growth which are in the course of the poem transformed or modified in accordance with the particular situation explored. This artistic device, which actually begins in *Masks* and reaches a height in *Islands,* underlines both the cyclical vision of history and the various instances of reclamation described in *Islands.* Thus, in *Masks,* when pathfinders grope their way in the forest in a second attempt at settlement and discovery, "the *moist* / stones, *warm* / pebbles of rain, // move into tossed leaves / of darkness,"[50] promising life and possibility. Similarly, as in "Coral" in *Islands,* the image of stone is from the beginning in a natural process of growth, like a "secret leaf" or a "curled embryo," awaiting fruition and birth, depending on the particular possibility uncovered in the exploration.

Indeed, as part of the paradoxical presentation of historical experience, the vision of growth also coexists with a vision of sterility, so that we have in *Islands* seemingly contradictory images of violence and sterility and of unraveling and growth; contradictions which are in themselves part of that exploratory technique which differentiates the use of image in *Islands* from the use of it in *Rights of Passage.* For in *Islands* Brathwaite is more anxiously concerned with the interaction between reality and possibility, between what the islands look like and what they could look like. Thus, often, the sterile Caribbean present is, as in the poem "Littoral," embodied in the image of the stone purged of all signs of life:

scuffed sand at my feet,

stone, roots of grass,
crushing scuttled sea shells,
claws of crabs.

In the poem's last stanza, the sterile and violent images are transformed into images of life and growth by virtue of the poet's special awareness and commitment. It is as if the sheer identification of stasis and the suggestion of direction contain within themselves hopeful possibilities for recovery. Brathwaite suggests throughout *Islands* that the burden of transformation may rest with the special perception and sensitivity of the poet,

whose marrow, whose toil
butting into this sweat-sweetened rot
will soften these roots,
loosen the shoots under pebble and shale?[51]

In *Islands,* the "limbo" sequences alternate in this way between such paradoxes, pointing to the life that could be reclaimed even from the most sterile and pessimistic images of the past and present. In a similar sense, the short poem entitled "Pebbles" enacts within its final, one-lined stanza the ambiguity and balance I have referred to:

You cannot crack a pebble,
it excludes
death. Seeds will not
take root on its cool sur-

face. It is duck's back
of water. A knife will not snap
it open. It will slay
giants

but never bear children.[52]

Following the mood of disillusion and despondency generated by the rejection of roots in "Caliban," the poem may seem definitive about the island's sterility and death; but the embryo image of the egg itself as well as the idea of death as regenerative do affirm a faint possibility. The idea of regeneration with its confident belief in the laws of the universe and in the recurrence of things underlies the section's insistent message that the sterile past must be bled to death before a movement forward can be achieved.

These paradoxical perspectives on history are not only embodied in the contradictions within images in particular poems; they are also demonstrated in a deliberate balancing and contrasting of moods and styles in the structuring of sections in *Islands*. Thus in the "limbo" section, for instance, the uncertainty and doubt of poems like "The Cracked Mother" and "Caliban" are balanced in the same sequence by the forward movement and perceptual achievements of poems like "Shepherd" and "Islands." In the earlier poems Brathwaite enacts the cyclic movements of the region's history, showing the beginning of colonization, the imposition of alien gods, and the consequent dislocation and maiming of aboriginal and African psyches, and although he moves forward in exploration and vision by deciphering the link between the history of subjugation and Caribbean schizophrenia, he never really overcomes the mood of uncertainty and doubt which pervade the two poems. The mother in "The Cracked Mother" is at the end still undecided about a direction for the present and future, and Caliban never explores the potential for perception and personal reintegration embodied in a recovery of roots.

Yet within the contrasting perspectives in which the limbo section is structured, the uncertainty and doubt of the two poems are balanced by the positive visions of "Shepherd" and "Islands." If Brathwaite stands halfway between despondency and possibility in the earlier poems, he now moves from doubt to vision and from dumbness to speech in "Shepherd." Indeed, as part of the increasingly dominant consciousness of the poet in *Islands,* "Shepherd" presents one possibility for the Caribbean. The poet-shaman's descent into the farthest reaches of memory, his recovery of submerged "history," and his acquisition of speech connect memory with history and creativity, enacting a process of reclamation. Thus, balanced and contrasted in this way, the entire limbo section may well sum up the message of its concluding poem, "Islands": that the truly creative and meaningful vision of the region's history is one that moves beyond its linear presentations to project its paradoxes and ambivalence.

> So looking through a map
> of the islands, you see
> rocks, history's hot-
> lies, rot-
> ting hulls, cannon
> wheels, the sun's

slums: if you hate
us. Jewels,
if there is delight
in your eyes.
. . . .
Looking through a map
of the Antilles, you see how time
has trapped
its humble servants here.
. . . .
But if your eyes
are kinder, you will observe
butterflies
how they fly higher
and higher before their hope dries
with endeavor
and they fall among flies.[53]

From now on in *Islands* it is the combined vision of growth and potential that informs the poet's consciousness as it becomes increasingly dominant and exhaustive in exploring the process of reclamation. As a prelude to this process, the poet persona becomes poet and shaman; and the poem "Shepherd" symbolically confirms him in the role as it enacts his symbolic descent into self and memory. Using the paradigm of the Pukkimina ritual of descent and possession, Brathwaite explores the enlightening and symbolic possibilities of Afro-Caribbean religion and ritual. Here the metaphor of descent becomes a mode of penetrating the ordinary realms of experience and acquiring new visions and energies. The experience enacted in "Shepherd" is therefore a distillation of all Brathwaite's explorations of history and creativity and of the artist's role in the creation of an aesthetic.

The idea of creation as a movement from dumbness to speech and as an uncurling of the artist's inner energies as well as the subtle presences of his world echoes the aesthetics of the drum and Word in *Masks*. In *Masks* the silence preceding the explosion of drum sounds is also the silence that conceals submerged presences. As in *Masks* the creative process also becomes a special sacrificial effort on the part of the poet, spurred on by the communal thrust and awesome energy of the drums and rituals. Again, as in *Masks,* vision precedes the birth of the Word, and the Word is the uncurled sound and shape, the thick gutturals and red, heavy consonants reclaimed from the pebble and shale and from the farthest reaches of the poet's memory. Here in "Shepherd" reclamation is a reclamation of the past and its spirit, of god and song and of the spiritual continuity from the past eroded by years of self-rejection and lack of awareness.

As one who would reclaim history, then, Brathwaite's weapon is "awareness," awareness of old ways and old gods as well as a reintegration of dead ancestors with the consciousness of the living. Throughout *Islands* Brathwaite opposes this kind of awareness to innocence and later on links it to his concept of the Word. Thus, in *Islands,* awareness as a weapon against innocence assumes a thematic significance and indeed clarifies those sections of the poem in which the poet communes with the gods and the dead.

> The streets of my home have their own gods
> but we do not see them
> they walk in the dust
> but are hidden from our eyes
> . . . .
> The streets' root is in the sea
> in the deep harbors;
> . . . .
> They speak to us with the voice of crickets
> with the shatter of leaves.[54]

The sea and the deep harbors make the connection between the Middle Passage and the New World, defying a history of amnesia and presenting the link against the whole complex intermingling of past and present in the awakened consciousness of the poet. The voices of crickets and the shatter of leaves relive the forest settlements in *Masks,* returning us to "leaves' sudden / betrayal of silence,"[55] to the aberration of slavery and to the moment of capture. Thus, in this way the very idea of god is expanded and secularized to include the spirit and consciousness of ancestors as they are reflected in people's lives. The gods are then brought so close to people's lives, to everything that has made them, that eventually their innocence becomes innocence not just of history but of the very substance of their being.

This kind of reclamation and reactivation is the basis of a personal aesthetic which Brathwaite extends to the New World of the Caribbean, an aesthetic which is also linked to his conception of the artist as priest and redeemer:

> You must spill me into the cracked ground
> . . . .
> I am the hot rum leaking from green

from the clanking of iron
I bleed with the fields' sweat
with the sweet backs of labor.[56]

Here the poet, without self and ego but with a clearer, more enlarged vision of history, takes on the challenge of the epilogue in *Rights of Passage* and defines the nature of that commitment which would usher in a new vision of the Caribbean. The new commitment is towards a more vigorous exploration and definition of the Afro-Caribbean heritage and its impact on vision and sociopolitical transformation in the region. Throughout the trilogy Brathwaite has maintained a cyclic view of history, continually enacting the intermingling of past and present in the circular, moving history of Africa and the West Indies. Now, in these final sections of *Islands*, his emphasis is on the actual components of this heritage and on their potential for vision and aesthetic extension in the arts of the imagination. The first poem in the sequence, "Wake," offers both a literal and symbolic illustration of the interplay between Old World and New World, between Africa and the West Indies.

For on one hand, the wake as an African burial rite is in a literal sense an African retention in the West Indies, a fact which validates Brathwaite's choice of it as an aspect of heritage and as a medium for exploration. In a major sense, however, its function as a preparation for transition into the world of the dead offers leeway for metaphorical interpretations. In its West African connotations, the principle behind the ritual relates to the concentric order of three worlds (the living, the dead, the unborn) and the continuous spiritual link between them. Thus, more than a medium of transition, the rite is also a mode of reconnection, a means by which the dead world and its life- and spirit-sustaining forces can intermingle with the living world to its renewed vitality and advantage.

Brathwaite's choice of the ritual as a medium for symbolic exploration, especially in a poem which also delineates the psychic destitution and spiritual poverty is especially significant. For "Wake" also functions as a mode of integration and an act of rediscovery. The "dead" in the poem are, therefore, the Caribbean dead: generations of ancestors, accumulations of history, storehouses of buried perceptions, in essence, all the lessons and illuminations embodied in a concept of heritage. Brathwaite outlines these hidden gems precisely in relation to the absences and enervation of the living world; the drifting ship of the islands, the insecurities, uncertainties, and concealed fears of its people; the absence of a grounded vision, of tradition, of native land and of that numinous element that raises life and living beyond the merely physical and banal.

Correspondingly, then, integration between living and dead worlds does not so much inspire shock and horror as retrieve aspects of heritage and perception which would inspire a sense of tradition and the potential for creating the Word.[57] Yet in "Wake" these features of heritage remain only possibilities. As with all Brathwaite's "circular" explorations, the discovery of possibility serves mostly to accentuate present absence and disability, since in the ongoing exploration the living world still seeks the creation of the Word that would save. It is for this reason that even at the end of such a promising vision in "Wake" the islands still remain

> Islands
> Islands
> stone stripped from stone
> pebbles
> empty shells.[58]

The aesthetic of renaissance is, therefore, more than a simpleminded restitution of dead gods, more than a recovery merely aimed at bridging the discontinuities of history. For the triumph over innocence and the recovery of god and song move beyond static restitution to be integrated into an ongoing exploration of Caribbean transformations. Indeed, unlike another reclaimer of history, Bryant in Harris's *The Secret Ladder,* the poet moves beyond allegiance to god and ancestor into a future in which the vision inspired by renaissance leads not to facile, romantic reconnections but to visions of change and reordering. It is for this reason that the recovery of god and song is differentiated from the birth of new language in the sequence entitled "Possession":

> My tongue is heavy with new language
> but I cannot give birth speech
> Pebbles surround me.[59]

"Pebbles" still symbolize silence and sterility even in the above extract, in which the poet persona is on the verge of new language. "Pebbles" could stall transformations unless awareness and art go further than personal vision to become media and agents for refashioning futures. For this reason, Brathwaite attempts to transform his new vision of heritage into a vital and meaningful self-expression that takes in experiences of landscape and history. Within this context, "Dawn" is crucial in enacting the processes by which the poet acquires a voice that speaks both for himself and his people, a voice more descriptive of his multiple selves than "waves whitest con- /

sonants,"[60] the syllables of subjugation and alienation which he had de-
cried in *Masks*. Thus, "Dawn," with all its connotations of awakening and
new perceptions, opens out all those sensations and possibilities of the island that can inspire both a poetic vision and a unique authentic voice. As
in the poem "South," in which seascape, fisherman's house, and starfish in
the pool suggest the limitless possibilities of identification with island and
people, "Dawn" moves even further than the dream and psychic vision of
"South" to encompass the actual processes of uncurling and speech, the
kind of poetic language in which the imagination is twined with the reality
it evokes, making artistic creation an honest fusing of imagination and
environment. "I watched the vowels curl from the tongue of the carpenter's
plane, / resinous, fragrant / labials of our forests,"[61] Walcott writes, enacting a similar uncurling and naming in *Another Life*. In Brathwaite, however, the vowels that come up encompass both perceived landscape and
reclaimed sounds and words: "the sea in its splendor," "fishermen's songs,"

> flowers knowing
> the sun-
> light
> . . . .
> red clay
> mud of volcanoes
> bristled with jewels
> . . . .
> . . . the cold fever of the day-
> light, thin man, knocking at doors, smile
> sharpened by the rats, tin can
>
> of pestilence, scruffulent scrubber,
> savior of the harbor's sepulchers of filth.
> . . . .
> frog songs
> the moth-organ drool of the snails'
> slow passage . . .
> . . . .
> the fat valley loads of my mother
> of water,
>
> spoken syllables: words salt on your lips
> on my lips. . . .[62]

These images of landscape, past history, historical scars, transformations in speech, song, and religion make up the larger images of the sea, the island, and the mother who is the source of the poet's identity and creativity.

Brathwaite's concluding statement in "Dawn" suggests that it is perhaps only from the acceptance and identification with the connotations of the sea image that the poet can recover a true poetic voice. The "wound- / ed gift-giver of sea"[63] who inspires the poet's spoken syllables in the final vision is certainly separate from the stones that give lips to the water in "Bosampra" ("The Return" sequence in *Masks*), just as the "salt words" she gives are differentiated from "waves' whitest con- / sonants," the syllables of subjugation and alienation in *Masks*.

The final sections of *Islands* are, therefore, celebrations and enactment of the "salt words," the spoken syllables recovered from the submerged history of the island. The grandmother's voice in "Ancestor," the blues song about Sookey's deprivation and death, the mask that the "Ogun" figure carves to express his life and hurts and anger, reflect a major creative thrust, one that is made possible by memory, by links and interrelationships between past and present, between history and possibility.

This base of memory and perception is both an aesthetic quest and a mode of liberation. That is why in spite of the comforting vision of self-acceptance and creative power achieved in "Ogun" the poet must nevertheless circle back to explore the possibility of his vision becoming a weapon for political liberation. Yet in the trilogy the relationship between artistic vision and political liberation is not a certainty but a debate with its own ambiguities and moral dilemmas which are enacted in the poems "Leopard" and "Anvil." In reversing the role of conqueror and victim and creating a situation in which

. . . Force
fashions force;
master makes over-
mastering slave

and cruelty breeds
a litter of bright
evils.[64]

The historical perspective here achieves subtle insights into the nature and quality of rebellion. The rebel leopard acquires illumination from the double situations of conqueror and conquered in which he is presented. The caged leopard caught in a paralysis of fear and inaction had once been a conqueror, too, preying on the weaker antelope and duiker in the African forests, unleashing its passion, slashing and mangling its victims and thriving on its brutal power in the manner of all conquerors.

. . . Yet had he felt
his supple force would fall

to such confinement,
would he, to dodge his doom
and guarantee his movement,

have paused from stalking deer
or striking down the duiker;
or would he, face to fate,

have merely murdered more?[65]

The integration of such opposite situations breaks down rigid perspectives and inspires moral insights into the whole process of rebellion, enabling the rebel to do more than expend rage and reverse his situation. Indeed, the rebel persona in "Anvil" opts out of sadistic repetition and vengeful assault:

. . . poised
in that fatal attitude

that would have smashed
the world, or made it, he
let the hammer

down; made
nothing, un-
made nothing;

his bright
hopes down,
his own
bright future
dumb,
his one
heroic flare
and failure
done.[66]

Was his inaction due to cowardice or humanity? Brathwaite does not debate the issue. Rather, he leaves the ambiguity simply as a base for further exploration. Whether the rebel's inaction was the result of cowardice or humanity, it still perpetuates the encircling cage, and the future of rebellion must now rest on the quality and impact of the newly reclaimed Word. At this point, the relationship between artistic vision and rebellion takes on wider, more subtle ramifications. The stone must confound the void, and the Word that must refashion futures, we now know, must move beyond vengeful rage and benefit from the enlargement of vision which the poet's exploration has achieved in the "Leopard" and "Anvil" sequences.

The Word of the Baptist preacher's double-edged sermon is in this sense an aspect of the rebellion that Brathwaite talks of. Steeped in ambiguity, it combines a Christian religious vision with a secular and political message that undermines that vision. Avowedly meant to praise God through the hymn, the stone sermon ends on a different affirmation that rejects the stranglehold of an oppressive Christianity and at the same time affirms a resilient faith unique to the folk. The "drowned faith" of the congregation is not drowned faith in God as such but a rejection of the orthodox church's parasitic and oppressive hold.

> Sookey dead
> Sookey dead
> Sookey drownded.
>
> Christ a-pick
> Christ a-peck
> Christ a-spite him.[67]

If the Baptist sermon enacts the special nuances of the reclaimed Word, the "stilts of song" and "masqueraded story" of the carnival ritual represent aspects of the Word with potentialities for catharsis, renewal, and vision. Tizzic's carnival dance may contain this potential in its desire for reconnection to "days of green unhur- / ried growing."[68] But unlike Achille's ritual dance in Omeros, which expresses the aggregate of his realities as he has explored them, Tizzic's ritual remains unproblematized and merely a response to melody and rhythm. For Walcott's Achille, the "goat-drums" and the "brass bells" around his ankle are not "chains from the Bight of Benin' / but those fastened by himself . . .":

> He was someone else
> today, a warrior-woman, fierce and benign.
> Today he was African, his own epitaph,
> his own resurrection.[69]

Brathwaite's Tizzic, on the other hand, is a figure of irony whom the poet delineates in order to castigate. His melodious carnival songs, even with the promise of heaven and the Madonna's sweet compassion, still turn him to "Lenten sorrows . . . Ash- / Wednesday, ashes, darkness, death." For the unrestrained ascents, the stars, and the bright, swinging heaven are borrowed glories unrelated to the realities of his life and history, and in their blazing apotheosis ". . . the good stilts splinter- / ed, wood legs broke, calypso steelpan / rhythm faltered," showing the difference between the illusion of a perfect heaven and the immediate and imperfect reality: "After the *bambalula bambulai* / he was a slave again."[70]

It seems then that for both Brathwaite and Walcott the reclaimed Word should reflect the meaning that one gives to the self and should be transformed, though perhaps through different ways and in different contexts. Achille's ritual dance in *Omeros* may not be too different from the enactment in "*Jou'vert*" which balances Tizzic's carnival fiasco in *Islands*. For the dialectical presentations that make up the basic structure of the poem "*Jou'vert*" enact a different relation to Carnival. Riveting back to rituals of prayer and sacrifice reminiscent of *Masks* but different in their aspirations, "*Jou'vert*" evokes carnival both as a ritual and as an uninhibited celebration of becoming that takes in the recurring processions of history and their transformations and paradoxes. Here, disintegration and death in the desert ("dust of desert / cries of arrows") repeat other instances of disintegration in the recurring history of West Indian people ("lightning flashes / man asunder / fangs of lightning / strike and / bite the bitter world of stone and sorrows")[71] are together balanced against the transformations and renewals in the New World. For it is the confrontation with such presences rather than an escape from them that leads to vision and liberation. The carnival consciousness that finally emerges in "*Jou'vert*" is therefore a consciousness that is purged of anger and bitterness, enlarged by a wider, more complex perception of history and by a renewed creativity:

hurts for-

gotten, hearts
no longer bound

to black and bitter
ashes in the ground.[72]

This manner of creation, which Harris has called "the art of the skeleton or cell, the lonely, diminished structure of man," is what Brathwaite had enacted in the birth of the Word in "Vèvè" and now celebrates in the renewed creativity of "*Jou'vert.*" His ritualistic and artistic innovations in "Vèvè" had defied annihilation and diminishment, and now his new exuberance in "*Jou'vert*" becomes a deliberate creative assertion in the face of these.

The sense of awakening and the general mood of exhilaration at the end of "*Jou'vert*" are therefore in keeping with the dialectical structure of *Islands* and with the affirmation of the general cyclical vision which is part of the trilogy's overall perspective. The belief in recurrence and the certainty of rebirth coupled with the sense of a tenacious growth in consciousness enacted throughout *Islands* gives a confident assurance to the poem's "resolution" that West Indians will make with their "history" and rhythms,

> . . . some-
>
> thing torn
>
> and new.[73]

The aesthetics of renaissance is thus what finally redeems the Caribbean broken ground "trampled with the bull's swathe of whips."[74] It is an aesthetic that involves a recovery or rather a reconnection to broken recollections, to earlier perceptions of the spiritual and sacred or other primordial realms of meaning not necessarily articulated; an aesthetic derived from that crack of possibility recoverable from the paralysis and stasis of Caribbean history and including the repossession of ritual, the recovery of the elemental, and of the graven Word:

> carved from Olodumare
> from Ogun of Alare, from Ogun of Onire
> from shango broom of thunder and Damballa Grand Chemin.[75]

Brathwaite draws on the connotations of "Olodumare," "Ogun," and "Shango" (as he has explored them in his poetry) as part of the forces, associations, and implications of the graven Word. But the specific nature of these symbols renders them susceptible to both literal and symbolic interpretations, and Brathwaite has sometimes been alluded to as artificially reinstating old and dead gods and creating a Caribbean vision from alien symbols.

> If the old gods were dying in the mouth of the old, they died of their own volition. Today they are artificially resurrected by the anthropologist's tape-recorder and in the folk archives of departments of culture . . . To believe in its folk forms the State would have to hallow not only its mythology but re-believe in dead gods, not as converts either, but as makers. But no one in the New World whose one God is

advertised as dead can believe in innumerable gods of another life. Those gods would have to be an anthropomorphic variety of his will. Our poets and actors would have not only to describe possession but to enact it, otherwise we would have not art but blasphemy, and blasphemy which has no fear is decoration.[76]

But Walcott's argument takes only a literal view of Brathwaite's symbols and appears to reject his fundamental assumption that discontinuity can be ameliorated through awareness of and reconnection to the spirit of the past. In his view the gods are dead, and dead gods of any mythology can only be artificially re-created.

Yet even from such literal considerations the fact that the connotations of these gods are recognizable and meaningful aspects of customs and rituals in Caribbean regions like Haiti validates Brathwaite's use of them as well as the implications of continuity and transformation they suggest. But the symbols are not entirely literal. The poet need not enact "possession" in order to validate it, since possession itself becomes a large metaphor of descent for a reconnection to a submerged past and sensibility. Brathwaite's "graven Word" in "Vèvè" is therefore not just the Word simplistically drawn from ancestor and god and facilely reinstated to bridge discontinuities of time. It is the emerged image, the reclaimed life and pain integrated into consciousness, "sundered from your bone / plundered from my breast // by ice, by chain, by sword, by the east wind,"[77] and merged with wind, fire, and dust, the elemental as well as the inarticulate presences of Caribbean space.

Brathwaite suggests his own intense and priestly commitment to this rebirth by conveying it through the metaphor of vodum possession, welcoming the reclaimed Word to mount his artist's consciousness as he communicates vision to his community and people. The metaphor of possession reveals several depths to his shamanistic commitment, for vodum possession has several symbolic implications. As Harris suggests, the dancer,

possessed by the muse of contraction dances into a posture, wherein one leg is drawn up into the womb of space . . . All conventional memory is erased and yet in this trance of overlapping spheres of reflection a primordial or deeper function of memory begins to exercise itself within the bloodstream of space . . . the dancer moves in a trance and the interior mode of the drama is exteriorized into a medium inseparable from his trance and invocation. He is a dramatic agent of subconsciousness. The life from within and the life from without now truly overlap.[78]

The trance of possession becomes, as Harris insightfully explains above, a crucial metaphor for the poet, because his own drama of consciousness involves the same process of revelation and unraveling of obscurity. But "whereas the territory of the dancer remains actually obscure to him within his trance whatever revelation or illumination his limbs may articulate in their involuntary theme," the "vision" of the poet, Harris argues (when one comprehends it from the opposite pole of "dance"), "possesses . . . a 'spatial' logic or 'convertible' property of imagination, making his drama of consciousness a slow unraveling of obscurity, a revelation or illumination within himself."[79] Harris's explanation clarifies for us the metaphors, parallelisms, and contrasts with the vodum dancer, illuminating the processes by which the writer becomes both a passive and a creative agent. As a creator, the writer's work is also a journey through territories of primordial but broken recollections in search of a "community" whose existence he begins to discern within a willed and intense visualization which carries him beyond ordinary natural boundaries into "overlapping capacities of nature where one breaks through, as it were, the one-sidedness of self-sufficient social character."[80]

This mode of apprehension, in which the writer seeks community and image through a drama of consciousness, represents an inner art which encourages the use of the imagination as a duty and as a major fact in the poet's evocation of images. The art of ascent and descent associated with Brathwaite's metaphor of possession are especially crucial for the artist seeking the "truth of community," because this truth, as Harris argues, is neither self-evident nor purely produced by economic circumstances,[81] and the creative artist needs to descend into the depths of his own consciousness in order, literally, to rediscover and reinform himself. Perhaps these kinds of depths and extensions are what Brathwaite refers to in "Eating the Dead" when he claims:

I . . .
can show
you what it means to eat
your god, drink his explosions of power
and from the slow sinking mud of your plunder, grow.[82]

Chapter Nine

Configurations of History in the Writing of West Indian Women

In the general context of a West Indian historical imagination, the writing of women not only reveals new and different perspectives but actually interrogates and problematizes some of the assumptions and perceptions already delineated in our earlier chapters on male writing. The commonly held idea that West Indian writing is almost exclusively male-centered[1] has generated the assumption that West Indian women writers and thinkers never entered the debate on history and identity. Yet a cross-section of the writing of older and younger women writers of the region reveals an equally vigorous engagement with issues of history, race, class, and gender. Indeed, the intersection of these issues in the writing of women reveals a unique relation to the region's history, and a separate chapter on the female historical imagination would present comparisons and contrasts that should reveal the complexity of the debate on history and its importance in shaping the nature of West Indian writing.

Although the woman writer's engagement with history is part of the general process of self-definition and reassessment in a postcolonial West Indies, the context of the writing presents a different order of imagination and representation since it is in the end inseparable from women's relation to history, culture, and political conditioning. The connection between these areas of experience and women's literary expression constitutes the special slant that gives a distinctive quality to the female imagination. In recent literary criticism this feminine framework has become a crucial basis for analyzing women's writing. Feminist research in history, anthropology, psychology, and sociology has identified a broad based community of values, institutions, relationships and methods of communication[2] which unifies women's experiences within and across cultures. In some women's literature this female world not only presents its own unique perceptions but actually intersects with, permeates, or even undermines the masculine systems that contain it. Thus analysis of writing by women involves a complex negotiation between female and male worlds and between women's personal, social, and political histories.

How then does the woman writer's perspective and representation of history intersect with all these aspects of our framework? First, this writing has its roots in the ways in which historical forces have shaped lives and destinies in the region and in how women writers have perceived and constructed this phenomenon. For instance, West Indian women, naturally differentiated from men by gender, were nevertheless undifferentiated from men in slavery since slave men and women were all defined as property and as accountable to their owners. Black women in the Caribbean have therefore a long history of work as field and house laborers, as producers of the labor force in the plantation society and in contemporary times, as workers in new industries. Such a history naturally creates a unique context of sexual and gender roles that may confuse relations between men and women. In the West Indies this situation is further complicated by the fact that from the early stages of slavery sexual exploitation and control of women were crucial elements in maintaining the power of colonists and planters, and this tendency has remained part of the dynamics of gender relations in West Indian societies.

Yet the dynamic is much more complex than it appears to be and was partly responsible for what Edward Brathwaite has described as the creolization and social ordering of society in the West Indies. For the paradox of the various sexual relationships between master and slave is that while these were in some respects exploitative they were in others mutual, humanizing, and sometimes even unifying. The separations of Creole society, Brathwaite has argued, were not rigidly maintained at the level of sexual relations,[3] and within the leeway of these liaisons the cultures of slave and master touched each other in a creolizing process that shaped both their lives. Thus historically, Afro-Caribbean women can lay claim not only to a past investment in the labor and economics of the region but also, significantly, to its social and cultural formation. West Indian women lived this history in all its ramifications and possessed intimate knowledge of their own movements through it. Generations of women have come to possess a better grasp of the deeper meanings of these processes, since as grandmothers and mothers they have transmitted what has always been a muted and submerged culture in women-centered forms often excluded from the domain of formal historiography. Thus, in the historical writing of West Indian women custom, tradition, myth, ritual, and belief are given new interpretations and meanings in forms that are inextricably linked with the narrative forms of an oral culture and with the language and metaphors of a different cosmology.

In this respect their writing is similar to and at the same time remarkably different from the perspectives of white Creole women, who also explored their relation to the region and its history in their writing. Like black women in slave societies, white Creole women also occupied ambivalent positions in a colonial ethos that was stridently patriarchal. On one hand, they were part of an oppressive system (some white women owned slaves themselves or managed slaves on behalf of their husbands);[4] yet on the other, their own positions in relation to a colonial and slave ethos rendered them vulnerable in several ways. Defined in contradistinction to black women as ideal wives and mothers, their positions and roles were nevertheless bound up with the dependency created by their subordinate roles as wives and mothers and with what Evelyn O'Callaghan has termed "the complicating factor of the black woman's *participation* in these roles."[5] To a large extent their dependence on black women for physical and emotional services destabilized the hierarchies of master/slave relationships and rendered white Creole women vulnerable; and it was in the end such abrogation of agency that revealed the paradoxes in their situation as oppressors and victims in the slave society.

White Creole women writers internalized and reflected these paradoxes in their writing, and their work may be read in conjunction with other writing as part of the female response to history in the West Indies. O'Callaghan has seen the significance of this writing in the insight it reveals on women's versions of the travel/adventure tale of the Caribbean, which was originally a male text. "The [women's] texts put forward 'versions' of the Caribbean already inscribed in colonial discourse—both positive and negative—to which the protagonists relate in a very personal way . . . [We must] pay attention [then] to the way in which these narratives by women depart from the conventional tropes of the travel story and the semantic and stylistic implications of such departures."[6]

Yet there is a larger sense in which this writing becomes an alternative version of colonial historiography itself, a representation of history from the other side, from the perspective of that construct of creolization in which white Creole women were more implicated than their men through their very proximity to black women and black "culture." Indeed, by representing this version of history from the perspective of their own vulnerability they expose the cracks within a colonial enterprise that is often represented in historiography as a bold, self-assured, and humanizing venture.

It is in this sense that a novel like Jean Rhys's *Wide Sargasso Sea* may offer contrasting insights into the confusing and contradictory epistemologies that make the perception of history in the region complex and paradoxical. The period of West Indian history which Rhys's novel explores encompasses that most significant period of transition when the West Indies stood on the threshold either of new social relationships or fragmentation into racial entities and confrontations. The historiography of the period offers several perspectives on the possibilities of this transition, and in spite of the general social direction of the writing, it was still dominated by historians like Carlyle, Trollope, and Froude, who still analyzed the society as an economic commodity and saw its social development not in terms of its own internal workings but in relation to its situation as a subordinate and marginal appendage to British interests.

Rhys's novel rewrites this period in different metaphors, configuring a more subversive history from a perspective of place and a specific social context with its own internal contradictions and competing ideologies. The metaphor of the Sargasso Sea, which provides the title of the novel,[7] evokes the historical contact between Europe and a vastly different West Indies, suggesting that a different set of preoccupations and dilemmas distinguish the special history of the region. Here it is the structuring vision of the female character that brings out the special nuances of this history, and the female perspective is significant not only, as Ramchand has long noted, "for its dramatic possibilities in creating a pattern of alienation within alienation"[8] but also for the leeway it provides for insight into other variables, often inarticulate and submerged, that constitute West Indian history.

Antoinette's perspective is, for instance, manipulated in such a way that it is at once an evaluative mirror of historical phenomena from the point of view of the growing child, the adolescent girl, and the woman and at the same time subject to unconscious revelation and to the novelist's interpretive ironies. It is from her observations and relationships that we get a double view of plantation society as a paradise that nevertheless conceals violent tensions within its social ordering. The ironies of her narrative reveal that the insecurity, disarray, antagonism, and despair into which the entire society is thrown at this time point to a far more fundamental rift in the social fabric than can be overcome by those objects of security to which white Creole women constantly cling.

But the female perspective represented by Antoinette is even more significant in combining the feminist and political dilemmas of the novel. For the vulnerability of the white West Indian woman which Antoinette's narrative reveals sheds a great deal of light on the foundations of colonial and slave society, revealing the essentially masculine and materialistic thrust of their ethos and their inevitable marginalization of women's priorities and sensibilities. There is a sense that within plantation society the idealization of the white woman's virtues—beauty, nimbleness, delicacy, emotion, help-lessness—is at variance with the harsh, materialistic, and brutal impera-tives of a society designed for the maximization of profit through exploita-tion. In such a world even the white woman suffers a disorientation which makes her both a victim and an oppressor and renders her perspective potentially susceptible to a wider and subtler apprehension of the circum-stances of history in the region.

In this sense both the marriages of Antoinette and Annette face the con-flicting priorities of plantation society as the female sphere clashes with the hard, money-making enterprise which determines plantation values. At the same time they make contrasting statements about women's capacity to con-front the divisions and conflicts of personal and public histories. Whereas Annette succumbs to her vulnerability and remains both oppressor and vic-tim, Antoinette retains some agency and achieves an understanding of her situation, so that her "madness" is not a total disorientation and defeat but wholly human and insightful.

This perspective on Antoinette's personal history is, of course, bound up with Rhys's complex and subtle delineation of her as a woman and a pro-tagonist. As already suggested, Antoinette's narrative perspective is ma-nipulated in such a way that it leaves room for ironical suggestions which reveal the romantic fantasies, self-deceptions, ambivalence, and internal contradictions of her situation both as a woman, marginalized and disre-garded, and as a member of an oppressive class. Thus, her perception of Coulibri as a paradise that was trampled upon and destroyed by Negroes is rendered open to question when the estate's Edenic qualities are juxtaposed both to the exploitation that keeps it a paradise and to its total dereliction when its exploitative framework is abolished by emancipation. Indeed, the entire evocation of landscape, place, and atmosphere in the second part of the novel in which, as seems obvious, Grandbois becomes a re-creation of the destroyed Coulibri, also presents its particular ironies. The narrative itself makes us aware that the vision of Eden is held over and above an amnesiac blindness to several relics of a brutal and violent past. The exotic hills and mountains and the blue-green sea coexist with the sad, leaning coconut palms, the silence and the dimness of the slave huts, and the suggestiveness and irony of a village named "Massacre," a reference too far down in the amnesiac past to be of consequence to any of the characters.

Antoinette's relationship with Tia and the entire black world is presented as similarly flawed, and the source of the falsification is demonstrated in the ambivalence with which Antoinette herself relates to a black world that is solidly around her and an English world that she can grasp only superficially. The relationships are presented within the wider social and psychological forces at work in a postemancipation West Indies and are thus subject to all the antagonisms, fears, and confusions of relationships within it. Yet significantly, it is only in Antoinette that these forces · create conflicts and ambivalence with which we are expected to empathize. Mr. Mason's uncomplicated and simplistic perception of the black world around him, for instance, is linked to the attitudes and values of a new plantocracy indifferent to the region's sordid history and incapable of seeing beyond its own anxiety to make the best economic gain out of a bad situation; Annette's relationships, though based on a more insightful understanding of the realities of slave society, are similarly uncomplicated, never questioning, never moving beyond makeshift relationships and preferring instead to accept dependence on black servants and let "sleeping curs lie."

It is such undemanding perceptions and relationships that stand in contradistinction to the ambivalence in Antoinette's relationships, and it is because she is the focus of Rhys's more serious grappling with the psychological toll of a fractured history that ambivalence becomes the outward manifestation of an inner division and trauma. In Antoinette such ambivalence is demonstrated as the pull between the ordinary human and familial relationships occasioned by the often unavoidable intimacies between master and slave and the cruel realities of a plantation culture that elicits hatreds, antagonisms, and fears. The thematic significance of Antoinette's relationship with Tia can be grasped within this context. Her perception of Tia as symbolizing the world she knows is another falsification, since the world she knows is not quite the world Tia knows and what she knows of Tia's world is sometimes limited and distorted.

Yet to identify such ambivalence and divisions is not merely to dramatize the circumstances and repercussions of history but to point rather to possibilities of human relationships that it overshadowed and the significance of our consciousness of this fact. In Rhys's novel "history" manifests itself in the inner processes of individuation and encapsulates the tensions, conflicts, and ambivalence that reveal the complex set of responses it elicits. It moves beyond the delineation of "historical" events and situations to demonstrate the possible set of relationships they can figure. Antoinette's internalization of Tia's situation ("we stared at each other, blood on my face, tears on hers. It was as if I saw myself. Like in a looking glass")[9] may be regarded then as an important new knowledge from which her own process of growth proceeds.

Such a process can be linked to the three stages of her dream, each of which reveals foreknowledge of future events and brings her nearer to an understanding and resolution of her conflicts; it is also evident in her responses to life at her convent school and in the subsequent traumas of her marriage and migration to England. Thus, although Louis James sees her period in the convent as an interlude of peace in a "charmed garden freed from all conflicts,"[10] the relative peace is also a climate for subversive thinking. The safety of the convent is the safety of a narrow religion and education which shut out evil in a contemplation of a static divinity. Its world of saints and relics evokes a religious fervor and enthusiasm which its restricted concerns and formal rituals cannot satisfy.

Antoinette's dream shows evidence of disappointment with her life and reveals a wish to move beyond the narrow world within its walls. For though it is clearly an intimation of her coming marriage to Rochester[11] and her subsequent "imprisonment" in England, it is at the same time a dream of expectation, a wish for an involvement in life beyond the safe and narrow concerns of the convent. It portends the passion and ecstasies of her experience of love and her later attempts to share her world with Edward (Rochester) and involve him in its hidden depths and magic. It condenses through metaphoric representation the two worlds that are later to meet in conflict within her own life: the world of the forest as opposed to the enclosed garden surrounded by a stone wall; the tall, dark trees she knows as opposed to the trees she does not know. In the dream Antoinette is anxious not to soil her beautiful dress yet actually ends up letting her skirt trail in the dirt, giving herself over to a new but hazardous experience much different from the safe life of the convent and preparing herself for what Harris has called "a dialogue with the 'other' in the garden, the strange, dark, terrifying voice she never forgets within her and without her."[12]

It is this otherness of her world that Antoinette first claims for herself then offers to Rochester as a vitalizing potential in the relationship between the two worlds. It is a world of paradoxes: a sensuous and exotic world that conjures up the New World before its fall, yet also a world already touched and corrupted by the old world, one whose legacies of alliances merge with the lingering aftermath of slavery and colonialism to present a distinct world central to Antoinette's conception of herself. Indeed, half the time it is Antoinette's trust and sympathies with this world that unnerves and destabilizes Rochester's very European self-apprehension, and there is a sense in which the novel's second section can be read as a contest between two perceptions and epistemologies represented by Rochester and by a black and Creole world symbolized by Christophine. Throughout their confrontation it is Christophine's insights and other knowledge that frequently startle and discomfit Rochester. Her confident assertion of the truth of other modes of perceiving and interpreting reality ("Read and write I don't know. Other things I know")[13] becomes a formidable, echoing presence in Rochester's consciousness, challenging not only his European certainties but also the stone mask which he wears as protection against the world symbolized by Christophine.

Antoinette herself is in some ways part of this world and in others ambivalent towards it. Her perceptions, language, songs, beliefs, and superstitions are all intertwined with the multiplicity of a worldview that perceives and interprets the world differently. Yet her ambivalence towards this world also shows in that apprehension of evil with which she perceives it and in the rather utilitarian way she resorts to Obeah only as a tool for restoring Rochester's love. Thus, Louis James's view of her actions as a "resort to the deepest intimations of the black world of her identity"[14] may be qualified in terms of these attitudes and her actions regarded rather as a pointer to the ambivalence central to her inner tensions.

Although Antoinette seeks in her own way to reconcile this ambivalence in the end, the text suggests it as part of the paradoxes of Caribbean history itself. Paradox and ambiguity are what *Wide Sargasso Sea* dramatizes in the end. Rhys herself suggests that they are the appropriate perception of a heterogeneous region and history which may be offered as a challenge to colonial historiography. There are several versions and interpretations of history which crisscross with each other in the text to resist a common, homogenous interpretation. Antoinette's version of events appears in a different perspective in Daniel Cosway's text, just as Cosway's own text is challenged both by Antoinette's version and Christophine's oral remembrance; Christophine's Obeah is seen differently in the text of *The Glistening Corronet of Isles* and in Frazer's legal account, and even the idea of justice, which for Rochester is clear-cut with regard to enslaved people, is problematized in Antoinette's mind in relation to the fate and suffering of her mother.

Paradox similarly underlies Antoinette's resolution at the end and the kinds of insights that emanate from them. On one hand, her action in bringing down the great house and perishing in the process may be seen as a leap into death, a statement of defeat, acknowledging the cycle of violence in the region's history as well as her own failure to resolve the ambivalence of her relationships with the black and metropolitan worlds. On the other hand, the subtle linking of her subconscious and conscious mind through dreams reveals several levels of perception and understanding. In Charlotte Brontë's *Jane Eyre* (to which Rhys's novel is textually related), the incident (which is merely reported) is the final destructive act of a lunatic, one which nevertheless provides Rochester with an opportunity for an expiation of wrongs, paving the way for a "clean" marriage to Jane. In *Wide Sargasso Sea* it becomes the culmination of a series of revelations and insights in which the various aspects of Antoinette's identity come together to define a distinctive West Indian self and history.

Thus, in her "madness" Antoinette may appear to possess no memory, but her mind works in other ways to replay scenes and imagine people and objects from her past; she may possess no abstract concept of time as progress, but a sense of history may be constructed and configured in other ways, and there is a kind of knowing, a mode of recollection through the senses in which various associations can fit into a meaning and understanding. Antoinette's red dress connotes the scents and colors of her West Indian world but also registers connections with the unrealized possibilities of a relationship with her mulatto cousin Sandi, a possibility that is stalled not only by the racial divide in the society but by Antoinette's own ambivalent attitudes towards the black side of her Creole identity.

Indeed, the symbolic associations stretch further down in the subconscious mind to induce the dream that completes her process of understanding and knowledge. It links up with the convent dream, revealing the moment of epiphany as also a moment of action. It is here in the course of her dream that Antoinette achieves insights into the paradoxes around her: the paradox which reveals the metropolitan world she yearns for as caught between "olive green water and tall trees looking into the water"[15] and a wooden (cardboard) world, a world of "mammon" without spirituality or passion. From now on Antoinette seems able to act and, contrary to her convent dream, able also to protect herself. Her act of self-assertion does not only give insights, it brings back the past as well: "Then I turned round and saw the sky. It was red and all my life was in it."[16] Fire as the image of rebellion is also the restorative image of a West Indian world with its Edenic possibilities and its history of fear and violence. Antoinette's leap away from Rochester towards her childhood friend Tia is thus not a simplistic acceptance and reunion but a recognition of that mixture of rebellion and self-assertion that had induced Tia's rejection of her and of the new understanding and possibilities of community that can come out of this insight.

In *Wide Sargasso Sea* it is the subconscious world of dream that illuminates with images from a heterogeneous Caribbean to provide insight and
prompt action on a conscious level. Such variables of the unconscious have
the capacity, as Harris suggests, to "challenge the imagination beyond ideal
formula," to descend beneath the "surface mind" of a "culture into other
structures that alter emphases upon vague and elusive formations suppressed by static gestalt institution."[17] In Rhys's novel such descents are
made possible by the distinctive realm of women's experience, which by its
multileveled nature can relate to the hard economic realities of public history as well as the domain of custom, myth, and ritual, an often submerged
area of history where narrative modes encompass depths of dream and the
metaphors of a different sensibility. It is to Christophine that Antoinette is
indebted for this mode of apprehension, and though Antoinette's ambivalence towards her world is never really resolved, the encoding of "history"
in this mode and its translation into a narrative that destabilizes the homogenous realist model of the novel is itself an affirmation of a distinct set of
cultural categories and figurative discourses, a statement on the possibilities of a West Indian history constructed from the perspective of women's
experience.

Among women writers of the West Indies, however, the perception of
history even from such a perspective is always mediated by racial and personal histories and by the kinds of claims that the past makes on a writer's
perception of the present. The modes of emplotment, of language and
figurative discourse that manifest the historical consciousness of a woman
writer may make several other statements on her apprehension of history.
Thus, a contrasting reading of Rhys's novel and Simone Schwarz-Bart's *The
Bridge of Beyond* reveals startling differences in conception and emphases,
even though both novels deal with the same postemancipation period and
inscribe the historical in geographic and matriarchal space rather than in a
more masculine political and public one. The three-part structure of narration in *Wide Sargasso Sea* (though unified somewhat by the central focus
on Antoinette's consciousness) frames the various pulls of locality and
metaphor, of racial worlds and their social and emotional demands, that
generate ambivalence in the novel and determine what substance is explored and what is left out. Thus, what Schwarz-Bart's text explores unam-
biguously as the substance, condition, and possibilities of black people's
lives in a postemancipation West Indies is in Rhys's novel subsumed in a
generalized and ambiguous view of Obeah. Christophine's mystical powers, which are damned by Rochester, threatened by the colonial district
commissioner, and prove unworkable for the white Antoinette, appear in a

larger framework and significance in *The Bridge of Beyond* as part of the fundamental cosmology that gives meaning and depth to life in the world created by the novelist.

The construction of history in *The Bridge of Beyond* is, as in *Wide Sargasso Sea*, predicated on a particular geographic space and on a family and its history. In Rhys this context becomes a framework principally for dramatizing the consequences of history: the disintegration of the plantation order and the disorientation and "terrified consciousness"[18] of white families marooned in a social world that no longer reflects their self-apprehension. Within the novel's paradoxes, however, it also becomes a base for the heroine's individuation and growth in a divided world. In *The Bridge of Beyond* the recollection of family history is on the contrary an act of reconstruction and revisioning. The breakdown of the plantation order is rather a chance to reconstruct physical and interior worlds and create historical myths as a base for continuity. Thus, in the novel several subtle links connect personal history with family and social history, linking the community with physical and spiritual landscapes so that "history" becomes the continuous intertwining of all these aspects of existence.

This kind of relation to history is not unique in West Indian writing. V. S. Reid makes similar connections between land, community, and identity in *New Day* as he explores the postemancipation world of Jamaica in 1865. But Reid's more overt and overriding political themes overshadow not only the interior lives and dilemmas of his characters but also the spirit, consciousness, and values which the novel's images suggest about the created world. Thus, for instance, rebellion in Morant Bay may be evoked in such a way as to signify the galvanized anger and assertive identity of a community of ex-slaves, yet at the same time be censured in the light of a more reasoned, nonviolent political ideal, deflating the impact of the cultural potential underlying the rebellion. History in this case is envisaged more as a political process, a lived historical experience that provides less leeway for imaginative and mythic extensions. It is also essentially a male history that traces West Indian genealogy and history through a male line, virtually excising the voices and impact of women as participants in the process. In concentrating on public and political action as the priorities of history, Reid deflates those images and sounds of women's expressivity which were the actual foundations of consciousness and the source of renewal in the West Indian world.

Schwarz-Bart's conflation of mythic and historical consciousness, her choice of material, point of view, and figurative language in *The Bridge of Beyond,* suggest that there are other ways of participating in history and other questions that can be asked of it. Here the merging of family and social histories and the framework of woman-centered experiences that link them valorize aspects usually submerged in academic considerations of history; it is as if Schwarz-Bart asks with Gerda Lerner: "What would history be like if it were seen through the eyes of women and ordered by values they define?"[19] Schwarz-Bart explores the nature of such a woman-centered history by separating it from "history" as it is academically understood and distinguishing it as "memory." For memory, unlike "history," has the capacity to reconstruct and transform in the interest of certain ends, and Telumée's act of recollection achieves this transformation in startling ways. As a griot, sifting through her own memories and connecting them with stories remembered by others, Schwarz-Bart's protagonist reconstructs a history that mythologizes, teaches, celebrates, acknowledges ambiguities, and finally gives back the past, in this way multiplying and extending the self in various ways. Indeed, these possibilities of the reconstructed memory are themselves significantly enacted in various experiences within the novel, paralleling the novel's own underlying purpose as an act of self-apprehension. Thus Telumée and Amboise, physically cut off from their past in their isolated cabin at La Follie, create such a "history" as they recollect and relate to all the events that had entered their lives: "There under the shelter we used to speak of all things past and present, of all the people we'd known, loved, and hated, in this way multiplying our own little lives and making each other exist several times."[20]

It is to acknowledge the capacity of memory to create such extensions of the self that Schwarz-Bart's novel is structured in the way it is. Telumée's recollection finds reference and meaning in the histories of the women before her, creating a historical space and time that encompass both interior and exterior space. The story of these foremothers is placed in the novel as a mythologized history (told so often and with such fervor and reverence as to become sacred and mythical) which Telumée uses for her own ends in her reconstruction and shaping of memory. Thus, if the stories of Minerva and Xango and of Toussine and Jeremiah appear unreal and even slightly sentimentalized, it is because Telumée transforms them into myth as a way of creating an ideal and model of possibility against which the ambiguities, uncertainties, and vagaries of the Negro's history can be related.

The style of the narrative answers to the purpose. Telumée's memory creates a perfect atmosphere for mythologizing, for harking back to the beginnings of visibility for Negroes, times when they could create not only communities, customs, and rituals but also make new myths for themselves out of the uncertainties and paradoxes of their lives. L'Abandonée itself mirrors these paradoxes in the narrative, becoming at once a place of refuge and the marginalized space of the displaced and rejected, where Negroes may evolve communities and rituals but are plagued by feelings of dread, uncertainty, and loss.

The mythologized history of Telumée's foremothers mirrors these paradoxes but at the same time represent the model, the possibility that exists with the uncertainties. Thus, against the rootless wanderings of Toussine's Dominican father is placed the commitment of the dark-skinned Xango, who names the abandoned Toussine and roots her firmly in the soil. Toussine's own youth and life-affirming temperament become a persistent possibility, as does the mythical story of her life with Jeremiah, which provides a model unreachable by most villagers yet available to them as a source for extending and multiplying their lives. For the mythical stories yield the implications deliberately built into them: the Negro's capacity to live with uncertainty and endure hurts without the acid bitterness that destroys; his ability to create a self-sufficient life without reference to whiteness; the collective nature of his life and its capacity to cushion and nurture; the enriching and ennobling possibilities of love and respect between Negro men and women; the power of human fantasy against sorrow and the vanity of things.

The implications reappear as reference points in Telumée's personal history, creating a body of precedents and a pattern of responses against which her individuation can be measured. History is then constructed not outwards from the perspectives of colonial and male master texts but inward from the familial and inner worlds of Negro women. The character of this history, its potential, paradoxes, and contradictions, are what create the historical consciousness that the protagonist acquires in the end, and though commentators have frequently seen this consciousness as part of a poetics of West Indian expressivity with distinctive values that define the black soul in the Caribbean, the narrative deemphasizes any monolithic view of "black soul" by ranging over several variables of West Indian responses to history.

Thus, on the face of it, one aspect of the narrative may privilege and valorize the homogenous, oral-centered world of Fond-Zombi, where communal perceptions, beliefs, rituals, and intimacies of a woman-centered world function as alternative avenues to knowledge; it may enact the power and efficacy of such a world by demonstrating how its Word can counter the precariousness and fragility of the Negroes' lives and the internal enslavement to which they are susceptible. Yet this world also exists and intersects in Telumée's personal history with other worlds whose circumstances and responses complicate the situation of the privileged black world and preclude a single position as the site of meaning in the exploration of history. For instance, the world of the cane fields, which merely hovers around L'Abandonée and Fond-Zombi as a dreaded world the Negro must avoid, surfaces in Telumée's narrative in a personal experience which reveals its power not only to reduce the Negro to the level of beast but actually to make her internalize this condition as her deserved fate.

Similarly, the white man's world, whether in Belle-Feuille or France, may be rendered irrelevant to the values of the privileged world. Yet the narrative admits in several subtle ways that its power to destabilize and confuse is something the Negro may have to deal with in ways other than what she has been taught. However much Telumée may neutralize white people's disregard and derision, however much she may dilute her pain, chop it into pieces, let it flow into song, sing "every part, every cry, possession, submission, domination, despair, scorn,"[21] certain psychic disturbances linger on and surface in nightmarish dreams in which she finds herself caught in a desire to prove herself to the white man, to show him she is at home in his world.

> my mistress often asked me how the climate affected me. I told her I liked it very much, and she would laugh, disbelieving. This laugh tore me in two, and one day when she started it again I said to her calmly: "I'm going to prove I'm not cold," and I took off my clothes and went out naked in the snow. She watched me in astonishment from behind the kitchen curtains. Then I felt my muscles stiffening until they turned to ice, and I fell down dead.[22]

This subconscious disturbance which Telumée cannot decipher, however much she tries, may indeed be linked to the general sad and questioning mood that comes upon her as she flees Belle-Feuille, the sadness which makes her question how "God had put me on earth without asking me if I wanted to be a woman or what color I'd like to be."[23]

Indeed, such disturbances are thematically connected with Amboise's narrative of his sojourn in France as retold by Telumée, a narrative which also encapsulates aspects of the unfinished stories of Regina, Victory, Elie, and, by ironic reference, the effaced story of Colbert Lanony, the white man whose singlehanded defiance of racism becomes that aspect of human fantasy that will always challenge "sorrow and the vanity of things."[24] Thus, while one point of view of the narrative (Toussine's) regards the wider white world as irrelevant to the Negro's self-apprehension, these outer dimensions intrude on the main narrative to hint at their impact and relevance both at the levels of personal and public histories. For instance, Amboise's narrative is the story of his flirtation with "whiteness," his rejection of self, and his final self-understanding and insight. As a parallel story it juxtaposes another, more real experience of history to the mythologized love story of Toussine and Jeremiah and finds echoes in the stories of characters literally excised from the novel. Amboise's experience in France chastens him into a recognition of the black man's real place in a white world and returns him to Guadeloupe to seek the Word that would save and comfort the Negro; though it may be argued that such an insight is one that a character like Toussine acquires intuitively and independently of France, Amboise's story, placed as it is in the overall narrative, works to extend the arena of history, propelling it into a more public and political experience.

Certainly the delineation of the ex-slave's sojourn in the metropolis is itself a political act that entails confrontations with structures of oppression and may be open to both political insight and action. Amboise's recognition in France that the Negro is a "tethered kid" whose fate lies not in himself but in the existence of the knife, is a political insight that reflects the socioeconomic and psychic reality of the Negro and holds a potential for rethinking and action. All Amboise's other insights, right up to his participation in the strike, proceed from this fundamental recognition, and his involvement in the strike is thus a logical action prompted by the questions he has always asked about the Negro's capacity to change his fate. The failure of the strike in which he takes a leading part is thus less significant than its symbolic indication of the "political" will to act.

Telumée's narrative yields these wider nuances of history and demonstrates the extent to which her own historical consciousness has been shaped and transformed by the act of ordering and retelling Amboise's story. Certainly, only the mature Telumée with years of experience and movement through history could have made such telling connections between the rebellion of the strikers and the age-old struggles of the Negro slave. Her deliberate manipulation of the narrative in those moments when the strikers give up, betraying Amboise's sacrifice, demonstrates how her own political point of view is involved in the sense of disappointment which the narrative conveys. History thus enters the woman's consciousness through the processes of her own inner journey, merging the personal and the public and expanding in various profound ways the geographic space, which in Rhys's novel is frequently celebrated as exotic and Edenic.

The woman's inner journey and individuation are also at another level processes of subjectification which defy the tendency in male texts to represent women as dormant and symbolic figures in history. Schwarz-Bart's text proves that a woman's inner journey can become the site of several contestations crucial to historical understanding. The conjunction of gender, ethnicity, and historical movement in this process often renders the

woman's perspective susceptible to a more complete grasp of the ramifications of history. The consciousness of self as woman and the processes of
relating to the male within a cultural milieu may create a situation in which
sexual politics may be closely aligned to cultural politics. For the nature of
woman's relation to man involves certain kinds of power relations which
are in turn part of the processes through which women themselves become
what they are through history.

Plantation societies differentiated little between men and women in their
definition of gender roles, and it was possible for a certain kind of equality
and shared understanding to exist between slave men and women. In
Schwarz-Bart's novel such a possibility is embodied in the mythologized
story of Jeremiah and Toussine, which becomes a model of possibility in
relationships between Negro men and women. Outside this history the
reality can be gleaned both from the myths created around women and
from the day-to-day relations between men and women. Even in newly
created communities where a pack of Negroes are in the same boat, "without any fathers and mothers before God" myths represent woman as the
spirit with the cloven hoof, a vampire that feeds exclusively on a man's
desire to live and drives him sooner or later to suicide.[25]

The view of woman conceptualized in such a vision may be linked to
that fundamental insecurity which is a constant source of destabilization in
relations between men and women in the novel. In spite of the novel's
constant affirmation of the power of love and kindness to transform and
ennoble lives, the general trend of male-female relationships demonstrates
a weakness linked to the precariousness of the Negro's existence and the
psychological toll of his enslavement. As Telumée's narrative points out,
"we pondered a lot about the personal lives of the grown-ups. We knew
how they made love, and we knew how they tore at and clawed and
trampled on one another afterwards, following an unchanging course that
led from the chase to weariness and downfall." In these relationships the
men appear to be victorious in the battle, but as Telumée's insight suggests,
they are subject to a vulnerability that is within them and probably outside
the battles themselves. "They broke bones and wombs, then they left their
own flesh and blood in misery as a crab leaves his pincers between your
fingers."[26] Telumée's Elie becomes part of this syndrome and is plagued by
a similar sense of insufficiency, a nagging fear of failure that transforms
itself into a dream of progress, an ambition to be a scholar, to bedeck his
woman in gold and lace, and though he sees this dream as an alternative to
enslavement in the cane fields he fails to see it as equally subject to the same
enslavement. This confusion of soul that paralyzes Elie and divides him

from himself engulfs Telumée's life as well, in such a way that her own internal struggles come to center on her relations with Elie.

Thus the processes of Telumée's individuation not only involve her ability to confront both the promise of love and its mutable and destructive possibilities but also the courage to chart an individual destiny as a woman. Here, it is sexual politics that open a way to a wider critical perception of the Negro in history, and it is Telumée's grappling with contradictory influences in her self-apprehension that makes possible the historical insights with which, as the older, more mature Telumée, she orders and presents her narrative. Thus initially, her definition of herself as a woman loved and cherished by a man reveals some ambiguities and contradictions.

> I seemed to have entered another world; it was as if I never lived before, never known how to. When Elie looked at me, then, only then, I existed, and I knew well that if ever one day he turned away from me I should disappear again into the void . . . The feeling I bore him overflowed on to every creature my eye lighted on . . . Life went on turning, suns and moons were engulfed and then reborn in the sky, and my continuing joy lifted me out of time. But meanwhile there were the dead children, the old who survived them, and friendships betrayed, razor slashes, the wicked waxing strong on their wickedness, and women with garments woven of desertion and want, and so on. And sometimes a long thorn slowly pierced my heart, and I'd wish I were like the tree called Resolute, on which it is said the whole globe and all its calamities could lean.[27]

On one hand, a woman's love for a man can extend and link her with the wider world; yet on the other, that same love can rob her of individuality and agency, virtually reducing her to the status of an object with no existence outside her function as wife and lover. Telumée's disequilibrium and breakdown spring partly from the implications of this self-perception, and the feminist dimension of the narrative delineates her confrontation with these contradictions and her growth into a complex, sensitive personality capable of individual critical perception and analysis.

It is this new perception of the female self that shapes Telumée's relationships and her understanding of the world around her. In the narrative it is evident in the ways in which her story sifts through the lessons of her grandmother's life and the communal wisdom of her people to plow a way towards a sense of self. If her way out of madness is through reintegration into her community's web of rituals and links, her self-definition proceeds from these inwards into an individual selfhood. From this individual female consciousness she achieves a wider, more pragmatic understanding of love as inseparable from life and its day-to-day corruptions. Her love for Amboise becomes not an exultation that lifts her out of time (as happens with her love for Elie) but a partnership to "bale life from the depths and set it up on earth,"[28] an invention of life through a sharing of space, work, consciousness, and history with a male partner. Thus Telumée inscribes herself in a much more complicated relationship to her male partner and her community,[29] expanding the situation of Toussine and Jeremiah, the ancestral lovers in whose mythologized love story the ideal love relationship appears merely as something given.

Telumée's inner struggle and female consciousness, on the other hand, widen to touch on issues of history, extending both their scope and ramifications and connecting the private domestic sphere with the public and political. In this sense the spiritual wisdom and the healing powers of the Obeah spiritualist, which she acquires as an old woman, combine with a wider, historicized vision of the Negro in history, a combination that surpasses the vision of previous Obeah women in her community. It is this complex, multidimensional vision that concludes her story and also frames the entire historical narrative and its figurative discourses.

This process of a female self-consciousness writing itself into history is a continuing trend in the writing of West Indian women. Fundamentally, all such processes involve what Evelyn O'Callaghan has called "the engineering [of] female subjectivity,"[30] a representation of the female as a historical agent and a participant in the economic, social, and political order. The nature of the inscription and the kinds of individuation achieved may differ from text to text, depending not only on how each woman writer experiences the historical legacy but also on how generational, class, racial, or color differences intersect in a woman writer's historicization of experience.

In Rhys's text subjectification of the female involves a wider negotiation between hegemonic and nonhegemonic traditions, and the rewriting of the female subject becomes part of a general rewriting of a different geographic space and history. Schwarz-Bart's *The Bridge of Beyond* achieves another kind of subjectification within a specific cultural context. The privileged world of women foremothers creates a space in which images frame spiritual and social values that provide the protagonist with definition and empowerment.

Houston Baker, writing in the context of African-American literary theory, sees this particular mode of New World subjectification as a negotiation of metalevels that privilege the role and figures of spiritual leaders.

Bereft of material, geographical, or political inscriptions of a state and a common mind, New World Africans were compelled to seek a personal, spiritual assurance of worth . . . Africans were compelled to verify a self's being-in-the-world. They were forced to construct and inscribe unique personhood in what appeared to be a blank and uncertain environment . . . The trajectory of this history is from what might be called the workings of a distinctively syncretic spirit to auto-biographical incorporation or expressive embodiment of such spirit work.[31]

Accepting this original negotiation as the basis of African-American intellectual discourse, Baker formulates a theory of African-American women's writing as that which seeks to arrive at the guiding spirit and consciousness of this original negotiation.

Yet African-American and Caribbean women's writing is more complex than simply the attempt to relate to this guiding spirit. Even in *The Bridge of Beyond,* in which this spiritual base becomes the center of values and revisions of history, other variables intervene to make female subjectivity a more complex and multifaceted phenomenon. Telumée's sense of herself as a woman who can "feel the beauty of [her] own two woman's legs"[32] and relate in various ways to the world around her contributes to a personal revaluation that not only leads to a wider perception of the Negro in history but also problematizes some of her community's own assumptions about love and relationships between men and women.

In the writing of other West Indian women, relation to this consciousness is even more drastically mediated by other variables. Class, racial, and gender tensions that surface but remain somewhat deflated in Schwarz-Bart's text reappear to complicate female subjectivity in a changing world. In the novels, stories, and poems of Merle Hodge, Erna Brodber, Michelle Cliff, Merle Collins, Olive Senior, Janice Shinebourne, Paule Marshall, Jamaica Kincaid, Velma Pollard, Grace Nichols, and Marlene Nourbese Philip, tensions, fragmentation, and competing ideologies dramatize the consequences of history; and "history" as an ideological perspective becomes, in Lamming's words, "a series of antagonistic situations"[33] which require different strategies of representation. They are occasioned by the process of female subjectification within a postcolonial ethos. While in the postemancipation world of *The Bridge of Beyond* it was possible to territorialize a world in which the privileged voices of foremothers defined a worldview and values which appeared homogenous and sufficient, the postcolonial worlds of these writers are fragmented not only by the divisions of class, color, and gender but by inner contradictions created by relations between the colonial "margin" and metropolitan "center." In *The Bridge of Beyond* the disorienting world of the school is rendered almost irrelevant to a homogenous world of other knowledge; in these postcolonial texts metropolitan epistemologies assume an overwhelming power that creates ambivalence both in self-perception and narrative enunciation. Thus, the matrilineal space and its guiding spirit, which Baker sees as fundamental, are themselves thrown into disarray in the changing landscape of a postcolonial world.

In Merle Hodge's *Crick Crack Monkey* a kind of ambivalence reveals itself in the differentiation the text makes between the ideal possibilities of the protagonist's childhood and the alienating world of her colonial experience. Tee's inscription of her personal history presents the unmediated world of childhood as that in which it is possible to be secure, whole, and integrated. Yet this world, like the mythologized story of Toussine and Jeremiah, is only an ideal against which the inevitable colonial experience is measured. As the adult Tee comments, "We roamed the yard and swarmed down to the water and played hoop around the breadfruit tree as if we would always be wiry-limbed children whose darting about the sun would capture like ember and fix into eternity."[34] Here the ironical relation between the child's perception and the adult's commentary prefigures the paradoxical mode in which the colonial experience would be delineated both as an exposure of the "illusionary nature of Tee's desire for assimilation" and as an indication of the ways in which the multiple worlds she inhabits can somehow be made to cohere. Simon Gikandi has argued that "the narrator draws our attention to the divisions and separations the child goes through in its struggle to become the 'other' and measures its loss against the narrating self which has, presumably, overcome its alienation by mastering its history through narration."[35]

Yet even here the narrating self of the adult is still an object of irony, and it is the text itself that points a way to possibilities of integrating Tee's multiple worlds. Gikandi's argument that Hodge sustains "both the creole and colonial cultures as opposed sites of cultural production which the 'modern' Caribbean subject cannot transcend entirely, nor reconcile"[36] must therefore be seen critically against the workings of the text itself. For in Hodge's novel the Creole world, centered mainly around women progenitors, is both privileged and negated. The narrative maintains a multiplicity of perceptual levels in which certain of its perspectives uphold its values at the same time as the protagonist's alienating experiences negate them. In a narrative in which the protagonist is a character, an object of irony and also a retrospective narrator, textual meaning should be located in the interplay between the character as character, as a child, and as an adult narrator. It is in the differentiation the text makes between the ideal possibilities of the child's vision and the adult's compromised narration that we can locate both the ambiguities and possibilities of history.

The authenticity and integrity of the child's vision affirms a creolized world which with all its ambivalence and insufficiencies is still a tangible reality. Ma's world becomes the older world of original cultural negotiation, where possibilities of continuity and change are suggested in the interplay between two perspectives of narration, allowing us to envisage from the very beginning a syncreticism in which Ma's cyclical vision of the world and the numinous quality of her relation to nature can have a place. The world of Tantie as perceived by Tee reveals other mutations: a new racial composition and its demands on relationships; a continuing colonial mentality and culture; and a new American presence which are all part of the dynamics of a social world the Caribbean subject must negotiate.

Commentators like Gikandi have seen this negotiation mostly in terms of the thematization of alienation. But Hodge's representation moves beyond exposure of the protagonist's alienation to point indirectly at possibilities of integration unrecognized by her. Thus the point of Hodge's delineation is not only that Tee rejects the tangible reality of the Creole world or that she is unfulfilled in either cultural world; it is also that the world of school allows her no creative connection between it and the world she knows, and she is herself unable to make the connection or draw insight from the emptiness and artificiality of Aunt Beatrice's world, which her own narrative indirectly exposes.

Gikandi's reading of *Crick Crack Monkey,* critically insightful and challenging as it is, tends occasionally to underestimate the monumental irony (tempered with sympathy) that Hodge constantly marshals against Tee. He argues, for instance, that "Tee, in an attempt to deal with her duality and crisis of identity, begins to apprehend herself as the other: she invents a double, a mirror image of herself, who is, nevertheless, white and thoroughly colonial, one who doesn't have to negotiate the dangerous chasm between Creole and colonial, self and other because she is ideal."[37] Yet it is precisely her inability to negotiate this chasm that becomes the significant irony against Tee. Though there is no immediate reconciliation or integration of her multiple identities, the text indirectly points to areas where possibilities exist, which the young confused Tee cannot see.

The structure of Tee's narrative suggests missing links in her organization of experience which reveal her inability even as an adult narrator to make connections between her multiple worlds. Ma's world is textually isolated in her narrative and projected as a world that must inevitably die. Yet the insights it offers on history, on beginnings, continuities, and transformations, could conceivably complement Tee's individuation. But Tee establishes no such links in her text, and the next chapter plunges the narrative into the esoteric mysteries of the school's written culture as though it represents the only possible source of knowledge and the import of the world revealed in Ma's universe has no correlation whatsoever with the world of school. Here, it seems to me, is a point of irony at the expense of Tee. For it is the absence or loss of such links and connections that contribute to her loss of confidence and spunk, and we have only to compare her first visit to Aunt Beatrice's house with her actual stay there to measure not only the extent of the loss but also the irony indirectly implied in her representation. In *Crick Crack Monkey* the presence of irony is also indirectly a hint of possibility. Thus, Ma's belief that Tee would grow up to become like her own proud, stubborn, unbending grandmother is rendered ironical in the context of Tee's alienation but at the same time also suggests the viability of such connections and continuities.

The text draws attention to other links and possibilities in Tee's relation to Tantie's world as it counterbalances its marginality and aggressive loudness with its "elemental toughness,"[38] warmth, and instinctive bonds of family and community. Tee's rejection of both worlds is loaded with nuances that censure her for failing to separate the marginality of these worlds from their spiritual and nurturing values. They are nuances that at the same time suggest possibilities for integrating what is sustaining and enriching in both worlds, and Gikandi's view that "Tee is structured by a set of oppositions, none of which offer her true identity: [that] her Creole world is makeshift and marginal; [and] her desired colonial universe . . . artificial," requires qualification. For though Tee's Creole world may be makeshift and marginal, it is significant in ways essential to her sense of self; it is the recognition of the value of its daily rituals not only an understanding of the "sources of marginality" and the "nature of artifice"[39] that will enable her to outgrow "Helen" and become a whole and integrated person.

In *Crick Crack Monkey*, the possibilities indicated exist in tension with several other forms of alienation, and though the protagonist never transcends hers, its inscription nevertheless evokes the space and voices of the Creole world, providing a ground of being that contests her alienation. The inscribed worlds of Ma, Tantie, Beatrice, and school enact creolization itself as a cultural negotiation between master and slave and between colonial and colonized, one which holds possibilities for a creative syncreticism but also harbors the threat of disorientation.

The loopholes of cultural negotiation that give rise to alienation such as Tee's are more drastically exposed and confronted in the texts of other West Indian women writers. Even as a character and a narrating consciousness Tee never understands her alienation or the possibilities inherent in her multiple identities. Hodge's text, while revealing this to the reader, suggests that Tee would only achieve subjectivity and integration when she has recognized and understood the factors that mediate her socializing process and contribute to her alienation. In Erna Brodber's *Jane and Louisa Will Soon Come Home* and Jamaica Kincaid's *Annie John,* the narrating protagonists continually interrogate these factors. Both writers inscribe the personal histories of their protagonists in more complicated and interrogative relation to the community, so that what Houston Baker calls the spirit of the original, metalevel negotiation of slave women, accommodates mutations and new attitudes generated by gender, class, color, and generational differences.

The larger social scene is in both novels deeply fragmented by contending ideologies, each with its own linguistic biases. Brodber's protagonist, unlike Hodge's, has to reconstruct self and history by making connections between different classes and gender groups. While Tee is defined by a different set of perspectives and linguistic forms in each of the different worlds she inhabits, Brodber's Nellie shifts fluidly between worlds and speech patterns within the Creole world. Her mode of narration enacts a collectivity that demonstrates the fundamental relatedness of a Creole world which encompasses both the living and the dead.

Hodge works through ironic delineations to expose her narrator's alienation in a fragmented world; Brodber on the other hand, presents a case study in which the protagonist's disassociation is rectified through a presentation of her multiple worlds as different but integral parts of a Creole world. Fragmentation is thus enacted against a textual background that suggests multiple, intersecting traditions within a shared ancestry. Because Nellie's narration proceeds from such an understanding, its structure deflates those boundaries and polarities that separate one world from another in Tee's narrative. The divisions she contends with are, like Tee's, real enough to cause disassociation and collapse, but the narration itself is a reconstruction of self from a point of knowledge and insight. The narrating consciousness is more aware of the separations of class and gender that mediate the socialization of the female subject: "God slackens the weave [of the community's homogenous web]. Separates us chicken from birds. Sends us to pick our way through crowded buses, electric wire and asphalt streets yet gives us no street map towards each other. No compass, no scale either. Leaves us no path, no through way, no gap in our circle."[40]

The narrative's objective, however, is not a simplistic linking of multiple worlds for a sentimentalized common identity; it is the hacking of a pathway, the opening of gaps in the circle. For Brodber the discovery of "street maps towards each other" begins from a recognition of the source of division and separation and from a probing of the fine *kumblas* woven to separate self from self and self from community. Nellie recognizes that the secrecy and repression that surround her socialization as an adolescent girl are themselves forms of subterfuge, ways of weaving fine *kumblas* to separate her from those "who would drag you down." Their basis is a polarization of sexuality and class that posits sensuality and earthiness as low-class desires that must be avoided by the young lady wishing to move up.

This distancing of sexuality is only one of several separations from the natural and "native" occasioned by upward mobility in West Indian society. The tendency seems as old as the beginnings of transformation itself. Even the earliest black ancestor in Brodber's novel, Tee Maria—the closest to a Creole worldview—annihilates her true self by weaving a *kumbla* around herself, denying her existence so that her children can prosper. "Two roads lay before her: none was kind. There were his people and there were her people and she knew who had power. Love, luck and strength were not enough. She'd have to learn to bob and weave."[41]

The narrating consciousness, writing from a position of insight, may explain this kind of annihilation with some sympathy, but her general perspective is paradoxical. The image of the *kumbla* carries a multiple meaning, signifying on one hand, an individual parachute, a temporary protection, and on the other, an indifference to the occupant's ability to act and control it. "It bounces anywhere . . . It blows as the wind blows it, it moves if it is kicked, if it is thrown . . . It makes no demands of you, it cares not one whit for you."[42] Neither Tee Maria nor her children's children, the narrator suggests, can achieve subjectivity and agency till they rip off the *kumblas* separating them from themselves and each other.

Although in the writing of West Indian women such alienation from the self are handled with a wide range of delineations, the world that is known and native is almost always the geographic and maternal space with its different perspectives on experience and history and its unique psychology and expressivity. In Jamaica Kincaid's *Annie John*, it is the young child's assertive individuality and consciousness of self and place that subvert the colonial invalidation of her world and expose the mother's imitative values as alienating and self-negating.

The seeming contradictions within the narrative are themselves para-doxical statements about the nature of the mother's alienation. Thus, on one hand, the narrative is framed within a colonial ethos that negates Annie's world and history; yet its substance affirms and validates the inti-mate relationships and domestic rituals of the world. The mother works assiduously to instill into Annie the manners and values of an imitative colonial world, yet the daily rhythms of her own life keep her solidly within the ordinary, real world of her community. She offers her daughter role models from a colonial world, yet the child's own narrative affirms a sig-nificant role model: the grandmother, whose stature and power derive from a native spirituality and a firm knowledge of self.

As in Hodge's *Crick Crack Monkey,* it is this intimate center of the child's world that intersects with the other worlds and texts of the colonial world. If Hodge's Tee succumbs to invalidation by erasing her real self from history, Jamaica Kincaid's Annie affirms the world she knows in spite of the major colonial presence that overwhelms it. Her rebellion against the knowledge that invalidates her world is also a rebellion against her mother's internalization of colonial paternalism. What the maturing Annie perceives as the thimble that weighed worlds, the dark cloud that was like an envelope in which she and her mother were sealed, is a construction that renders her powerless and stops her from re-creating herself and her world: "I could not be sure whether for the rest of my life I would be able to tell when it was really my mother and when it was really her shadow standing between me and the rest of the world."[43]

Craig Tapping describes Annie's unseating of this epistemic and familial power in terms that invite comparison with Hodge's Tee: "in this figuration of the European conqueror/instigator of history, Annie reads her own people and is moved to joy at the reversal of roles—a fantasy she enter-tained in the immediately preceding paragraph: 'If the tables had been turned we would have acted differently' . . . Thus [the] history book, rather than imposing its discourse on Annie, invades her discourse but, paradoxi-cally, offers her the image and model of how to confront and decenter—to trope—the very domination it probes."[44]

What Tapping perceives as a refiguration of the history of conquest be-comes evident in Annie's changed perspectives on history. If in her child-hood games she had unthinkingly imbibed the dichotomies of discoverer/discovered, savage/civilized, as an adolescent she is more fluidly engaged in reimagining received history and extending the frontiers of its assumptions. For it is within this refiguration that Annie can actually write the histories of women like Ma Chess, ordinary black women who nevertheless exude a spiritual power and knowledge derived almost entirely from their "native" worlds.

Yet even within this new perception of environment and history several subtle contradictions emerge to render Kincaid's relation to this world less straightforward. On another level, the world affirmed is also the world from which the protagonist must be separated in order to become her own individual person. The conflicting, often ambiguous relationship between the protagonist and her mother, between her and the world she so sensuously evokes, reflects these other sides of the relationship. Thus the Edenic and protective world of childhood—the loss of which is repeatedly mourned both in *Annie John* and *At the Bottom of the River*—is also a world of subtle adult manipulation and control. The magical world of the grandmother's Obeah, enacted sympathetically in *Annie John* as a mysterious healing power, presents its paradoxical side in *At the Bottom of the River* as a sinister force within the multiple faces of the night. For the landscape is one that contains both the innocuous and the sinister, and the night reveals a magical world that is also evil, destroying and annihilating rather than protecting and healing. The mother's magical powers, which appear in the piece "My Mother" as knowledge and power transmitted to the daughter for survival and self-protection, becomes part of the night's sinister powers in "In the Night," so that the "jablesse" light, connoting her power, strength, and ability to manipulate reality, is at the same time also a power that functions to the detriment of the daughter's personality.

The daughter's own need for separation from family and home, explored in her constant attempts to privilege her own personal history, is similarly fraught with paradox and ambiguity. For the desire to achieve distance from island and family holds two contradictory pulls: the pull towards appropriation of place and history and the pull towards separation and individuality. Thus two similar incidents of a girl's going away from home and parents present different ramifications and endings. In *At the Bottom of the River* the young girl's surreal evocation of departure reflects a subconscious desire to remain part of the mother and her world ("we were in complete union in every other way ... my mother and I walk through the rooms of her house. Every crack in the floor holds a significant event"),[45] while in *Annie John* the realistic story of departure presents a healthy and forceful sense of severance in spite of the protagonist's emotional trauma and her fear of the unknown ("I dragged myself away from her and backed off a little and then I shook myself, as if to wake myself out of a stupor").[46]

In Kincaid this multileveled relation to colonial and "native" worlds is part of the protagonist's anxiety not to be fixed in any particular mold, part of a desire to question each relation to the historical experience. Hodge's Tee never achieves this maturation. Though her narrative gives form and visibility to the Creole world she inhabits, she is as an adult, unable to imagine them in ways other than what are defined by the colonized perspectives of Aunt Beatrice and school. Hodge's purpose in Crick Crack Monkey is principally to enact the complete alienation of the protagonist, leaving the text itself an ironic pointer to the gaps and loopholes that cry out for examination and connection.

In Brodber's Jane and Louisa such connections are indeed the crux and structuring vision of the novel. The protagonist's reconnection to the world from which she is alienated is not as insurmountable as it appears to be in Crick Crack Monkey. For Nellie, unlike Tee, recognizes that the barriers that divide people and groups are not only artificial but actually hide the most natural and fundamental social bonds. Her narrative deflates these barriers by consciously reconstructing experience and history and by recalling ordinary communal interactions and domestic rituals: voices of the living and the dead, sounds of music, smells of food, smells of plants and trees. And in this conscious activation of memory, history, folklore, song, and dance function thematically as relevant referents that contest her alienation. The text enacts their adaptation and creolization as "native" forms in the way it intertwines them into the narrative structure. Thus the children's ring game, "Jane and Louisa Will Soon Come Home," actually enacts the fusion of the English quadrille dance with the transformational power of Afro-Caribbean conjuring, just as the Ananse tale functions as both a narrative device and a moral insight.[47] Its coexistence in the same novel with other creolized forms dramatizes the multiple worlds of the novel as integral rather than oppositional. Above all, the piecing together of family history becomes in itself a revelation of the combinations of race, class, and cultures that mingle in the protagonist's ancestry, illustrating even more glaringly the reality and possibilities of this multiple heritage.

In Brodber's novel such insights about history are grasped from the delineation of community and family and the relationships within them. As in the works of other women writers, the intimate contexts of family and community rather than the public and individual arenas are the domains for exploring female subjectivity. The topography of intimate human space that images of community and family connote links female subjectivity with the distinctive values of rootedness, nurturing, and renewal.

But the ways in which these writers conceive of female space is far more complicated and radical than the feminine matrix envisioned in the world of West Indian male writers. In Brathwaite's *Mother Poem* and Walcott's *The Star-Apple Kingdom* woman is not always a character in her own individual right but a representative figure: a manipulable victim of history in *The Star-Apple Kingdom* and in *Mother Poem* a waterless rock seed, the porous limestone of the land whose rootedness shows up the outward pulls and wanderings of the male figures. In *Mother Poem* woman is conceived in the context of "home," which is again defined as a plot of ground, and her precious seedlings, the children through whom she stakes a "personal" future in the region. Throughout the poem she is seen in contradistinction to the men in her life and her emotional state explored as responses to pressures from them. Thus, while the male goes out among "bicycle bells" and "gunfire of donkey carts" and becomes part of the merchant's material and enslaving world, the woman sits and calls on Jesus' name, awaiting his return "with her gold rings of love / with the miner's trove that binds her to his world."[48]

Bev Brown has argued strongly that such representations take away women's agency:

> there are no women-links of either physical or metaphysical relation-
> ships among women that are comparable to creolization mystified as
> masculine, creationist theory. According to Brathwaite, "son" does,
> "mother/woman" is. On one hand, "son" can move in time and
> space to remember to maneuver his process of adaptation. On the
> other hand, "mother" is part of that which "son" maneuvers.[49]

But it is easy to see the contrasting representation as Brathwaite's way of identifying the woman's world and vision as the center of Afro-Caribbean memory and expressivity. Within her apparent lack of agency the woman retains what is valuable and crucial to the historical experience. On one hand, she is a victim of history in the way Walcott's female persona is envisioned in *The Star-Apple Kingdom:* "She wears on her wrist the shadow of the chain / history of flesh / written by whip of torture / legacy of bribe." Yet

> she will remember the eyes
> sinking into the night of dead water

cries of flame when there was gun
fire, gong beat and the cripple footsteps running from the tribe

from the sickness of the plantation
she gathers sticks
gutters then to fashion pipes, flutes siphons
rambles of herb she touches and sniffs

offering them prayers and names.[50]

Ironically, however, it is this burden of an idealized symbol and the exteriority of representation that West Indian women's writing attempts to deconstruct.[51] As Mae Henderson argues in the context of African American women's writing,

The real status of black women and their relationship to the rest of society—cannot be captured in "felicitous images." Such a representation would suggest that black women inscribe themselves in nonadversarial relationships with both community and the society at large. Such images have the potential to reinforce and maintain the status of currently marginalized and subdominant groups. The power of black women's writing is precisely its ability to disrupt and break with conventional imagery.[52]

Women writers in the West Indies have begun to valorize and problematize the woman's sphere of experience. As this chapter has demonstrated, the female sphere in women's writing is the site of several contestations and the fundamental source of cultural negotiation and transformation. Its structuring vision provides leeway to explore submerged and inarticulate variables of history transmitted orally through generations of women. Yet it is also the site of women's own individuation, where self-understanding and growth illuminate a sense of their place in the community and where sexual politics is intertwined with the wider politics of history and transformation as women writers consistently deconstruct the divisions between domestic and public domains.

There are thus complex variations in the conception of female space in the women writers represented here. In Jean Rhys's *Wide Sargasso Sea* sexual and political themes are combined in the protagonist's individuation. Antoinette's feminine self-assertion, even in her madness, becomes a political statement, an assertion (however doomed) of a different geographic space and history. Schwarz-Bart's protagonist in *The Bridge of Beyond*, like Brathwaite's persona in *Mother Poem*, embodies an Afro-Caribbean historical and spiritual consciousness, but her wider perception

of the Negro's place in the world is made possible by a feminist reorientation of her self-perception as a woman. In the various crises of the protagonists in the novels of Brodber and Kincaid, a rejection of sensuality and
earthiness is part of a colonialist rejection of self and history, and women's
individuation in Kincaid's *Annie John* and Brodber's *Jane and Louisa* and
Myal involve reconceptualizations of the feminine different from the re-
pressions, self-negations, and imitative culture which are part of the whole
"young woman business." Indeed, even in *Crick Crack Monkey,* in which
the focus of delineation is more historically centered, there is a feminist
dimension to the thematization of alienation that locates Tee's crisis of self-
perception within the crisis of femininity experienced by the protagonists in
the works of Kincaid and Brodber.

These variations in the representation of the women's sphere confirm
Henderson's statement that the power of women's writing resides in its
ability to disrupt and break with conventional imagery. They also affirm
the chapter's underlying idea that the intersection of generational, class,
race, and color differences necessarily affect a woman writer's representation of the women's sphere; that the difference of women's writing resides
in a complex intersection of gender perspectives and a host of other factors
related to a woman's distinctive historical, cultural, and personal experience.

Chapter Ten

Africa in the Historical Imagination of the West Indian Writer

In the imagination of the Afro–West Indian writer Africa has always loomed large as a reality and an idea, and the writer's relationship to it has often been defined by a sense of origin, of the past and its impact on West Indian people and their place in history. The striving to achieve this relationship is itself an aspect of a deep psychological need that creates a nameless yearning for origins in most peoples of the African diaspora. West Indian writers, particularly Brathwaite, Lamming, and Harris, see this link with origin as a necessity that could put West Indian man in a meaningful context of space and time and enlarge his consciousness of self.

In response to this necessity the writer's imaginative relationship to Africa and the ancestor has in the last two decades progressed from self-conscious evocations of a private and mythical Africa to mature and subtle probing into the ways in which an African consciousness modified and transformed itself in the physical and psychological situation of slavery and colonialism. Correspondingly, critical emphasis has shifted from unsubtle categorization of the use of African survivors in Caribbean writing towards an identification of an Afro-Caribbean tradition and aesthetic. The crucial question being raised now in relation to the subject is not simply what scope exists for the Caribbean novelist wishing to evoke Africa, but also whether or not an Afro-Caribbean tradition survives in the Caribbean and can provide gateways for redefinition.[1]

For Brathwaite such continuities and transformations are part of a submerged West Indian history and self which could generate an art of renaissance: "In the Caribbean, whether it be African or American, the recognition of an ancestral relationship with the folk or aboriginal culture involves the artist and participants in a journey into the past and hinterland which is at the same time a movement of possession into present and future. Through this movement of possession we become ourselves, truly our own creators, discovering word for object, image for the word."² The awareness that psychic wholeness and creativity in the region depend on a confrontation with the past and with the ancestor is a common idea in West Indian thinking and has different ramifications in different writers. Thus, if for Brathwaite the confrontation is an act of memory and a possession of submerged continuities, it is for Harris a chance to "immerse ourselves in a new capacity or treaty of sensibility," a chance "to bring into play a new variable imagination, a renaissance of sensibility steeped in caveats of the necessary diversity and necessary unity of men."³

In Harris's explorations a relationship to the ancestor is thus much more than a restoration of links with origin; it is also a chance to create new sensibilities, to move into a future and to reintegrate ancestral memory into the West Indian psyche in order to achieve that wholeness which is the prerequisite for self-knowledge and creation. Memory, Harris insists, must liberate and transform the past by linking itself with the continuous cycles of change and renewal that goes on throughout history.

For other thinkers and writers of the region the imaginative confrontation with Africa has not yielded the positive results of recognition, recovery, and transformation. But the confrontation itself has been an act of exorcism, a purging of delusions that led to insights into the West Indian man's relation to his ancestors and to his own hybrid and unique evolution. In this sense the confrontations with Africa in Denis Williams's *Other Leopards* and Derek Walcott's *Dream on Monkey Mountain* present different ramifications of West Indian attitudes to the ancestor and to origins.

The sense of guilt and insufficiency, the deep psychological needs that impel these novels' protagonists towards Africa are not too different from the needs that motivate the protagonists of Brathwaite, Lamming, and Harris. Yet in both Williams and Walcott the imaginative contact with Africa reveals rather the negative ramifications of these needs, particularly the self-doubt and self-abnegation that inspire the West Indian man's filial relationship to the ancestor. As Williams has remarked, posing the problem with remarkable clarity: "In our relationship to the ancestor we of the New World are judged by the pedigree consciousness of the old; our mongrelism is abhorred by the thoroughbred sensibilities of the world . . . to the old world 'pure' races the specter of miscegenation is the specter of the loss of pedigree, the corruption of the thoroughbred, the destruction of the ancestor, the emergence of the mongrel . . . Attuned to an Old World culture, one has come to view one's own condition as mongrel, one's own being, in fact, with the racial biases of pedigree man."[4]

This sense of loss and taint which characterizes the West Indian man's self-perception is, in Williams's view, the basis of that nameless hankering after origin which besets and confuses the West Indian consciousness. In *Other Leopards* it is the starting consciousness of Williams's protagonist and part of that monumental sense of guilt which characterizes his relationship to Africa's past and present. The need that sends Froad on a quest to Johkara and which makes him susceptible to his white boss's constant goading about proving his place in history is one that is tinged with defensiveness and guilt. "All along, ever since I'd grown up, I'd been Lionel looking for Lobo. I'd felt I ought to become this chap, this alter ego of ancestral times that I was sure quietly slumbered behind the cultivated mask."[5] Indeed, Froad's work as an archaeological draftsman is an indication of his inner need to find a positive relation to the past and to origin, but the expression of this need is also a reflection of the quality of his quest, of the fundamental defensiveness and insecurity that inspire the search in the first place. Though this defensiveness is part of his own divided psychology, it is also in a major sense a reflection of his ambivalent relationship with his white boss, Hughie, of his deep-seated respect for him on one hand and, on the other, of his bitterness against him for suggesting his lack of a link with civilized history.

Hughie's obsession with responsibility to race, history, and the future, his relentless drive to prove and establish a distinctive aesthetic as the life force in Meroitic art, has a tinge of superiority as well as a contempt for Froad, since he is also aware that such a distinctive aesthetic may never be established. In a similar way it is possible to argue that the entire archaeological and historical interpretation in which Froad is engaged reveals that his relation to history and Africa is inspired by feelings of inferiority and guilt in the face of what he perceives as the great European historical assurance symbolized by Hughie. Indeed, his response to Meroe history and art reveals not only tentativeness and defensiveness, but also self-doubt and guilt. "Maybe the Old Queen of Meroe will have something to say to me . . . I feel like a supplicant off to consult an oracle."[6] Such expectations, however tentative, represent a lot more than the expectations with which we generally relate to history, and it is as if for Froad the discovery of Meroe civilization will establish that sense of history and memory which he is convinced he lacks. He invests so much of his own personal stability and sense of equilibrium in the effort that identification with the Meroe past becomes the all-encompassing panacea that would resolve his crises of temperament and relationships.

Yet ironically, Froad's contact with the figure of Queen Amanishakete stirs up only confusion and distaste, revealing again the ambivalence and division that are part of his divided mulatto personality. As he runs his fingers greedily over the steatopygous body, the African (Lobo) in him speaks, insisting, "this is your woman." At the same time, his mulatto strain confesses: "I am a man most profoundly attracted by light-colored, copper-colored, mestizo, West Indian mulatto women. Sun in the blood, copper in the skin; that's my thing . . . this queen was bronze; close as the sweat on my skin. Too close, not my thing."[7] More crucial than this confusion and ambivalence is Froad's shocking realization that the Meroe statue cannot talk to him; that he himself cannot claim that past and significance which she symbolizes. "I wished for the words to assault those stone ears with some claim of my very own, mine, me. But time passed, wind blew, sand settled, gloom deepened, and I could think of nothing, nothing at all."[8]

Although part of Froad's entire relation to Meroitic civilization had been (as Hughie wanted it) to demonstrate the creativity of the ancient kingdom and establish the ego of his race, he discovers no creative identification with the past. On the contrary, he finds himself confused and agitated to discover the hatred and cruelty embodied in the whole aura of Amanishakete and by implication the racial history she symbolizes. Such a discovery throws into disarray Froad's own romanticized assumptions about racial purity and about the moral certainty of thoroughbred cultures and unbroken histories.

Throughout his relationship with Africa Froad assumes a pose of inferiority, believing that his mulatto condition robs him of links to the moral certainty of the pure African. In describing a local *tirah* player he is anxious to bring out the African's authenticity as it shows up in his animistic relationship with his environment. "Yes, he drew out the sound as though it were already there in the darkness waiting to be uncoiled at the touch of his leaping fingers, he standing before me showing the music down my face, singing in his hoary Tigre tongue, me confronting him with face marked by store of senseless knowledge stamped all over by three hundred years of error."[9] By Froad's reckoning the correlation between environment and art becomes part of the African's authenticity and strength, characteristics which he is convinced show up his own bastard, fake, morally tainted condition.

But such a view about the cultural wholeness and moral strength of the thoroughbred is not the novel's vision. Indeed, the certainties of race, religion, history, and culture appear throughout as rigid enclaves that admit of no flexibility or sensitiveness and inspire the hatreds, antagonisms, and disintegration in the novel. Arab, Christian, African, English—all appear inflexible, caged in the structures and certainties of creed, race, and culture and excluding some of the most fundamental human bonds that bring men together beyond these structures. The chief's filial response to Africa, embodied in his simplistic interpretation of the myth of Zagreus,[10] is, for instance, the most criticized and devastatingly flayed in the novel: "(He) said that Zagreus had to perish because as a bastard he lacked the moral force to pit against the Titans, i.e. titanic nature, i.e. evil; because the link with his people had been broken. He said: What's the use quibbling, no man can live without this link, this moral certainty, a man must live in time, it is his nature."[11]

The self-assured dogmatism of the chief's interpretation of the Zagreus myth (linked in the novel with universal relationships between men and historical circumstances) reveals several ironies that comment on his perspective and point to Williams's own stand on the issue of relationships to the ancestor. The chief's easy condemnation reveals a serious insensitivity on his part to the human situation of Froad, who is, like Zagreus, a mongrel. It is an insensitivity which Williams also links to the chief's unbending and almost inhumane treatment of his daughter, as well as to the other rigidities of belief and assumption which diminish human factors in personal relations.

In contrast to these rigid systems of pure race and culture, Froad's faltering self-confrontations and self-assessments push him towards a more honest relationship to the past and to origin, one that recognizes and accepts that unique mulatto identification which he had spent all his life running away from. For Froad, self-confrontation and self-assessment include, on one hand, a reinterpretation of the Zagreus myth and a new relationship to it in his own consciousness. His reworking of the myth rejects both the chief's fatalistic interpretation of Zagreus' circumstances as well as Hughie's rationalist acceptance that struggle and opposition to history are the only conditions for man's liberty on earth. As Hughie rationalizes, determined to blame Froad's defensive dishonesty on his bastard situation, "The story of Zagreus was significant only in so far as Zagreus took account of his historic circumstance and opposed it . . . Zagreus was a figure of historic circumstance (and) opposition is the fundamental attitude of being for Homo sapiens . . . there is no liberty except in spurning circumstance with self."[12] This idea of struggle and opposition to historical circumstance is the burden of responsibility which, goaded by Hughie, Froad takes on in his reconstruction of history. To prove himself into history and therefore into existence is, like Zagreus' many disguises, an opposition to personal history and a way of transcending its bastard and tainted origins.

Yet paradoxically, it is partly through his opposition to his hybrid condition that Froad comes to recognize its uniqueness and validity, so that when he finally stabs and kills Hughie he eliminates the burden of time and history into which he had to prove himself in order to earn parity with him. It is Hughie, after all, who deliberately goads him into an attitude about history in order to make it a condition for equality with him, knowing at the same time that a reconstruction of it would only reveal Froad's inferior place in history and confirm the superiority of his own thoroughbred race and culture. For Froad the elimination of the specter of Hughie is not just a chance to exorcise a filial relation to history but also an opportunity to assess the implications of the present and the unique possibilities of his hybrid origins, a chance to explore at the same time possibilities for an autonomous self-image not derived from any ancestor. Indeed, Froad comes nearer to this discovery when, after desperately trying to identify with both, he recognizes at last the mulatto divide (the desert) between Africa and Europe makes him neither "infra" nor "supra": it puts him outside the contending claims of both parent cultures.

Although the novel ends with Froad burrowing to primal time, returning to the very origins of life as if he has given up on time and context, there are enough indications of the processes of thought and perception that have pushed him towards awareness of an autonomous self-image to suggest the possible emergence of a new consciousness, one that may not invest so much in connections with ancestral parent cultures but in "reservoirs of creativeness whose content might be as much environmental as they are racial." Thus, for someone like Froad with an artist's temperament and quest, the problem of autonomous image and autonomous culture will be one, as Williams himself claims, "of exploring our peculiar psychic heritage in concepts for which there might be no ancestral warrant."[13]

Yet ironically, and in spite of this perception and effort, Froad is still caught in the old self-image based on a long-accepted relationship between him and Hughie, the "Prospero" figure in the novel. Every move of Froad's, even after he has killed Hughie, reckons with his superior knowledge, systems, and understanding, although he continually reminds himself to plan "outside the limits of Hughie's intelligence." Thus in the end it appears as if to extricate himself from the various systems and contexts that imprison people in structures of race, religion, and politics, Froad must relinquish all time, must insulate himself against all encroachments of time, even though he is aware that symbolically this is a denial of life. But perhaps for Williams this momentary blotting out of life is a chance to begin again (like Zagreus, with whom he identifies) to reemerge in a different mold and frame of mind, having shed all contexts and all traces of history and their implications.

Although Williams's novel works towards this final realization, the entire engagement with Africa and history becomes a catharsis in which the burden and fear of history are exorcised and the whole idea of origin and its relation to the present are given a new realistic qualification. Yet, whereas in Brathwaite such an engagement leads to an awareness of the wider historical and ancestral links in the creation of a West Indian identity, a similar engagement in Williams and Walcott leads rather to an exorcism, to a sense of freedom from historical links and contexts. In their essays and works both Williams and Walcott see this freedom positively as a freedom from witness and from destiny, one that allows West Indian man to invest rather in the present and its creative possibilities: Williams has argued forcefully "that among us of the Caribbean who hold no warrant for a destiny it is the present which is our only witness, the present as it has been determined in the complex womb of which we are the issue."[14]

In a more imaginative way, Williams explores this perspective positively in *Other Leopards* when he weans his protagonist from a negative relation to the present to a positive awareness of its creative potential. Throughout the novel, Froad, in line with his defensiveness, has viewed his relation to the present (what he calls "the void of his perennial present") negatively, as an abnegation of duty to the past and history. By the end of the novel, however, he has come to realize that in some liberating sense the "present without contour" represents a freedom which could be finally creative.

As in *Other Leopards*, Walcott's protagonist in *Dream on Monkey Mountain* ends his dream experience purged and cleansed and ready to return to the present, to the green beginnings of his world, in effect, to his own independent self. For Walcott, as for Williams, the obsession with origin and the pursuit of birthright are finally futile because, inspired by filial relationships to the racial ancestor, they are also impelled by assumed identities, by illusions of identity either of European whiteness or African blackness. Makak's experience in *Dream on Monkey Moutain*, though following the disjointedness of a dream sequence, becomes in the end part of a collective cathartic experience in which the division and peculiar psychosis of the West Indian consciousness are laid bare and confronted. Makak's relationship with Africa is given a background and perspective which links it to his own personal self-contempt and to his secret longings for a white identity. Cast as a warrior "redeemer" figure, he is put through a process through which his messianic vision is compromised and tainted by his particular schizophrenia. His original (first) dream makes him out, in Fanon's words, as a white mind in a black skin. His dream vision is both inspired and colored by an antithetical image of his surroundings and by his ordinarily negative perception of himself. The black charcoal burner, alone, at one with the forest and his god, dreams one day of a white woman, "the loveliest thing on this earth, floating towards him just like the moon," a vision which, as Lestrade is later to warn, is as unattainable as the moon itself. Makak's other vision of himself as an African king is likewise given by the same tantalizing white apparition and has therefore a similar base of falseness, defensiveness, and insecurity. "She say I should not live here so any more, here in the forest, frighten of people because I think I ugly. She say that I come from the family of lions and kings."[15]

The vision of himself that the white woman offers Makak has within it a paradoxical combination of positive perceptions and romantic fantasies and represents the confused longings and delusions of the ordinary West Indian. There is on one hand the positive and revolutionary vision she offers Makak of his hidden powers as healer and leader, and there is on the other the romantic, confusing vision she gives him of his warrior and regal role in Africa. The vision of an inner spiritual force and power is, of course, the dream of self-realization and revolutionary change which is the common dream of the colonized and which in the play is shared by characters as far apart in status and consciousness as Lestrade, Makak, and Souris. In spite of his being against the force represented by the strikes and the cane burnings, Lestrade's other self longs for the chance to see his people "challenge the law, show they alive . . . prove they are not paralyzed because they born slaves and they born tired."[16] In the dramatist's way of linking characters' consciousness and dreams, Lestrade's wish echoes Makak's earlier hope in the healing scene, in which he too stresses the need for his people to believe in themselves and in the power of their spirit. In the overlapping ramifications of these dreams, Walcott demonstrates the various ways in which the revolutionary dream degenerates or is confused by the colonials' other longings and obsessions about origins and ancestors.

In *Dream on Monkey Mountain* the drama of part 2, involving Makak's apotheosis as an African chief, represents one level of this degeneration. The fact that Makak's deification is initiated by Lestrade, the middle-class mulatto who had vigorously championed white civilization in earlier scenes, sounds a note of falseness in the new African identity assumed by both Makak and himself. Walcott's comic parody of African rituals, customs, and songs presents a background within which Makak's dream of chieftainship in a precolonial African community could be assessed. In the first place, Makak's desire to find his origin in the African kingdoms of the past is, as in the case of Froad, inspired by his fantasies about the white apparition and by his anxiety to prove his place and validate his existence to the white world. Thus, throughout the drama, the romanticized evocations of Africa are continually balanced against visions of turmoil and disarray to illustrate the confused and illusionary nature of Makak's relation to Africa. The Africa of "the golden sands and rivers, where lions come down to drink lapping at the water with their red tongues" is deflated by "the wrangling of the tribes snarling at their shadows, snapping their own tails."[17] In Africa, Makak's dream of community, inner strength, and salvation degenerates into a dream of power, destruction, and eventually of revenge against the entire white world. His thunderous voice commanding Souris to feed his armies and his fierce determination that squabbling tribes must be crushed reflect aspects of this degeneration. The trial scene is linked to these earlier scenes, especially in the way it reveals Makak's revolutionary dream as more revenge against the history of colonialism and exploitation than a creative perception and transformation of a colonial situation. Indeed, the indiscriminate lumping of the condemned prisoners, all connected in various exploitative human and creative ways with the colonial experience, is the dramatist's critical judgment of the narrowness and intransigence of Makak's revolution. "Some are dead and cannot speak for themselves, but a drop of milk is enough to condemn them, to banish them from the archives of the bo-leaf and the papyrus, from the waxen tablet and tribal stone."[18]

Makak, too, like Lestrade, moves from extreme love of the moon to extreme hatred of it, leaving no leeway for creative assessment and transformation. His beheading of the apparition is thus on one hand a cold-blooded rejection of whiteness and on the other a final coming to terms with the burden of origin and a relationship to the ancestor. It is as if in that private moment of confrontation with the apparition Makak recognizes the extent to which his dream of African origins has been prompted by feelings of inferiority and self-rejection and by a very real psychological need to compensate for these. Making the decision to behead the apparition is for Makak also a deep and poignant confrontation with his innermost consciousness. That is why, in opposition to Lestrade's prompting for a quick and decisive action, Makak lingers to search his memory for clues to the exact nature of his relations with the apparition.

> I remember, one day, when I was younger, fifty year old or so, I wake up, alone, and I do not know myself. I wake up, an old man that morning, with my clothes stinking of fifty years of sweat . . . and I ask myself, in a voice I do not know: who you are, negre . . . I say, your name is what—an old man without a mirror. And I went in the little rain barrel behind my hut and look down in the quiet, quiet water at my face, an old cracked, burn-up face, with the hair turning white. And it was Makak. So I say, if you died now . . . No woman will cry for you, no child will look at your face in death as if it was for the first time . . . you will go under this earth and burn and change as if you were a coal yourself.

It is important that at this point Makak should link the burden of his relationship with the apparition to the critical moments of his own feelings of inferiority and crisis of identity: "A big, big loneliness possesses me, as if I was happy once, and strong, but could not remember where, as if, in some way, I was not no charcoal-burner . . . but a king, and I feel strongly to go down the mountain, and to reach the sea, as if the place I remember was across the sea."[19]

It becomes clear at this point that it is Makak's own psychology which merges with the prompting of the apparition and which makes him highly susceptible to her manipulations. Indeed, the entire unraveling of Makak's dream is a progress from one kind of manipulation to another: manipulation first by the apparition, then by Moustique, by Souris, and finally by Lestrade. Thus Makak's final and private act of beheading the apparition has a dramatically double-edged implication, representing on a less subtle level his rejection of the white world (as prompted by Lestrade) and on a deeper, more psychosomatic level, a freedom from the burden of proving his existence by reference to ancestral greatness. The illumination of his experience has led rather to a sense of self-acceptance—acceptance of his own individual potential, of his non-African name (Felix Hobain) as well as his West Indian home and all its possibilities: "now this old hermit is going back home, back to the beginning, to the green beginning of this world."[20] The reference to "green beginnings" relates, of course, to Walcott's own view that the West Indian can, like a second Adam, begin again to build a sense of self and identity without too much reference to the ancestor.

Makak, supposedly purged of his dreams, illusions, and false identities, returns to his original home, his original name, and to possibilities of new beginnings and new self-conceptions.

For Walcott, the imaginative relationship to Africa and Africa's past serves mostly to accentuate the illusionary and false nature of the West Indian's assumed African identity and the necessity of forging a separate self from his own unique situation and circumstances. Because the relation is geared towards this purgation it is perceived mostly in terms of parody and ridicule, and Makak is in the end unable to work out a cleansing, realistic, positive relation to Africa in the way that Brathwaite's persona is able to do in *Masks*. In Brathwaite's imaginative relation to Africa there is a certain amount of romance, even of sentimentality, but it is a sentimentality that is sustaining and which is reassessed for a more realistic revaluation of the multiple sources of identity. In *Dream on Monkey Mountain* sentimentality, ridicule, and corruption leave little room for reassessment, since the entire basis of the relationship is shown as false. The drama of Makak's putting on the rage of the lion in *Dream on Monkey Mountain* is, for instance, purely a spectacle of fantasy, showing the ludicrous nature of his delusions and hallucinations and ridiculing the falseness of his presumed African identity without really exploring its deep-seated complexities and the possibilities it could yield for self-understanding.

Yet in "Wings of a Dove" (*Rights of Passage*) Brathwaite presents a similar hallucination in the poem's persona, Brother Man, without necessarily negating the value of his African and grounded self-perception. For while Makak's rage is pure delusion, Brother Man's "dream" has a paradoxical mixture of hallucination and clarity, showing the irony of a clear vision trapped in delusions and religious ritual. Thus, although at the end of his walk through the "now silent / streets of affliction . . ."[21] Brother Man's dream is nowhere near fulfillment, he has at least clarified a vision of himself as well as a view of the ungrounded, middle-class West Indian.

As Brathwaite demonstrates in *Rights of Passage, Masks,* and *Islands,* African continuities and transformations exist in the Caribbean, and memory trunked up in the attic of the mind can be activated and transformed into a new future. Indeed, Brathwaite's own aesthetic of renaissance derives from such a relation to memory and the ancestor, and a great deal of his explorations in *Islands,* as demonstrated in chapter 8, is committed to activating West Indian memory for the creation of new and fuller sensibilities in Afro-West Indian people.

It seems that a West Indian relation to Africa, then, conceived wholly from a situation of neurosis, may yield only a satiric delineation that laughs away fantasies without exploring the ancestral links that intersect with others in the creation of a unique West Indian identity. The fruitful thrust of exploration is that which views this relation in the contexts of displacements, transformations, and coexistence with other realities in the Caribbean itself. There is, for instance, a revealing contrast of presentation and insight in a comparison of the dream journey of Makak in *Dream on Monkey Mountain* and Achille in *Omeros* which may illustrate and validate the points raised about the thrust of exploration.

Whereas in *Dream* the context, images, and symbols of the *mas* combine to heighten Makak's African "trip" in carnival parlance, as a big *mas* and fantasy Achille's dream voyage is explored in the context of poetic reflection as part of a larger enterprise in which Walcott explores a concept of home and identity with explicit reference to the various sources of his West Indian heritage. The dream voyage to Africa occurs after Achille and other characters have been named and located within their West Indian landscapes and in the context of the rituals and realities of their own worlds, thus presenting a perspective of "home" from which the experience in Africa is then explored.

As in Brathwaite's *Masks,* in which two sets of consciousness operate within the poet-persona's mind—one daring the ships of separation and the other recognizing the wounds of history—Achille inhabits several other minds and perspectives in Africa which push him to resist a simplistic bridging of the discontinuities. His dream experience, while revealing continuities, also sharpens his awareness of a separate history and future. If it exorcises sentimentality it at the same time integrates the tragedy of African disintegration and West Indian displacement into his consciousness, so that the two histories of disintegration and displacement are accepted as related parts of an African tragedy. The connections made between Achille's dream and his everyday life are much more natural and meaningful than those made between Makak and his dream. Makak's return to the elemental beginnings of his West Indian forest is, in spite of his new self-understanding, a return to further isolation in a relatively unchanged world; Achille's African experience, however, becomes part of a larger dialectic aimed at exploring the complex nature of Afro-Caribbean identity. Linked to Philoctete's story and to the self-healing process by which shame, fear, and self-hatred are cured, the dialectic explores the African presence not as a fad that characters take on to hide from feelings of self-rejection but as continuities traced back through the long trail of ants (generations of coal-carrying ancestors) to

"All the unburied gods, for three deep centuries dead," who
                                   swarmed in the thicket
of the grove, waiting to be known by name.[22]

In *Omeros* this idea of transformation is central to Achille's dream vision and to the dialectic on the African presence in the West Indies. A tree carried across the Atlantic shoots "fresh leaves as its dead trunk washes on our beaches."[23] The images of transformation that surround the weed that finally cures the wounds of history also reverberate with irony regarding Achille's naive anxieties to find a place in Africa. They satirize his desire to claim back Africa's gods and demonstrate why in spite of the peace on the "waveless" African river the "surf roared in his head."[24] Achille's liberation is thus in the end a liberation not from roots in Africa but from bondage to the idea of his place in Africa. His final ritual dance towards the end of *Omeros* may resemble rituals in Africa but represents his own West Indian rituals, just as he retains his given name, Achille, symbolizing the transformed system of alliances in his new Antillean home.

But there is still a dominant satiric thrust in *Omeros* that threatens to overshadow some of the subtle continuities and connections of which Achille becomes aware in his dream visit to Africa. The tendency to see the two worlds and histories as dichotomies blurs those subtle links and continuities that were crucial to the survival of African slaves in the first place. We do not have in *Omeros* those subtle paradoxes of *Masks*, in which both the gains and losses of Africa's history are integrated in the West Indian consciousness as a way of liberating and reconstituting historical spaces in the West Indian psyche.

Yet removing the darkness that encircles Africa in the West Indian mind is also a form of liberation, a way of infusing a new self-apprehension in the West Indian mind. In *Masks* this freedom is achieved precisely because Africa and its past are more than what is in *Omeros* symbolized by the "snaking river," the "mud without shadow," and the raids that lead to disintegration and displacement. In a text in which intertextuality is a consistent phenomenon, the images of a closed world and the bend in the snaking river recall the African worlds of Conrad and Naipaul without expanding on those Eurocentric creations in new and radical ways.

Still, in terms of the place and meaning of Africa in West Indian definition, the explorations in *Omeros* identify a new focus which negotiates other social and cultural spaces encountered by African people in the New World. The midshipman drowned in the Atlantic, the sojourn of Dennis and Maud Plunkett, the fate of the Aruaks, even the narrator's own love-hate relationship with the worlds that had enslaved and colonized him, are stories that represent the complexity which makes up the "roaring surf," contrasted with the "waveless [African] river" of Achille's dream vision.

Other West Indian texts that explore the African presence emphasize different aspect of it, though they all invariably stress transformation rather than the rhetoric of evocation. Harris's *Secret Ladder* explores the significance of integrating the ancestor into consciousness but stresses a transformation of his image into a fluid future rather than a static celebration of the relationship for its own sake. The death of the African ancestor is thus a release that ushers in a new future, though ironically that future represents hardly any input from the ancestor himself.

In Dennis Scott's *An Echo in the Bone* an important duality exists in the very use of an African ritual that nevertheless explores West Indian history. On one hand, the ritual of the wake, which structures the drama of remembering, affirms an African survival; on the other, the phenomenon of spirit possession, which facilitates the recall and piecing together of Afro-Caribbean experience, becomes a metaphorical reliving, assessment, and possession of West Indian rather than African experience. The conflation of time and place afforded by spirit possession allows an easy connection between the "present" of the play and the different periods of West Indian history as a way of demonstrating how present states of consciousness and personality relate to moments in history which characters have wiped out of their consciousness. The play's catharsis is thus one of self-revelation, knowledge, and renewal derived from the piecing together and integration of experiences which illuminate Afro-Caribbean history from the moment of displacement to the present of the play.

In George Lamming's *Season of Adventure*, Edward Brathwaite's *Islands*, and Paule Marshall's *Praisesong for the Widow*, exploration of the African presence is in a major sense a reclamation of psychocultural space through the activation of memory. The thrust in these works is always psychological and "spiritual," though differentiated from the spiritual perspectives of Harris's works. The drums of the forest reserve and the Haitian ceremony of souls in *Season of Adventure* are, for instance, symbols of cultural links with Africa which have different connotations from those of the isolated figure of the runaway African slave and his buried community in Harris's *The Secret Ladder*. In both novels the protagonists have to confront either the African ancestor or African continuities. But in *The Secret Ladder* the central character actually wills the death of the ancestor to prevent a static relationship with the kind of isolation and freedom he represents, which Harris finds incongruous with the heterogeneous ground of community in the Caribbean. Thus Poseidon is integrated into Fenwick's consciousness not merely to bridge gaps in discontinuity but to transform his symbolic import into a fluid future. In *Season of Adventure* the symbols of the submerged past are actually symbols of African continuities and transformations very much alive in the peasant world of the novel, though they exist in tension with another, middle-class world. As in Harris's novel, the protagonist confronts the ceremony of souls not as a new experience but as with some hidden part of herself; and though the confrontation is redemptive in the way it purges shame and fear of the past, the vision it affords is rooted within the political realities of the material world. Its transformation is political, with different connotations from the kind which Harris refers to as the authority of freedom.

It seems that even where West Indian writers engage with Africa historically as a source of origin, their perception of it in relation to West Indian identity is dependent on the conceptual framework that informs their thinking on history. The ambivalence of Harris and Walcott relates both to their emphasis on transformation and their primary view of the West Indies as a unique construct with a separate future. For Brathwaite, Lamming, and Paule Marshall, the first priority is unearthing the submerged continuities in the Afro-Caribbean experience. There is in all three writers a sense of the connections between cultural space and subjectivity, and continuities suppressed through shame and embarrassment represent for them the submerged and buried self. In their works freedom consists in a knowledge of the value of what is submerged, and delineations are a way of coming to terms with the "past" within the self.

In Marshall's *Praisesong for the Widow* the submerged world exists in tension with the demands of survival and progress in a wider culture that can overshadow what is after all a minority culture. Yet the remarkable thing about Marshall's novel is the way it pieces together fragments of ritual, mythology, and custom to create a psychocultural space that connects areas of the diaspora with each other and ultimately with Africa. The larger meanings imbued in the rituals extend beyond Africa to embrace the larger confraternity of community which African people created in the New World with the "bare bones" of remembered culture. The conception and imaging of Africa in the novel is probably the least sentimental and most realistic recent example in West Indian literature.

The protagonist's spiritual odyssey and descent into the furthest reaches of memory are structured through the ritual of remembrance, which celebrates generations of New World ancestors and the memory of the African homeland. Yet the realities of the celebration also define the fact of discontinuity and separation from Africa. The entire scenario of the ritual enacts not the romance of a phantom Africa or even the embodiment of the ritual as it is performed in Africa but rather the sadness and pain of the community's own life, "its long trial by fire."[25] The restrained and understated movements of the dance reverberate with meanings that tell a peculiarly New World story of separation, loss, and transformation. What the ritual at Carioucou enacts in remembrance is thus the essence of something rather than the thing itself, since "All that was left were a few names of what they called nations which they could no longer even pronounce properly, the fragments of a dozen or so songs, the shadowy forms of long-ago dances and rum kegs for drums. The bare bones. The burnt-out ends. And they clung to them with a tenacity she suddenly loved in them and longed for in herself."[26]

The tenacious clinging to fragments of memory may suggest the links and continuities that are crucial for the people's sense of themselves. But in the novel these continuities also represent transformations. In the criss-crossing and linking of memories in the protagonist's mind the more personal and intimate memories are those that connect two areas of the diaspora: the Caribbean and the southern United States. The memories connected in this way demonstrate a new thrust: the reassembling and creation of a new sense of community. In a similar sense the god Legba is refigured in *Praisesong* not as an African god per se but as a human ancestor of the New World, a godlike man of many sides and possibilities. These transformations, rather than the mere evocation of an African ritual, are impressed upon the clean state of the protagonist's consciousness. Marshall suggests that it is in integrating aspects of such continuities that characters can keep track of their own spirits and those of their communities.

Although Africa and the idea of Africa have featured strongly and consistently in the historical imagination of the West Indian writer, it is only in the last two decades that the engagement has moved to such a mature level of subtlety and seriousness. The controversy it has generated is thus a measure of the complexity of the West Indian's relationship to the past as well as the complex cultural forces that create an ancestral African past. Where the engagement has provided a perspective and vision, the writer has often explored ways in which a relation to the ancestor and to ancestral history can lead to new self-conceptions and sensibilities in the region. But even where the exploration has yielded no positive identification, the engagement has, as in the case of writers like Williams, helped in the formulation of a valid perception of Caribbean identity.

Conclusion

In this study of the interplay between historical perception and imaginative writing what has emerged as remarkable is the extent to which conceptions of history outside the intrinsic methodologies of historiography can unleash several levels of meaning and perspective. Harris's call for reconceptualizations of Caribbean history in imaginative literature appropriately coincides with a new skepticism about the discipline of history itself. The claims that are made for it as an intrinsic discipline are based on methodologies that emphasize sources, records, and evidence. Yet such requirements do not stop historical writing from intersecting with other variables. As Lowenthal has argued, historians "go beyond the actual record to frame hypotheses in present-day modes of thought,"[1] and analytical concepts like time, cause and effect, and continuity can be ideological constructs that elicit particular, even partisan perceptions of the past. Their potential biases have in fact encouraged thinking on what might happen if other concepts were used to organize the field of history. Keith Jenkins has recently argued that "the fact that history per se is an ideological construct means that it is constantly being re-worked and re-ordered by all those who are variously affected by power relationships; because the dominated as well as the dominant also have their versions of the past to legitimate their practices, versions which have to be excluded as unproper from any place on the agenda of the dominant discourse."[2]

Jenkins's observation is particularly pertinent to the first chapter of this book. The evaluation of West Indian historiography from the sixteenth century to the twentieth century has revealed the ways in which discourses on the region's history have been written and rewritten from all kinds of economic, political, and imperial biases. It is not surprising then that their conceptions of the region's history should be so different from the perceptions in the imaginative literature. For the re-creation of history in imaginative terms is actually a construction of meanings outside the restrictions of history as discipline. In the literature of the West Indies this kind of engagement is also ideological, a way of interrogating and re-creating identity. The impulse of subjectification which moves V. S. Reid to fictionalize the Morant Bay rebellion and link it with the constitutional struggles of the 1940s is the same impulse that leads Naipaul into an imaginative reconstruction of the East Indian's progress in colonial Trinidad. It is the same impulse that drives Walcott, Lamming, Brathwaite, and Harris through the long, tortuous probing of the meaning of history in the West Indies.

Yet there are differences even in the kind of understanding these writers have achieved in their engagement with history. A historical sense is in the final analysis a subjective vision, influenced not only by a writer's ideals but also by how historical legacies intersect with several other factors in a writer's historicization of experience. Thus, if Reid's reconstruction of history in *New Day* projects a vision of the West Indian as a man who progresses from slave to free man and whose freedom has to be assessed and contained within the framework of his links with empire, Naipaul's evocation of the colonial's evolution highlights on the other hand the crippling limitations of his status as a colonial. His protagonist's movement in *A House for Mr. Biswas* from the obscure sugar estates to the wider colonial society may sharpen his perceptions and increase his understanding of his condition as colonial, but the experience does not necessarily exempt him from the consequences of his condition. Indeed, the colonial experience heightens even more glaringly the limitations of his historical situation. For Harris the idea of history becomes part of a transcendental philosophy that provides an understanding both of the historical process and of the spiritual capacities of man himself. Indeed, for all the writers considered here, a discourse on history is both a dialogue with and an interrogation of the assumptions of historicism as well as an exploration of other ways of conceiving history.

The book's contrasting perspectives reveal a shift from a literal engagement with linear history to a figurative configuration in which writers extract other meanings as they grapple with questions of history and subjectivity. The difference between a literal and figurative view of history has been explained at length by Harris as the difference between a material vision, which views particular events as occurring continuously at a particular place, and a metaphysical view, which endows real events with symbolic implications beyond their factual meanings.[3] In the reimagining of history in West Indian writing, the implications of such a differentiation are immense, ranging from conceptions in which history is simply the historical memory that creates room for speculation and innovation, or inarticulate and submerged experience the activation of which may create new sensibilities, or simply, in Walter Benjamin's words, "a conception of the present as the time of the now which is shot through with clips of messianic time."[4]

In West Indian imaginative writing, the engagement with history, as can be judged from this study, began as an engagement with literal and material history. The simple realism in which the physical world was evoked as a background to narrative and character created a perspective of order and coherence which was not commensurate with the discontinuities of the region's history, steeped in what Harris has called "broken conceptions as well as misconceptions of the residue and meaning of conquest."[5] De Lisser and Mittelholzer created fiction in which the material world was presented as simply given and in which the big issues of slavery and colonization become only part of the backdrop of an essentially unmediated reality. In contrast, Reid's construction of actual history in *New Day* and Naipaul's narrative of Biswas in colonial Trinidad are actually transformed in accordance with particular purposes: to create an optimistic story of West Indian political evolution as in Reid or, in Naipaul, to dramatize Biswas's repeated struggles and unfulfilled aspirations as symptomatic of the inherent disabilities of the colonial and displaced character. Although Homi Bhabha has argued persuasively that such a representation of the colonial's primary lack shatters "the mirror of representation and its range of western bourgeois social and psychic identifications,"[6] this study identifies a historicist and deterministic streak in the representation which consolidates Biswas's status as victim without venturing, in Harris's words, into "a revolutionary or alien question of spirit."[7]

The "revolutionary question of spirit," which can transpose the West Indian novel out of a static perception of history, is what Harris himself experiments with. The novel ways in which he alters the boundaries of realism and naturalism to suggest dimensions of historical perception available to the Caribbean imagination are experiments in this direction. For instance, his belief in the possibilities of integrating contrasting consciousness in characters enables him to envision paradoxes in Caribbean history and frees him from the temptation to regard the region and its people only as victims of European greed and brutality. His characters integrate not only other states of consciousness but also appropriate other spaces and spiritual seasons, in this way forestalling the usual polarization of historical situations and cultural identities in material history. Yet, as the study has revealed, Harris's ecumenical vision can sometimes blur the social contexts it seeks to transform, as happens, for instance, in *The Secret Ladder,* in which Poseidon's transformation from the static symbol of ancestry to integral part of the future community is subsumed in a spiritual vision that virtually excises his own consciousness.

It is obvious then that Harris's idea of renaissance, arguing the need to retrieve vestiges of pre-Columbian and ethnic imagination, works towards different ramifications from the idea of renaissance envisioned in the works of other West Indian writers. Though, like Harris, all the other writers explore the nature and function of memory in a West Indian context and investigate how it can be transformed, their relation to it registers differing variations. In Harris's work memory liberates only when it is linked with immateriality and with the continuous cycle of change and renewal that goes on in all his novels. In similar other senses, Walcott, Brathwaite, and Lamming have all engaged with memory in an effort to free themselves from imperial and linear history. Lamming's restlessness within the realistic medium shows up in his increasing use of myth as an enlightening and transforming medium. His subjective refiguration of the past actually constructs a version of history that not only destabilizes received history but also creates new meanings from the past with an eye on the future.

Walcott's philosophical essay "The Muse of History" is similarly as much a plea for a figurative vision of history as Harris's "History, Fable, and Myth." His distrust of linear time and his desire to see the past as timeless and mythical are explored in the book as the climax of his groping in the early stages of his career. The concept of a timeless history in which an elemental and Adamic West Indian roams unencumbered, grasping, in Walter Benjamin's words, "the constellations which his own era has found with a definite earlier age,"[8] widens into other perceptions of history in the poet's drama and in later works like *Omeros.* But a vision of history based on the idea of an Adamic man creates its tensions in Walcott's poetry, since it coexists with the poet's awareness of a historically determined disability created by the absences of history in the region. Walcott's problem, then, as his vision of history unravels is one of reconciling a perception that annihilates history with a condition that is determined by it. As this study demonstrates, he attempts such a reconciliation through his concept of the "Word," born when the artist makes a psychic return to the elemental to create a language beyond mimicry that would give his people a new image of themselves.

Yet Walcott's poetry, particularly in *Another Life,* has appeared to struggle with an ambiguous relationship between the artist's words and the people's consciousness. In some sense, his poetry dramatizes the poet's difficulty in activating the consciousness of his people in spite of his "elation" and his rooted language. The problem as it reveals itself in *Another Life* rests on the tensions in his conception of the imagination both as a reflection of the people's life and as a transcendental and self-igniting phenomenon. Although such an ambiguity may appear to question the sufficiency of "elation"[9] as a historical vision of the West Indies, Walcott accepts it as a valid enough basis for his function as a poet. In his poetry the poet is not a priest, as he often appears to be in Brathwaite's *The Arrivants,* nor is his imagination purged entirely of ego, as it appears to be in Brathwaite's trilogy. In Brathwaite's *Islands* the poet has the character of a shaman with the burden of recovering the Word and moving the people to self-awareness and revolution. In Walcott's poetry, he carries both the burden of the Word and the burden of the imagination, which by its very nature also carries his ego, his sheer joy and exhilaration at the mind's power to stretch itself and transform reality.

Only Reid, Naipaul, and Brathwaite engage with the actual substance of history as events in time. Reid's reconstruction of historical events in *New Day* had been an attempt to put a shape on Afro-Caribbean progress in the West Indies; it was a kind of social history, a substitute for the continuity which he thought was crucial for West Indian identity. The piecing together of events gave him a sense of progress but also deflated other areas of experience and tension equally relevant to West Indian self-conception.

Brathwaite engages with the substance of history on a slightly different level. His "history" in the trilogy is more of an epical re-creation of a wide stretch of African and diasporan history, and in spite of the precise focus on some aspects, particularly of African history, his "history" is more a conjectural evocation that exploits the freedom of myth in order to rearrange, interpret, and suggest possibilities in the Caribbean historical experience. It is the fluid nature of the re-creation that allows him to delineate Afro-Caribbean experience in history by suggesting links and continuities with Africa. The conflation of the mythic and the historical creates extended spaces, particularly in *Rights of Passage,* and breaks ground for the aesthetics of renaissance which becomes the underlying motif in *Islands.* Thus, in order to write a different perspective into Afro-Caribbean slavery and displacement, Brathwaite mythologizes and reimagines it in a different form. For though imaginative re-creation in *The Arrivants* and historical methodology in *The Development of Creole Society* have appeared to work towards similar conclusions, revealing the extent to which historiography itself may be susceptible to ideological construction, it is still only in *The Arrivants* that Brathwaite is able to break away from the confines of historical methodology to present history as the interrelationship of past, present, and future. *The Development of Creole Society* may be slanted towards anthropological and oral history, yet "history" still restricts itself to particular spaces and times and the specific institutions within them, and we have only to contrast it with *The Arrivants* to observe the radical perspectives which the freedom from linearity and conclusions affords the imaginative writer.

In Naipaul, there is a definite and closer correlation between historical writing and fiction writing. *The Loss of El Dorado* may satisfy a methodological requirement for records, sources, and evidence, but its actual narrative is framed by an underlying perspective which has been constant in all Naipaul's writing. That he should call it a history is itself an irony that hints at history's own fragile methodology and the untenability of its claim as an objective social science. Hayden White has argued that the "'chronicle' of events out of which the historian fashions his story of 'what really happened,' already comes preencoded."[10] In *The Loss of El Dorado* even the selection and placing of incidents come encoded, and analysis of cause and effect is colored by what is already known to be violation and loss. The generally linear mode of his perception of history means that Naipaul is unable to offer an ameliorating vision of history that would overcome a sense of loss and displacement. But his determinism grasps other equally important meanings from history. The awareness of loss and the sense of regret at the disintegration of custom are themselves assessments that overcome illusions about place and the unity of experience as well as the innocence that an unexamined sense of continuity might create in the Caribbean consciousness.

The configurations of history in the writing of West Indian women immediately throw a new and ironic light on the entire discussion. There are several layers in women's writing that show their experience of history as culturally different and markedly influenced by the politics of gender. Their contrasting representations and modes of individuation ironize the tendency in male writing to present women as symbols and metaphors. They demonstrate that women sometimes inscribe themselves in adversarial relationships to their communities[11] and that their works reveal a complex intersection of historical, class, and ethnic situations that are as varied as those in the writing of men. On another level the range of experience, insight, and perspective that women's relation to history introduces valorizes an area of Afro-Caribbean traditions which has remained submerged in the postcolonial worlds of Caribbean societies.

Aside from the contrasting perspective on history revealed in these chapters, the space and range of the period covered by the book permits us to demonstrate the various ways in which relations to history have matured or changed either in response to further exploration or to a change of genre. The shifting relations to history in the early and later works of Reid, Naipaul, Lamming, and Walcott; the differing perspectives in the poetry and drama of Walcott; and the shifting ways in which Africa as an idea has impacted on the historical imagination of West Indian writers prove the benefits of the book's methodology. The engagement with history is an ongoing discourse that explores the phenomenon of history as a means of self-understanding and definition. A concluding chapter can perhaps only present deductions as it places writers in relationships of comparison and contrast and reveals how the attempt to interpret the region's history has also been a spur to innovative thinking and writing.

Notes

Preface and Acknowledgments

1. Froude, *The English in the West Indies*, 306.
2. Naipaul, *The Middle Passage*, 29.
3. See Ramchand, "History and the Novel," 103–13, and Wynter, "Novel and History," 95–102.

Introduction: The Critical Context

1. Althusser, *Lenin and Philosophy and Other Essays*, 155.
2. Foucault, "What Is an Author?" 198.
3. Dash, "In Search of the Lost Body," 18.
4. Harris, "Carnival of Psyche," 131. While noting Harris's affinity to post-structuralist perspectives, it is important to mention that the thrust of this essay separates itself from the structuring impulse of their methodologies.
5. Belsey, "Literature, History, Politics," 406–7.
6. See Foucault, "What Is an Author?"
7. Dash, "In Search of the Lost Body," 18–19.
8. Naipaul, *The Middle Passage*, 73.
9. Naipaul, *The Mimic Men*, 243.
10. See Naipaul's discussion of Indian perceptions of and attitudes to history in *An Area of Darkness*, 113–17.
11. In *The Mimic Men* the order of the medieval world and the world of Central Asian horsemen are posited against what Naipaul's protagonist sees as the New World's disorder.
12. For an extended discussion of the theoretical issues in representing colonial reality, see Bhabba, "Representation and the Colonial Text," 93–122.
13. Harris, "Interior of the Novel," 14.

14. Ibid.

15. Ibid., 12.

16. See White, "The Historical Text as Literary Artifact," 81–100.

17. See Harris's discussion of how Naipaul restricts this arena of experience in "Tradition and the West Indian Novel," 40.

18. Harris, "Form and Realism in the West Indian Artist," 13–15.

19. Walcott, *Another Life,* 75.

20. Brathwaite, *The Arrivants,* 219.

21. Baker, "There Is No More Beautiful Way," 136.

22. Williams, *Image and Idea in the Arts of Guyana,* 5–14.

Chapter 1: The Scope and Limits of West Indian Historiography

1. See especially, Herder, *Reflections on the Philosophy of the History of Mankind.*

2. Colon, *The History of the Life and Actions of the Admiral Christopher Columbus;* Valdes, *Natural History of the West Indies;* Casas, *The Spanish Colonies* and *The Tears of the Indians;* Herrera, *The General History of the Vast Continent and Islands of America.*

3. Du Tertre, *Histoire Générale des Antilles Habitée par les Français;* Rochefort, *Natural History of the Islands of the Antilles.*

4. Goveia, *A Study on the Historiography of the British West Indies,* 171.

5. Long, *The History of Jamaica;* Edwards, *The History, Civil and Commercial, of the British Colonies in the West Indies.*

6. Burke and Burke, *An Account of the European Settlement in America.*

7. Raynal, *A Philosophical and Political History of the Settlement and Trade of the Europeans in the East and West Indies.*

8. Martin, *The British Colonies: Their History, Extent, Condition, and Resources.*

9. See also Rodway and Walt, *Chronological History of the Discovery and Settlement of Guiana.*

10. Stubbs, "The Purpose and Methods of Historical Study," 42.

11. Macaulay, *The History of England from the Accession of James II;* Acton, *Lectures on Modern History;* Freeman, *The Growth of the English Constitution;* Gobineau, *The Inequality of Human Races.*

12. Acton, Review of *History of Ireland,* 54.

13. Sewell, *The Ordeal of Free Labour in the West Indies.*

14. Carlyle, *Occasional Discourse upon the Nigger Question;* Trollope, *The West Indies and the Spanish Main;* Froude, *The English in the West Indies.*

15. Thomas, *Froudacity.*

16. Ibid., 70.

17. James, "Introduction," *Froudacity,* 26.

18. Harris, "History, Fable, and Myth," 24.

19. James, "Introduction," *Froudacity,* 46.

20. James, *The Black Jacobins,* 19, 246.

21. Ibid., 288.

22. Ibid., 394.

23. Goveia, *Slave Society in the British Leeward Islands;* Williams, *Capitalism and Slavery;* Patterson, *The Sociology of Slavery;* Smith, *The Plural Society in the British West Indies;* Brathwaite, *The Development of Creole Society in Jamaica.*

24. Brathwaite, "Caliban, Ariel and Unpropero in the Conflict of Creolization," 43.

25. See Smith, *The Plural Society in the British West Indies,* for a discussion of this paradigm.

26. Brathwaite, *The Development of Creole Society in Jamaica,* 298–305.

27. Brathwaite, "Caliban, Ariel and Unprospero," 44, 42.

28. Brathwaite, "Caribbean Man in Space and Time," 4.

29. Harris, "History, Fable, and Myth," 24.

30. Ibid., 24.

31. Harris, *Tradition, the Writer, and Society,* 30–31.

32. Ibid., 32.

33. Ibid.

34. Ibid., 35.

35. Walcott, "The Muse of History," 3.

36. Ibid., 5.

37. See Dash, "Introduction," *Caribbean Discourse,* xxvii.

38. White, "The Historical Text as Literary Artifact," 82.

39. Hutcheon, "Historiographic Metafiction," 100.

Chapter 2: The Novel as History: Edgar Mittelholzer and V. S. Reid

1. See Lukàcs, *The Historical Novel,* 94.

2. Ibid., 42.

3. Harris, "Interior of the Novel," 14.

4. The trilogy is made up of the following: *Children of Kaywana, The Harrowing of Hubertus* (republished as *Kaywana Stock* in 1959), and *Kaywana Blood.*

5. Long, *History of Jamaica;* Edwards, *The History, Civil and Commercial, of the British Colonies in the West Indies.*

6. The Morant Bay rebellion, a historical event, took place in the parish of St. Thomas, Jamaica, in October 1865. It was inspired by black resentment against the local and British governments, both of which had ignored the suffering caused by the severe draughts of 1863, 1864, and 1865. For the fullest account, see Heuman, *The Killing Time: The Morant Bay Rebellion.* The 1944 Jamaican constitution guaranteed self rule under crown supervision. This was a major change from the crown colony status imposed on Jamaica after the 1865 rebellion.

7. Reid, *New Day,* 18, 102.

8. Reid, *Sixty-Five,* 36–37.

9. Reid, "Author's Preface," *New Day.*

10. Augier, "Before and After 1865," 21–40.

11. Ramchand, "History and the Novel," 102.

12. Reid, *New Day*, 19.

13. White, "The Historical Text as Literary Artifact," 92.

14. Williams, *Image and Idea in the Arts of Guyana*, 7.

15. Reid, *The Leopard*, 47.

16. Ibid., 96.

17. Ibid., 95.

Chapter 3: History as Loss: Determinism as Vision and Form in V. S. Naipaul

1. Raymond Williams, *The English Novel from Dickens to Lawrence*, 13.

2. Butterfield, *History as the Emancipation from the Past*, 16–17.

3. Naipaul, *An Area of Darkness*, 133.

4. Ibid., 136–37

5. Naipaul, *The Enigma Of Arrival*, 142.

6. Naipaul, *The Loss of El Dorado*, 319.

7. Ibid., 266.

8. Bhabha, "Representation in the Colonial Text," 118–19. For the full discussion, see 93–122.

9. Ibid., 119.

10. "Language, Counter-memory, Practice," quoted in Bhabha, 119.

11. Bhabha, 119–20.

12. See Harris, "Tradition and the West Indian Novel," 40.

13. Naipaul, *The Mimic Men*, 126–27.

14. There seems to be a hidden intent, a historical irony suggested in the fact that Naipaul's fictional island is called *Isabella*. The first island founded by Columbus in the Caribbean was also called Isabella, and it proved to be a disastrous settlement, a total failure. Is there no correlation here between the novelist's naming and the central character's obsessions about taint and wrongness?

15. Naipaul, *The Mimic Men*, 204–5.

16. Ibid., 167. Singh's distaste and horror is an ironic undercutting of his own romantic delusions about Aryan horsemen. If Gurudeva's fantasies can descend to such depths, Singh's could conceivably suffer a similar degeneration.

17. Ibid., 238.

18. Ibid., 279.

19. Ibid., 282.

20. Ibid., 185.

21. Ibid., 296.

22. Naipaul had first written a factual account of the life of "Michael X," the London-based *black*-power leader in "The Killings in Trinidad" before fictionalizing the "history" in *Guerrillas*.

23. Naipaul, "Conrad's Darkness," in his *The Return of Eva Peron*, 210.

24. Naipaul, "The Circus at Luxor," in his *In a Free State*, 121.

25. Naipaul, *The Enigma of Arrival*, 145.

26. Naipaul, *Guerrillas*, 36.
27. Naipaul, *A Bend in the River*, 18–19.
28. See Glissant's comments on this perspective in *Caribbean Discourse*, 64.
29. Naipaul, *A Bend in the River*, 15.
30. Ibid., 135.
31. Ibid., 23.
32. Ibid., 15.
33. Ibid., 162, 262.
34. Naipaul, *The Enigma of Arrival*, 53.
35. Ibid., 50.

Chapter 4: Lamming and the Mythic Imagination: Meaning and Dimensions of Freedom

1. Naipaul, "Conrad's Darkness," 211.
2. Ibid., 209.
3. Glissant, *Caribbean Discourse*, 66.
4. Bhabha, "Representation and the Colonial Text," 116, 118.
5. Lamming, *The Pleasures of Exile*, 15.
6. Rohlehr, *Pathfinder*, 14–15.
7. Brathwaite, "The New West Indian Novelists," 273.
8. Glissant, *Caribbean Discourse*, 71.
9. Naipaul, *The Mimic Men*, 92, 97.
10. Righter, *Myth and Literature*, 32.
11. Naipaul, *The Mimic Men*, 146.
12. White, "The Historical Text as Literary Artifact," 85.
13. Lamming, *Of Age and Innocence*, 357.
14. Ibid., 174.
15. Ibid., 179.
16. See Lamming, "The Negro Writer and His World," 32.
17. Harris, "Tradition and the West Indian Novel," 37.
18. Lamming, *Of Age and Innocence*, 412.
19. Harris, "Tradition and the West Indian Novel," 34.
20. Lamming, "The West Indian People," 64–65.
21. Lamming, *The Pleasures of Exile*, 229.
22. Bhabha, "Representation and the Colonial Text," 96.
23. Lamming, *Season of Adventure*, 220, 316.
24. Glissant, *Caribbean Discourse*, 65.
25. Lamming, *The Pleasures of Exile*, 15.
26. Lamming, "The Negro Writer and His World," 327.
27. Lamming, *Of Age and Innocence*, 206.
28. Ibid., 308, 309.
29. Kent, "A Conversation with George Lamming," 89.
30. Shakespeare, *The Tempest*, I:ii.

31. Lamming, *Water with Berries*, 205.

32. Lamming, *The Pleasures of Exile*, 24.

33. Shakespeare, *The Tempest*, I:ii.

34. Lamming, *Water with Berries*, 205, 248.

35. Lamming, *The Pleasures of Exile*, 115.

36. Lamming, *Water With Berries*, 320.

37. For further amplification of this perspective on history, see White, "The Historical Text as Literary Artifact," 81–100.

38. Lamming, *Natives of My Person*, 71.

39. Ibid., 325.

40. Ibid., 334.

41. Lamming, *The Pleasures of Exile*, 15.

42. Lamming, *Natives of My Person*, 310.

Chapter 5: Beyond Realism: Wilson Harris and the Immateriality of Freedom

1. Naipaul, *The Enigma of Arrival*, 142. It is much later in this autobiographical book that Naipaul reveals the idea behind the writing of *The Loss of El Dorado*.

2. Ibid., 142.

3. Lamming creates his mythology from the legend of the mass suicide of Carib Indians.

4. Naipaul, *The Loss of El Dorado*, 107.

5. Harris, "Tradition and the West Indian Novel," 35–36.

6. Ibid., 34, 36.

7. Harris, *Palace of the Peacock*, 20.

8. Ibid., 54.

9. Ibid., 30.

10. Harris, "A Talk on the Subjective Imagination," 60.

11. Harris, *Palace of the Peacock*, 63.

12. Ibid., 58.

13. Ibid., 59.

14. Ibid., 84.

15. Read, ed., *The Collected Works of Carl Jung*, 21.

16. Harris, *Palace of the Peacock*, 106.

17. Ibid.

18. Ibid., 116.

19. Ibid., 149.

20. Ibid.

21. Drake, "Language and Revolutionary Hope," 77. Sandra Drake takes the quote from Fredric Jameson's *Marxism and Form* in an attempt to establish the nature of hope in Harris's world, where linear time is called into question as a valid category for perceiving Caribbean history.

22. Harris, "Tradition and the West Indian Novel," 30.

23. Harris, "History, Fable, and Myth," in his *Explorations*, 19.

24. Harris, "The Native Phenomenon," in his *Explorations*, 50.

25. Harris, *The Whole Armour and The Secret Ladder,* 49.

26. Ibid., 51.

27. Ibid., 58.

28. Ibid., 9, 61.

29. Ibid., 22–23.

30. Ibid., 91.

31. Ibid., 206.

32. Ibid., 174.

33. Ibid., 170.

34. Ibid., 171.

35. Ibid., 199.

36. Ibid., 182.

37. Brathwaite, "The African Presence in Caribbean Literature," 88.

38. Harris, *The Whole Armour and The Secret Ladder,* 155.

39. Ibid., 164.

40. Ibid., 152.

41. Ibid., 239.

42. Gilkes, *Wilson Harris and the Caribbean Novel,* 92.

43. Harris, *The Whole Armour and the Secret Ladder,* 242.

44. Ibid., 246.

45. Ibid.

46. Ibid., 250.

47. Ibid., 253.

48. Ibid., 171.

49. Ibid., 258.

Chapter 6: Transcending Linear Time: History and Style in Derek Walcott's Poetry

1. Walcott, "The Muse of History," 6.

2. See Walcott, "What the Twilight Says," 31–32.

3. Ibid., 17.

4. Ibid., 5.

5. Walcott, *The Castaway,* 35.

6. Ibid., 35.

7. Ibid., "The Swamp," 11.

8. Walcott, *The Gulf,* 69–70.

9. Walcott, *The Castaway,* 11.

10. Ibid., 50.

11. Ibid., 9.

12. See Walcott, "Return to D'ennery, Rain," in his *In a Green Night,* with its reference to the poet's individual consciousness: "Nor have you changed from all of the known ways / To leave the mind's dark cave, the most. / Accursed of God's self-pitying creatures" (34).

13. Walcott, *Another Life,* 4.

14. Walcott, *In a Green Night,* 19.

15. Ibid., 19.

16. Ibid., 61.

17. Walcott, *Another Life,* 70.

18. Ibid., 70.

19. Ibid., 71–72.

20. Walcott, *Sea Grapes,* 9.

21. Walcott, *The Castaway,* 36.

22. Ibid., 51.

23. The Daphne myth intensifies the link with the almond trees. Apollo, watching and mourning Daphne's transformation into a tree with beautiful, shining leaves, also affirmed a perpetual link between it and him: "You shall be my tree. With your leaves my victors shall wreathe their brow. You shall have your part in all my triumphs. Apollo and his laurel shall be joined together wherever songs are sung and stories told" (Hamilton, *Mythology,* 144–45).

24. Walcott, *The Castaway,* 37.

25. Ibid., 51.

26. See Izevbaye, "The Exile and the Prodigal," 70–82.

27. Walcott, *The Castaway,* 37, 52.

28. Walcott, *Another Life,* 75.

29. See "Return to D'ennery, Rain," *In a Green Night,* 33–34.

30. Walcott, *The Gulf,* 10.

31. Ibid., 12.

32. Walcott, *Another Life,* 4, 7, 9.

33. Walcott, *The Castaway,* 57.

34. Walcott, *The Gulf,* 71.

35. Ibid., 9.

36. Walcott, *In a Green Night,* 55.

37. Walcott, *The Gulf,* 29.

38. Ibid., 37.

39. Ibid., 43.

40. Ibid., 22.

41. Ibid., 50.

42. Ibid., 16.

43. Ibid., 19.

44. Ismond, "Walcott Versus Brathwaite," 61.

45. Walcott, *The Gulf,* 19.

46. Walcott, *The Castaway,* 31, 56–57.

47. Walcott, *The Gulf,* 70.

48. Ibid., 37.

49. Ibid., 42.

50. Walcott, *Another Life,* 53.

51. Ibid., 54.

52. Brathwaite, *The Arrivants,* 233.
53. Ibid., 234.
54. Walcott, *The Castaway,* 9.
55. Ibid., 37.
56. Naipaul, *The Mimic Men,* 175–76, 204–6.
57. Walcott, "The Muse of History," 7.
58. Ibid., 2.
59. Walcott, *Another Life,* 66.
60. Walcott, *The Gulf,* 67.
61. Walcott, *Another Life,* 74.
62. Ibid., 75.
63. Walcott, *The Castaway,* 21. Note the parallels between this poem and the reference to the "horned, sea-snoring island" in *Another Life.* Walcott establishes a contrast between mythology and history, between the island in its original state and as a conquered and defeated island, the island of history.
64. Walcott, "The Caribbean: Culture or Mimicry?," 6.
65. The poem appeared separately (before the publication of *Another Life*) in the *New Yorker,* 28 October 1972, 30–33.
66. See Baugh, *Derek Walcott,* 73.
67. Walcott, *The Castaway,* 37.
68. Walcott, *Another Life,* 146.
69. Walcott, "The Caribbean: Culture or Mimicry?," 8.
70. Walcott, *Another Life,* 146.
71. Ibid., 9.
72. Walcott, *The Gulf,* 12.
73. Ibid., 67.
74. Walcott, *Another Life,* 58.
75. Ibid., 59.
76. Ibid., 88.
77. Ibid., 85.
78. Ibid., 92.
79. Ibid., 95–96.
80. Ibid., 101.
81. Ibid., 105.
82. Ibid., 108, 109.
83. Ibid., 139.
84. Ibid., 8.
85. Walcott, *The Star-Apple Kingdom,* 8.
86. Ibid., 9.
87. Ibid., 51.
88. Ibid., 56
89. Ibid., 57.
90. Ibid., 25.

91. Ibid., 57.
92. Brown, *West Indian Poetry*, 140.
93. Walcott, *The Star-Apple Kingdom*, 16.
94. Ibid., 20.
95. Ibid., 19.
96. Walcott, *Omeros*, 319.
97. Ibid., 31.
98. Ibid., 97.
99. See Brathwaite, *The Development of Creole Society*, 297–311.
100. Walcott, *Omeros*, 97.
101. Ibid., 72.
102. Ibid., 142.
103. Ibid., 151.
104. Ibid., 139.
105. Ibid., 242–43.
106. Ibid., 248.
107. Ibid., 249.
108. Ibid., 239.

Chapter 7: From Myth to Dialectic: History in Derek Walcott's Drama

1. Walcott, "What the Twilight Says," 4.
2. Ibid., 6.
3. Ibid., 7.
4. Ibid., 16.
5. Walcott, *Henri Christophe*, 1.
6. Ibid., 50.
7. Walcott, "What the Twilight Says," 12.
8. Walcott, *Henry Christophe*, 50.
9. "What the Twilight Says," 14.
10. Ibid., 23–24.
11. See Breiner, "Walcott's Early Drama," 77.
12. Walcott, *Ti-Jean and His Brothers*, 149.
13. Glissant, *Caribbean Discourse*, 199.
14. I use this term in the sense of a carnival masquerade in which masks and costumes are used to enact certain personalities and situations. See Walcott, "Mass Man," in *The Gulf*. See also Earl Lovelace, *The Dragon Can't Dance*.
15. Walcott, *Dream on Monkey Mountain*, 304.
16. Ibid., 326.
17. Walcott, "What the Twilight Says," 5.
18. Walcott, "The Muse of History," 2.
19. Walcott, *Remembrance and Pantomime*, 138.
20. Walcott, "A Season of Plays."
21. Walcott, "The Caribbean: Culture or Mimicry?," 6.

Chapter 8: Edward Brathwaite and Submerged History: The Aesthetics of Renaissance

1. Brathwaite, *The Development of Creole Society,* 307.
2. Harris, "History, Fable, and Myth," 22.
3. Brathwaite, *The Arrivants,* 221.
4. Ibid., 14.
5. Brathwaite, *Folk Culture of the Slaves in Jamaica,* 4–5.
6. Brathwaite, *The Arrivants,* 6.
7. Ibid., 13.
8. Ibid., 15.
9. Ibid., 83.
10. Walcott, "The Muse of History," 10, 12. Walcott's recent long poem *Omeros* (1990) presents a slightly different emphasis. See my discussion in chapters 6 and 10.
11. Ibid., 12–13.
12. See Brown, "Mansong and Matrix," 68–121.
13. Yet interestingly, see Walcott's *The Star-Apple Kingdom,* in which this pull of memory, embodied in the female figure of the region, is seen as part of the revolution's hankering for ancient remembrances ("but she would not understand that . . . / he wanted a history without memory" [51]).
14. Brathwaite, *The Arrivants,* 32.
15. Ibid., 33.
16. Ibid., 43.
17. Ibid., 57.
18. See Brown, "Mansong and Matrix," 68–120, for a differing view.
19. See Brathwaite, "Caribbean Man in Space and Time," 35–44.
20. Brathwaite, *The Arrivants,* 78.
21. Ibid., 79.
22. Walcott, *The Castaway,* 35.
23. Brathwaite, *The Arrivants,* 164.
24. Ibid., 165.
25. Ibid., 83.
26. Ibid., 84.
27. Ibid., 102.
28. Ibid., 105.
29. Ibid., 122.
30. Ibid., 132.
31. Ibid., 136.
32. Ibid., 13.
33. Ibid., 83.
34. Ibid., 148.
35. Ibid., 149.
36. Ibid., 150.
37. See Ismond, "Walcott Versus Brathwaite," 54–75.

38. Brathwaite, *The Arrivants,* 149.
39. Ibid., 153.
40. Harris, *Tradition, the Writer, and Society,* 13.
41. See Brathwaite, "Sir Galahad," 8–16.
42. Harris, *Tradition, the Writer, and Society,* 13–14.
43. Brathwaite, *The Arrivants,* 162.
44. Ibid., 163.
45. Ibid., 165.
46. Ibid., 75.
47. Ibid., 82.
48. In "What The Twilight Says" Walcott argues that the West Indian soil is not a soil that has been long fed with the mulch of cultures, "with the cycles of tribalism, feudalism, monarchy, democracy, [and] industrialization . . . [that] Death, which fastens us to the earth, remains pastoral or brutish, because no single corpse contributes to some tiered concept of a past" (20–21). Brathwaite's enactment in "Coral" suggests the building up of such a tier of history, a different kind of history.
49. Brathwaite, *The Arrivants,* 233.
50. Ibid., 119 (emphasis mine).
51. Ibid., 172.
52. Ibid., 196.
53. Ibid., 204.
54. Ibid., 189–90.
55. Ibid., 136.
56. Ibid., 187.
57. In *Masks* the kind of integration suggested in "Wake" inspires shock and horror in the returned New World persona. See "Korabra" and "Crossing the River," *The Arrivants.*
58. Brathwaite, *The Arrivants,* 212.
59. Ibid., 221.
60. Ibid., 137.
61. Walcott, *Another Life,* 74.
62. Brathwaite, *The Arrivants,* 235–38.
63. Ibid., 238.
64. Ibid., 250.
65. Ibid., 245.
66. Ibid., 251–52.
67. Ibid., 257.
68. Ibid., 261.
69. Walcott, *Omeros,* 273.
70. Brathwaite, *The Arrivants,* 262.
71. Ibid., 267, 268.
72. Ibid., 269.
73. Brathwaite, *The Arrivants,* 270.

74. Ibid., 265.
75. Ibid.
76. Walcott, "What the Twilight Says," 8.
77. Brathwaite, *The Arrivants*, 265.
78. Harris, *Tradition, the Writer, and Society*, 51.
79. Ibid., 52.
80. Ibid., 48.
81. Ibid., 60.
82. Brathwaite, *The Arrivants*, 221.

Chapter 9: Configurations of History in the Writing of West Indian Women

1. See Davies and Fido, *Out of the Kumbla*, 2.
2. See Lerner, *The Majority Finds Its Past: Placing Women in History*.
3. Brathwaite, *The Development of Creole Society*, 305.
4. See *History of Mary Prince*. See also Carby, *Reconstructing Womanhood*, 37, and O'Callaghan, *Woman Version*, 26.
5. O'Callaghan, *Woman Version*, 27.
6. Ibid., 27–28.
7. See Athill's informative view of this metaphor in her notes to *Wide Sargasso Sea*, 112.
8. Ramchand, *The West Indian Novel and Its Background*, 231.
9. Rhys, *Wide Sargasso Sea*, 19.
10. James, *Jean Rhys*, 55. See also Ramchand, *The West Indian Novel and Its Background*, 233–34.
11. Although Jean Rhys's "Rochester" is not named as such, most commentators refer to him as Rochester to stress the intertextual connection with Brontë's *Jane Eyre*.
12. Harris, "Carnival of Psyche," 130.
13. Rhys, *Wide Sargasso Sea*, 88.
14. James, *Jean Rhys*, 58.
15. Rhys, *Wide Sargasso Sea*, 100.
16. Ibid., 103.
17. Harris, "Jean Rhys's *Wide Sargasso Sea*," 130, 131.
18. See Ramchand, *The West Indian Novel and Its Background*, 235.
19. Lerner, "The Challenge of Women's History," 52.
20. Schwarz-Bart, *The Bridge of Beyond*, 147.
21. Ibid., 63.
22. Ibid., 74.
23. Ibid., 76.
24. Ibid., 12. All the effaced stories involve the Negro's more intimate relationship with the white world, a thematic aspect of the novel which is deliberately deflated in order to give prominence to the theme of the Negro's self-sufficiency and survival.

25. Ibid., 5.

26. Ibid., 44–45.

27. Ibid., 95–96.

28. Ibid., 141.

29. Telumée's growth and self-perception as an individual separate from her husband, Elie, goes contrary to what the community has always understood. "It was as if they'd always known in their minds that my destiny was to live on a branch in Fond-Zombi, under Elie's wing" (*Bridge of Beyond,* 121).

30. O'Callaghan, *Woman Version,* 69.

31. See Baker, "There Is No More Beautiful Way," 136.

32. Schwarz-Bart, *The Bridge of Beyond,* 116.

33. Lamming, *The Pleasures of Exile,* 36.

34. Hodge, *Crick Crack Monkey,* 18.

35. Gikandi, "Narration in the Post-Colonial Moment," 17.

36. Ibid., 19.

37. Ibid., 20.

38. Narinesingh, introduction to *Crick Crack Monkey,* viii.

39. Gikandi, "Narration in the Post-Colonial Moment," 21.

40. Brodber, *Jane and Louisa,* 17.

41. Ibid., 138.

42. Ibid., 123.

43. Kincaid, *Annie John,* 107.

44. Tapping, "Children and History in the Caribbean Novel," 10.

45. Kincaid, *At the Bottom of the River,* 60.

46. Kincaid, *Annie John,* 147.

47. See Carolyn Cooper, "Afro-Jamaican Folk Elements in Brodber's *Jane and Louisa Will Soon Come Home,*" 279–88.

48. Brathwaite, *Mother Poem.*

49. Brown, "Mansong and Matrix," 71. For a similar perspective on Walcott and Brathwaite, see Johnson, "A-beng: (Re) Calling the Body In(To) Question," 111–42.

50. Brathwaite, *Mother Poem,* 47.

51. Brathwaite's woman gains an individual voice in the final section of *Mother Poem,* but curiously, she is still perceived in a general sense, as the people of the island, as a conch, a lobster, and a flying fish.

52. Henderson, Response, 161.

Chapter 10: Africa in the Historical Imagination of the West Indian Writer

1. Ramchand, *The West Indian Novel and Its Background,* 119.

2. Brathwaite, "Caribbean Man in Space and Time," 35–44.

3. Harris, "History, Fable, and Myth."

4. Williams, *Image and Idea,* 3–4.

5. Williams, *Other Leopards,* 20.

6. Ibid., 129.

7. Ibid., 135.

8. Ibid., 155.

9. Ibid., 178.

10. In Williams's novel the myth of Zagreus features symbolically as an illumination of the novelist's theme and style. Zagreus, bastard son of Zeus and Persephone, is a horned infant. On his father's throne the Titans attack him with knives. For a time he evades their assaults by turning himself into various shapes, assuming the likeness of Zeus, of a young man, a horse, and a serpent; finally, in the form of a bull, he is cut to pieces by the murderous Titans. Williams uses the myth in the novel as an illustration of the major characters' views of man's relation to historical circumstances. Their various subjective interpretations of the myth reflect their positions in respect to the argument as well as Williams's implied commentary. The differing interpretations of Catherine, Froad, Hughie, and the chief are therefore crucial to the central argument in the novel.

11. Williams, *Other Leopards*, 178.

12. Ibid., 120.

13. Williams, *Image and Idea*, 9.

14. Ibid., 19.

15. Walcott, *Dream on Monkey Mountain*, 235, 236.

16. Walcott, 261.

17. Walcott, 291.

18. Walcott, 305.

19. Walcott, 318.

20. Walcott, 326.

21. Braithwaite, *The Arrivants*, 44.

22. Walcott, *Omeros*, 242.

23. Ibid., 243.

24. Ibid., 141.

25. Paule Marshall, *Praisesong for the Widow*, 240.

26. Ibid.

Conclusion

1. Lowenthal, *The Past Is a Foreign Country*, 216.

2. Jenkins, *Re-thinking History*, 17–18.

3. See Harris, "History, Fable, and Myth," 20–42.

4. Benjamin, "Theses on the Philosophy of History," 255.

5. Harris, "Tradition and the West Indian Novel," 31.

6. Bhabha, "Representation and the Colonial Text," 119.

7. Harris, "Tradition and the West Indian Novel," 40.

8. Benjamin, "Theses on the Philosophy of History," 255.

9. See Walcott, "The Muse of History," 1–27 (particularly 13–19).

10. White, "The Historical Text as Literary Artifact," 90.

11. Henderson, Response, 161–63.

Bibliography

Acton, John E. S. *Lectures on Modern History.* Edited by J. V. Figgis and R. N. Laurence. London: Macmillan, 1906.

———. Review of *History of Ireland* by Godwin Smith. *Rambler* (March 1862). Quoted in Eric Williams, *British Historians and the West Indies,* 54.

Adam, Ian, and Helen Tiffin, eds. *Past the Last Post: Theorizing Post-colonialism and Post-modernism.* London: Harvester Wheatsheaf, 1991.

Aiyejina, Funso. "The Death and Rebirth of African Deities in Edward Brathwaite's *Islands.*" *World Literature Written in English* 23, no. 2 (1984): 397–404.

———. "Derek Walcott and the West Indian Dream and Veneration of Africa." *Literary Half-Yearly* 36, no. 1 (1985): 180–93.

———. "The Poet as a Federated Consciousness." *World Literature Written in English* 27, no. 1 (1987): 67–80.

Alleyne, Mervyn. *Roots of Jamaican Culture.* London: Pluto, 1988.

Allfrey, Phyllis. *The Orchid House.* 1953. Rpt., London: Virago, 1982.

Althusser, Louis. *Lenin and Philosophy and Other Essays.* Translated by Ben Brewster. Harmondsworth: Penguin, 1985.

Angier, Carole. *Jean Rhys.* London: Viking, 1985.

Anyidoho, Kofi. "Divine Drummer: Drum Poetics in Brathwaite and Okai." In *Black Culture and Black Consciousness,* edited by E. Emenyonu. Ibadan, Nigeria: Heinemann, 1987.

Asein, Samuel Omo. "The Concept of Form: A Study of Some Ancestral Elements in Brathwaite's Trilogy." *Bulletin of the African Studies Association of the West Indies* 4 (December 1971): 9–38.

———. "Symbol and Meaning in the Poetry of Edward Brathwaite." *World Literature Written in English* 20, no. 1 (1981): 96–104.

Athill, Diana. Introduction to *Wide Sargasso Sea,* by Jean Rhys. London: Hodder and Stoughton, 1989.

Attridge, D., G. Bennington, and R. Young. *Post-Structuralism and the Question of History*. Cambridge: Cambridge University Press, 1987.

Augier, F. R. "Before and after 1865." *New World Quarterly* (1966): 21–40.

Augier, F. R., S. C. Gordon, D. G. Hall, and M. Reckford. *The Making of the West Indies*. London: Longman, 1960.

Baker, Houston A., Jr. "There Is No More Beautiful Way: Theory and the Poetics of Afro-American Women's Writing." In his *Afro-American Literary Study in the 1990s*, 135–63.

Baker, Houston A., Jr., and Patricia Redmond. *Afro-American Literary Study in the 1990s*. Chicago: University of Chicago Press, 1989.

Bakhtin, Mikhail M. *The Dialogic Imagination: Four Essays*. Translated by Caryl Emerson and M. Holquist. Austin: University of Texas Press, 1981.

Barker, Francis, ed. *Literature, Politics, and Theory: Papers from the Essex Conference, 1976–84*. London: Methuen, 1986.

Barker, Francis, Peter Hulme, and Margaret Iverson, eds. *Uses of History: Marxism, Post-Modernism, and the Renaissance*. Manchester: Manchester University Press, 1991.

Barthes, Roland. *Mythologies*. Translated by Annette Lavers. London: Jonathan Cape, 1972.

Baugh, Edward. *Derek Walcott: Memory as Vision: Another Life*. London: Longman, 1978.

———. "Metaphor and Plainness in the Poetry of Derek Walcott." *Literary Half-Yearly* 2, no. 2 (1970): 47–58.

———. *West Indian Poetry, 1900–1970*. Kingston, Jamaica: Savacou, 1970.

———. "The West Indian Writer and His Quarrel with History." *Tapia* (February 25 and 27, 1977).

Baugh, Edward, and Mervyn Morris, eds. *Progressions: West Indian Literature in the 1970s*. Mona, Jamaica: University of the West Indies Press, 1990.

Beckles, Hilary. *Natural Rebels: A Social History of Enslaved Black Women in Barbados*. London: Zed, 1984.

Belsey, Catherine. "Literature, History, Politics." In *Modern Criticism and Theory*, edited by David Lodge. London and New York: Longman, 1988.

Benjamin, Walter. "Theses on the Philosophy of History." In his *Illuminations*, edited by Hanna Arendt and translated by Harry Zohn. 1968. London: Fontana, 1992.

Berrian, Brenda F. *Bibliography of Women Writers from the Caribbean*. Washington, D.C.: Three Continents Press, 1989.

Bhabha, Homi K. "Representation and the Colonial Text: A Critical Exploration of Some Forms of Mimeticism." In *The Theory of Reading*, edited by Frank Gloversmith. London: Harvester, 1984.

Blackburn, Robin. *Ideology in Social Science: Readings in Critical Social Theory*. London: Fontana, 1972.

Bolland, N. "Creolization and Creole Societies: A Cultural Nationalist View of

Caribbean Social History." In *Intellectuals in the Twentieth-Century Caribbean*, edited by A. Hennessy, 2 vols. London: Macmillan Carribbean, 1992.

Boyce-Davies, Carole, and Elaine Savory Fido, eds. *Out of the Kumbla: Caribbean Women and Literature*. Trenton, N.J.: Africa World Press, 1990.

Brathwaite, Edward Kamau. "The African Presence in Caribbean Literature." *Daedalus* 103, no. 2 (Spring 1974): 73–109.

———. *The Arrivants: A New World Trilogy*. London: Oxford University Press, 1973.

———. *Black and Blues*. 1976. Reprint, Benin City, Nigeria: Ethiope, 1978.

———. "Caliban, Ariel, and Unprospero in the Conflict of Creolization: A Study of the Slave Revolt in Jamaica, 1831–32." In *Comparative Perspectives on Slavery in the New World Plantation Societies*, edited by V. Rubin and A. Tuden, 41–62. New York: New York Academy of Sciences, 1977.

———. "Caribbean Critics." *New World Quarterly* 5, nos. 1–2 (1969): 5–12.

———. "Caribbean Culture: Two Paradigms." In *Missile and Capsule*, edited by Jurgen Martini. Bremen: Caribbean Festival of the Arts, 1980.

———. "Caribbean Man in Space and Time." *Savacou* 11/12 (September 1975): 1–11.

———. *The Colonial Encounter: Language*. Mysore, India: University of Mysore Press, 1984.

———. *Contradictory Omens*. Kingston, Jamaica: Savacou, 1979.

———. "The Controversial Tree of Time." *Bim* 30 (1960): 104–14.

———. "Creative Literature of the British West Indies during the Period of Slavery." *Savacou* 1 (1970): 46–73.

———. *The Development of Creole Society in Jamaica, 1770–1820*. Oxford: Clarendon, 1971.

———. *Dreamstories*. London: Longman, 1994.

———. *Folk Culture of the Slaves in Jamaica*. London: New Beacon, 1970.

———. "Gods of the Middle Passage." *Caribbean Review* 11, no. 4 (1982): 18–19, 42–44.

———. *History of the Voice: The Development of Nation Language in Anglophone Caribbean Poetry*. London: New Beacon, 1984.

———. "History, the Caribbean Writer, and X/Self." In *Crisis and Creativity in the New Literatures in English*, edited by G. Davies and H. Mais Jelinek, 23–45. Amsterdam and Atlanta: Rodopi, 1990.

———. *Islands*. London: Oxford University Press, 1969.

———. "Jazz and the West Indian Novel." *Bim* 44 (1967): 275–84.

———. *Masks*. London: Oxford University Press, 1968.

———. *Mother Poem*. London: Oxford University Press, 1977.

———. "The New West Indian Novelists." *Bim* 31 (1960): 199–210; 32 (1961): 271–80.

———. *Our Ancestral Heritage: A Bibliography of the English-Speaking Caribbean*. Kingston, Jamaica: Carifesta, 1976.

————. "Race and the Divided Self." *Caribbean Quarterly* 14, no. 3 (1974): 127–39.

————. *Rights of Passage*. London: Oxford University Press, 1967.

————. "Roots." *Bim* 37 (1963): 10–21.

————. *Roots: Essays in Caribbean Literature*. 1986. Ann Arbor: University of Michigan Press, 1993.

————. "Sir Galahad and the Islands." *Bim* 25 (1957): 8–16.

————. "Submerged Mothers: Militant Black Women in Historical Perspective." *Jamaica Journal* 9, nos. 2–3 (1975): 48–49.

————. *Sun Poem*. London: Oxford University Press, 1982.

————. "Timehri." *Savacou* 2 (1970): 35–44.

————. "West Indian Prose Fiction in the Sixties." *Caribbean Quarterly* 5, no. 4 (1970): 5–17

————. *X/Self*. London: Oxford University Press, 1987.

Breiner, Laurence. "Tradition, Society, and the Figure of the Poet." *Caribbean Quarterly* 26, nos. 1–2 (1980): 1–2.

————. "Walcott's Early Drama." In *The Art of Derek Walcott*, edited by Stewart Brown. Bridgend, Wales: Poetry Wales, 1991.

Breslin, Paul. "I Met History Once but He Aint Recognize Me: The Poetry of Derek Walcott." *Triquarterly* 68 (Winter 1987): 168–83.

Brodber, Erna. *Jane and Louisa Will Soon Come Home*. London: New Beacon, 1980.

————. *Myal*. London: New Beacon, 1988.

————. *Perceptions of Caribbean Women: Towards a Documentation of Stereotype*. Cave Hill, Barbados: Institute of Social and Economic Research, University of the West Indies, 1982.

Brown, Bev E. "Mansong and Matrix: A Radical Experiment." In *A Double Colonization: Colonial and Post Colonial Women's Writing*, edited by Kirsten H. Peterson and Anna Rutherford, 68–79. Mundelstrup, Denmark: Dangaroo Press, 1986.

Brown, Lloyd W. *West Indian Poetry*. Boston: Twayne, 1978.

Brown, Stewart. *The Art of Derek Walcott*. Bridgend, Wales: Poetry Wales, 1991.

————. *The Art of Kamau Brathwaite*. Bridgend, Wales: Poetry Wales, 1995.

————. "Derek Walcott: The Poems." In *A Handbook for the Teaching of Caribbean Literature*, edited by David Dabydeen. London: Heinemann, 1988.

————. "Walcott's Fortunate Traveller: A Patriot in Exile." *Carib* (Kingston), no. 5 (Winter 1989–90): 10–15.

Brydon, Diana. "The Myths That Write Us: Decolonizing the Mind." *Commonwealth* 10, no. 1 (1987): 1–14.

————. "Rewriting the Tempest." *World Literature Written in English* 23, no. 1 (1984): 75–88.

Burke, William, and Edmund Burke. *An Account of the European Settlement in America*. 2 vols. London: R. and J. Dodsley, 1757.

Burton, R. D. E. "Derek Walcott and the Medusa of History." *Caliban* 3, no. 2 (1980): 3–48.

Busia, Abena P. A. "This Gift of Metaphor: Symbolic Strategies and the Triumph of Survival in Simone Schwarz-Bart's *The Bridge of Beyond.*" In *Out of the Kumbla,* edited by Carole Boyce Davies and Elaine Savory Fido. Trenton, N.J.: Africa World Press, 1990.

———. "What Is Your Nation? Reconnecting Africa and Her Diaspora through Paule Marshall's *Praisesong for the Widow.*" In *Changing Our Own Words: Essays on Criticism, Theory, and Writing,* edited by Cheryl A. Wall. New Brunswick and London: Rutgers University Press, 1989.

Butterfield, Herbert. *History as the Emancipation from the Past.* [Address delivered at the London School of Economics, December 9, 1955.] London: London School of Economics, 1955.

Calder, Angus. "Darkest Naupaulia." *New Statesman* 82 (October 8, 1971): 482–83.

Carby, Hazel V. *Reconstructing Womanhood: The Emergence of the Afro-American Woman Novelist.* 1987. Oxford and New York: Oxford University Press, 1989.

Carlyle, Thomas. *Occasional Discourse upon the Nigger Question.* London, 1889.

Carmichael, A. C. *Domestic Manners and Social Condition of the White, Colored, and Negro Population of the West Indies.* 1833. 2 vols. New York: Negro Universities Press, 1969.

Carpentier, Alejo. *The Kingdom of This World.* 1957. Translated by Harriet de Onis. London: Victor Gollancz, 1967.

———. *The Lost Steps.* Translated by Harriet de Onis. London: Victor Gollancz, 1956.

Carr, E. H. *What Is History?* 1961. Harmondsworth: Penguin, 1964.

Casas, Bartolomé de las. *The Spanish Colonie, or Briefe Chronicle of the Acts and Gestes of the Spaniards in the West Indies.* London: Thomas Dawson, 1583.

———. *The Tears of the Indians.* Translated by John Philips. London: Longman, 1743.

Césaire, Aimé. *Discourse on Colonialism.* Translated by Joan Pinkham. New York: Monthly Review Press, 1972.

———. *Return to My Native Land.* Translated by John Berger and Anna Bostok. Harmondsworth: Penguin, 1969.

———. *Une tempête: D'apres "La tempete" de Shakespeare.* Paris: Editions du Seuil, 1969.

Clark, Arthur M. *Studies in Literary Modes.* London: Oliver and Boyd, 1937.

Cliff, Michelle. *Abeng.* New York: Crossing Press, 1980.

———. *No Telephone to Heaven.* New York: Dutton, 1987.

Collingwood, R. G. *The Idea of History.* Edited by T. M. Knox. Oxford: Clarendon, 1946.

Colon, Ferdinand Don. *The History of the Life and Actions of the Admiral Christopher Columbus and of His Discovery of the West Indies Called the New World*. 4 vols. London: Johan and Awnsham Churchill, 1704.

Cook, J. "A Vision of the Land: A Study of V. S. Naipaul's Later Novels." *Journal of Caribbean Studies* 1, nos. 2–3 (1980): 140–61.

Coombes, Orde, ed. *Is Massa Day Dead? Black Moods in the Caribbean*. New York: Anchor, 1974.

Cooper, Carolyn. "Afro-Jamaican Folk Elements in Brodber's *Jane and Louisa Will Soon Come Home*." In *Out of the Kumbla: Caribbean Women and Literature*, edited by Carole Boyce Davies and Elaine Savory Fido. Trenton, N.J.: Africa World Press, 1990.

———. *Noises in the Blood: Orality, Gender, and the "Vulgar" Body of Jamaican Popular Culture*. London: Macmillan, 1993.

———. "'Something Ancestral Recaptured': Spirit Possession as Trope in Selected Feminist Fictions of the African Diaspora." In *Motherlands: Black Women's Writing from Africa, the Caribbean, and South Asia*, edited by Susheila Nasta, 64–87. London: Women's Press, 1991.

———. "Writing Oral History: Sistren Theatre Collective's *Lionheart Gal*." *Kunapipi* 2, no. 1 (1989): 49–57.

Croce, B. "Historical Determinism and the Philosophy of History." In *Theories of History*, edited by Patrick Gardiner. New York: Free Press, 1959.

Cudjoe, Selwyn. *Resistance and Caribbean Literature*. Athens: Ohio University Press, 1980.

———. *V. S. Naipaul: A Materialist Reading*. Amherst: University of Massachusetts Press, 1988.

Dabydeen, David, ed. *A Handbook for Teaching Caribbean Literature*. London: Heinemann, 1989.

Dash, J. Michael. "Edward Brathwaite." In *West Indian Literature*, edited by Bruce King. London: Macmillan, 1979.

———. "In Search of the Last Body: Redefining the Subject in Caribbean Literature." In *After Europe*, edited by Stephen Slemou and Helen Tifin. Mundelstrup, Denmark: Dangaroo, 1989.

———. Introduction to *Caribbean Discourse* by Edouard Glissant, i-xiv.

———. "Marvelous Realism: The Way Out of Negritude." *Caribbean Studies* 12, no. 4 (1973): 57–70.

D'Costa, Jean. "The Poetry of Edward Brathwaite." *Jamaica Journal* 2, no. 3 (1968): 24–28.

De Lisser, H. *Morgan's Daughter*. London: E. Benn, 1952.

———. *The White Witch of Rosehall*. London: Oliver and Boyd, 1937.

Drake, Sandra. "Language and Revolutionary Hope." In *The Literate Imagination: Essays on the Novels of Wilson Harris*, edited by Michael Gilkes. London: Macmillan Caribbean, 1980.

Du Tertre, Jean Baptiste. *Histoire Générale des Antilles Habitée par les Français*. 4 vols. Paris, 1667.

Eagleton, Terry. *Criticism and Ideology.* London: New Left Books, 1976.

Edwards, Bryan. *The History, Civil and Commercial, of the British Colonies in the West Indies.* 2 vols. London: J. Stockdale, 1793–94.

Fabre, Michael. "Adam's Task of Giving Things Their Names: The Poetry of Derek Walcott." *New Letters* (Fall 1974): 91–107.

Fanon, Franz. *Black Skin, White Mask.* Translated by Charles L. Marhmann. New York: Creole, 1967.

———. *The Wretched of the Earth.* Translated by Constance Farrington. Harmondsworth: Penguin, 1967.

Fernández de Ovieto, Gonzalo. *Natural History of the West Indies.* 1557. Translated and edited by Sterlin A. Stoudemire. Chapel Hill: University of North Carolina Press, 1959.

Foucault, Michel. *The Archaeology of Knowledge.* Translated by A. M. Sheridan. London: Tavistock, 1972.

———. *Language, Counter-Memory, Practice.* Oxford: Blackwell, 1977.

———. "What Is an Author?" In *Modern Criticism and Theory,* edited by David Lodge. London and New York: Longman, 1988.

Freeman, E. A. *The Growth of the English Constitution from the Earliest Times to the Present.* London, 1872.

Froude, James A. *The English in the West Indies.* London: Longman, 1988.

Gardiner, Patrick, ed. *Theories of History.* New York: Free Press, 1959.

Gates, Henry Louis, Jr., ed. *Black Literature and Literary Theory.* New York: Methuen, 1984.

Gikandi, Simon. "Narration in the Post-Colonial Moment: Merle Hodge's *Crick Crack Monkey.*" In *Past the Last Post: Theorizing Post-colonialism and Postmodernism,* edited by Ian Adam and Helen Tiffin, 13–21. London: Harvester Wheatsheaf, 1991.

———. *Writing in Limbo: Modernism and Caribbean Literature.* Ithaca: Cornell University Press, 1992.

Gilkes, Michael. *The Literate Imagination: Essays on the Novels of Wilson Harris.* London: Macmillan Caribbean, 1989.

———. *Wilson Harris and the Caribbean Novel.* London: Longman, 1975.

Glissant, Edouard. *Caribbean Discourse: Selected Essays.* Translated by M. Dash. Charlottesville: University Press of Virginia, 1989.

Gloversmith, Frank, ed. *The Theory of Reading.* London: Harvester, 1984.

Gobineau, Arthur de. *The Inequality of Human Races.* Translated by Adrian Colling. London: Heinemann, 1915.

Goldstraw, Irma. *Derek Walcott: A Bibliography of Published Poems.* Port-of-Spain, Trinidad: Research and Publication Committee, University of the West Indies, 1979.

Gordimer, Nadine. "White Expats and Black Mimics: In a Free State." *New York Times Book Review* (October 1971): 482–83.

Goveia, Elsa V. *Slave Society in the British Leeward Islands at the End of the Eighteenth Century, 1780–1800.* New Haven: Yale University Press, 1978.

————. *A Study on the Historiography of the British West Indies to the End of the Nineteeth Century.* Mexico City: Instituto Panamericano de Geografia e Historia, 1956.

Grant, Damian. "Emerging Image: The Poetry of Edward Brathwaite." *Critical Quarterly* 12, no. 2 (1970): 186–92.

Griffiths, Gareth. *A Double Exile: African and West Indian Writing between Two Cultures.* London: Marion Boyars, 1978.

Hakluyt, Richard. *The Principal Navigations, Voyages, Traffiques, and Discoveries of the English Nation.* 12 vols. 1589. Glasgow: MacLehose, 1903–5.

Hamilton, Edith. *Mythology: Timeless Tales of Gods and Heroes.* New York: New American Library, 1940.

Hamner, Robert. *Critical Perspectives on Derek Walcott.* Compiled and edited by Robert D. Hamner. Washington, D.C.: Three Continents Press, 1993.

————. *Derek Walcott.* Boston: Twayne, 1981.

————. "Derek Walcott: His Works and His Critics—An Annotated Bibliography, 1947–1980." *Journal of Commonwealth Literature* 16, no. 1 (1981): 142–84.

————. "Exorcising the Planter-Devil in the Plays of Derek Walcott." *Commonwealth Essays and Studies* 7, no. 2 (1985): 95–102.

————. "Mythological Aspects of Derek Walcott's Drama." *Ariel* 8, no. 3 (1977): 35–58.

Harris, Wilson. *Ascent to Omai.* London: Faber and Faber, 1970.

————. *Black Marsden: A Tabula Rasa Comedy.* London: Faber and Faber, 1972.

————. *Carnival.* London: Faber and Faber, 1985.

————. "Carnival of Psyche: Jean Rhys's Wide Sargasso Sea." Lecture given to British Studies, University of Texas at Austin, 22 February 1980. Published in *Explorations,* 125–33. Also published in *Kunapipi* 11, no. 2 (1980): 142–50.

————. *Explorations: A Selection of Talks and Articles, 1966–1981.* Edited by Hena Maes-Jelinek. Mundelstrup, Denmark: Dangaroo, 1981.

————. *The Eye of the Scarecrow.* London: Faber and Faber, 1965.

————. *Heartland.* London: Faber and Faber, 1964.

————. "History, Fable, and Myth in the Caribbean and Guianas." 1970. In his *Explorations,* edited by Hena Maes-Jelinek. Mundelstrup, Denmark: Dangaroo, 1981.

————. "The Interior of the Novel: Amerindian/European/African Relations." *Explorations: A Selection of Talks and Articles, 1966–1981.* London: Faber and Faber, 1970, 10–19.

————. "Literacy and the Imagination." In his *The Literate Imagination: Essays on the Novels of Wilson Harris,* 13–30.

————. "The Native Phenomenon." In *Common Wealth,* edited by Anna Rutherford, 144–50. Reprinted in *Explorations,* 49–56.

————. *Palace of the Peacock.* London: Faber and Faber, 1962.

————. "The Question of Form and Realism in the West Indian Artist." In his *Tradition, the Writer, and Society,* 13–20.

————. *The Secret Ladder.* London: Faber and Faber, 1963.

————. "A Talk on the Subjective Imagination." *New Letters,* 40, no. 1 (1973): 37–48. Reprinted in *Explorations,* 57–67.

————. "Tradition and the West Indian Novel." In his *Tradition, the Writer, and Society: Critical Essays,* 28–47.

————. *Tradition, the Writer, and Society: Critical Essays.* London: New Beacon, 1967.

————. *Tumatumari.* London: Faber and Faber, 1968.

————. *The Waiting Room.* London: Faber and Faber, 1967.

————. *The Whole Armour.* London: Faber and Faber, 1963.

————. *The Whole Armour and The Secret Ladder.* London: Faber and Faber, 1973.

Hearne, John. "The Snow Virgin: An Inquiry into V. S. Naipaul's Mimic Men." *Caribbean Quarterly,* 23 no. 3 (June–September 1977): 31–37.

Henderson, Mae G. Response to Baker's "There Is No More Beautiful Way," in Baker, *Afro-American Literary Study,* 155–63.

Herder, Johann Gottfried Von. *Reflections on the Philosophy of Mankind.* Edited by Frank E. Manuel, translated by T. O. Churchill. Chicago and London: University of Chicago Press, 1968.

Herrera, Antonio de. *The General History of the Vast Continent of America.* 6 vols. Translated by John Stevens. London: Longman, 1743.

Herskovits, Melville J. *Trinidad Village.* New York: Octagon, 1964.

Heuman, Gad. *The Killing Time: The Morant Bay Rebellion.* London: Macmillan Caribbean, 1994.

Hodge, Merle. *Crick Crack Monkey.* 1970. London: Heinemann, 1981.

Hughes, Peter. *V. S. Naipaul.* London: Routledge, 1988.

Hulme, Peter. *The Colonial Encounters: Europe and the Native Caribbean, 1492–1797.* London: Methuen, 1986.

Hutcheon, Linda. "Historiographic Metafiction: The Pastime of Past Time." In her *A Poetics of Postmodernism: History, Theory, Fiction.* London: Routledge, 1988, 105–23.

Ismond, Patricia. "Another Life: Autobiography as Alternative History." *Journal of West Indian Literature* 4, no. 1 (1990): 41–49.

————. "Derek Walcott: The Development of a Rooted Vision." Ph.D. diss., University of Kent, 1974.

————. "Naming and Homecoming: Walcott's Poetry since *Another Life.*" *Literary Half-Yearly* 24, no. 1 (1985): 3–19.

————. "Walcott Versus Brathwaite." *Caribbean Quarterly* 17, nos. 3–4 (1971): 54–71.

————. "Walcott's Later Drama: From Joker to Remembrance." *Ariel* 16, no. 3 (1985): 89–101.

Izevbaye, D. S. "The Exile and the Prodigal: Derek Walcott as West Indian Poet." *Caribbean Quarterly* 26, nos. 1–2 (1980): 70–82.

Jacob, H. P. "The Historic Foundations of New Day." *West Indian Review* (14 March 1949): 21–22.

Jahn, Janhainz Muntu. *An Outline of the New African Culture.* New York: Grove, 1961.

James, C. L. R. *The Black Jacobins: Toussaint L'Ouverture and the Saint Domingue Revolution.* Revised edition. New York: Vintage, 1963.

———. Introduction to *Froudacity: West Indian Fables by James Anthony Froude,* by J. J. Thomas, 23–60.

James, Louis. "Brathwaite and Jazz." In *The Art of Kamau Brathwaite,* edited by Stewart Brown, 62–74. Bridgend, Wales: Poetry Wales, 1995.

———. "Caribbean Poetry in English: Some Problems." *Savacou* 2 (1970): 78–86.

———. *Jean Rhys.* London: Longman, 1980.

———. "Midsummer." In *The Art of Derek Walcott,* edited by Stewart Brown, 115–20. Bridgend, Wales: Poetry Wales, 1991.

———, ed. *The Islands in Between: Essays on West Indian Literature.* London: Oxford University Press, 1968.

Jameson, Fredric. *Marxism and Form: Twentieth-Century Theories of Literature.* Princeton: Princeton University Press, 1972.

———. *The Political Unconscious.* Ithaca: Cornell University Press, 1978.

Jenkins, Keith. *Re-thinking History.* London and New York: Routledge, 1991.

Johnson, Lemuel. "A-beng: (Re) Calling the Body in (To) Question." In *Out of the Kumbla,* 111–42.

Jung, C. G. *The Collected Works of C. G. Jung,* edited by Herbert Read et al. Vol. 9, pt. 1: *The Archetypes and the Collective Unconscious, 1954.* Translated by R. F. C. Hull. 2nd edition. London: Routledge and Kegan Paul, 1967.

———. *The Collected Works of C.G. Jung,* edited by Herbert Read et al. 2nd edition. Completely revised. Vol. 12: *Psychology and Alchemy, 1944.* London: Routledge and Kegan Paul, 1952.

Kent, George. "A Conversation with George Lamming." *Black World* 22, no. 5 (March 1973): 4–14, 88–97.

Kincaid, Jamaica. *Annie John.* New York: Farrar, Straus and Giroux, 1985.

———. *At the Bottom of the River.* New York: Vintage, 1985.

King, Bruce. *West Indian Literature.* London: Macmillan, 1979.

Klass, Morton. *East Indians in Trinidad.* New York: Columbia University Press, 1961.

Lamming, George. "Caribbean Literature: The Black Rock of Africa." *Africa Forum* 1, no. 4 (1966): 22–55.

———. *The Emigrants.* London: Michael Joseph, 1954.

———. *In the Castle of My Skin.* London: Michael Joseph, 1953.

———. *Natives of My Person.* London: Longman, 1972.

———. "The Negro Writer and His World." *Presence Africaine* (June–November 1956): 318–25.

———. *Of Age and Innocence.* 1958. Reprint, London: Allison and Busby, 1981.

———. *The Pleasures of Exile.* 1972. Reprint, London: Allison and Busby, 1984.

———. *Season of Adventure.* 1960. Reprint, London: Allison and Busby, 1982.

———. *Water with Berries.* Trinidad: Longman, Caribbean, 1971.

———. "The West Indian People." *New World Quarterly* 2, no. 2 (1966): 63–74.

Lerner, Gerda. "The Challenge of Women's History." In her *The Majority Finds Its Past: Placing Women in History,* 168–80.

———. *The Majority Finds Its Past: Placing Women in History.* New York: Oxford University Press, 1979.

Lewis, Gordon. *The Growth of the Modern West Indies.* New York: Monthly Review Press, 1968.

———. *Main Currents in Caribbean Thought.* Baltimore: Johns Hopkins University Press, 1983.

Lewis, Maureen W. "Cultural Diversity, Disintegration, and Syncretism in V. S. Naipaul's *A House for Mr. Biswas.*" *Caribbean Quarterly* 16, no. 4 (1970): 70–79.

———. *Notes on Masks.* Benin City, Nigeria: Ethiope, 1977.

———. "Odomankoma Kyereme Se." *Caribbean Quarterly* 19, no. 2 (1973): 51–99.

Lodge, David, ed. *Modern Criticism and Theory.* London and New York: Longman, 1988.

Long, Edward. *The History of Jamaica.* 3 vols. London: T. Lowndes, 1774.

Lovelace, Earl. *The Dragon Can't Dance.* London: Longman, 1979.

Lowenthal, David. *The Past Is a Foreign Country.* Cambridge: Cambridge University Press, 1985.

Lukàcs, Georg. *The Historical Novel.* Translated by Hannah and Stanley Mitchell. Harmondsworth: Penguin, 1971.

———. *The Meaning of Contemporary Realism.* London: Merlin, 1972.

———. *Studies in European Realism.* Translated by Edith Bone. New York: Grosset and Dunlap, 1964.

Lyotard, J. F. *The Postmodern Condition: A Report on Knowledge.* Translated by Geoff Bennington and Brian Massumi. Manchester: Manchester University Press, 1987.

Macaulay, Thomas B. *The History of England from the Accession of James the Second.* 1883. Edited by T. F. Henderson. London: Oxford University Press, 1931.

Macherey, Pierre. *A Theory of Literary Production.* Translated by Geoffrey Wall. London: Routledge and Kegan Paul, 1978.

Maes-Jelenik, Hena. *The Naked Design: A Reading of Palace of the Peacock.* Mundelstrup, Denmark: Dangaroo, 1976.

Marshall, Paule. *Brown Girl, Brownstones.* New York: Avon, 1959.

———. *The Chosen Place, the Timeless People.* New York: Harcourt, Brace and World, 1969.

————. *Praisesong for the Widow.* 1983. New York: Penguin, 1983.

Martin, Montgomery. *The British Colonies: Their History, Extent, Condition, and Resources.* 6 vols. London and New York: London Printing and Publishing, 1851–57.

Maxwell, Marina. "The Awakening of the Drum: A Review of *Masks.*" *New World Quarterly* 23, nos. 2–3 (1977): 91–301.

McDonald, B. "The Birth of Mr. Biswas." *Journal of Commonwealth Studies* 9, no. 3 (1977): 50–54.

McDougall, Russell. "Something Rich and Strange in the Poetry of Edward Kamau Brathwaite's *The Arrivants.*" In *(Un)Common Ground: Essays in Literatures in English,* edited by A. Taylor and R. McDougall, 63–74. Adelaide: CRNLE, 1990.

McNeill, William H. *Mythistory and Other Essays.* Chicago: University of Chicago Press, 1986

McWatt, M., ed. *West Indian Literature and Its Social Context.* Cave Hill, Barbados: University of the West Indies, 1985.

Memmi, Albert. *The Colonizer and the Colonized.* London: Souvenir, 1974.

Millett, J. *The Genesis of Crown Colony Government: Trinidad, 1783–1810.* Port-of-Spain, Trinidad: Moko Enterprises, 1970.

Mittelholzer, Edgar. *Children of Kaywana.* London: Peter Nevill, 1952.

————. *The Harrowing of Hubertus.* London: Secker and Warburg, 1954.

————. *Kaywana Blood.* London: Secker and Warburg, 1958.

Moore, Gerald. *The Chosen Tongue.* London: Longman, 1969.

————. "East Indians and the Novels of V. S. Naipaul." *Black Orpheus* 7 (June 1960): 11–15.

Morris, Mervyn. "Niggers Everywhere." [Review of *Rights of Passage* by Edward Kamau Brathwaite.] *New World Quarterly* 14 (March–June 1968): 9–24.

————. "Some West Indian Problems of Audience." *English* 16, no. 94 (1967): 127–31.

————. "This Broken Ground: Edward Brathwaite's Trilogy of Poems." *New World Quarterly* 23, nos. 2–3 (1977): 91–103.

Morris, Robert K. *Paradoxes of Order: Some Perspectives on the Fiction of V. S. Naipaul.* Columbia: University of Missouri Press, 1975.

Munroe, Trevor. *The Politics of Constitutional Decolonization: Jamaica, 1944–62.* Mona, Jamaica: Institute of Social and Economic Research, University of the West Indies, 1972.

Naipaul, Seepersad. *The Adventures of Gurudeva and Other Stories.* Foreword by V. S. Naipaul. London: Andre Deutsch, 1976.

Naipaul, V. S. *An Area of Darkness.* London: Andre Deutsch, 1963.

————. *A Bend in the River.* London: Andre Deutsch, 1980.

————. "Conrad's Darkness." In his *The Return of Eva Perón with the Killings in Trinidad,* 206–28.

————. *The Enigma of Arrival: A Novel in Five Sections.* London: Viking, 1987.

————. *Finding the Centre: Two Narratives.* New York: Knopf, 1987.

————. *A Flag on the Island.* London: Andre Deutsch, 1967.

————. *Guerrillas.* London: Andre Deutsch, 1975.

————. *A House for Mr. Biswas.* London: Andre Deutsch, 1961.

————. *In a Free State.* London: Andre Deutsch, 1971.

————. *India: A Wounded Civilisation.* London: Andre Deutsch, 1977.

————. *The Loss of El Dorado.* London: Andre Deutsch, 1969.

————. *The Middle Passage.* London: Andre Deutsch, 1962.

————. *Miguel Street.* London: Andre Deutsch, 1959.

————. *The Mimic Men.* London: Andre Deutsch, 1967.

————. *The Mystic Masseur.* London: Andre Deutsch, 1957.

————. *The Overcrowded Barracoon.* London: Andre Deutsch, 1972.

————. *The Return of Eva Perón: With the Killings in Trinidad.* New York: Knopf, 1980.

————. *The Suffrage of Elvira.* London: Andre Deutsch, 1958.

————. *A Turn in the South.* Harmondsworth: Penguin, 1989.

————. *A Way in the World: A Sequence.* London: Heinemann, 1994.

Narinesingh, N. Introduction to *Crick Crack Monkey* by Merle Hodge.

Nasta, Susheila, ed. *Motherlands: Black Women's Writing from Africa, the Caribbean, and South Asia.* London: Women's Press, 1991.

Nichols, Grace. *Whole of a Morning Sky.* London: Virago, 1986.

Nketia, K. "African Roots of Music in the Americas: An African View." *Jamaica Journal* 43 (March 1979): 12–18.

————. *Drumming in Akan Communities.* Accra: University of Ghana Press, 1963.

————. *Funeral Dirges of the Akan People.* Achimota, Ghana, 1955.

Noel, Jessie. "Historicity and Homelessness in Naipaul." *Caribbean Studies* 11, 83–87.

O'Callaghan, Evelyn. *Woman Version: Theoretical Approaches to West Indian Fiction by Women.* London: Macmillan, 1993.

Oliver, Paul. *The Story of the Blues.* London: Cox and Wyman, 1969.

Omotoso, Kole. *The Theatrical into Theatre: A Study of Drama and Theatre in the English-Speaking Caribbean.* London: New Beacon, 1982.

Pastor Bodmer, Beatriz. *The Armature of Conquest: Spanish Accounts of the Discovery of America, 1492–1589.* Stanford: Stanford University Press, 1992.

Patterson, Orlando. "Rethinking Black History." *Harvard Educational Review* 41, no. 3 (1971): 41–48.

————. *The Sociology of Slavery.* Rutherford, N.J.: Fairleigh Dickinson University Press, 1967.

Pouchet-Paquet, Sandra. *The Novels of George Lamming.* London: Heinemann, 1982.

Prince, Mary. *History of Mary Prince, a West Indian Slave, Related by Herself.* 1831. In *The Classic Slave Narratives*, edited by Henry Louis Gates Jr. New York: New American Library, 1987.

Questel, Victor. "Dream on Monkey Mountain in Perspective." *Tapia* (September 1, 1974): 2–3; (September 8, 1974): 6–7.

———. "Walcott's Major Triumph." [Review of *Another Life* by Derek Walcott.] *Tapia* (December 23, 1973): 6–7; (December 30, 1973): 6–7.

Ramchand, Kenneth. *Acts of Possession: The New World of the West Indian Writers.* Port-of-Spain, Trinidad: Bank of Trinidad and Tobago, 1991.

———. "The Fate of Writing." *Caribbean Quarterly* 28, nos. 1–2 (1982): 76–84.

———. "History and the Novel: A Literary Critic's Approach." *Savacou* 5 (June 1971): 103–13.

———. *An Introduction to the Study of West Indian Literature.* London: Nelson, 1976.

———. "Parades, Parades: Modern West Indian Poetry." *Sewanee Review* 87, no. 1 (1979): 99–117.

———. "West Indian Literary History: Literariness, Orality, and Periodization." *Callaloo* 2, no. 1 (1988): 95–110.

———. *The West Indian Novel and Its Background.* 1970. Reprint, London: Heinemann, 1984.

———. "The World of *A House for Mr. Biswas*." *Caribbean Quarterly* 15, no. 1 (1969): 60–72.

Rattray, R. S. *Religion and Art in Ashanti.* 1927. London: Oxford University Press, 1959.

Raynal, Abbé. *A Philosophical and Political History of the Settlement and Trade of the Europeans in the East and West Indies.* Translated by J. Justamond, 5 vols. London: Printed for T. Cadell, 1779.

Read, Herbert, ed. *The Collected Works of Carl Jung.* London: Routledge and Kegan Paul, 1979.

Reid, V. S. *The Leopard.* London: Heinemann, 1980.

———. *New Day.* 1949. London: Heinemann, 1950.

———. *Sixty-Five.* London: Longman, 1960.

Rhys, Jean. *Wide Sargasso Sea.* 1966. Reprint, London: Hodder and Stoughton, 1989.

Righter, William. *Myth and Literature.* London: Routledge and Kegan Paul, 1975.

Risden, W. "*Masks*: Edward Brathwaite." *Caribbean Quarterly* 14, nos. 1–2 (1968): 145–47.

Robertson, William. *History of America.* 3 vols. London: W. Straham, 1977.

Rochefort, Charles de. *Natural History of the Islands of the Antilles.* London, 1966.

Rodriguez, Illeana. *House/Garden/Nation: Space, Gender, and Ethnicity in Post-Colonial Latin American Literatures by Women.* Translated by Rodriguez Robert Carr. Durham: Duke University Press, 1994.

Rodway, T., and I. Walt. *Chronological History of the Discovery and Settlement of Guiana.* 2 vols. Georgetown, 1886.

Rohlehr, Gordon. "Background Music to *Rights of Passage.*" *Caribbean Quarterly* 26, nos. 1–2 (1980): 32–40.

———. "Bridges of Sound: An Approach to Edward Brathwaite's 'Jah.'" *Caribbean Quarterly* 26, no. 112 (1980): 13–31.

———. "A Carrion Time." *Bim* 15, no. 58 (1975): 92–109.

———. "Character and Rebellion in *A House for Mr. Biswas.*" *New World Quarterly* 4, no. 1 (1968): 66–72.

———. "Dream Journeys." *World Literature Today* 68, no. 4 (1994): 765–74.

———. "Flowers of the Harmattan: Brathwaite's *Black and Blues* Examined." In *West Indian Poetry: Proceedings of the Fifth Annual Conference on West Indian Literature,* edited by J. Jackson and J. B. Allis, 201–17. St. Thomas: College of the Virgin Islands, 1986.

———. "The Historian as Poet." *Literary Half-Yearly* 11, no. 2 (1970): 171–78.

———. "History as Absurdity." In *Is Massa Day Dead? Black Moods in the Caribbean,* edited by Orde Coombes, 69–109. New York: Anchor, 1974.

———. "The Ironic Approach: The Novels of V. S. Naipaul." In *The Islands in Between,* edited by Louis James, 1–48. London: Oxford University Press, 1968.

———. "Islands." *Caribbean Studies* 10, no. 4 (1971): 173–202.

———. "Islands: A Review." *Caribbean Quarterly* 16, no. 4 (1970): 29–35.

———. "Megalleons of Light: Edward Brathwaite's *Sun Poem.*" *Jamaica Journal* 16, no. 2 (1983): 81–87.

———. *My Strangled City and Other Essays.* Port-of-Spain, Trinidad: Longman, 1992.

———. *Pathfinder: Black Awakening in the Arrivants of Edward Kamau Brathwaite.* Port-of-Spain, Trinidad: Privately published, 1981.

———. "The Problem of the Problem of Form." *Caribbean Quarterly* 31, no. 1 (1985): 1–52.

———. "The Rehumanization of History: Regeneration of Spirit, Apocalypse, and Revolution in Brathwaite's *The Arrivants* and *X-Self.*" In his *The Shape of That Hurt and Other Essays,* 248–92. Port-of-Spain, Trinidad: Longman, 1992.

———. "West Indian Poetry: Some Problems of Assessment." *Bim* 14, no. 54 (1972): 80–88; 14, no. 55 (1972): 34–43.

Schwarz-Bart, Simone. *The Bridge of Beyond.* 1975. Translated by Barbara Bray. London: Heinemann, 1982.

Scott, Dennis. *An Echo in the Bone: Plays for Today.* Edited by Errol Hill. Port-of-Spain, Trinidad: Longman, 1985.

Seacole, Mary. *The Wonderful Adventures of Mary Seacole in Many Lands.* 1857. Reprint, London: Falling Wall, 1984.

Selvon, Samuel. *A Brighter Sun.* London: Longman, 1957.

Senanu, Kofi. "Brathwaite's Song of Dispossession." *Universitas* 1, no. 1 (1969): 59–63.

Senior, Olive. *Summer Lightning and Other Stories.* London: Longman, 1986.

Sewell, W. G. *The Ordeal of Free Labour in the West Indies.* London, 1862.

Shinebourne, Janice. *Timepiece.* Leeds: Peepal Tree, 1986.

Slemon, S., and H. Tiffin, eds. *After Europe: Critical Theory and Post-Colonial Writing.* Mundelstrup, Denmark: Dangaroo Press, 1989.

Smith, M. G. *The Plural Society in the British West Indies.* Berkeley: University of California Press, 1965.

Spivak, Gayatri C. *In Other Worlds: Essays in Cultural Politics.* London: Methuen, 1987.

———. "Three Women's Texts and a Critique of Imperialism." *Critical Inquiry* 12, no. 1 (1985): 243–61.

Stanford, Michael. *The Nature of Historical Knowledge.* Oxford: Basil Blackwell, 1986.

Stubbs, William. "The Purpose and Methods of Historical Study." Lecture delivered at Oxford University, 15 May 1887. Quoted in F. Williams, *British Historians and the West Indies,* 42.

Tapping, Craig G. "Children and History in the Caribbean Novel: George Lamming's *In the Castle of My Skin* and Jamaica Kincaid's *Annie John.*" *Kunapipi* 11, no. 2 (1989): 51–59.

Thomas, J. J. *Froudacity: West Indian Fables by James Anthony Froude, 1889.* London: New Beacon, 1969.

Thorpe, Marjorie. "*The Mimic Men*: A Study in Isolation." *New World Quarterly* 4, no. 4 (1968): 55–59.

———. "The Problem of Cultural Identification in *Crick Crack Monkey.*" *Savacou* 13 (1977): 31–38.

Trollope, Anthony. *The West Indies and the Spanish Main.* London: Longman, 1888.

Walcott, Derek. *Another Life.* London: Jonathan Cape, 1972.

———. *The Arkansas Testament.* London: Faber and Faber, 1987.

———. "Caligula's Horse." In *After Europe,* edited by Stephen Slemon and Helen Tiffin. Mundelstrup, Denmark: Dangaroo, 1989.

———. "The Caribbean: Culture or Mimicry?" *Journal of Interamerican Studies and World Affairs* 16, no. 1 (1974): 3–13.

———. *The Castaway.* London: Jonathan Cape, 1965.

———. "The Figure of Crusoe." Open Lecture Series, University of the West Indies, St. Augustine, Trinidad, October 27, 1965.

———. *The Fortunate Traveller.* London: Faber and Faber, 1982.

———. *The Gulf.* London: Jonathan Cape, 1969.

———. *Henri Christophe: A Chronicle in Seven Scenes.* Bridgetown, Barbados: Advocate, 1950.

———. *In a Green Night.* London: Jonathan Cape, 1962.

———. *The Joker of Seville and "O Babylon."* London: Jonathan Cape, 1979.

———. "Meanings." *Savacou* 2 (1970): 45–51.

———. "The Muse of History." In *Is Massa Day Dead? Black Moods in the Caribbean,* edited by Orde Coombes, 1–27. New York: Anchor Doubleday, 1974.

———. *Omeros.* London: Faber and Faber, 1990.

———. "On Choosing Port of Spain." In *David Frost Introduces Trinidad and Tobago*, edited by Michael Anthony and Andrew Carr, 14–23. London, 1971.

———. "The Poet in the Theatre." *Poetry Review* 80, no. 4 (1990–91): 4–8.

———. *Remembrance and Pantomine*. New York: Farrar, Straus and Giroux, 1980.

———. *Sea Grapes*. London: Jonathan Cape, 1976.

———. *A Season of Plays*. Handbook of the Trinidad Theatre Workshop's Production of *Ti-Jean and His Brothers* and *Dream on Monkey Mountain* at the Creative Arts Centre, Mona, Jamaica, in April 1971.

———. *The Star-Apple Kingdom*. London: Jonathan Cape, 1979.

———. *25 Poems*. Bridgetown, Barbados: Advocate, 1949.

———. "Ti-Jean and His Brothers." In *Dream on Monkey Mountain*. 81–166.

———. "What the Twilight Says: An Overture." In his *Dream on Monkey Mountain, and Other Plays*. New York: Farrar, Strauss and Giroux, 1970.

Walnsley, Anne. "Dimensions of Song: A Comment on the Poetry of Derek Walcott and Edward Brathwaite." *Bim* 13, no. 51 (1970): 152–57.

Walsh, William. *V. S. Naipaul*. London: Oliver and Boyd, 1973.

Webb, Barbara. *History and Myth in Caribbean Fiction*. Amherst: University of Massachusetts Press, 1992.

White, Hayden. *The Content of the Form: Narrative Discourse and Historical Representation*. Baltimore: Johns Hopkins University Press, 1987.

———. "The Historical Text as Literary Artifact." In *Tropics of Discourses: Essays in Cultural Criticism*. Baltimore and London: Johns Hopkins University Press, 1978.

———. *Metahistory: The Historical Imagination in Nineteenth-Century Europe*. Baltimore: Johns Hopkins University Press, 1973.

White, Landeg. *V. S. Naipaul: A Critical Introduction*. London: Macmillan, 1975.

Williams, Denis. *Image and Idea in the Arts of Guyana*. Georgetown: Ministry of Information, 1969.

———. *Other Leopards*. London: Heinemann, 1963.

Williams, D. A., ed. *The Monster in the Mirror: Studies in Nineteenth-Century Realism*. London: Oxford University Press, 1978.

Williams, Eric. *British Historians and the West Indies*. London: Deutsch, 1966.

———. *Capitalism and Slavery*. New York: Russell and Russell, 1961.

Williams, Raymond. *The English Novel from Dickens to Lawrence*. London: Chatto and Windus, 1970.

Wilson-Tagoe, Nana. "The Backward Glance: African Continuities as Gateways to Definition in Caribbean Writing." In *Black Culture and Black Consciousness in Literature*, edited by E. Emenyonu. Ibadan, Nigeria: Heinemann, 1987.

———. "Edward Brathwaite: Poems." In *A Handbook for Teaching Caribbean Literature*, edited by David Dabydeen, 104–15. London: Heinemann, 1989.

———. "No Place: V. S. Naipaul's Vision of Home in the Caribbean." *Caribbean Review* 11, no. 2 (Spring 1980): 37–41.

———. "Tradition and the Creative Imagination: The Poetry of Christopher

Okigbo and Edward Brathwaite." In *Comparative Approaches to Modern African Literature*, 133–52. Ibadan, Nigeria: Ibadan University Press, 1982.

Wood, Donald. *Trinidad in Transition: The Years after Slavery.* London: Oxford University Press, 1968.

Wynter, Sylvia. "Beyond Miranda's Meanings: Un/silencing the 'Demonic Ground' of Caliban's Woman." In *Out of the Kumbla,* edited by Carol Boyce Davies and Elaine Savory Fido, 355–72. Trenton, N.J.: Africa World Press, 1990.

———. "Novel and History, Plot and Plantation." *Savacou* 5 (June 1971): 95–102.

Young, Robert. *White Mythologies: Writing History and the West.* London: Routledge, 1990.

Index

to, 132; and West Indian geography, xii. *See also Guiana Quartet*
"Hawk" (Walcott), 142–43, 145
Henderson, Mae, 251, 252
Henri Christophe (Walcott), 171–72
Herrera, Antonio de, 16
"Historian as Poet, The" (Rohlehr), xi
Historical determinism. *See* Determinism
Historical event, the, 35
Historical novel, 39–53; defined, 9; as fusion of history and the novel, 40; imagination and truth in, 9; imaginative possibilities in, 40–41; Lukàcs on historicism and the, 40; of Mittelholzer, 41–43; of Reid, 43–53; in West Indian literature, 40–41, 54
Historicism: emergence in nineteenth century, 15; fundamental principle of, 33; the historical novel and, 42, 54; Naipaul's *A Bend in the River* challenging idea of, 74; the novel's emergence and, 39–40; postmodernist critiques of, 37; and representation of the colonial, 90; West Indian writers and assumptions of, 270
"Historicity and Homelessness in Naipaul" (Noel), xi
Historiography: the arts for transforming, 35–36; historical texts as fictions, 38, 84, 151; historical writing as resembling the novel, 40; idea of progress in British, 21–22; postmodernist critiques of, 37; time as conceived in, 32; transcendence in European, 15. *See also* History; West Indian historiography
History: Brathwaite's cyclic view of, 213; as a construction, 90, 269; Harris's mythic construction of, 110, 112; the historical event, 35;

imagination's intersection with, 7–9, 270; literal and figurative views of, 270–71; man as agent of, 54; memory contrasted with, 234; Naipaul on sense of history as sense of loss, 54, 55–56, 70, 75; as nightmare and challenge for writers, 4; nineteenth-century American perceptions of, 129–30; the novel as, 39; as preencoded, 274; separation of past and present, 71; as series of antagonistic situations for Lamming, 241; Walcott on debt of history, 129, 173; Walcott on history as myth, 128; West Indian writers as traumatized by, 2; women's figurations of, 12, 234, 274–75. *See also* Historiography; Linear history
History and Myth in Caribbean Fiction (Webb), x
"History, Myth, and Fable in the Caribbean and Guianas" (Harris), x, 33, 272
Hodge, Merle: complicating factors in female subjectification, 241. *See also Crick Crack Monkey*
"Homecoming: Anse la Raye" (Walcott), 142
House for Mr. Biswas, A (Naipaul): Bhabha on narrative disturbance in, 59–60, 79; Biswas as symbolic colonial, 58; Harris on, 60; on inherent limitations of colonial situation, 270, 271; Naipaul's ideal vision in, 68; the past as shaping characters of, 58–59; as romance of purity, 78; the Tulsis, 58
Humanism, 17, 19, 21, 140

Ideology: in construction of history, 269; form as influenced by, 1
Image and Idea in the Arts of Guyana (Williams), x

Nana Wilson-Tagoe recently joined the Department of Africa, School of Oriental and African Studies, University of London. Her publications include *A Reader's Guide to West Indian and Black British Literature* and various chapters and articles in books and journals. This book represents a thoroughly revised version of her 1984 Ph.D. thesis from the University of the West Indies.